Vessels for the Ancestors

Vessels for the Ancestors

Essays on the Neolithic of Britain and Ireland
in honour of Audrey Henshall

Edited by
NIALL SHARPLES and ALISON SHERIDAN

EDINBURGH UNIVERSITY PRESS

© Edinburgh University Press, 1992

Edinburgh University Press
22 George Square, Edinburgh

Typeset in Lasercomp Times Roman
by Alden Multimedia Ltd, Northampton, and
printed in Great Britain by The Alden Press Ltd,
Osney Mead, Oxford

A CIP record for this book is available
from the British Library

ISBN 0 7486 0341 7

Contents

Contributors

Dr Ian Armit Centre for Field Archaeology, University of Edinburgh, Appleton Tower, Level 5, Crichton St, Edinburgh EH8 9LE.

Mr John Barber AOC (Scotland) Ltd., 1A Lansdowne Crescent, Edinburgh EH12 5EQ.

Mr Gordon Barclay Historic Scotland, 20 Brandon Street, Edinburgh EH3 5DX.

Professor Richard Bradley Department of Archaeology, University of Reading, Reading RG6 2AA.

Ms Ann Clarke Department of Archaeology, University of Glasgow, Glasgow G12 8QQ.

Dr Rosamund Cleal Trust for Wessex Archaeology, Portway House, South Portway Industrial Estate, Old Sarum, Salisbury SP4 6EB.

Dr Gabriel Cooney Department of Archaeology, University College Dublin, Belfield, Dublin 4.

Mr Trevor Cowie National Museums of Scotland Archaeology Department, Royal Museum of Scotland, Queen St, Edinburgh EH2 1JD.

Dr Mark Edmonds Corpus Christi College, University of Cambridge.

Professor George Eogan Department of Archaeology, University College Dublin, Belfield, Dublin 4.

Dr Ian Kinnes Department of Prehistoric and Romano-British Antiquities, British Museum, London WC1B 3DG.

Ms Frances Lynch University College of North Wales, Bangor, Gwynedd LL57 2DG.

Dr Ann MacSween, AOC (Scotland) Ltd., 1A Lansdowne Crescent, Edinburgh EH12 5EQ

Mr Roger Mercer Royal Commission on the Ancient and Historical Monuments of Scotland, 54 Melville Street, Edinburgh EH3 7HF.

Ms Jane Murray Department of Archaeology, University of Edinburgh, 16–20 George Square, Edinburgh EH8 9JZ.

Ms Rachael Ransom School of Geography, Archaeology and Palaeocology, The Queen's University of Belfast, Belfast BT7 1NN.

Mr Colin Richards Department of Archaeology, University of Glasgow, Glasgow G12 8QQ.

Mr Roy Ritchie Grant Institute of Geology, University of Edinburgh, Edinburgh EH8 9LE.

Mr Niall Sharples Historic Scotland, 20 Brandon Street, Edinburgh EH3 5DX.

Mr Jack Scott Woodrow Bank, Creebridge, Newton Stewart, Galloway DG8 6NR.

Dr Alison Sheridan National Museums of Scotland Archaeology Department, Royal Museum of Scotland, Queen Street, Edinburgh EH2 1JD.

Professor Derek Simpson School of Geography, Archaeology and Palaeoecology, The Queen's University of Belfast, Belfast BT7 1NN.

Dr Julian Thomas Department of Archaeology, Saint David's University College, Lampeter, Dyfed SA48 7ED.

Preface

This book is presented, with affection and gratitude, to Audrey Henshall on the occasion of her 65th birthday. Eschewing personal tributes in favour of a set of essays which it is hoped will be of interest to her, the Editors pass on the good wishes of all her friends, colleagues and admirers.

The papers presented here have all been stimulated, directly or indirectly, by Audrey's many and substantial contribution to prehistoric archaeology. The accent is unashamedly and appropriately Scottish, although essays concerning English, Welsh and Irish material, sparked by her funerary and ceramic work, are also included. The range of topics covered in the volume is witness to Audrey's broad-ranging interests, and we would not wish to embarrass her by listing her many and varied publications here; the numerous references to her works made within the text speak for themselves.

To Audrey
Happy Birthday

Note on Radiocarbon Dates and Terminology

Reference to absolute dates within the text are given according to the following conventions: unless stated otherwise, individual radiocarbon determinations are cited in their calibrated form, to one sigma, and labelled 'CAL-BC'. General references to calendrical dates are labelled as 'BC'. References to uncalibrated dates are cited as 'bc'. The calibration was carried out by Magnar Dalland of Historic Scotland (Kinnaird Park), and is based on high-precision C14 measurements of Irish oaks as published by Pearson et al. in *Radiocarbon* 28, 2b, 1986. The Editors thank Magnar and also Anne Crone of HS (KP) for providing calibrated date lists.

In accordance with the wishes of individual contributors, no attempt has been made by the Editors to impose a standardised terminology related to megalithic funerary monuments here: hence references to 'passage graves', 'passage tombs', 'chambered tombs', 'chambered cairns' etc.

1

Introduction: The State of Neolithic Studies in Scotland

Alison Sheridan and Niall Sharples

INTRODUCTION

As indicated in the Preface, this volume is offered as a tribute to Audrey Henshall in recognition of her major contribution to Scottish Neolithic studies over the last four decades. Although some of the papers do not deal primarily with Scottish material, all are nevertheless relevant to the central issues facing Neolithic studies in Scotland. The aim of this chapter is to set out what we feel these issues are, to review the current state of knowledge and the past and current approaches to the subject matter, and to recommend some possible future directions for Scottish Neolithic studies.

THE CURRENT STATE OF KNOWLEDGE

Ian Kinnes' review article of 1985 provides a useful starting point, offering a summary of the state of knowledge at that time and an attempt, through a thematic approach, to make some sense of the rich but variable database. Since 1985 there have been several significant additions to this database; these are summarised below.

In the Northern Isles, Colin Richards' excavations at Barnhouse (1989; 1990) have indeed provided 'a new perspective on the Orkney landscape' (Kinnes 1985, 27), with the uncovering of a multi-phase, Grooved Ware-associated site featuring both 'domestic' structures and a large 'ceremonial' building close to the Stones of Stenness; whilst at Pool and Tofts Ness, the results of the Bradford University excavations are currently nearing publication (Hunter et al. forthcoming), and a preview of some of the results for Grooved Ware and coarse stone tools is offered here (MacSween this volume; A. Clarke this volume). Regarding Orcadian funerary monuments, Jim Davidson and Audrey Henshall's revision of their chambered tomb *corpus* (1989) provides a welcome updating of this class of evidence, as does their similar exercise in Caithness (J.L. Davidson and Henshall 1991). Further north, for Shetland, Alasdair Whittle's full publication of the Scord of Brouster excavation results (1986) amplifies the evidence alluded to by Kinnes (1985, 28).

In the Hebrides, a major addition to our knowledge of the Neolithic period has been provided by Ian Armit's excavations at Eilean Domhnuill, Loch Olabhat, North Uist (Armit this volume). Amongst other significant contributions, this site provides valuable information regarding house structures and serves to remind us of the diversity of Neolithic settlement types (cf. Eilean an Tighe, a closely comparable island site, whose status as a settlement – rather than as Lindsay Scott's 'pottery workshop' (1951a) – is confirmed by the even larger ceramic assemblage recovered at Eilean Domhnuill). Most importantly, the latter constitutes an all-too-rare well-stratified and (eventually) absolutely-dated sample of pottery which promises to provide the key to understanding the nature and development of conventionally-termed 'Unstan' and 'Hebridean' pottery in the Western Isles. Anne Crone's site at Bharpa Carinish on North Uist (1989; forthcoming), which produced similar pottery, draws attention to the possibilities for recovering datable sub-peat occupation evidence, whilst the ongoing Sheffield University 'SEARCH' project in the Hebrides is providing useful palaeoenvironmental information and the hint of further Neolithic settlement sites (e.g. on Barra: SEARCH 1989).

In south-west Scotland, Alison Haggarty's excavations of stone circles Nos. I and XI on Machrie Moor, Arran have provided evidence for a long sequence of activity including cultivation and the erection of timber circles prior to their replacement by stone counterparts; Grooved Ware sherds were found in one posthole of the timber circle at Circle I (Haggarty forthcoming). On Islay, Rod McCullagh's site at Newton (McCullagh 1991) offers a well-contexted and dated Early Neolithic assemblage to add to the sparse yet important evidence for Neolithic activities on that island.

Moving east, the recent activities of the Lanark and District Archaeology Society have recovered evidence for a Neolithic and later landscape on Biggar Common, Lanarkshire, including a non-megalithic long mound containing a secondary individual inhumation with a 'Seamer axe' and bifacially-worked object of flint, almost certainly imported from Yorkshire (D.A. Johnston 1990; Sheridan 1989; this volume). This information was obtained after the area had been ploughed for commercial forestry, and the exercise highlights not only the importance of co-operation between developers and archaeologists, and between Local Society volunteers and 'professionals', but also the amount and quality of evidence which is currently being destroyed or under threat in Scotland. At nearby Blackshouse Burn, excavations by Peter Hill in 1985-6 (unpublished) revealed what may be a Late Neolithic circular enclosure (RCAHMS 1978, no. 171); the amount of information obtained from these investigations was, however, frustratingly sparse.

Elsewhere, work at individual sites has provided evidence useful to the study of several types of monument. Barclay and Maxwell's 1989 excavations at the suspected long mortuary enclosure at Inchtuthil help to fill out the picture for this site (Barclay and Maxwell 1991; cf. Kinnes 1985, 40 and this volume), whilst Barclay's report for the Balfarg sites, now nearing publication, adds detail on these enigmatic structures (Barclay and Russell-White forthcoming). The significance of Roger Mercer's excavations at Sketewan (Mercer and Tipping 1989) to the study of Clava monuments is explained by Barclay in this volume, and the results of the 1990 investigations at Miltown of Clava (Sharples 1990) are outlined here too. The recognition of the Cleaven Dyke in Perthshire as a probable cursus (RCAHMS in press) extends the known distribution of this type of monument northwards by a significant distance, and emphasises the need for a coherent model of Neolithic activities in central and eastern Scotland.

Further information germane to such a model is provided by the recent fieldwork directed by Mark Edmonds at the stone extraction and working site at Creag na Caillich, near Killin, Perthshire (Edmonds, Sheridan and Tipping forthcoming; Sheridan this volume). This detailed survey and excavation project has gone a long way towards addressing Kinnes' demand for an 'active search for débitage and quarrying traces' (1985, 25), and helps to create and realise 'a framework for both production and utilisation' of Scottish stone axeheads (ibid., 24). Other advances in Scottish stone axe studies since 1985 include Roy Ritchie's detailed survey of the source of riebeckite-felsite (Gp XXII) in the Northmaven district, Shetland, and its products (P.R. Ritchie and J.G. Scott 1988 and P.R. Ritchie pers. comm.); and fresh information fuelling the debate on the use of Irish flint in south-west Scotland has been provided by the discovery of a hoard of five axeheads and almost 200 flakes near Campbeltown, Argyll, in 1990 (Saville and Sheridan forthcoming; Sheridan this volume). Other recent and important discoveries of stone axeheads in Scotland are discussed by Sheridan in this volume.

Advances in the palaeoenvironmental record since 1985 have been sub-stantial. Many results, however, remain unpublished and the published reports are scattered widely throughout the literature, making overviews difficult. Richard Tipping's diagram for Creag na Caillich (Edmonds, Sheridan and Tipping forthcoming) is the first substantial sequence for central Scotland, whilst the work of palaeoenvironmentalists from Birming-ham, Cambridge and Sheffield Universities in the Hebrides (e.g. Bohncke 1988) provides a firm basis for modelling environmental change in this part of Scotland. The integration of palaeoenvironmental work within the rescue archaeology programme since 1988 has provided further much-needed infor-mation in diverse parts of Scotland (Carter 1989; Maté 1988; Mills 1988; 1989).

Other additions to our knowledge of Neolithic Scotland have arisen from the many rescue excavations undertaken since 1985, and further contribu-tions (such as Jane Murray's review of Henshall's group of 'Bargrennan' cairns) are presented in this volume. However, it must be said that a great deal of excavated information still remains locked up in unpublished reports, too plentiful (and embarrassing) to be enumerated here.

PAST AND PRESENT APPROACHES TO THE STUDY OF NEOLITHIC SCOTLAND

Four main traditional approaches to the study of Neolithic Scotland can be discerned, namely: (i) the site-orientated approach, usually taking the form of an excavation report, in which broader discussion is often limited to placing the site in its regional context (e.g. Isbister: Hedges 1983; Scord of Brouster: Whittle 1986); (ii) the regional study, often focusing on a specific category of evidence (e.g. Orcadian tombs: Fraser 1983; 'Clyde cairns': J.G. Scott 1969); (iii) the national-based study, again usually limited to one type of site or artefact (e.g. chambered tombs: Henshall 1963; 1972; pottery: McInnes 1969; stone axeheads: P.R. Ritchie and J.G. Scott 1988); and (iv, overlapping with ii and iii) the artefact-type or resource-based study, whose geographical scope varies according to the distribution of the material under study (e.g. carved stone balls: Marshall 1977; pitchstone: O.W. Thorpe and R.S. Thorpe 1984). A major characteristic of most of these studies is the way in which attention is limited to one specific aspect of the archaeological record, usually for the purpose of describing its properties, classifying it and mapping its distribution and variability.

Truly synthetic studies, attempting to build a narrative of the events and processes of Neolithic Scotland by integrating information on material culture, economy, environment, social organisation, settlements, monuments and beliefs, are remarkably few since Atkinson's 1962 attempt (see Kinnes 1985, 15 for a list). Kinnes' own version in 1985 limited itself to the issue of social change during the Later Neolithic (ibid., 41–4), while Renfrew's contributions (1976; 1979) focused on putative socio-economic changes in Orkney. Graham and Anna Ritchie's *Scotland: Archaeology and Early History* (1981) demonstrated how difficult it is to construct a coherent, Scotland-wide narrative given such an incomplete and unevenly-distributed database. It also raised the question, taken up by Kinnes (1985) and addressed again in this volume, principally by Sharples, of how (and indeed whether) the Scottish Neolithic can be understood in terms of a set of regional developments.

The range of approaches in current use, to a large extent encapsulated within the present volume, is striking in its diversity. In addition to the four main variants described above, one finds that the newer perspectives of recent and current archaeological theory are beginning to be applied to Scottish data. Early examples of this include Sharples' 1985 study of the role of chambered tombs in maintaining Orcadian Neolithic social order, and Hodder's (1984) study of the parallelism between houses for the living and tombs for the dead. A current trend, represented in this volume by (for example) Mark Edmonds' and Colin Richards' contributions, focuses on the ways in which material culture, social practices and humanly-managed space (in the form of buildings, monuments and landscapes) are used to maintain, manipulate or undermine the social order. Specific reference is sometimes made to the approach, borrowed from general social theory, whereby an analogy is made between the humanly-created world and the written text – with all the attendant scope for alternative 'readings', explicit and hidden meanings, and nuances of detail (for an explanation of what this means, see Hodder 1989). This approach admits of the inevitable subjectivity of the archaeologist in making sense of the remains of past societies; and while it neither enjoys universal acceptance nor constitutes the new 'wonder-paradigm', it does nevertheless encourage the integration of various strands of evidence in the search for a meaningful interpretation of the archaeological record.

KEY ISSUES IN, AND FUTURE DIRECTIONS FOR, SCOTTISH NEOLITHIC STUDIES

Of the many problems facing Scottish Neolithic studies, the two most important remain the incomplete and uneven nature of the database, and the apparent reluctance of scholars to attempt coherent, synthetic, interpretative model-building. While many might argue that the former precludes the latter activity, we feel that the traditional compartmentalisation of Scottish Neolithic research into artefact- or site-orientated studies, and the strong emphasis on description rather than interpretation, misses many opportunities for advancing our understanding. Such a view lies behind Sharples' attempt in this volume to hazard broad-brush comparisons and contrasts between patterns of Neolithic activity in different regions of Scotland.

It is not necessary to enumerate all the areas in which the Scottish Neolithic database is inadequate (cf. Kinnes 1985); suffice it to mention but a few. The gross geographical imbalance in knowledge, with Orkney occupying a pre-eminent position thanks largely to several decades of intense attention, is beginning to be redressed by work elsewhere (e.g. in the Hebrides), but for large areas of Scotland – e.g. the Borders, the Lothians, Central, Fife, Tayside and Grampian Regions – the patchiness of the record remains a severe handicap. This is perhaps most regrettable in lowland Scotland, where the available evidence suggests intensive use of agriculturally-rich land and a variety of ceremonial, funerary and domestic activities, many of which are represented by currently 'anomalous' (within the Scottish context) or poorly-understood structures (e.g. the Cleaven Dyke probable cursus: RCAHMS in press; the Balbridie massive timber house: Ralston 1982; the timber en-closures at Forteviot and Meldon Bridge: Burgess 1976; and the various non-megalithic monuments discussed by Kinnes in this volume, Chapter 7).

Other shortcomings of the database include the continuing paucity of evidence relating to the 'Mesolithic-Neolithic transition' in Scotland (Kinnes 1985, 18–21), despite advances in our knowledge of the Mesolithic (Woodman 1979) and a geomorphology which should be favourable to the preservation of relevant evidence. There is a similar shortage of information about, and discussion of, the processes of social and economic change during the period when metal items and Beaker pottery began to be used.

Three key issues will be discussed briefly below, although others could be suggested; lack of space, and the desire not to duplicate comments made by Kinnes (1985) or by the contributors to this volume, preclude a more exhaustive treatment of this subject. The three issues chosen for discussion concern the following: a) the ceramic record and its wider significance; b) the use of lithic resources; and c) the formulation of overall models for Neolithic Scotland.

Scottish Neolithic pottery

It is perhaps ironic that Isla McInnes' brief article in 1969 remains the latest published overview of Scottish Neolithic pottery (*pace* Kinnes 1985, 21–4), despite a lot of invaluable site-based work since then (much of it by Audrey Henshall), together with an attempt at a regional sequence in the South-West by Jack Scott (1969), a *corpus* of Neolithic pottery from the North-East by Audrey Henshall (1983c), and a similar *corpus* for the eastern and central Scotland by Trevor Cowie (forthcoming). The need for further *corpora* of the existing material is obvious, although increasingly harder to achieve given the massive excavated assemblages of recent years. Certain specific gaps in the record are easily identified: Ann MacSween's contribution in this volume underlines the need for more Grooved Ware assemblages in mainland Scotland to elucidate the origins and development of this pottery type, while many more examples of Late Neolithic Scottish 'Impressed Wares', the northern counterpart of the 'Peterborough' tradition, are needed before an adequate characterisation and evaluation of this type of pottery can be made. Expansion of this particular database is useful for several reasons, not least for understanding the development of the Food Vessel tradition in Scotland (Cowie personal communication), and for making more informed assessments of relationships with Irish Late Neolithic pottery and its producers (Sheridan 1985).

Rosamund Cleal's contribution to this volume makes the important point that the *way* in which pottery is approached is just as important in understanding the material as the sherds and vessels themselves. In Scottish pottery studies, two distinct approaches have been used, and yet the difference between them (and the fact that they are often applied simultaneously) has rarely been acknowledged. The first classifies 'types', 'styles' or 'wares' on the basis of recurrent sets of distinctive morphological and decorative criteria (e.g. 'Beacharra bowls', 'Achnacree bowls': Henshall 1972); the second defines groups of pottery on the basis of their assumed cultural affiliations (e.g. to the first agricultural settlers in an area, or to a particular group of tomb-builders – 'Unstan ware': S. Piggott 1954, 'Beacharra ware': J.G. Scott 1969). Hence the confusion and shifting definitions of 'Unstan' pottery, where a specific vessel type – the collared 'Unstan bowl' – can be identified over a wide area in the Northern and Western Isles and on the northern mainland, although the broader assemblages within which such bowls are found in Orkney (i.e. Stuart Piggott's 'Unstan ware': 1954) are not replicated *in toto* elsewhere (see J.L. Davidson and Henshall 1989, Henshall 1972 and Sharples 1981 for a discussion). Clearly, then, future Scottish ceramic studies will need to set out explicitly the aims and methods of the chosen approach, as done for example by MacSween in this volume.

Finally, one can identify aspects of the Scottish ceramic record which would repay closer attention. First, for example, among Stuart Piggott's broader class of 'Unstan ware' in Orkney are a few vessels resembling those which appear in larger numbers in the Hebrides: these are from Sandyhill Smithy, Bigland Round and the Point of Cott (Henshall 1963, MacSween forthcoming a); compare these with vessels from Eilean an Tighe (W.L. Scott 1951a) and Eilean Domhnuill (unpublished). (It remains to be seen whether Hebridean counterparts for the plain vessels from various Orcadian sites such as Isbister (Henshall 1983b) or Knowe of Craie (Henshall 1963) will be found.) Second, these and other vessels in the Hebrides and elsewhere in Scotland (e.g. Mid Gleniron II: Corcoran 1969b, Figure 11) share some features in common with north-east Irish pottery of roughly similar date (Sheridan 1985). This is all the more interesting in view of the fact that two sherds of deep-bellied, neck-decorated carinated Hebridean-type bowl turned up at Portstewart, Co. Derry (Sheridan 1985, 203 and Figure 5.56), and porcellanite axeheads from Co. Antrim have turned up in the Hebrides (Sheridan 1986b).

Lithic resource use

Although valuable work regarding the nature and distribution of some of Scotland's diverse lithic resources has been done (e.g. A. Clarke 1990b, O.W. Thorpe and R.S. Thorpe 1984; Wickham-Jones 1981, Wickham-Jones and Collins 1978), much still needs to be clarified about their exploitation during the Neolithic. Setting aside for a moment the various well-known problems associated with lithic studies, such as the sourcing of flint and chert and the identification of worked quartz, two points of interest emerge from a brief review of the currently available information.

First, in marked contrast to most known Mesolithic sites (such as Kinloch, Rhum: Wickham-Jones 1990 or Newton, Islay: McCullagh 1991), assemblages of small stone tools from Neolithic settlement sites and chambered tombs are strikingly sparse in Scotland. Relevant figures are as follows:

- Auchategan, Argyll: 100 pitchstone and 25 flint pieces (Marshall 1978);
- Balloch Hill, Argyll: 58 pitchstone and 118 flint pieces (Peltenburg 1982);
- Eilean an Tighe, North Uist: 27 pieces of flint, chert and quartz (W.L. Scott 1951a);

- Eilean Domhnuill, Loch Olabhat, North Uist: few (as yet unquantified) pieces of flint; quartz assemblage yet to be investigated (Armit this volume, Chapter 22);
- The Knap of Howar, Orkney: 105 pieces of flint and chert (A. Ritchie 1983);
- Boghead, Moray: 68 pieces of flint (Burl 1984).

Only on the Grooved Ware settlements of Orkney does this picture change. At the Links of Noltland, an assemblage of several thousand pieces of flint has been recovered from David V. Clarke's excavations (Wickham-Jones personal communication), and at Skara Brae a considerable amount of effort has gone into creating a heat-treated rock which could be knapped into morphologically distinct tools. Building 8 seems to have been deliberately designed to function as a furnace in which the raw material could be heated at a controlled temperature (D.V. Clarke and Sharples 1985). The products of this semi-industrial process were, however, restricted to the settlement of Skara Brae. There is no evidence for this very characteristic material at Barnhouse (Richards personal communication) or at the more distant settlements of Rinyo and the Links of Noltland (Wickham-Jones personal communication).

Clearly, collector bias cannot be ruled out as a factor in explaining this rather odd pattern, but the paucity of the Boghead material seems surprising in view of the proximity of the rich flint source in the Buchan area.

Second, it appears that there was no *substantial* movement of stone artefacts or their raw materials around Scotland: although artefacts of materials such as pitchstone occur in Neolithic contexts at considerable distances from the source area (e.g. Barnhouse: Richards personal communication, or the Borders: Finlayson personal communication), nevertheless these quantities are never great. The same appears true of axeheads from the Creag na Caillich source: although extensive, their distribution is nowhere dense, and the fieldwork results at the source suggested small-scale exploitation quite unlike the level witnessed in the later phases of activity at Great Langdale (Edmonds, Sheridan and Tipping forthcoming; Sheridan this volume, Chapter 15). Such a pattern makes the widespread and, in some areas, relatively dense distribution of imported Group VI and IX axeheads (amongst other exotics) all the more interesting.

Finally, as Ann Clarke and Derek Simpson point out in this volume, a marked use of local materials appears to be the case (for Orkney, at least) with both coarse stone tools and maceheads; and the former appear in much larger numbers per site in Orkney than elsewhere.

Clearly, the reasons for these phenomena need to be investigated further.

Towards overall models for Neolithic Scotland

As suggested above, there is a pressing need for new interpretative studies which attempt to knit together the diverse strands of available evidence: despite Colin Renfrew's attempts to inject the 'New Archaeology' into Orcadian studies in 1976, there has been little debate at the interpretative, synthesising level.

The basic frame(s) of reference with which to construct interpretative models still needs clearer definition. In economic terms, for example, what 'Neolithic' means for the south of England is far removed from what it means in Orkney, with its apparently semi-domesticated deer population and rich variety of wild and domesticated resources (D.V. Clarke 1976a; D.V. Clarke and Sharples 1985), and indeed within Scotland there appears to be great diversity in 'Neolithic' subsistence strategies (e.g. Sharples this volume, Chapter 23; Whittle 1986). Maclean and Rowley-Conwy's survey of Scottish cereal evidence (1984) illustrates both these points well.

Similarly, there is still a need for basic definitions of what forms of change took place in the various parts of Scotland over the fourth millennium BC, and for debate on how these may have arisen. Kinnes' 1985 paper makes one attempt at this, but more discussion is badly needed (cf. Thomas 1989 and Whittle 1990 for southern England).

The question of 'regionalising' the Scottish Neolithic is one which has occupied a prominent role in much of past and present work, most notably in ceramic and funerary studies (e.g. Henshall 1963; 1972), but needs yet more attention (see, for example, Sharples this volume, Chapter 23). Clearly, as a device in helping to make sense of the large and diverse archaeological record, it is useful to divide Scotland into regions. Unfortunately, however, the regional boundaries for the various classes of evidence are neither coincident nor stable over time, so that as a tool for understanding processes of social and economic change, it has its limitations. A classic example of where a supra-regional as well as a local perspective is required is offered by the evidence relating to Grooved Ware pottery in Scotland. While its use *seems* to coincide with the appearance of henges and stone or timber circles in diverse parts of Scotland (e.g. Orkney: J.N.G. Ritchie 1976; Fife: Mercer 1981; Arran: Haggarty 1981), and may well be symptomatic of the kind of Later Neolithic social change (i.e. hierarchisation) alluded to by Kinnes in 1985, it would be unwise to assume that its appearance is universally associated with such changes.

An allied point, and one which again bears on the issue of Later Neolithic social changes in particular, is the importance to be ascribed to the evidence for inter-regional and external contacts. While there is some justification for Kinnes' (1985) appeal for explanations more sophisticated than those which equate external contacts with colonisation, there are some cases in which the jury must remain out on this matter (e.g. the issue of passage tomb origins in the west of Scotland: not an easy matter to resolve). That there is scope for integrating evidence for long-distance contact with models of social change in which such activities were part of a *strategy* is clear from Bradley and

Chapman's study of Orkney-Boyne contacts (1986; see also Sheridan 1986a). Clearly, more use could be made of the evidence which is already available.

CONCLUSIONS

This brief review of the state of Scottish Neolithic studies has revealed some heartening progress since 1985; continuing work on some major unpublished excavation assemblages (e.g. Skara Brae and the Links of Noltland) promises further improvements. Clearly, however, several basic questions need urgent attention, and it remains to be seen whether Scottish Neolithic research in the twenty-first century AD can match the contribution of twentieth-century workers such as Audrey Henshall. We present this volume in the hope that it will.

Part 1
Funerary Studies

2

Megalithic Architecture

John Barber

INTRODUCTION

Chambered cairns survive in large numbers in Scotland and more particularly in Orkney (Davidson and Henshall 1989, Figure 1), where they have been a focus of antiquarian interest for two centuries. Ranging in size from 48 to 970 cubic metres (Fraser 1983, 354), stone cairns survive as low, irregular, spread mounds. The angles at which their sides slope down to the surrounding land surface are often gentler than the maximum angle of repose (see Figure 2.1) of the stones which make up their bulk (Figure 2.2), implying that they have been extensively robbed and denuded.

Earthen mounds or cairns composed of earth and stone, such as Maes Howe, Orkney or Knowth and Dowth, Co. Meath, Ireland, are usually more steep-sided than their stone equivalents. Despite recent disturbance at Maes Howe and Dark Age remodelling at Knowth, the mounds were clearly conceived of as tall, steep-sided structures. It is equally clear that many of the stone cairns must have been higher than their surviving remnants suggest, if only to cover and enclose their chambers. Given that they are bounded by kerbs, or walls, they must also have been much steeper.

The apparent requirement for high cairns with steep external faces may have been largely a matter of aesthetics, arising from a desire to create imposing mortuary structures. It was, in part, forced on the cairn-builders by the need to encompass tall corbelled chambers. Corbelling produced chambers which were two or three times higher than they were wide, and thus very large, high and steep-sided cairns were needed to enclose them. Because their external faces were steeper than the angle of repose of their stone component, they were inherently unstable (Figure 2.3).

The absence of developed soil profiles under the collapsed margins of excavated cairns indicates that their external wall faces collapsed before a pedogenetic profile had time to develop on the stripped ground that surrounded them. Undeveloped profiles underlay the cairn collapse at Newgrange (O'Kelly 1982, 72–3), at Tulloch of Assery A (Corcoran 1966),

Figure 2.1: Schematic diagram showing the angle of repose (or 'rest') of material of three different sizes. This may be envisaged as the slope angle of the sides of a cone formed by dumping a large sample of the material at one point. The size of the angle is determined by a range of factors among which particle size and shape and inter-particulate friction are important.

at Quoyness (Childe 1952, 125) and at the Point of Cott, Orkney. An A-horizon would have formed on most of the soil-types involved in less than a decade or two, and would have been well-established within the span of a lifetime. This implies that Neolithic builders must have witnessed the collapse of steeply-piled cairns and been aware of the need to counteract this problem. Indeed, the development of much of Neolithic architecture appears to have been conditioned by the need to reconcile the demand for tall chambers with the need for stability in the dry-stone cairns which enclose them.

INTERNAL WALLS

In many cairns, one or more lines of wall-facing have been noted within the body of the cairn, apparently unconnected with the construction of the chamber (Figure 2.4). These are often visible even in unexcavated cairns. Before excavation, at least two lines of walling were visible on the west side of the Point of Cott. Where access to the chamber is via a passage that penetrates the cairn, the lines of intra-cairn wall-faces are often revealed as vertical 'building breaks' in the masonry of the side walls of the passage (Figure 2.5).

These wall-faces are usually single-faced walls which have been interpreted as revetments to the amorphous bulk of cairn material which they enclose. Intra-cairn walls with two faces have been noted at Quanterness and at the ruined site at the Howe (Davidson and Henshall 1989, 41).

Davidson and Henshall note (ibid., 40) that in all cases where the cairn has been examined, chambers of Maes Howe type are 'enclosed within and supported by a core of cairn material which was faced by masonry'. It was, they suggest, the minimum size necessary to contain the chamber; its outer face is sometimes only a metre from the cell walls. Where examined, the core-cairns are composed of densely-packed, horizontally-laid slabs which form very stable structures. These core-cairns are delimited by a wall-face,

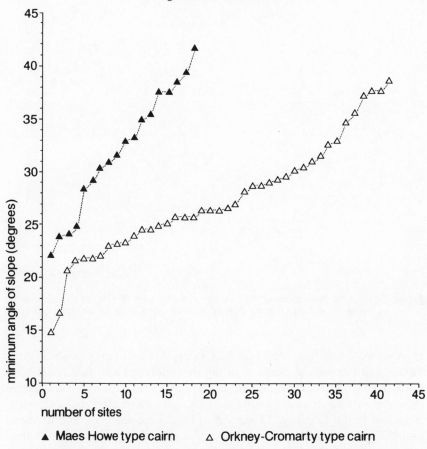

Figure 2.2: Graph showing minimum angle of cairn slope for Maes Howe (MH) and Orkney–
Cromarty (O–C) type chambered cairns.

usually of particularly good masonry, which is the most commonly observed
intra-cairn wall-face.[1]

Wideford Hill, Quanterness and other sites, such as the Point of Cott, have
further wall-faces between the core-cairn face and the outermost walling
(ibid., 41). It seems very probable that future excavations will show that this
is the rule rather than the exception.

EXTRA-REVETMENT MATERIAL

Vertical or near-vertical stones have been noted at several sites, set in or on
the old ground surface surrounding chambered cairns and abutting their
outermost wall faces. These, described as 'extra-revetment' material in the
early literature (see Daniel 1950, 41–3, for discussion) have been interpreted
as deliberate attempts to stabilise tall but amorphous cairns, by buttressing

JOHN BARBER

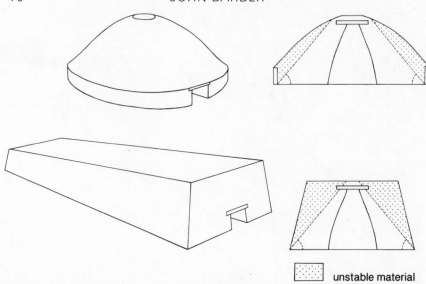

unstable material

Figure 2.3: Unstable material revetted by the external wall faces of MH and O–C cairns. Its instability is due to it being piled up more steeply than its natural angle of repose.

the outermost wall-faces. At Tulloch of Assery A, Corcoran concluded (1966, 29–30) that the vertical stones abutting the outermost wall-face could have fallen from the top of the wall, but that the horizontal slabs which lay outside these represented *extra-revetment material*, introduced after the outer wall-faces had begun to decay. This material blocks the entrance, and its interpretation as revetment material implies that the cairn was being maintained as a structure after it had gone out of use as a funerary site. It seems more probable, as Collins (1954, 21–3) has suggested, that all such material had fallen from the cairn walls after their abandonment.

PRIMARY STRUCTURES

Corbelling is the technique whereby successive courses of stones are laid so that each course slightly oversails the one beneath it, progressively narrowing the gap to be roofed until it can be closed off with relatively small slabs. A corbelled dome relies on an internal balancing act to dispose of the forces created by the weight of the roof and any superincumbent material (Figure 2.6).

The simplicity of corbelling is more apparent than real. In the simplest example, we may consider the case where all the stones are the same size and weight and the oversail is kept constant. The possible closure is the length of a stone less the length of the oversail (Figure 2.6a). Once this point is reached, the mass of material to one side of the first pivotal edge ('P' on Figure 2.6)

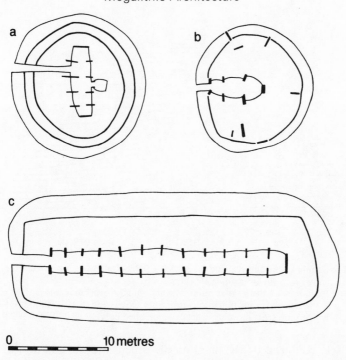

Figure 2.4: Intra-cairn wall lines at the sites of: a) Unstan, b) Bigland Round and c) Midhowe.

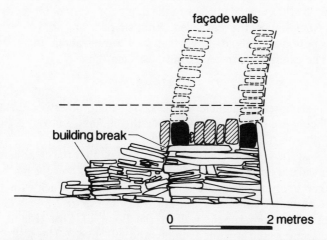

Figure 2.5: Building breaks (arrowed) in the western passage wall at the Point of Cott. These correspond to the intra-cairn wall-faces. Note also that the most massive lintels (in solid black) are those which carried the wall-faces of the façade across the passage.

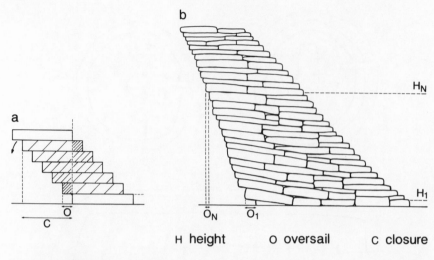

Figure 2.6: Simplified (a) and realistic (b) models of a corbelled structure. The shading in (a)
shows how the oversailing elements are balanced by the embedded parts. Here, all
the stones are the same size and thickness and the oversail is constant. In reality (b),
stone size and oversail reduce with height (compare H1 with Hn and O1 with On,
which represents more realistically a corbelled curve).

is precisely balanced by the mass on the other, and the addition of even a
single further block will bring the entire structure crashing down.

Height and closure can only be increased by varying the length and the
thickness of the stones used (Figure 2.6b). This implies a relationship between
the inner and outer faces of a corbelled structure, and is merely a qualitative
statement of the mathematical relationship implied by the balance of the
oversailing by the embedded parts of the dome for every point on its internal
surface. Analysis of the corbelled, boat-shaped oratories of the Early
Christian period in Ireland shows that they are parabolic in vertical cross
section. The external diameter D_e must be such that:

$$D_e \geqslant D_i (1 + \sqrt{5})/2$$

where D_i is the internal diameter at the same height, otherwise the corbelled
dome will collapse (Barber and Angell forthcoming; see also Cavanagh and
Laxton 1990, on the curves used in *tholoi*).

The prehistoric corbeller did not have to know that the chambers' curves
were elliptical or parabolic, nor indeed did he have to know the mathematical
basis of their analysis. There are several rules of thumb which would be used
to achieve a suitable curve. The one illustrated in Figure 2.7 was used in the
rebuilding of a compartment wall at the Point of Cott (Figure 2.8), in
parabolic section, and operated simply and effectively. The wall/roof of a
corbelled chamber does not need to curve inwards, but can form an inclined
plane, as many of the best Orcadian examples demonstrate. There is still a

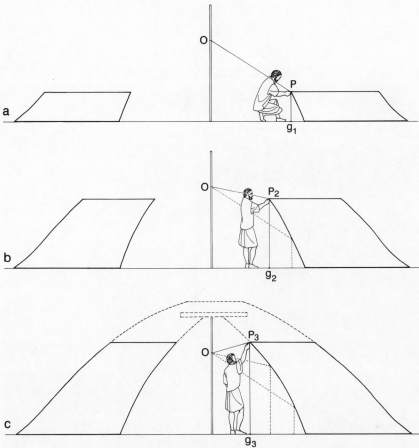

Figure 2.7: One rule-of-thumb for marking out a parabolic vertical section. A pole is set
vertically at the centre, or on the centre line, of the structure, with a weighted piece
of string attached at O. By placing a finger inside the string and sliding it out in such
a way as to keep the weight just touching the ground (g1, g2, g3 etc.), a parabola is
made by the path described by the finger (p1, p2, p3 etc.).

fixed relationship between closure and wall-thickness, i.e. between the
distances from the midpoint of the floor and the inner and outer wall-faces,
if stability is to be maintained.

SOME IMPLICATIONS OF CORBELLING

The principal advantage to the prehistoric builder of using corbelling was
that no internal supports were necessary during construction. Indeed, it is not
possible to build the inner face of a corbelled chamber and then pile cairn
material up on its exterior; rather, the inner and outer faces rise together in
a single coherent structure (Figure 2.9). A corbelled structure is, necessarily,

Figure 2.8: Compartment wall at the Point of Cott, 'rebuilt' in a few hours using the rule-of-thumb described in Figure 2.7. The vertical curve is parabolic and closely approximates to the chamber's original profile.

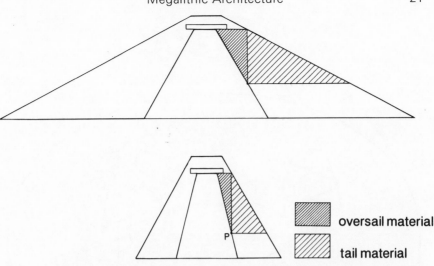

Figure 2.9: Two variants of rectilinear-profile corbelled structures, showing how the oversailing part must be counterbalanced by tail material. In the lower example, floor width is 42% of the total width, and 1.3 cu m of building material is required for every cu m of chamber space. In the upper example, which is only slightly shallower, the chamber width is reduced to 27% of the total width and just over twice as much building material is required per cu m of chamber space. The Orcadian tomb chambers suggest that structures of the lower type were considered more appropriate; these would have been much less labour intensive than the wider, shallow, but more massive forms.

stable at every level, and, as the structure rises, the inner face is readily constructed from the sides and top of the rising core-cairn. In other words, what Davidson and Henshall call the 'core-cairn' is not a cairn (in the accepted sense of a covering pile of stones) but the corbelled structure of the chamber.

Burying the core-cairn with its chamber, deep inside a large cairn, only serves to strengthen it (Figure 2.10), unless the weight pushes down the inner faces of individual stones, forcing them to slope downwards to the interior. If that happens, the oversailing mass above the sloping corbel is free to slip inwards, causing the chamber to collapse (Figure 2.11). This results more commonly from the crushing of poor-quality stone or settlement of the foundation courses than from the overloading of the structure.

Some settlement after construction was inevitable as the heavily-loaded walls settled into the ground below, or as weaker stones were crushed or broken by the superincumbent weight. Neolithic builders were conscious of this potential weakness and provided for it, usually by placing small stone spalls under the inner faces (i.e. those forming the chamber 'walls') of the corbels so that they sloped downwards as they radiated out into the mass of core-cairn. The presence of these spalls is usually attributed to the builders'

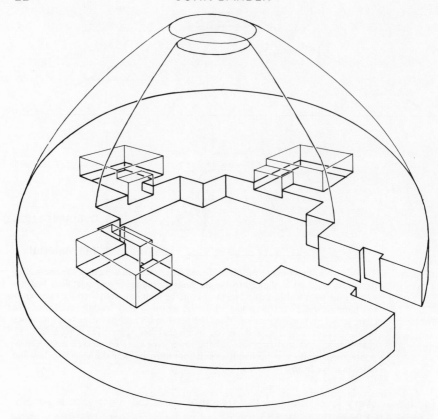

Figure 2.10: A Maes Howe type tomb at an early stage of construction. No internal props are
needed and access to the internal faces was readily gained over the mass of the
core-cairn already *in situ*. As the core-cairn and chamber rose, ramps of external
cairn material would have provided access and then be subsumed within the final
cairn.

desire to present a fair wall-face, but many unfilled voids and gaps occur
among the corbelled courses, and this suggestion seems improbable.

These spalls, by tilting the corbels of a course upwards, facilitated the
creation of 'horizontal arches'. The builders usually set the corbels in each
course so close together that their inner corners touched. Subsequent settlement, pushing the inner faces downwards, would crush the corners together,
locking the stones of the course into a rigid ring commonly (but incorrectly)
called a horizontal arch (Figure 2.12a). By creating a series of horizontal
arches, tremendous strength and resistance to deformation could be imparted
to the structure. Corbelled horizontal arches were used to revet massive loads
and were made stronger in the process.

It is not essential that the horizontal arch be a full circle. In the case of the
stalled cairns (Figure 2.12b), short, shallow arcs of walling provide structural

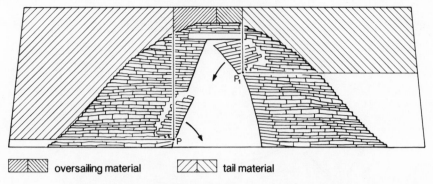

oversailing material   tail material

Figure 2.11: Collapse of a corbelled structure. The shapes of corbelled structures are such that
            burying them in a larger cairn will always add more weight to the 'tail' than to the
            oversailing material. Thus burial within a larger cairn or mound usually strengthens
            the structure. If, however, the additional weight causes some corbels to tilt
            downwards into the chamber, the conditions for stability are rapidly breached and
            the chamber will collapse.

integrity in a rectangular ground plan. Davidson and Henshall propose the
following structural sequence for Orkney-Cromarty (O-C) chambers:

> The logical procedure in constructing a tripartite or stalled chamber, after
> stripping the turf and marking out the plan, would be to set up the backslab
> on the ground surface, supported behind by a sufficient depth of cairn and
> in front by the side walls of the terminal compartment built to a sufficient
> height, then to add a pair of transverse slabs and the next section of side
> wall, so continuing to the portal slabs, and then the passage walls. (1989, 20)

However, the evidence from the Point of Cott indicates an alternative structural sequence. Here, it was clear that, as the first stage of building, the
chamber area had been stripped of turves and topsoil, shallow sockets had
been dug and the transverse stones erected. The chamber's side walls were
slightly bowed, the masonry courses were tilted downward into the core-cairn
and the edges of adjacent stones were crushed. All of these features indicate
the builders' deliberate creation of horizontal arches in the chamber's side
walls. The transverse stones provided fixed abutments against which the
thrust of the adjacent arcs of walling cancelled each other out. Thus the
structure arose, course by course, from ground to closing slabs, as a complete
entity and probably not from one end to the other as Davidson and Henshall
suggest.

The use of horizontal arches does not necessarily mean that the chambers
were roofed by corbelling. Indeed, Henshall suggests that the long chambers
of the O-C group were closed with lintels. However, despite a very careful
excavation, no lintels were found at the Point of Cott. Examination of the
admittedly opaque records of earlier excavations has failed to provide
evidence for lintels in the chambers. Passage lintels survive in many instances
and are readily identified, even when broken, and are commonly illustrated

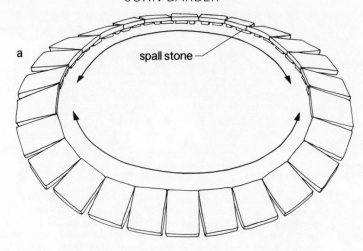

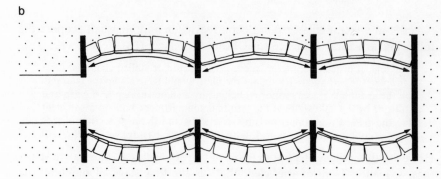

Figure 2.12: Creation of a 'horizontal arch'. A slight upward tilt is often imparted to the corbels in one course, usually by inserting small stone spalls under their front edges. Settlement of the corbels under the weight of the completed structure crushes the edges of adjacent corbels together, creating a 'horizontal arch'. This can be a complete circle (a), for example in the roof of a circular corbelled chamber, or a shallow arc (b) between successive transverse stones in a segmented chamber.

in plans, sections and photographs. This suggests that, were the chambers commonly roofed with lintels, these would also have been unambiguously identified. The absence of supporting evidence for lintelling indicates that dry-stone chamber roofs were commonly corbelled for the greater part of their closure.

The retrieval of human bone from positions high in the stones of the chamber-roof collapse at the Point of Cott raises the possibility that aumbries, or pigeon-holes, were built into the upper chamber walls and used to house human bones.

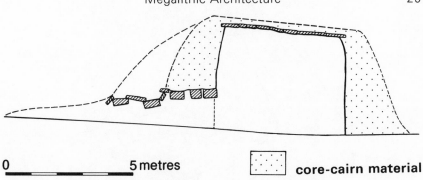

0 _____ 5 metres   core-cairn material

Figure 2.13: Section through the Knowe of Lairo, Rousay, showing the use of substantial lintels
to support the weight of the core-cairn above the passage.

ENTRANCE PASSAGES

The creation of openings in corbelled structures posed a particularly difficult
problem for the megalithic architect. Clearly, any entrance passage must pass
under the core-cairn and must support the weight of that part of the core-
cairn which overlies it. The simplest architectural adjustment to this problem
has been the use of the narrowest passages possible. The widths of entrance
passages are recorded as ranging from 45 to 95 cm wide, with the majority
between 50 and 70 cm (Fraser 1983, 122–5). Other architectural responses
include the use of massive lintels or of lintels turned on edge and the use of
massive entrance portal stones. The trabeate doorway, a doorway with
inclined jambs characteristic of Early Christian corbelled structures (Leask
1977, 24), also seems to have been used in Neolithic structures. The doorway
to Side Chamber 1 at Isbister, as illustrated, has markedly inclined jambs
(Hedges 1983, Figure 6).

Massive lintels commonly cover the entrance passages to Maes Howe type
cairns where they pass beneath the core-cairn (Figure 2.13). Outwith this,
smaller slabs were often employed, and often failed, reducing the outer edges
of the passages to open trenches. The sites of Maes Howe, the Knowe of
Lairo and Quanterness all have massively thick passage-lintels under the
core-cairn. Where stones of suitable thickness were not available, or perhaps
where insufficient labour was available to handle larger stones, the lintels
were sometimes set on edge (see the passage lintels at the Point of Cott, for
example, in Figure 2.5).

Massive entrance portals, like those at the Ord North (Sharples 1981,
Figures 2.4 and 2.5) are sometimes used to carry thick, heavy lintels whose
weight might otherwise prove destabilising for dry-stone passage-walls. It is
possible that the two other pairs of portals in the passage also supported large
lintels which were required to carry intra-cairn walls across the passage. No
such walls were noted by the excavator at the Ord North, but the thickest

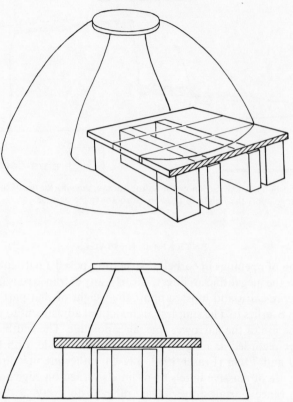

Figure 2.14: Schematic diagram of the relieving structure at Newgrange. Such structures were
used where the weight of the core-cairn could not be supported by the passage
walls. Here, a massive lintel is supported on large stone sleepers which, in turn, rest
on cairn material behind the passage. The passage orthostats do not carry any
weight at this point.

lintels, set on edge, across the passage at the Point of Cott were set along the
lines of the façade walls (Figure 2.5).

Relieving structures become necessary where the lintels required to support
the core-cairn above the passage or entrance become so large that the
passage-walls alone could not support them. The best example of a relieving
structure is that excavated by Professor M.J. O'Kelly at Newgrange, in
Ireland. This is the largest cairn in Europe, with a very large chamber
enclosed within a superbly built core-cairn. The lintels supporting the core-
cairn, over the passage, are so massive that their weight had to be borne on
two very large horizontal slabs set on either side of the passage and supported
on built plinths (Figure 2.14). This is currently the only example known, but
so few cairns have been excavated that further examples, and even alternative
strategies, probably remain to be discovered.

DRAINAGE

If the soils underlying megalithic cairns were to be softened, by percolating rainwater for example, large-scale settlement of the great mass of the chamber/core-cairn would ensue, probably resulting in the collapse of the chamber. We should not be surprised to find, then, that some pains were taken to keep the chambers waterproof and to divert any downward trickle of water off into the looser and lighter mass of the enclosing cairn. The tilt of the corbels – downwards away from the chamber – facilitated this. The quality of the core-cairn's outer face, commented upon by several writers, also acts as a barrier to the percolation of rain into the chamber area. Newgrange is, again, the only large megalithic chambered tomb to have undergone large-scale excavation in recent times (apart from Knowth site 1), and here the tops of the passage-lintels and of the lintels of the relieving structure have rain-gullies cut along their sides with further gullies running out from these to discharge percolating rain out into the body of the enclosing cairn, behind the passage walls.

Clearly, the builders' concern that the chamber should be kept dry could have a liturgical[2] basis; they may have seen the chambers as the homes of the dead. However, the original stimulus for the efforts expended in rain-proofing may well have been an awareness of the potential for destabilisation which the percolation of water could pose to the whole structure.

O'Kelly observed at Newgrange that the core-cairn and passage were erected as free-standing structures, within a keyhole-shaped area, around which the great bulk of the external cairn was amassed and stabilised with turf layers to prevent it from falling into the central work area (M.J. O'Kelly 1982, 89 and Figure 2.14). A bank of clay at the Howe (Carter et al. 1984, 61–3) similarly surrounds the area within which the core-cairn would have been erected.

THE ENVELOPING CAIRN

The size and shape of the chamber roof, the access passage and the core-cairn were all, to a great degree, predetermined by the selection of the chamber's ground plan. If the builders diverged from the optimum structure for that plan, stability was rapidly compromised and the entire structure was in danger of collapse. The Neolithic architect had a greater degree of freedom in the design of the enveloping cairn. Whether a cairn had horns or multiple walls, or extended beyond the chamber by 1 m or 100 m, are matters which the builders could have decided virtually at their whim. The enveloping cairn therefore allowed the builders to express changes in fashion, religion or liturgical practice without the great constraints which the need for structural integrity placed on the architecture of the chambers.

This freedom for expression is reflected in the strangely ephemeral nature of the structures used to bulk out and form the external cairn. Hornworks and enveloping cairns were composed of layers of 'onion-skin' walls enclosing the core-cairn (Barber 1988, 58). The spaces between these walls were largely void, and the voids account for a very large part of the apparent volume of the cairn. At the Point of Cott, for example, the voided areas facilitated colonisation of cairn and chamber by a range of creatures including otters, sea eagles, voles, rabbits and a variety of birds. These, in turn, disturbed and contaminated the chamber-floor deposit (ibid., 60). It does not strain the syllogism to suggest that the radiocarbon evidence for chamber-floor disturbance at Quanterness implies a similar ease of access to deposits which appear, deceptively, undisturbed. Ease of access to intra-cairn and chamber-floor deposits, via voided structures, may prove the rule rather than the exception.

Tulach an t-Sionnaich and the Point of Cott are both long cairns of O-C type. In each, the heart of the enveloping cairn is made up of irregular patterns of orthostatic slabs. These, at the Point of Cott, were roofed over with lintels on which stood the uppermost, and innermost, pair of longitudinal, onion-skin walls. At both sites, the aim has been to make the cairns appear more massive than they really are. This may have been a standard Neolithic building technique. It was also observed in the construction of the enclosing bank at the Neolithic enclosure of Blackshouse Burn (Hill personal communication).

Fine masonry faces and patterned walling were used to enhance the appearance of the finished cairns. In Orkney, four O-C cairns have outer wall-faces with decorative stonework (J.L. Davidson and Henshall 1989, 30–1). As Kilbride-Jones has noted, there can be little doubt that these features were intended to be seen (1973, 95). An impression of the grandeur of patterned walling and its varying appearance under different conditions of light and shade can be gained from Andy Goldsworthy's 'Slate Stack' at Stone Wood, Penpont, Dumfriesshire (Goldsworthy 1990, 148–9).

'THEY HAVE THEIR ENTRANCES AND EXITS'

The core-cairn and passage are structurally joined to the enveloping cairn in the area of the entrance. In a majority of cases, the outermost cairn wall-face curves inwards to meet the passage. This indentation varies from slight dimples (e.g. at Bigland Round, Knowe of Craie and Wideford Hill) to substantial indentations (e.g. at the Ord North and Rudh' an Dunain), and may have provided the stimulus for the creation of the elaborate façades of the horned cairns (e.g. Mid Gleniron I, Garrywhin and South Yarrows). Where multiple wall lines have been used in the external cairn, elaborate façade terraces were created which emphasise the entrance. Camster Long Cairn and the Point of Cott are of this type. Even where the entrance is set in the long wall of a rectangular cairn, its presence can similarly be emphasised by the vertical terminals of the enclosing walls. Recent work at

Isbister has revealed such an arrangement (Smith personal communication), as has work at Gavrinis, Brittany (O'Kelly 1989, 103, Figure 51).

THE DEVELOPMENT OF NEOLITHIC ARCHITECTURE

The relatively ephemeral construction of enveloping cairns implies that their ease of construction and destruction have been consistently underestimated. Fraser's estimates of construction times, ranging from 672 to 13,636 work-hours (1983, 354–7), should be reduced by up to forty per cent, on the basis of the evidence for structural voids at the Point of Cott. That the cairns still represent a significant social commitment cannot be doubted, but it is a commitment which could readily be met by relatively small communities. Reduced to sixty per cent, and assuming a workforce of say ten persons, these estimates imply that a small chambered tomb could be built in forty-one hours, i.e. a small site represents roughly a week's work. The largest site, allowing for a ten-hour day, could have been built in eighty-two days by a ten-person team. If the larger sites were built to service larger communities with a greater labour force available, they could have been built in periods of only a few weeks each.

What goes up quickly can come down quickly! It is salutary to reflect for a moment on what would be left if we were to remove all the stone on a megalithic cairn which was not set in sockets. At the Point of Cott, we would have four pairs of transverse stones and a straggle of orthostatic slabs at the north end. At Maes Howe, we would probably have nothing but the four corner orthostats. From many of the smaller sites, we would simply have nothing at all. The import of this for archaeological studies is that we are studying a residual population of sites biased by the accidents of its survival (*contra* Fraser 1983).

The solidity of core-cairns contrasts strongly with the ephemeral enveloping cairns. Some of the smaller cairns may be residual core-cairns from which all enveloping material has been stripped, and this should be considered when assessing their construction times. Some of the very large cairns are of a particularly dense construction, even in their enveloping material, and their construction times may be close to Fraser's estimates.

Henshall recognises some seventy cairns in the Orkney archipelago. These, with their mainland counterparts, are dated over the fourth to mid-third millennia BC (Kinnes 1985, Figure 7). This reflects a calibrated range of 1340 calendar years. Evenly spread, this implies a building-rate of roughly one site every twenty years.

Neolithic architecture must have evolved as a pragmatic art, not as a structural science. Its development and retention necessarily required the practice of this art on a regular basis. The rate of building implied by both the surviving population of sites and their gross chronology is too slow to allow either for the accumulation of the expertise required or for the retention of that expertise if it were introduced to the islands. Indeed, it seems improbable that tomb-construction alone would have generated or maintained the necessary expertise, and we must wonder what the contribution of the vernacular architecture of the day may have been.

Although not roofed by corbelling, horizontal arching was used in the construction of the Neolithic houses at the Knap of Howar (A. Ritchie 1983) together with slight corbelling of the upper courses. Therefore, some of the architectural expertise we are seeking could be found in these early domestic structures. At Skara Brae, both horizontal arching and corbelling are evidenced, the latter intended to narrow the gap to be roofed rather than to furnish a roof in its own right, but nonetheless present. The houses on Shetland investigated by Calder (1963) are, as Henshall has noted (1963, 151), structurally similar to the cairns of her Zetland Group. The house site at the Ness of Gruting (Calder 1956) has a range of features which, McInnes (1971) argues, relate it both to houses of the Shetland, Stanydale type and those of Skara Brae, and maintains its structural similarities with the chambered cairns.

Removal of the stones of these domestic structures would leave even less for the archaeologist than the removal of the chambered cairns; little more than the earthfast stones of the hearths (Crone forthcoming). Excavations at Barnhouse (Richards 1989, 66–7) have revealed a number of sites, apparently constructed of onion-skin walls, which on the available interim information seem architecturally closer to the great cairns than to the houses at Skara Brae and the Links of Noltland. Similar structures have been revealed in the excavations at Pool, Sanday (Hunter et al. forthcoming).

Even if the first megalith-builders introduced the requisite empirical expertise from elsewhere, it would quickly have been lost if its use were restricted to the small number of chambered cairns which survive. It seems inescapable that chambered cairns were far more numerous than we have previously allowed and that the architecture of the cairns was also that of the contemporaneous domestic sites.

ARCHITECTURE AND SOCIETY (FORM AND FUNCTION)

Binford et al. (1970, 1) have noted that archaeological sites should exhibit a complex formal-spatial structure in direct correspondence to the degree of differentiation of activities and social units performing the various activities. Goldstein interprets this as meaning that mortuary sites should exhibit 'a complex formal-spatial structure' (1981, 57). The implication appears to be that the architecture of chambered tombs should reflect the liturgical practices of their users. However there are several significant obstacles to the archaeological retrieval of the relationship between the architectural form and liturgical functions of these monuments.

To begin with, liturgical changes of considerable scale can take place with little or no architectural adjustment to sacred structures. While it is true that newly-built post-Reformation churches in Scotland reflect in their architecture the liturgical processes favoured at the time of their construction (Hay 1957), existing churches were very rarely abandoned. As Gerit Berckheyde's painting (1673) of the Dutch Reform Church meeting in Haarlem's Grote Kerke eloquently demonstrates, existing churches could accommodate the formal requirements of this liturgical revolution by a simple rearrangement of the seating!

The common re-use of, for example, Irish passage tombs for Beaker burials, suggests that liturgical changes were also accommodated in existing formal contexts in the early prehistoric period. The implication for chambered cairns seems to be that only the very last sites built will reflect a single liturgical tradition; all the earlier sites will present a palimpsest, a conflation, of the formal accommodations of the several liturgies in vogue during the currency of their use and subsequent re-use.

The unreliability of single radiocarbon dates, or even of small numbers of dates, from the disturbed chamber floors of chambered cairns adds to our difficulties, as does the 'bunching' of dates around 2400 bc, which is an artefact of the calibration curve. The effect of both has been to reduce chronological resolution and, consequently, to produce apparently overlapping date-ranges for the different cairn-types.

Precisely dated structural and depositional assemblages from a statistically significant number of cairns may distinguish between successive liturgical practices and separate stages in a single, but complex, and contemporaneous, liturgy. Until then, the relationship between liturgical practice and architectural form must remain hidden from us. Fortunately, this does not impair our appreciation of chambered cairns as expressions of a well-developed, sophisticated and, above all, impressive architectural tradition.

ACKNOWLEDGEMENTS

I am indebted to Christina Unwin for the drawings in this chapter and for discussion of their content. Patrick Ashmore, Gordon Barclay, Ann MacSween, Olwyn Owen and Finbar McCormick commented on a first draft of this chapter, and I am grateful to them for their helpful suggestions. I would also like to acknowledge the assistance of the volume's editors, Niall Sharples and Alison Sheridan, whose various comments and criticisms have been most helpful.

NOTES

1. In an earlier paper, I have referred to core-cairns as construction-cairns (Barber 1988, 58). Davidson and Henshall's term 'core-cairn' is much better, and I am happy to adopt it in this text and to abandon my somewhat clumsy term.
2. I have used 'liturgical' and 'liturgy' throughout this text to avoid the omnibus terms 'ritual' and 'rite', not least because I feel that the latter terms imply that a single rite or a continuity of ritual behaviour charac-

terised the use of chambered tombs, and this I believe to be highly improbable.

This chapter is based on the Society of Antiquaries of Scotland Buchan Lecture, presented by the author at Kirkwall, Orkney in 1990.

3

The Bargrennan Group of Chambered Cairns: Circumstance and Context

Jane Murray

INTRODUCTION

The Bargrennan Group was first identified by Audrey Henshall in the second volume of her *magnum opus*, *The Chambered Tombs of Scotland* (1972), and her account (pp. 1–6, 249–56, 278), together with the individual plans and descriptions in her Catalogue of Sites, remains the only detailed treatment accorded to this somewhat unusual set of passage graves in south-west Scotland. It is hoped that this chapter, discussing both the specific circumstance and the broader context of the group, may provide some measure of the further analysis which the initial study was intended to provoke.

HISTORY OF RESEARCH

Before publication of Henshall's volume, recognition of the Bargrennan Group was hampered by a shortage of published plans of chambered cairns in Galloway and Ayrshire, where the 'gallery grave' of Clyde-Solway type was taken to represent the norm (Daniel 1962, 52). Chambers in both types of tomb are rectangular, simple in plan and in uncorbelled elevation, while cairn shapes are often idiosyncratic (e.g. Mid Gleniron II; Cairnholy II). It can be unclear whether outlines, distorted through the passage of time, represent round or long cairns. Presenting the Wigtownshire Inventory, A.O. Curle attempted to impose order on this somewhat featureless material by suggesting a sequence of attenuation, from long chambered cairns, through oval and round, to the round cairns with closed cists of the Bronze Age (RCAHMS 1912, xxxviii).

Curle's model of progressive degeneration was accepted by Gordon Childe, who treated all the Galloway chambered cairns as members of a 'Solway Group', a sub-group related to the neighbouring Clyde cairns. He noted as distinguishing features the small size of the Solway chambers and the presence of 'an ante-chamber or even a built passage' (1935a, 31). Childe was clearly conflating structural features at the two Cairnholy cairns, where tall portal stones mark the entrance to high-roofed 'ante-chambers', with those at the King's Cairn on the Water of Deugh, where passages diminish in size towards an entrance almost impossible of access. Of the latter site, Childe commented: 'Here we see the collective tomb turning into individual sepulchre' (1946, 40).

It was with the expressed intention of elucidating this relationship that, in 1949, Professor Stuart Piggott and T.G.E. Powell, having completed investigation of the Cairnholy cairns, devoted two days to excavation of the exposed chamber and passage at the round White Cairn of Bargrennan, 30 km to the north-west. They showed that this massively-built structure consisted of a 'truncated wedge' 7·3 m in overall length, narrowing internally from 1·3 m at the inner end to 0·6 m at the outer. Despite the lack of differentiation between chamber and passage, they could unhesitatingly assign the monument, with its circular cairn, to the passage grave group. Confirmation of cultural difference from the 'Clyde-Carlingford' tombs at Cairnholy was found both in the presence of a cremation pit at the entrance to the Bargrennan passage, for which parallels were suggested in Late Neolithic ritual pit settings such as Cairnpapple, and in the character of the impressed pottery sherds from the passage floor which were compared to finds from Irish passage graves at Carrowkeel and Loughcrew. In contrast, an upright carinated bowl from Cairnholy I was said to relate to Carlingford tomb wares (S. Piggott and Powell 1949, 119, 152).

The only other certain passage grave in south-west Scotland cited by Piggott and Powell was the King's Cairn on the Water of Deugh, excavated by Curle in 1929 (Curle 1930), although they mentioned as possibilities two other round cairns, Cairn Kenny and Cave Cairn. In his *Neolithic Cultures of the British Isles* (1954), Stuart Piggott made only passing reference to 'scattered sites of passage grave type' in Galloway (p. 223). In 1972, however, Henshall could list twelve probable and two or three possible members of a Bargrennan Group, and further sites have more recently been identified (The Druid's Grave: Masters 1981a; Baing Loch: RCAHMS 1983, 8, no. 23; Claywarnies: RCAHMS 1987, 10, no. 27). Bargrennan cairns now seem to be more numerous in Galloway and south Ayrshire than Clyde cairns.

PROBLEMS OF CLASSIFICATION

Following Piggott and Powell, Henshall defined the Bargrennan Group on the basis of the passage grave format. The cairns were said to be characteristically round, although at least two long cairns (Cuff Hill and the Caves of Kilhern) were included; the chambers were described as being rectangular or wedge-shaped, sometimes merging into the passage without structural distinction (1972, 6–7). As theories of multi-period construction developed during the 1960s (Corcoran 1969a), the importance of the shape of the cairn as a guide to classification diminished. Further, if chambers of different types could all be subsumed within the final form of an enveloping long cairn, this raised doubts as to the validity of the distinction between passage graves and gallery graves. Henshall felt it necessary to accept the 'theoretical possibility' that an originally small, simple chamber could have undergone extension to become an elongated Bargrennan-style, wedge-shaped chamber set in an enlarged round cairn (1972, 249–50). Such a local process of evolution was, however, difficult to reconcile with the undeniably 'international' character of the monuments, closely allied, for example, to the undifferentiated passage graves which appear to cluster around the great mound at Knowth (ibid., 276). The Bargrennan Group 'posed problems', and Henshall's favoured solution came to be one of the 'hybridisation' between two early, simple forms of monument, Clyde tombs and Orkney-Cromarty-Hebridean passage graves (Henshall 1974, 153). The sequence envisaged could accommodate recognition of passage grave influence both in the initial impetus to monument-building and in later developments, while acknowledging the importance of local evolutionary processes in accounting for regional peculiarities.

To the present writer, it seems that an ingenious solution has been found to a morphological puzzle which could itself have been avoided by the use of a different basis of classification. The presence of a passage does not necessarily indicate typological, let alone cultural relatedness, but may be no more than a simple structural device. The round White Cairn at Bargrennan with its undifferentiated chamber and passage must certainly be distinguished from the trapezoidal cairns with simple or segmented chambers of the Solway area; it need not be any more closely related to those long cairns with chambers approached through narrow passages included in Henshall's Bargrennan Group. The three surviving chambers at Cuff Hill and the axial, east chamber at the Caves of Kilhern all have distinctly separate passages, while the remaining three chambers at the latter site have entrances marked by transverse portal stones. These long cairns contain no undifferentiated structures comparable to that at Bargrennan, and there seems no reason to suppose any cultural or even structurally imitative relationship between the two site-types. Jack Scott has aptly remarked (1969, 211–12) on the resemblance between Cuff Hill and the laterally-chambered Cotswold-Severn cairns, sites now considered to be early in their local sequence (Thomas 1988), and not necessarily the product of phased accumulation (see Gwernvale: Britnell and Savory 1984). Exclusion of long cairns from the Bargrennan Group leaves a coherent set of circular passage graves, morphologically repetitive and spatially discrete. These monuments are most probably of a single phase, planned and executed to a recognisable and replicated pattern by a homogeneous social group.

STRUCTURAL CHARACTERISTICS

Table 3.1 lists eleven probable and two possible members of a Bargrennan Group of round cairns, and their distribution is shown on Figure 3.1. (Readers seeking further details are referred to the appendix to this chapter.) All the sites have been examined and planned in 1989–90, and will be

Table 3.1: Round Cairns of the Bargrennan Group (County numbers after Henshall 1972)

1. Balmalloch AYR 3
2. Cave Cairn AYR 4
3. The Druid's Grave AYR 7 (Masters 1981a)
4. Baing Loch, Ayrshire (RCAHMS 1983, 8, no 22)
5. White Cairn, Bargrennan KRK 5
6. Cairnderry KRK 6
7. King's Cairn, Kirriemore KRK 10
8. Sheuchan's Cairn KRK 11
9. King's Cairn, Water of Deugh KRK 13
10. Cairn Kenny WIG 4
11. Claywarnies, Wigtownshire (RCAHMS 1987, 10, no 23)

Possible sites
12. Arecleoch AYR 2
13. Craigairie Fell, Wigtownshire (Yates 1984 6, 182 EW1)

discussed in a forthcoming thesis (Edinburgh University). Most are in a very poor condition. Cairn material had sometimes been collapsing before the construction of sheepfolds or pens which are found on or against ten of the thirteen sites, and which have caused serious damage. Ten cairns are in forestry where vegetation obscures details. One entire site at Arecleoch has been quarried away. Nevertheless, each cairn could originally have been circular, usually between 16 m and 20 m in diameter, with Cairnderry and Kirriemore reaching 24 m and 26 m respectively. These are high mounded cairns, very different from the small oval or kidney-shaped structures, 7 m in maximum diameter, enclosed within the long cairns at Mid Gleniron (Corcoran 1969b). The Auld Wife's Grave (WIG 3), a 9–10 m cairn, has therefore been rejected as being uncharacteristic of the Group, and the destroyed chamber at Arecleoch, which may also have been in a cairn no more than 10 m in diameter (OS records NX17 NE2), is listed only as a possible member. These two cairns, together with a 13–14 m round cairn on Craigairie Fell, where only one stone of a probable chamber survives *in situ*, have been excluded from the following analysis.

Figure 3.2 depicts the six most regular chamber layouts with projected original circumference lines imposed. These cairns contain one, two or three chambers, axially and symmetrically arranged, and the double- or multi-chambered examples are clearly not simple extensions of single-chambered cairns. Number 8, Sheuchan's Cairn, may still conceal a second chamber under its mound. Figure 3.3 shows the rather more variable layouts of the remaining cairns, mostly badly damaged or less fully exposed. These examples could include some expanded cairns (e.g. No. 7, Kirriemore) or alterations of layout (e.g. No. 3, The Druid's Grave) but, where evidence is best-preserved, designs are regular and deliberate and appear to be of a single phase.

The chambers, apart from one polygonal example at Balmalloch, are all

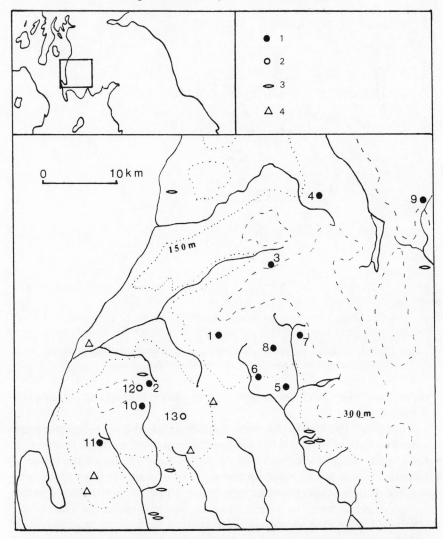

Figure 3.1: Distribution map: Bargrennan round cairns and other Neolithic cairns in south-west
Scotland. Key: 1. Bargrennan cairns; 2. Possible Bargrennan cairns; 3. Long cairns,
chambered and unchambered; 4. Possible long cairns and other chambered cairns.
Numbers refer to Table 3.1.

rectangular and all seem to be undifferentiated from their passages, except in
the occasional appearance of a low sill-stone. At least four examples,
including the White Cairn, Bargrennan, are constructed of four pairs of large
orthostats, a regularity itself suggesting intended design rather than fortuitous extension. The unity of the structure at the White Cairn is further
demonstrated by the combined support which the three inner orthostats of

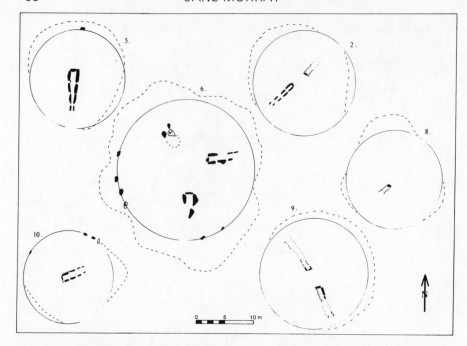

Figure 3.2: Bargrennan round cairns: chamber layout and projected original outline. Most
           typical examples. Numbers refer to the Appendix.

the east wall give to an upper layer of big blocks (S. Piggott and Powell 1949,
Figure 12).

About half the visible chambers employ an alternative technique using
long, thin slabs of stone laid flat and sometimes stacked on top of one another
rather than being bonded into walling. At the King's Cairn on the Water of
Deugh, six such layers make up one portion of wall. At Cave Cairn, one
chamber is orthostatic, the other largely slab-built, showing that local stone-
type did not dictate the style employed but that deliberate choice was
involved. Use of long slabs could have recalled the laminar sandstone flags
of the northern passage graves or, in more local vein, the timber planks of
mortuary chambers such as Lochhill (Masters 1973; and cf. Haddenham:
Shand and Hodder 1990), presumably also used in domestic buildings.

If later extension has affected Bargrennan cairns, this could most plausibly
be expected to have taken the form of concentric outer revetments concealing
original passage-entrances, none of which is now visible. No archaeological
excavation has examined cairn structure, but extensive casual denudation has
failed to reveal any inner wall-faces. At the White Cairn, Bargrennan, excavation showed the passage to terminate 1·8 m from the cairn edge. Between the
east wall and the cairn perimeter, a burnt area and a cremation pit were
sealed under cairn stones which were probably in position when the passage

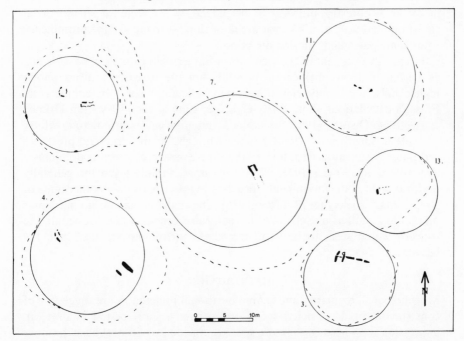

Figure 3.3: Bargrennan round cairns: chamber layout and projected original outline. Severely damaged and irregular examples. Numbers refer to the Appendix.

was infilled (S. Piggott and Powell 1949, Figure 12). The excavators suggested that entry could have been made from above, perhaps by steps. It seems at least possible that the cairn was originally constructed to its full present dimensions with the entrance deliberately concealed. Given the morphological similarity between Bargrennan cairns and the undifferentiated passage graves in the Boyne Valley, it is worth recalling Frances Lynch's projected reconstruction of Cairn L at Newgrange, as well as of other passage graves in Ireland and Anglesey, involving a 'roof-box' feature for ritual communication with the interior (F.M. Lynch 1973). The small opening envisaged, although visible from the exterior, would not have provided a functional entrance. The concept of the chamber as an inaccessible shrine rather than as a tomb for recurrent deposition of remains seems particularly appropriate in relation to the narrow Bargrennan passages, their entrances concealed, and leading to no large, corbelled central space.

SITUATION AND OUTLOOK

Five Bargrennan cairns are on rounded knolls, clearly chosen as sites for circular cairns. These locations are often inconspicuous, but the use of a natural mound undoubtedly adds to the visual impressiveness of the cairn, particularly when approached from lower ground. The consistent preference, in so far as forestry allows it to be judged, is for secluded sites of local elevation – a knoll, a ridge, or a break in slope – giving skyline prominence from some particular, limited direction.

Twenty-five per cent of the views from Bargrennan cairns can be classified as 'Distant' in terms of extending beyond 5 km; the five eastern cairns, among higher hills, have only eleven per cent 'Distant' views. In comparison, Fraser's calculations show thirty-eight per cent of the views from Orkney cairns to be 'Distant' (1983, 301). No Bargrennan cairn appears to overlook any other member of the Group, although, again, forestry precludes certainty. These cairns were not, by their mere presence, asserting dominance over others (cf. Fraser 1983, 379), nor, more suitably given the generally uniform scale of the monuments, proclaiming peer parity with other units of a segmentary society (cf. Renfrew 1976). The chambers favour no particular orientation, and, as one chamber in each cairn generally faces downhill, the concern would seem to be with immediate surroundings rather than the heavens.

DISTRIBUTION

Morphological regularity and shared locational preferences are suggestive of construction by a restricted social group over a short period of time, an impression supported by the close spatial coincidence of the set once the more scattered long cairns are excluded (Figure 3.1). Distribution extends over 60 km in a belt stretching from near Loch Ryan in the west to the Water of Deugh in the east. Although only a proportion of original numbers may have survived and, given the large numbers of round cairns in the South-West, been recognised, the compactness of the surviving distribution indicates a close approximation to original limits.

Six of the eleven cairns are almost exactly 4 km from their nearest Bargrennan neighbour, with none at a closer distance if the doubtful Arecleoch chamber is omitted. This regularity supports the suggested contemporaneity of use. The dispersed pattern, very different from that of the clustered passage graves of Ireland, would accord with a settlement-based, territorial system, such as that postulated by Renfrew in relation to Arran (1976, Figure 6). The three north-eastern cairns are more widely dispersed, 11 to 14 km apart, probably because of restricted settlement opportunity in more rugged hill country.

The two largest cairns, Cairnderry and Kirriemore, both with chambers of massive orthostatic construction, lie only 8 km apart within the central cluster of sites. This spatial pattern is not necessarily a reflection of centralised authority: the most isolated sites contain two chambers, a complexity which could derive not from rank but from the need for cooperation between small, scattered social units.

ENVIRONMENT

The inland and upland (120 m–300 m OD) distribution of the sites has led to suggestions that their environment was inhospitable and perhaps only suitable for pastoralists (Childe 1946, 40–1; Henshall 1972, 6). Isobel Hughes (1988) has argued that the Ayrshire cairns could relate to mobile exploitation of upland resources by coastal communities (but see Murray forthcoming). However the potential of this hill country for permanent settlement should not be underestimated.

The shallow blanket bog covering the moors in the western half of the distribution area is likely to have originated in later prehistory (P.D. Moore 1973), and during the fourth to third millennium BC these low hills probably carried light mixed oak forest (A.G. Smith 1981, 125–7) attractive to Neolithic farmers. To the east the more rugged Galloway hills offer a harsher environment; nonetheless, analysis of pollen cores from the valley of the Black Water of Dee has shown that during the early to mid-fourth millennium BC the regional vegetation picture was varied with much open ground offering scope for pastoral use as well as opportunities for the exploitation of wild resources (Birks 1975, 207).

A few of the cairns seem to be particularly isolated and are located on or above steep hillsides. Monuments, however, do not necessarily coincide directly with settlement. All the sites are within 2 km of modern farms in valleys which offer some arable potential, and it would seem that the relationship to settlement may have been peripheral only to the extent that the cairns lay at the limits of individual catchment areas. The consistent proximity to hill-country is nonetheless striking, and, although perhaps an aspect of ritual practice, it also argues for concern with pastoralism or hunting.

SETTLEMENT EVIDENCE

Despite cairn locations which often seem unpropitious for settlement and agriculture, evidence for prehistoric land use in the vicinity has occasionally survived the effects of peat-growth and afforestation. Small cairns were recorded beside Bargrennan White Cairn before the area was planted (F.R. Coles 1897, 5), and they survive, partly peat-submerged, close to Balmalloch cairn (RCAHMS 1981, 13, no. 76). Cairn Kenny is surrounded by deep peat, but at 500 m to 2 km distant, on the better-drained hillsides that remain unplanted, a remarkable series of hut circles, buried walls, small cairns and enclosures has been recorded (RCAHMS 1987, 40–1, nos. 214, 216). From a terrace 600 m to the north of Claywarnies, a small hut-circle still enjoys a skyline view of the cairn on the newly planted, southern side of the valley (RCAHMS 1981, 19, no. 129).

Most of these remains probably pertain to the Bronze Age, with the small cairns offering the best prospect of a Neolithic origin (Yates 1984a, 225–6). The dispersed settlement that they represent, however, conforms to common

Neolithic patterns and is likely to have been of long continuity. If a suggested minimum half a dozen family units were farming within a 2 km radius of each cairn, population over the whole distribution area would have reached several hundreds, a viable level for a reproduction network.

ARTEFACTUAL EVIDENCE

Artefacts which could derive from Bargrennan settlement are a rarity, reflecting the poor recovery potential of upland, peat-covered country. The total absence from the area of polished stone or flint axeheads furnishes, however, such a contrast with the dense distribution of stone axeheads in the coastal lowlands (P.R. Ritchie 1987, 11) as to suggest cultural difference. It may indicate not merely exclusion from particular exchange networks, but the prevalence of contrasting attitudes to axes as appropriate items for deposition.

Reported finds of leaf-shaped arrowheads from the shores of Loch Doon (*Discovery Excav Scotl* 1968, 14; 1969, 31), midway between Bargrennan cairns at Baing Loch and on the Water of Deugh, suggest hunting activity, although coincidence with areas of Mesolithic recovery may link the finds to episodes of Early Neolithic seasonal exploitation rather than to settlement by cairn-builders (cf. Hughes 1988). Two separate finds of flint knives have been made within 1·5 km of Bargrennan White Cairn, one with part of a leaf-shaped arrowhead (*Proc Soc Antiq Scotl* 89 (1955–6), 458; 90 (1956–7), 260), and these items, together with the fabricator from the excavation, suggest access to supplies of flint, perhaps from Ireland. The pottery sherds from the passage find parallels among the prolific coarse, decorated wares from Luce Sands, 28 km to the south-west (McInnes 1964, 49ff.).

CHRONOLOGY

No secure dating evidence is available for the cairns. Sherds from the passage paving in the Bargrennan White Cairn cannot be associated with construction, even if Scottish decorated pottery could itself offer chronological precision (A.M. Gibson 1984, 79). The cremation pit at the entrance is not usefully to be compared to Late Neolithic pit settings; 'ritual pits' recur at Neolithic sites of all periods, including Irish court cairns with early dates (E.E. Evans 1953, 67).

Indications of date may be derived from comparative morphology, local settlement sequence and environmental evidence, but, since these approaches are merely inferential, the information from each must be combined to give mutual support. The passage grave classification is, in itself, unhelpful since such monuments appear to have been constructed along the north-western seaboard of the British Isles from at least the early fourth millennium BC (Burenhult 1984), and probably into the second half of the third millennium BC. Chronological sequences have been postulated for passage graves in Ireland by Alison Sheridan (1986a), and in northern Scotland by Niall

Sharples (1985), both suggesting a model of progressive aggrandisement from small and simple to large and complex, with lesser discussion of late developments. Undifferentiated passage graves in Ireland, comparable in size to the Bargrennan cairns, are assigned to Sheridan's Stage 3 with dates of about 3500–3000 BC. Developed tripartite tombs in Caithness of an equivalent scale have produced dates between c. 3600 BC and c. 3400 BC (Sharples 1986).

In the extreme south-west of Scotland, there is no similar context of passage grave building. The earliest dated monuments here are rectangular 'boxes' of timber or of megalithic construction destined to be enclosed within trapezoidal cairns. A plank, presumably of mature timber, from the mortuary structure at Lochhill, Kirkcudbright, has given a date of 4005–3770 CAL-BC (I- 6409: Masters 1973), while charcoal from below an orthostat of the axial chamber at Glenvoidean, Bute, a very similar site to the Mid Gleniron cairns, was dated to 3775–3540 CAL-BC (I- 5974: Marshall and Taylor 1977). In the Solway valleys, long cairns lie consistently at least 9 km south of Bargrennan sites, and the physical separation is chronologically uninformative. In south Ayrshire, however, the steep-sided Stinchar valley offers no suitable settlement niches, and here Clyde cairns penetrate inland onto the moors. A trapezoidal cairn with orthostatic façade on Loch Hill, Ayrshire (RCAHMS 1981, 7, no. 5), is only 1·3 km from Cave Cairn. If spatial contiguity is indicative of chronological disparity, the Bargrennan cairn should be the later, although the interval of time is not easy to estimate.

In view of the divergent local traditions, it would be inappropriate to transfer dating evidence from the morphologically similar Irish passage graves to the Galloway series. Emulation of the passage grave format must, however, be a factor in the appearance of the isolated Bargrennan enclave in south-west Scotland, having no obvious cultural affinities with any 'host' region. If the aim were to establish status by demonstrating knowledge of contemporary structures of power (Bradley 1985, 8–9), an appropriate context should shortly post-date the construction of major monuments in the Boyne Valley and in the Orkneys in the late fourth millennium BC. While there is a danger here of reliance on self-sustaining typological assumptions of unilinear sequence (Kinnes 1985, 31), it may be ventured that the assured confidence of the replicated Bargrennan style would fit happily into this relatively late context. Such dating would mean that the cairns could have been contemporary with the stone circles of the Solway Peninsula, which do not occur in their vicinity.

The late fourth to early third millennium BC offers an appropriate context for the expansion of settlement into the Galloway uplands in terms of the ecological diversification of the 'secondary Neolithic' already recognised by Stuart Piggott (1954, 365–6) and characterised by the spread of settlement into new environments (Bradley and Hodder 1979, 96), reaching even such extremities as the infertile hillsides of Scord of Brouster in Shetland (Whittle

1986). Chapman has commented on the coincidence between the construction of megalithic tombs and agricultural expansion into difficult, upland environments in several parts of Europe (1981, 78–9), and the small, heel-shaped cairns of Shetland may similarly have accompanied the intensification of land use here in the late fourth to early third millennium BC (Müller 1988, 7–8). The Bargrennan Group could be a comparable instance of regional diversity and social fragmentation in the same period.

Environmental sequences from the Galloway Hills do not register major and permanent clearance until levels considerably post-dating the Elm Decline (Birks 1975), and this development has conventionally been ascribed to the late third to early second millennium BC, largely on the basis of comparisons with the rather different lowland environment at Bloak Moss in north Ayrshire (e.g. Price 1983, 188–9). However, a dated pollen core now available from the Round Loch of Glenhead, only 9–10 km from the cairns at Kirriemore and at Bargrennan, exhibiting a very similar sequence to that of the earlier studies, shows the onset of major clearance to occur just before c. 2800 BC (V.J. Jones, Stevenson and Batterbee 1989). Diatom analysis of sediments from the same loch detected two specific episodes of catchment disturbance and inwash dated to c. 2870 and c. 2600 BC. Intensification of activity in the Galloway Hills during the Late Neolithic would appear to have been unequivocally demonstrated.

If the Bargrennan Group can be assigned to the late fourth or early third millennium BC, it can be accommodated within a local sequence offering greater credibility than any model which invokes concepts of passage grave 'intrusion' into an alien cultural milieu. Despite chronological uncertainty, the evidence seems strong enough to warrant assessment of the role of the monuments on this basis.

SOCIAL AND SYMBOLIC SIGNIFICANCE

Acceptance of the local context obviates the need to search for Bargrennan origins in population movements or missionary conversions (cf. Herity 1973). In certain respects, there is apparent continuity between local long cairns and the Bargrennan sites. They share a simplicity of chamber design and construction, comparable patterns of distribution, and locational preference for enclosed valley sites lacking prominence. Nonetheless, the progression from Clyde cairns to passage graves cannot be viewed as simple replacement over time. Chambered cairns are not a ubiquitous component of the Neolithic, and their appearance in any particular settlement phase requires further explanation.

Theoretical models which emphasise the role of chambered cairns as an aspect of the agriculturalist's investment of effort in land (Meillassoux 1973) have had to take account of the frequent association of such monuments with marginal land (Bradley 1984, 15–17). Attention has turned to the stresses induced by population pressure (Renfrew 1976), or critical resource levels

(Chapman 1981) in the stimulation of public and sometimes competitive display (Cherry 1978; 1981; Hodder 1979). Alternatively, marginality could be interpreted as a simple function of dispersed settlement, the cairns serving as 'social integrative facilities' for units of a scattered population (Adler and Wilshusen 1990, 133). Bargrennan cairns lack functional space for group participation at ritual performances but, nonetheless, the standardisation of design across the set demonstrates the existence of social contact and the maintenance of an active information network. The combination of architectural replication and ritual exclusiveness may suggest that the relationships serviced by this facility were not those of immediately local families, but concerned a specialised segment of the whole regional population.

In many respects, the Bargrennan cairns appear to be the product of an egalitarian society. The monuments are largely uniform in scale, lack internal demarcation of space and are not associated with prestige artefacts. Nonetheless, in a non-literate society, knowledge of and control over the secrets of the tomb can provide a potent substitute for material symbols of power (Bourdieu 1977, 187–9). The cairns themselves with their attendant ritual may have constituted a 'mode of domination', symbolising and actively regulating social order. The barely accessible passages, angled downwards to admit little light, set a distance between the living and the dead, between sacred and profane, a separation which some would see as redolent of a patriarchal social organisation (cf. Grøn 1989, 103 on domestic spatial ordering).

When social diversity is manifested in the form of distinctive material culture traits, such as Bargrennan cairns, this may itself be an indication of the existence of competitive stress generating an attachment to cultural identity and a need for expression of difference (Hodder 1978). The establishment of settlement in the Galloway uplands is likely to have disrupted long traditions of seasonal activity, resulting in rivalry between upland and lowland communities. The achievements of earlier megalith-builders still retained a role in the Late Neolithic, posing a challenge to the new settlers, who could choose to emphasise 'schism' by the adoption of a new style of monument (Bradley 1985, 13). The round cairn, an economical way of producing an effect as impressive as that of the sealed long cairn, also embodied a display of knowledge of modes current among other power systems, and it proclaimed difference from the lowland sequence of Clyde cairns and stone circles.

Finally, it must be significant that Bargrennan cairns failed to attract the later ritual and funerary activity that clusters round and impinges upon the long cairns of the region. Apart from small cairnfields, the closest Bargrennan 'satellites' are two round cairns 300–400 m south-west of the King's Cairn on the Water of Deugh (RCAHMS 1914, 63 no. 90), and these were not positioned to obtain a view of the chambered cairn. This avoidance could be interpreted as a failure of the Bargrennan ritual to maintain its power over succeeding generations. Alternatively, in the Bronze Age landscape of large round cairns, the identical outward appearance of the sealed Bargrennan mounds may have continued to command respect in contrast to the long cairns, which, as obsolete historical monuments, could be used to confer prestige on a new order.

CONCLUSION

It is hoped that the Bargrennan Group as defined in this paper may be regarded not as a problem but as the monumental expression of a well-defined and cohesive social group. Despite drawing inspiration from the international family of passage graves, the society that built the cairns appears to have been inward-looking, even isolated. In view of the restricted distribution of the monuments and their occurrence within a limited environmental range, they would seem to represent the achievement of a people with a shared subsistence strategy and world-view, a sizeable community entirely likely to have evolved locally. Such a context for the Group would seem to offer as close an approximation to an archaeological 'culture' as may be expected to be encountered among the fragmented circumstance of Neolithic survival in Scotland.

ACKNOWLEDGEMENTS

I would like to thank Roger Mercer for discussions of Bargrennan cairns and Dr Richard Tipping for information on environmental evidence.

APPENDIX: BARGRENNAN ROUND CAIRNS

(Numbers correspond with those on the map (Figure 3.1) and plans (Figures 3.2 and 3.3). Key to abbreviations: DES = *Discovery and Excavation in Scotland*; ONB = Ordnance Survey Object Name Books; NMR = National Monuments Record; NSA = The New Statistical Account of Scotland 1845.

1. *Balmalloch* AYR 3   NX 2638 8453
   Diameter: 17 m, spread to 23 m.
   Two chambers, one with capstone *in situ*, one dislodged.
   Refs: ONB Ayrshire 10, 93–4; J. Smith 1895, 219; Childe and Graham 1943, 33–5; J.G. Scott 1969, 318; Henshall 1972, 398–9; RCAHMS 1981, 7, no. 2.
2. *Cave Cairn* AYR 4   NX 1831 7924
   Diameter: 17·5 m, spread to 21 m; under sheepfold.
   Two chambers, one with capstone *in situ*, one dislodged. Refs: ONB Ayrshire, 6, 52; G. Wilson, MS Notes NMR 457; J. Smith 1895, 224–5; Childe 1934, 21; 1946, 101; S. Piggott and Powell 1949, 144 no. 14; W.L. Scott 1951b, 71, appendix 3; Gray 1956, 13; J.G. Scott 1969, 318; Henshall 1972, 399–400; RCAHMS 1981, 7, no. 3.
3. *The Druid's Grave* AYR 7   NX 3477 9439

Diameter: 16 m; under sheepfold.

One chamber, two capstones *in situ*; possible second chamber, only north side surviving.

Refs: M'Bain 1929, 120–1; McDowall 1947, 469–70, 542; DES 1976, 21; Masters 1981a; RCAHMS 1983, 9, no. 23.

4. *Baing Loch*, Ayrshire   NX 4128 0276

Diameter: 20 m, spread to 24 m; under sheepfold.

One probable chamber; second structure, possibly a passage.

Refs: ONB Ayrshire, 60, 116; RCAHMS 1983, 8, no. 22.

5. *White Cairn, Bargrennan* KRK 5   NX 3524 7835

Diameter: 16·5 m, spread to 19 m.

One chamber, two capstones *in situ*.

Excavation: S. Piggott and Powell 1949.

Refs: NSA IV, 132; ONB Stewartry of Kirkcudbright, 49, 10; Wilson 1851, 61; F.R. Coles 1894, 64; 1897, 4–5; RCAHMS 1914, 186–8, no. 350; S. Piggott 1954, 265; Daniel 1962, 63; J.G. Scott 1969, 323; Henshall 1972, 445–7.

6. *Cairnderry* KRK 7   NX 3159 7994

Diameter: 24 m, spread to 28 m.

Three chambers, one with capstone dislodged.

Refs: F.R. Coles 1894, 63–4; 1897, 2–7; RCAHMS 1914, 184–6, No. 346; S. Piggott and Powell 1949, 143, 144, no. 6; DES 1958, 25–6; Daniel 1962, 52; J.G. Scott 1969, 212, 324; Henshall 1972, 448–9.

7. *The King's Cairn, Kirriemore* KRK 10   NX 3773 8545

Diameter: 26 m, spread to 34 × 30 m.

One chamber, one capstone and one lintel *in situ*

Refs: ONB Stewartry of Kirkcudbright, 25, 28; RCAHMS 1914, 188, no. 351; J.G. Scott 1969, 323; Henshall 1972, 452–3.

8. *Sheuchan's Cairn* KRK 11   NX 3379 8387

Diameter: 16·5 m.

One chamber, capstone dislodged.

Refs: RCAHMS 1914, 188, no. 352; J.G. Scott 1969, 323; Henshall 1972, 454–5.

9. *The King's Cairn, Water of Deugh* KRK 13   NX 5542 0114

Diameter: 18·5 m, spread to 20 × 21 m; within sheepfold.

Two chambers, one lintel *in situ*.

Excavation: Curle 1930

Refs: RCAHMS 1914, 63–4, no. 91; Childe 1933, 129; 1935a, 31; 1946, 40; S. Piggott and Powell 1949, 152; S. Piggott 1954, 243; Daniel 1962, 52; Henshall 1972, 455–6.

10. *Cairn Kenny* WIG 4   NX 1746 7526

Diameter: 15·5 m.

One chamber, capstone dislodged.

Refs: ONB Wigtownshire, 5, 11; G. Wilson, MS Notes NMR 457;

RCAHMS 1912, 99, no. 271; S. Piggott and Powell 1949, 144, no. 13; J.G. Scott 1969, 328; Henshall 1972, 538–9. Plan: Atkinson and Ritchie 1952, NMR WGD/74.

11. *Claywarnies, Wigtownshire*   NX 1034 7171
Diameter: c. 19–20 m; under sheepfold.
One chamber (possible).
Refs: Smith 1895, 227; RCAHMS 1987, 10, no. 27.

Possible Sites

12. *Arecleoch* AYR 2   NX 1742 7827
Diameter: possibly 10 m (OS records); site destroyed.
One chamber.
Refs: ONB Ayrshire 6, 51, 75; G. Wilson, MS Notes NMR 457; J. Smith 1895, 224; OS records NX 17NE 2; Gray 1956, 12; J.G. Scott 1969, 318; Henshall 1972, 397, 399; RCAHMS 1981, 7, no. 1.

13. *Craigairie Fell, Wigtownshire*   NX 2324 7439
Diameter: 13–14 m; under sheepfold.
One chamber (possible).
Refs: DES 1977, 39; Yates 1984b, 182 EWI.

4

Cumulative Cairn Construction and Cultural Continuity in Caithness and Orkney

Roger Mercer

INTRODUCTION

Caithness is at once one of the most beautiful counties in the British Isles and one of the most intimidating. The severity of the landscapes and the ferocity of its rain are matched only by the glory of its light and the generous warmth of its people. It is a quite separate and individual element of the Scottish mainland which can never fail to impress itself on the visitor as he or she swings down from the hill-country to west and south onto the plateau with its sharply contrasting geology, vegetation, architecture, agriculture and coastline. This must always have been so, creating in Caithness a space quite apart within the cultural landscape of Scotland. Beyond it lies a further entity, as we see it today – the Orcadian archipelago closely similar in almost every regard to Caithness but divorced from it in our minds by different, and relatively new, concepts of centrality and proximity. With a constant focus upon the 'Central Belt' of Scotland, Orkney seems distant and isolated yet invested with a degree of curiosity and romanticism that provokes enquiry and visitation. Caithness is simply distant and relatively unknown.

Centrality in Scotland has differentiated Orkney from Caithness in our minds in a way quite at variance with the ancient close parallelism of the two areas. Modern concepts of proximity have set the seal upon this divorce. It is now more difficult in some ways to move between Thurso and Kirkwall than between Edinburgh and Kirkwall. The increasingly ineffectual 'Jellicoe railway' renders communication with Thurso a penance (if one with beautiful interludes), while aeroplane or boat renders Kirkwall a less daunting prospect (if still an expensive one). We no longer have a society, either in Orkney or in Caithness, where small-boat passage is routine, and thus communion between the two areas, while still far greater than immediately apparent, is far less than has ever been the case in the past.

For predominantly southern and urban-based archaeologists, these factors have led to a quite artificial, and the writer will argue conceptually dangerous, perceived divorce between two parts of one geographical, cultural and economic whole. Orkney has become a 'laboratory' – a proposed, though unimplemented, 'World Heritage area'. Caithness remains in its shadow, under-appreciated but more importantly under-investigated. This is not to imply that Orkney is over-valued – rather, that any understanding of Orkney in prehistoric and historic terms can only ever be partial and blinkered without a parallel development of understanding of Caithness. The disparity in understanding of the prehistory of the two areas has increased over the last four decades to a point where research design must be seriously distorted in either area by the imbalance between the two. That imbalance ought now to be actively diminished.

There are two ironies in this situation that perhaps ought to be briefly explored. The first is that it was Caithness which set the pace of archaeological investigation in the nineteenth century, with a distinguished pedigree of excavation and fieldwork by such as Rhind, Anderson and Tress Barry on those most eye-catching monuments within the Caithness landscape – chambered tombs and brochs. Sadly, there was not, nor could there be, according to modern standards, a published outcome of these exercises, which has naturally diminished their impact upon a modern academic audience.

The second lies in the extent to which the nature of sites in Caithness has been understood, and for how long. In 1909, Alexander Curle conducted the second RCAHMS county Inventory, recording sixty-two chambered cairns in the county. By 1963, Henshall was only able to add to that total two extant monuments (plus three documented but destroyed sites that could not fall within Curle's remit). A more recent survey by the writer has, interestingly, added only one or two extra sites plus some details to those already known in a very extensive 'landscape' coverage of a large part of the county (Mercer 1980b; 1985; forthcoming). In Orkney, the RCAHMS Inventory published in 1946 listed fifty-six monuments, to which Henshall was able to add four by 1972. Since that date, as a result of the prodigious effort of fieldwork by David Fraser and Raymond Lamb among others, the number has risen in the recent reassessment of the Orcadian chambered tombs (J.L. Davidson and Henshall 1989) to eighty-one, an additional twenty-one monuments (of which fourteen had been noted, but not recognised as chambered tombs, by RCAHMS in 1946).

Such a recitation of fieldwork achievement serves to illuminate two important observations in the context of this essay. The first relates to the intensification of fieldwork effort seen in Orkney but not in Caithness during the last two decades. The second is the suggestion that, in both areas, we have as secure a basis for distributional study of chambered tombs as anywhere. Intensity of work in Orkney and recent wide-ranging work in Caithness suggest that few monuments of hitherto recognised type now elude us.

But what does this latter statement mean to the prehistorian? We have been brought by Henshall among others to the clear understanding that multi-phase complexity is to be expected as a feature of chambered tomb construction. In Caithness, Corcoran's excavation at Tulach an t-Sionnaich (CAT 58) (Corcoran 1966) has made this process abundantly clear, while in Orkney Dr Anna Ritchie's excavations at Holm of Papa Westray North (ORK 21) (A. Ritchie forthcoming), a stalled cairn, and John Barber's investigation of a very similar tomb at the Point of Cott (ORK 41) (Barber forthcoming), have also shown the complexity of construction processes.

Barber has, however, made the point that the 'voided box' construction at the Point of Cott (and hinted at on long cairn and other stalled cairn sites) both reduced the effort of construction and facilitated the ultimate dismantling and removal of the monument. Long cairns were systematically robbed (for example, Brawlbin Long (CAT 6) and Tulach Baile Assery (CAT 59)), apparently for the later construction of other elements on site. A particularly fine example of this process, first recognised by Patrick Ashmore and recorded in 1983, is at Warehouse South (CAT 64), where the long-recognised round cairn sits atop a barely visible long-cairn remnant reduced to its basal structure.

'CUMULICITY' AND LONG CAIRNS IN CAITHNESS AND ORKNEY

Thus our northern distributions are accorded their due fragility. But a further layer of suggestion is possible here. The evidence for multi-phase 'cumulicity' (and de-construction) is so far limited to monuments of types that lie at the smaller scale of labour input. It is in the long cairn, and its typologically undeveloped regional variations, that we observe, by both excavation and superficial examination, this tendency towards progressive development involving construction and destruction towards ends quite (apparently) at variance with initial intention. Such random cumulicity has not yet been demonstrated in the instance of the structures of the larger, more regionally specialised cairns of larger stalled or 'Maes Howe' type in Orkney.

The field record, however, offers clear indications of a fairly consistent sequence in both Caithness and Orkney. The key is perhaps best given at Warehouse South (CAT 64), but also by a number of other sites in Caithness, including Brawlbin Long (CAT 6); Cnoc Freiceadain (CAT 18); Tulach Baile Assery (CAT 59) and significantly, as we shall see, Na Trì Shean (CAT 41), as well as Henshall's later (J.L. Davidson and Henshall 1989) appreciation and plan of Head of Work (ORK 18), 4·5 km north-east of Kirkwall in Mainland.

The sequence which recurs throughout this group is of a low long cairn with a chamber of Orkney-Cromarty (O-C) type (in Henshall's terminology). The low long cairn (at least in its ultimate condition) is furnished with protuberant horns at either the proximal or the distal end or both, with, where the horns are proximal, much of their outline covered by spread from the later round cairn. The suggestion has been made that, in a number of instances, consistent and orderly quarrying has been undertaken on the body of the long cairn and that care seems to have been exercised to define the 'distal' arc of the later round cairn so as to indicate that the long cairn was robbed to allow construction of the round cairn (a suggestion seemingly beyond confirmation by either non-interventionist or excavational methods).

Given this primary articulation of a demonstrable sequence which occurs in about twenty-five per cent of all long cairns in both Caithness and Orkney, we may wonder if the development can be perceived over a greater range of types. In 1985 the writer argued, and still does argue, that it can, both forwards and backwards in time. In both directions, his evidence now becomes less secure, but remains secure enough to suggest both an extended sequence and thereby a model for development (in monumental terms) in this northern cultural zone.

Firstly, backwards in time finds superficial interrogation of the sites at a disadvantage – it is not easy on the basis of field observation to divine what may be concealed underneath a long cairn. Our principal evidence therefore must be the monument at Tulach an t-Sionnaich, excavated by Corcoran during a truly heroic season in 1961 when, with paid labour, he explored the structure and chamber contents of three cairns, threatened with inundation by the development of Loch Calder as a water supply, producing an excellent report within three years. Tulach an t-Sionnaich was a long cairn, oriented (unusually) south-south-west to north-north-east. Corcoran managed to complete a contour-survey which would have enabled the superficial observer to infer that the tail of the long cairn was added secondarily (and slightly askew on axis) to the proximal higher cairn. This latter feature appeared from superficial survey to be oval, but excavation revealed it to be a heel-shaped cairn, itself the product of at least two phases of construction and orientation almost directly south-south-west to north-north-east. Heel-shaped cairns are not by any means unknown in northern Scotland, and Henshall has suggested eleven possible examples in Caithness and Sutherland (see Mercer 1985, 12). Three more examples have been noted as a result of the writer's surveys in northern Ross-shire (Henshall ROS 15 and 17 and LOU 8 – Mercer 1980b, 70). Their orientation ranges widely between due north and south-south-west (through east), with Tulach an t-Sionnaich at the latter extreme, and a heavy emphasis in the south-east quadrant of the compass. The chamber at this site is of simple polygonal form and is approached by a short 'passage' which parallels a similar possible chamber at Coille na Borgie North (SUT 22). In the case of the Tulach an t-Sionnaich heel-cairn, from forecourt to the axial rear point of the cairn was less than 10 m – a very small cairn indeed enclosing a chamber 2 × 1·5 m – little larger than a cist (cf. SUT 22: 2·5 × 1·5 m). This primary heel-cairn was approximately 1·75 m high and must be contrasted in its diminutive extent with the altogether larger round cairns which surmount the proximal end of long cairns such as that at Brawlbin Long (25 m diameter × 2·5 m high, CAT 6) or at Warehouse (20 m diameter × 2·5 m high, CAT 64). For the significance of these seemingly relatively minor variations of height and diameter to be appreciated, it should be remembered that a cairn 25 × 2·5 m contains four times as much material as one 10 × 1·5 m and therefore represents a significantly greater labour investment. From the field evidence, we may be able to indicate Sordale Hill Long (CAT 52) (see Figure 4.1) as a further possible long cairn with sub-stratified heel cairn.

The long cairn added to the heel cairn at Tulach an t-Sionnaich exhibits the vertical-slabbed box construction indicated by many traces visible as field remains in other long cairns in the area. As we have seen, this technique of construction is perhaps to be related to the form of construction noted by John Barber at the Point of Cott (ORK 41), where he has argued that construction, and subsequent dismantling, are much eased by this 'house of cards' constructional technique. Traces of such a technique are visible at Brawlbin Long (CAT 6), Tulach Buaile Assery (CAT 59), Brounaban (CAT 9) and Cnoc Freiceadain (CAT 18), and may well help to explain the apparently ordered robbing traces noted above.

There can be no doubt, on the basis of the field drawings of cairns such as Brawlbin Long (CAT 6), or the questionable site at Torr Ban na Gruagaich (CAT 56), Cnoc Freiceadain (CAT 18) or Warehouse South (CAT 64), that round cairns have been constructed over and above the proximal ends of long cairns. Less rigorously demonstrable as a sequence are instances such as South Yarrows North (CAT 54) and Tulach Buaile Assery (CAT 59), where the robbed nature of the long-cairn element set beside the relatively intact current state of the round cairn strongly suggests a sequential development.

These round-cairn additions set atop the earlier horned long cairns produced a composite outline to a new kind of monument, a round/long-cairn composite. The outline, both in plan and in elevation, is redolent of earlier composites (see Tulach an t-Sionnaich) – part of a continuing tradition of cumulative architecture which may well have expressed dynastic, territorial or simply monumental seniority. The monumental whole, this cumulative outcome, seems perhaps to have stimulated an *architectural* conception which combines these cumulative elements into a rationalised and pre-designed whole. It is thus perhaps that we see the emergence of the Na Trì Shean (CAT 41)/South Yarrows South (CAT 55) type of cairn with its 'one-off' designed framework which expresses the diversity and temporal cumulicity of the Brawlbin Long-type monuments. It is certainly difficult to conceive the process occurring in reverse.

There is, however, supporting evidence for the sequential nature of this process. The tripartite O-C chamber, defined by Henshall in 1963, occurs only in the round cairns superimposed upon pre-existing long cairn complexes (South Yarrows North (CAT 54), Brawlbin Long (CAT 6), Warehouse South (CAT 64)). It never occurs in the underlying long cairn in Caithness, and at Coille Na Borgie South (SUT 23), the level of the chamber

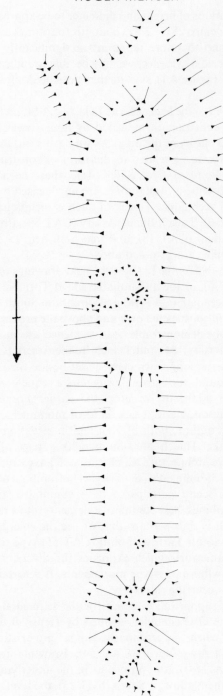

Figure 4.1: Plan of Sordale Hill Long (CAT 52).

and the form of the proximal end of the cairn suggest that here it pertains to a later and added terminal round cairn.

At Na Trì Shean (CAT 41), this sequence is apparently broken in that, once again, a round cairn is built quite clearly over the cairn at both distal and proximal ends, the secondary context emphasised by the non-axial positions of both. A chamber exists within the proximal mound of uncertain form. This instance may serve only to refine the sequence, however, as the fully-developed form of Na Trì Shean-type long cairn occurs at South Yarrows South (CAT 55), which has integrally built within it an O-C chamber validating the sequence suggested. At CAT 55, the whole cairn is built to respect the requirements of the O-C chamber with its preference for a south-east axis.

This of course leads us in the direction of that most isolated and difficult of the long cairns, Camster Long (CAT 12) with its unique format. The enveloping cairn is identical to the now dilapidated plan of Na Trì Shean and South Yarrows South. This great cairn is very strikingly close to these monuments in its lateral dimensions, all three being just over 60 m in length and between 22 and 25 m across the proximal horns – a further factor perhaps suggesting an 'architectural', preconceived and planned, stimulus to their construction. At Camster, however, one might suggest that the siting of the long cairn was determined not only by the lie of the land – as indeed at South Yarrows and Na Trì Shean – but also by the putative pre-existence of a cairn encapsulating the clearly primary easternmost chamber – polygonal, about 2 m in width, and comparable with the primary chamber at Tulach an t-Sionnaich. Its predetermined orientation demanded that the O-C chamber with its required south-east axis had to be accessed from the southern flank of the cairn, elegantly exemplifying the contrast which may have existed between the monumental impact and ritual exigency that complicated the construction of these monuments. We must await the publication of investigations on this site before verifying these comments or embarking upon further conjecture.

From this point, we are led towards the other feature quite peculiar to this northern 'Kulturkreis' – the short horned cairn. This equally 'architectural' monument could not have been conceived without the pre-existence of the Na Trì Shean type of preconceived and planned long cairn. The type stands at the end of a long regional and national sequence whence it can only be derived.

Significantly, in this context, the chambers of all known and explored short horned cairns are of integral O-C type and represent that chamber-type at its most developed in technical and architectural form. Comparison of all known (at that time) chamber proportions in both Orkney and Caithness (Mercer 1985, 50) indicates quite clearly that the corbelled width of all three short horned cairn chambers in Caithness lies in the top twenty per cent of all chambers in both regions, with the Garrywhin chamber (CAT 26) being the greatest corbelled span in the region short of the quite exceptional Maes Howe. Furthermore, there can be little question, even in their not totally excavated state, that *all* of these monuments are 'one-off' and are architecturally planned to reflect a certain preceding vocabulary of design features. Once again, it is very difficult to imagine the process taking place in reverse.

So far, we have pursued a very old-fashioned 'typological' argument of the kind discredited in the early 1960s as a result of the ultra-diffusionism of the late Professor Daniel (Daniel 1958) and of those upon whom he founded his pan-European arguments. Let us briefly scrutinise the rights and wrongs of such arguments. Carried across geological/geomorphological/geographical and historiographical boundaries, such arguments exhibit the same obliviousness to reality as indiscriminate use of an international railway timetable. It is the writer's contention, however, that he is not making this error. In using the material remains which are expressed within one very individual geological/geographical and indeed historiographical medium, it is quite appropriate to compare, within this very narrow and well-defined frame, this kind of material. What may emerge is primarily the kind of distinction versus similarity that is the basis of human culture at any stage of its development.

DISCUSSION AND CONCLUSIONS

If we accept the broadly-brushed sequence as sketched above, then a number of other conclusions follow, based principally upon the distribution of sites in the two regions (see Figure 4.2).

First, on presently understood distribution, and based, necessarily, upon the uneven evidence of both excavation (of all types) and surface field survey, no cairns of heel-shaped form occur in Orkney. Henshall suggests a total of eleven examples from northern Scotland and seven from Sutherland (SUT 15, 16, 17, 18, 22, 34 and 45), to which the writer would wish to add three from Ross and Cromarty (ROS 15, ROS 17 and his LOU 8 (Mercer 1980b, 70, 153)). In Caithness, Henshall suggests four examples, including Tulach an t-Sionnaich (CAT 58). Na Tri Shean (CAT 41), Gallow Hill CAT 25 and Fairy Hillock CAT 24 are the others, to which the writer might add one possible example – Sordale Hill Long (CAT 52). Ten of the sites have orientation of forecourt axis between east and south, with Tulach an t-Sionnaich varying to south-south-west (perhaps by virtue of the exigencies of its situation). This directional preference may be regarded as significant, and, if so, it will be seen to be of interest in noting a similar preference among Shetland heel-shaped cairns. The distribution within Caithness is absolutely nodal to all later distribution, as will be seen from the distribution map. It might be seen to indicate an initial occupation of Caithness in the area around and inland from Thurso with little penetration elsewhere. It might also be seen to suggest that extension of monument-construction to Shetland took place at this early juncture, possibly even prior to the introduction of this cultural medium to Orkney with, perhaps, its persistence in isolation there as a tradition thenceforth. Nothing in the presently available radiocarbon evidence would conflict with this suggestion.

Second, the tradition of long-cairn construction, it might be suggested, arrived in the north secondarily to this initial impulse. Simple long cairns are rare, if known at all (although examples have been suggested: see Mercer 1985, WAR 5 and WAR 49). In those cases where long cairns are known, they are usually associated with earlier and later monuments to make up cumulative monumental complexes. Initially, this cumulative format appears to have developed, and then, by virtue of typological considerations that it is difficult to reverse, we observe the generation of northern, architecturally consolidated forms exemplified at Na Trì Shean, South Yarrows North and Camster Long. The distribution of such monuments shows a clear expansion on that indicated by suggested heel-cairn forms. Once again, the valley of the Forss Water and Thurso river form a focus, but two other major concentrations emerge – one to the south-west of Wick in the area surrounding the Loch of Yarrows reaching from Camster in the west to Loch Sarclet in the east, and the others clustered around the Dunbeath Water.

Within these localities, however, the distribution is revealing. In each instance, the concentration of monumental remains is set, quite clearly, to one side of the area of maximum fertility. In the instance of the Thurso River assemblage, the monumental group is set on high ground to the north-east of the south-west-facing valley slopes – on marginal land at locally high altitude. Relatively speaking, the situation is precisely similar south-west of Wick where high ground above fertile valley slopes and marginal ground by the sea coast is utilised; while at Dunbeath, the cairns again occupy a marginal zone on the north side of the valley above the south-west-facing lower slopes. It is, of course, open to us to argue that monuments on the lower, optimally agricultural ground have been destroyed. The argument is of course irrefutable but with two provisos. First, these are very major monuments – difficult to destroy *in toto* (see the example close by Stemster House). Second, some of these monuments (e.g. Sordale Hill) are now under cultivation and have been for at least 150 years, and yet have survived to tell the tale.

The notion of nodal areas of Neolithic occupation is therefore developed: according to presently available evidence, firstly in the Thurso/Forss River area and then into the Wick River and Dunbeath basins – some but by no means all of the points of access to Caithness through the steep coastal façade.

Only at this point is monumental tradition established (or recognised as established) in Orkney. The recognised monuments are those at the Head of Work (ORK 18), just outside Kirkwall, and Earl's Knoll on Papa Stronsay (ORK 14), with a possible third example at Hacksness (Haco's Ness) (ORK 62) situated on the southernmost point of the island of Shapinsay. The Head

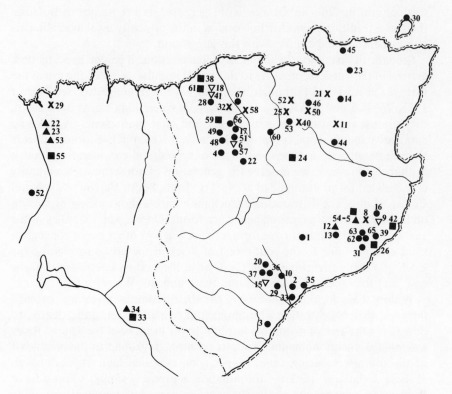

Figure 4.2: a. The distribution of chambered tombs in Sutherland and Caithness (see next page for Figure 4.2b). The numbers refer to Henshall's county-based system. Key: ● round cairn with Orkney-Cromalty chamber; × long cairn with terminal round cairn(s); ▲ horned long cairn; ▽ horned long cairn with terminal round cairn; ■ Na Trì Shean type long cairn; —— long cairn.

of Work is quite clearly a cumulative structure with a sub-circular cairn built atop it with a likely O-C type chamber within it. Earl's Knoll is a long cairn oriented east to west with a substantial mound at its east end. Like all the Orkney long cairns except that at Staney Hill (see below), it is set very close to the present-day coastline on land which, in the island context, would presumably be marginal – too spray-dominated for successful cultivation to take place. We must note the extraordinary division of such cumulative long cairns into those oriented south-east to north-west in Caithness east of the Thurso River and into north-east Caithness (and followed in Orkney), as

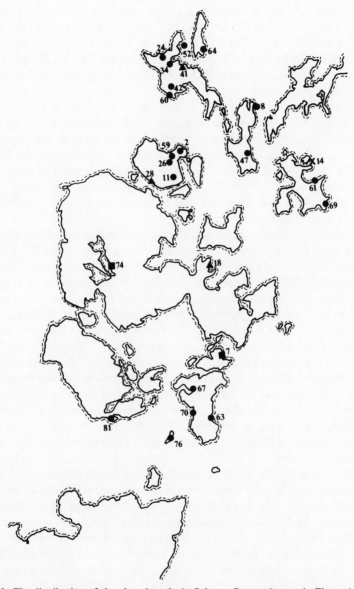

Figure 4.2: b. The distribution of chambered tombs in Orkney. Conventions as in Figure 4.2a.

opposed to the north-east to south-west orientation west of the Thurso River and to the south in the Wick and Dunbeath area.

The third point of our conclusion is that we see the development of the architecturally conceived version of the cumulative long cairn in Caithness, with examples at Na Trì Shean (CAT 41), South Yarrows South (CAT 55) and Camster Long (CAT 12). In some instances, this new design is covered by a round cairn with a bi- or tripartite chamber (Na Trì Shean); otherwise, such a chamber is integral (CAT 55, CAT 12). In Orkney, we see further development with the construction of the Knowe of Lairo (ORK 28) on Rousay, where the distinctive outline and double wall-facing is of the type associated with an integral tripartite chamber of somewhat adventurous design. Similar construction is exhibited in the cairn at the Point of Cott, but on this occasion with an integrally-built stalled cairn. At Staney Hill (ORK 74), situated in Mainland, a cairn nearly identical in form to Na Trì Shean and South Yarrows South, and of near-identical size, has an apparently integrally-built O-C chamber and a misaligned possible stalled chamber which may therefore be secondary.

Fourth, the consistent stratigraphical sequence noted above, evident from field recording in at least ten instances in both Orkney and Caithness, is the superimposition of circular cairns about 20–25 m in diameter, containing an integral O-C bi- or tripartite chamber. If one accepts this generalised sequence, then the distribution of such tombs (twenty-five in Orkney, thirty-seven in Caithness) offers further possible insights. Caithness sees an apparent outward movement of the distribution of such tombs, both on the microcosmic scale at each focus of distribution – Forss Water, Dunbeath Water – and on the macrocosmic scale as these tombs see an expansion into north-east Caithness. In Orkney, the distribution is heavily biased, with an apparent extension of the north-east Caithness distribution into southern Hoy, Stroma, South Ronaldsay and Swona. Thence the distribution in Orkney is northern, on Stronsay, Eday, Westray, Rousay and the northern-most reaches of Mainland, with the mass of Mainland and Shapinsay apparently avoided.

Fifth, and finally, short horned cairns are found following a very similar distribution. The only known intrusion into central Mainland by structures in this ritual continuum is the newly-discovered tomb of apparently South Yarrows/Na Trì Shean type at Staney Hill (ORK 74).

This interlinking of the architectural development of Caithness and Orkney sets the background for the development in Orkney of stalled cairns which, where relationships are apparent (as at Calf of Eday Long, ORK 8), are secondary to cairns and chambers of O-C type. During this stage, changes take place in structural traditions, leading to clear distinctions developing in the technical detail of chamber-construction (see Mercer 1985, 50). Ultimately, only one possible stalled cairn appears back in Caithness, at Shurrery Church (CAT 49).

Such a brief exploration of one aspect of relationships between Caithness and Orkney may have accomplished little other than to open a new aspect of questioning the archaeological record in the north and perhaps throw some light on cultural interaction in the region in the Earlier Neolithic. Its debt to Audrey Henshall's extraordinary dedication and skill is obvious at more or less every point. The writer can only hope that she does not feel that he has abused her data and that she will accept this short tribute to her seminal contribution to northern Neolithic studies.

5

Doorways into Another World:
The Orkney-Cromarty Chambered Tombs

Colin Richards

INTRODUCTION

The Orkney-Cromarty group of megalithic chambered tombs, as defined by
Audrey Henshall (1963), maintains a distribution restricted to north-east
Scotland and the Northern Isles. The distribution is, however, extensive,
spanning an area of approximately 250 kilometres and crossing a notorious
stretch of ocean, the Pentland Firth (Figure 5.1). This situation is but a single
strand in the total 'megalithic phenomenon'. Our lack of understanding of its
significance is governed on the one hand by the inadequacy of the empirical
data and on the other by the limits of our interpretative abilities. Whichever
epistemological stance is assumed, an understanding of the circumstances
surrounding the construction of megaliths and the mechanisms responsible
for their distribution remain, for archaeologists, an obsessive attraction.
These problems cannot merely be pushed aside, as the initial response of
archaeologists and public alike, when confronted with a 'megalithic tomb', is
to question what it is and why it was built, with at least a brief thought given
to how we can ever answer such questions. With regard to the chambered
tombs examined in this chapter, Joseph Anderson expressed a similar
concern in 1868:

> The archaeologist can have as little knowledge of the design of the cairn-
> builders, with reference to the peculiarities of form and varieties of type
> exhibited in the construction of cairns of different classes, as they could have
> had of his special theory on the subject. He can see, however, that they had
> fixed ideas which they wrought out with great persistency, both in the
> external configuration and in the internal arrangements of their sepulchral
> structures. (1868, 481)

Apart from the obvious inconsistency of assumed function, the question
remains regarding the ability of archaeologists to obtain any knowledge of
the 'design' or 'special theory' of the cairn-builders.

Regardless of statements to the contrary (e.g. Renfrew 1976, 204), it
appears to have been an extremely difficult task to shed the idea of megalithic
chambered tombs constituting a unitary phenomenon. However, it should

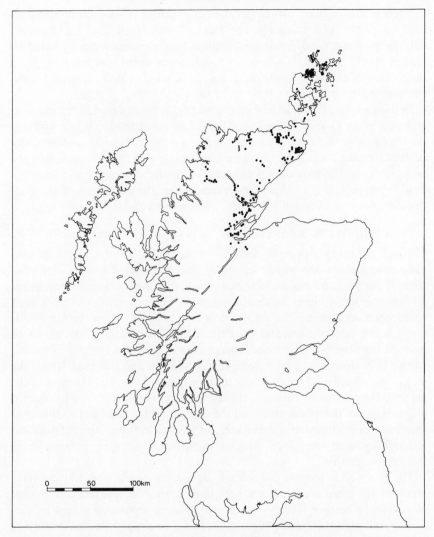

Figure 5.1: The distribution of Orkney–Cromarty chambered tombs (drawing by J. Downes).

not be forgotten that, despite the consistent usage of the term 'megalithic chambered tomb', which tends to support the 'certain homogeneity' noted by Renfrew (1976, 199), these monuments are defined and classified according to architectural variation. At times, these differences are either emphasised or suppressed according to the desired objective: for instance, in discussing the Orcadian megalithic tombs, Renfrew (1979, 211) provides an amended typology based on architectural variation. Later in the discussion, however, this variation is ignored, and all types of tomb, irrespective of architectural difference, are suggested to constitute equal-access communal monuments (ibid., 216–17). Unfortunately, the lack of consideration of architectural differences, apart from typological studies, has been inadvertently aided by Kinnes' (1975, Figure 7) scheme of modular chamber construction. By a simple manipulation of modules, some of the most complex forms of architecture become reduced to little more than a shuffling of boxes.

In this chapter, I wish to examine a particular tradition of architecture as revealed in the Orkney-Cromarty (O-C) chambered tombs. While realising that to focus attention on a single group of tombs tends to bypass the wider problems of the 'megalithic phenomenon', it is hoped that by examining the architecture of the monuments in terms of spatial experience and architectural representation, a deeper understanding of the intentions of the constructors may be obtained (see also Thomas this volume, Chapter 11).

THE FIRST MEGALITHS IN NORTH-EAST SCOTLAND

Through the many aspects of debate surrounding megalithic enquiries, two basic assumptions are widely accepted: that chambered tombs were constructed for the containment of the dead, and that they constitute monumental construction. Neither assumption is particularly contentious; hence their widespread acceptance. The implication of this belief is that the megalithic tomb is the first monumental construction (in north-east Scotland) to be inserted into the landscape and, therefore, the geography of the Neolithic world. It is also a material statement about death and the dead. Thus, the megalithic chambered tomb constitutes an objectification of the past in the present. How different pasts are chosen to be represented is visually charted in the design of the monuments and the many modifications and additions to their basic appearance. It is the concept of the past in the present, of time and temporality fused into 'place', which is of particular relevance in considering the first megaliths.

The assumed sedentism of the early agriculturists will undoubtedly have involved far more profound changes than a growing awareness and urge physically to mark a territory (Renfrew 1976) or legitimate claims to particular resources (Chapman 1981). Sedentism, or simply the idea of staying in the same place, provokes an altered perception of the outside world; it also focuses attention on temporality and the apparent ontological contradictions inherent within a 'lifetime'.

The life of the hunter-gatherer is one of movement. In north-east Scotland, little is known of the indigenous Later Mesolithic inhabitants. Potential habitation sites at Freswick Bay, Caithness and along the Sutherland coastline between Golspie and the Dornoch Firth (Morrison 1980, 164), and in the Mainland, Orkney (Richards 1985), have yet to be fully investigated or confirmed (Masters 1989, 25). Nevertheless, Later Mesolithic inhabitants would quite probably have practised a trans-resource subsistence cycle entailing the movement of people between different topographic zones and plant and animal species (cf. Ingold 1986, 190). Such movement is locked into the cycle of the seasons. In this way of life, physical *movement* from place to place defines life and, therefore, cosmology. This in turn entails a distinctive world-view, akin to that of many Australian groups, whereby the ancestral past is seen as part of a physical process of moving through the world, involving a recognition of specific places or locales (Thomas forthcoming). It is, however, the action of moving between such places which defines existence. Thus, Ingold (ibid., 153) can suggest that, for hunter-gatherers, 'the road or track has a past, described by the people, ancestors and spirits who – in an unbroken succession – have travelled it and left their mark on the countryside'. Hence movement, and its spatial and temporal classification, embodies both a religious passage and the means of subsistence: in short, life itself (ibid.).

The mechanism behind the introduction of agriculture to north-east Scotland is unknown. However, on the basis of pollen assemblages from the Northern Isles (Keating and Dickson 1979; D.A. Davidson and Jones 1985), it occurred in the early fourth millennium BC. Even if this change involved little arable cultivation with the emphasis placed on animal husbandry, the sedentary nature of farming fosters the illusion of staying in a single place for ever, inducing a profound effect on the way people see their own presence in the world. The existence of the farmer is governed by a perceived attachment to a single area radiating from the centre of the world, in other words the house and home (Richards forthcoming). Observation from a primary locale necessarily sees time passing, for Neolithic people, according to the annual agricultural cycle of birth – growth – maturity – death – rebirth, an enforced analogy with the human life-cycle and past generations. Thus, existence becomes fused with place.

It is in this context that megalithic architecture should be seen. Death and monumentality: the physical objectification of the past in the present. For the first time, a permanent architecture is brought into existence, and, through the necessary sanction of religion, the world is transformed.

DOORWAYS AS A METAPHOR: THE ORKNEY-CROMARTY CHAMBERED TOMBS

Although having round, rectangular, or horned long mounds, the O-C chambered tombs are currently identified as a separate tradition on the basis of chamber form. Opposed upright stone slabs or orthostats project inwards from the side walling of the chamber and passage, creating a distinctive method of partitioning which is best visualised in its Orcadian variant, the Stalled cairn (Figure 5.5). This tradition of chambered-tomb architecture has been subdivided by Henshall (1963, 45–121) to include four main types:

1. Rectangular chambers (Figure 5.2).
2. Polygonal chambers (Figure 5.3).

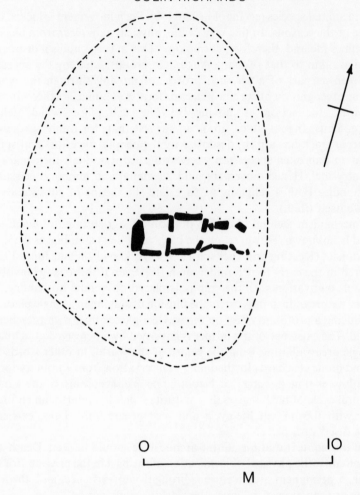

O   IO
M

Figure 5.2: Carn Glas, Ross-shire: a rectangular-chambered Orkney–Cromarty tomb (after A.A. Woodham and M.F. Woodham 1957).

3. Camster chambers (Figure 5.4).
4. Stalled chambers (Figure 5.5).

These differences, based on shape and method of chamber-construction, maintain a certain geographic integrity. Various reasons for this divergence have been presented, ranging from chronological progression (Henshall 1963) through to technological limitations (Sharples 1980). Given this variation, however, there remains a consistency of architecture which is followed through all the above subdivisions. Interestingly, this architecture is also a feature of the contemporary house, as demonstrated at the Knap of Howar, Papa Westray, Orkney (Figure 5.6; Traill and Kirkness 1937; A.

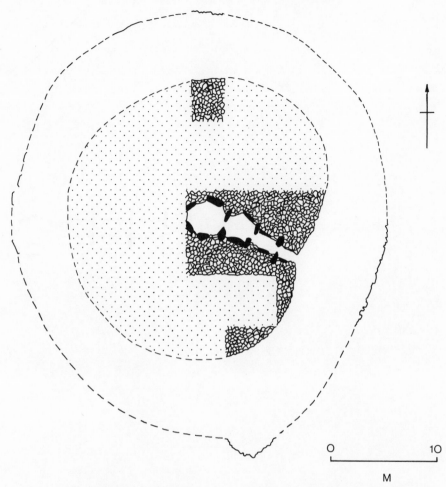

Figure 5.3: The Ord North, Sutherland: a polygonal-chambered Orkney–Cromarty tomb (after Sharples 1981).

Ritchie 1983). In this respect, it is well to remember when attempting to understand the architecture of the O-C chambered tombs that they were constructed by people who were engaged in the creation of a spatial representation which embodied and spoke of religious ideas which lay beyond everyday experience. Hence, by definition, the architecture of a chambered tomb relied on analogy and metaphor for its understanding and interpretation.

In utilising the architecture of the house, the builders were drawing on a particularly potent metaphor (Blier 1987, Hodder 1990), since as a model it provides a concrete expression: a physical sense of order to cosmological themes and beliefs. The house and its constituents are central to human

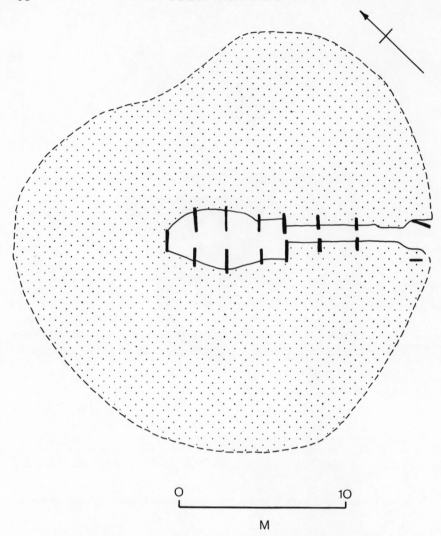

Figure 5.4: Hill of Shebster, Caithness: a Camster type Orkney–Cromarty tomb (after Henshall 1963).

experience: people 'live' in houses, and the principles of order and classification embodied within their architecture are realised in the order and classification of people, things and events which constitute daily life (Richards forthcoming). In viewing the house as a metaphor which allows an understanding of the unknowable, we appreciate the significance of claims that religious architecture is simply a development of that found within the habitation (Eliade 1959, 58).

However, the O-C tomb is not a house, although, through its imagery,

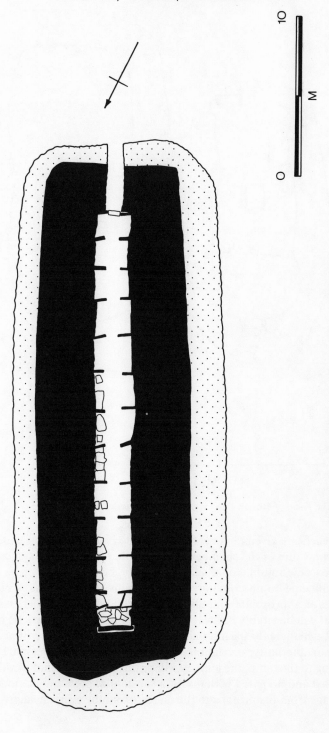

Figure 5.5: Midhowe, Orkney: a stalled Orkney–Cromarty tomb (after Callander and Grant 1934).

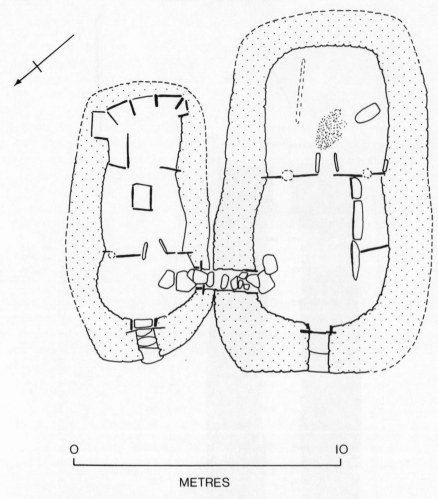

O   IO
METRES

Figure 5.6: The Knap of Howar, Papa Westray, Orkney (after A. Ritchie 1983).

complex beliefs are given tangible form. Only by Neolithic people experienc-
ing the architecture of the chambered tomb, either directly through entry or
indirectly by description, could such knowledge be imparted.

The chambered tomb contains and constrains the dead. As a place of
death, it has an appropriate situation in the world. It is simply where it should
be, and that will inevitably be away from the living. Visiting it will be heavily
sanctioned, whethere for the interment of a corpse, the extraction of ancestral
remains or an alternative revelation. It will be done at the right time. For the
people going to the tomb, the journey will be one of consequence; it will have
been planned and prepared perhaps for a substantial preceding period, since
it is a passage from the profane to the sacred, from the everyday activities of

life to the religious experience of death. For those who will enter the monument and move into the domain of the dead, the experience will be magnified; perhaps they will be afraid. However, regardless of the deeds to be undertaken, all will possess a clear image of their goal. At this time, the route and direction of movement is fully part of the ritual process, since it will involve transformation which is defined not only in religious awareness but also in spatial and temporal terms.

The forecourt or external perimeter wall represented the end of the journey for some of the participants. They may never have entered the chamber, or only cautiously viewed the internal proceedings (see Richards 1988, 54), perhaps never to cross the entrance, relying instead on verbal accounts, myths and revelations. The experience, for them, is imaginary; for those entering the tomb, the experience is physical and real.

Within the enhanced façade of the later tombs, drama was surely enacted (Fleming 1973). Even outside the smaller tombs, the focus of attention was to be reflected back onto the watchers. When powerful words were spoken and rituals enacted, it was by individual representatives. When facing the onlookers situated in and beyond the forecourt area, these individuals commenced a discourse with the living, drawing on the sanctity of the dead. On turning and entering the chamber, a reversal occurred: the individuals were now wholly mortal, and a rather more dangerous discourse was set to begin.

The view confronting those moving into the tomb was one of gloom and darkness: after negotiating a narrow entrance passage, the chamber expands before the subject. Perhaps aided by fire, the chamber sides would still lie in shadow. Ahead, out of the darkness, a familiar sight would appear: stone doorways through which a path leads towards the goal in the furthest, deepest part of the tomb. This is the image which the architecture presents to the subject, one of a series of doorways (Woodham and Woodham 1957, plate 6).

What is normally and unquestioningly (but see Boast 1987) accepted as being merely stone partitioning to define a series of compartments within a main chamber is suggested to be a completely different representation. Of course, an open area is required between the doorways. However, here megalithic logic is reversed. No longer do the stone uprights define the compartment but the compartments define the doorways. Occasionally, the doorways have threshold slabs set on edge across the bottom (e.g. Camster Long, Knowe of Yarso, Carn Glas, etc.). In some cases, as at South Yarrows, Warehouse South and Allt Nam Ban, a stone 'door' was set between the door jambs, blocking the pathway. If the O-C 'chambered' tombs are principally conceived as a series of doorways, the question arises: where are they leading? To what goal?

In discussing the rectangular O-C tombs, Henshall notes that the end stone is 'nearly always taller than the other stones' (1963, 62). In some examples, this stone is almost a metre taller than the other orthostats. Moreover, the end stone is generally pointed at the top, a feature which dominates the monuments on the Black Isle, Easter Ross (Woodham and Woodham 1957, 111), and the majority of single standing stones in north-east Scotland. For the rectangular tombs, there can be little doubt that the final goal is the huge monolith placed at the end of the pathway which, it should be noted, often exceeds the height of the subject. Indeed, the tomb is in some ways no more than a covered pathway through a series of doorways to the ultimate goal: a symbol of the divine or an impassable gateway to another world?

The end stone is less clearly defined in the polygonal tombs, although the innermost 'compartment' is always of larger area in assuming a more circular shape. However, things are not always as they appear, for in describing the end chamber at the Ord North, Sutherland, Sharples notes that 'the largest orthostat, no. 9, was built with the dry-stone walling running behind it unlike all the other orthostats where the walling abuts on to the stone' (1981, 28). Here, within a different 'sub-type', we find the same emphasis placed on the free-standing, tallest monolith, situated directly at the end of the pathway through the tomb. As with the end stones within the rectangular tombs, the stones or orthostats composing the end compartment in the polygonal tombs are taller than the other uprights. Henshall (1963, 65) identifies this charac-teristic: 'it seems likely that the small, low, outer compartment was lintelled (as is typical of most Camster-type chambers) and the inner polygonal chamber was corbelled'. The largest stone, however, does not always occupy the rearmost position: 'the backslab is sometimes the tallest stone in the chamber, but as often as not it is topped by one of the others [in the rear chamber] which can be a very prominent stone as at Ballachnecore or Leachkin' (ibid., 66).

Of further relevance is the condition of the internal floor-deposits of the O-C tombs, particularly those of the Camster type of Caithness. Consistent-ly, the clay, earth and ash floors, incorporating small and broken fragments of cremated human bone, are compressed to form a dark, greasy deposit described as compacted 'and bearing that trodden appearance so characteris-tic of all the floors of these cairns' (Anderson 1868, 499). In some tombs, such as South Yarrows North, South Yarrows South and Ormiegill, a layer of paving was laid down to create a new floor surface (Henshall 1963, 90). The thick layer of soil included in the basal deposits of the Orkney and Caithness tombs may also be interpreted as a continual process of covering the burnt remains of the dead and recreating the pathway.

The noted wear and compaction of the chamber floor, together with the examples of resurfacing, relates to more than just the occasional deposition of the few individuals represented in the tombs by fragmentary skeletal material. It demonstrates that people frequently entered the tomb and moved through its interior on a formidable journey, following the many previous footsteps taken in awe and trepidation towards an ultimate goal.

It has been suggested that the innermost compartment of the Orcadian Stalled cairns maintains a distinctive quality in terms of architecture and deposits (Richards 1988, 52–3; J.L. Davidson and Henshall 1989, 19). As within the Camster-type tombs, with the exception of Carriside (Henshall 1963, 267), a tall monolith is absent from the inner area of the Orcadian Stalled cairns. However, a massive backslab – the largest orthostat within the chamber – is virtually always present. The special nature of this stone slab is effectively demonstrated at Knowe of Yarso, Unstan and Midhowe, where the massive backslabs were inserted after the walled construction of the tomb-chamber (Callander and Grant 1935, 332). This observation is particularly significant when it is remembered that the opposed orthostats creating the internal doorways or 'stalls' would normally be a primary element of tomb-construction (Henshall 1963, 80), and the later addition of the backslab would have been a formidable task. Nevertheless, for a certain period of time, the line of doorways formed by the orthostats would have been free-standing stones and completely visible.

Regardless of the number of doorways or the length of the path through the tomb, this characteristic use and arrangement of orthostats marks a consistency discernible in the architecture of all the O-C tombs. A series of doorways which define a path, one which is taken to extreme lengths in the Stalled tombs of Orkney (Figure 5.5), leads to the inevitable representations of the doorway to immortality and another world, the door which is always closed to humanity.

THE WEIGHT OF AGES: RECONSTRUCTING THE TOMBS

Outward appearances are important; they are meant to be seen, but, as we all know, they can be deceptive, and they frequently are in the case of the O-C tombs. The massive long horned cairns, which have confounded past typologies (Childe 1934; S. Piggott 1954), are now revealed as composite structures which, through their alterations, betray a continued but changing attitude on the part of Neolithic people to time and the past (see also Mercer this volume, Chapter 4). The modifications represent a reconstitution of the past and also a redefinition of 'place'.

At Tulach an t-Sionnaich (Corcoran 1966, 5–22), as with many other examples, an extended sequence of tomb-reconstruction can be demonstrated. Similarly, at Camster Long, a sequence of incorporation reinforces the view that the earliest O-C tombs were small circular constructions and that the many long mounds of Caithness and Sutherland are merely reconstructions, adding enormous masonry shells to this basic circular-tomb form (Henshall 1972, 241; Sharples 1986, 9). In assuming this primary position, the smaller circular tombs combine a striking architectural opposition between what Hodder (1990) terms the inside-linearity (i.e. culture) and outside-circularity (i.e. nature). Such a spatial representation may be consistent with

the profundity of committing the first permanent architecture to the world
and hence physically altering it.

The consequences of such action are difficult to realise; however, through
time, changes occur to both the external world and, necessarily, people's
perceptions of their place within it. On the Scottish mainland, the tombs are
altered and the treatment of the corpse changes. No longer are the purificat-
ory properties of fire used in the interior of tombs as part of the rituals
surrounding interment (Henshall 1963, 88–9). Complete bodies are now
inserted and placed inside the monuments in positions which would impede
or even prohibit movement through the interior. Coincidentally, the exterior
of the monument is transformed, sometimes through a series of stages, from
a small circular cairn to a massive linear construction with outstretching
monumental hornworks situated at either end. These changes are undoubtedly concerned with display, since their enlargement and reconstruction often
involved subtle and deceptive building techniques to achieve monumental
grandeur (see Barber 1988, 58 and this volume, Chapter 2). Internally, no
major architectural changes accompany this process of monumentalisation;
indeed, it is as though the interior is forgotten, perhaps relegated to myth,
and the entrance passages are frequently blocked by masonry as part of the
external modifications.

The linearity of the pathway is now sealed within the tomb. Individuals are
unable physically to approach the sacred goal or door, and the mound itself
becomes the embodiment of the idea of linearity. Proximity to the sacred is
now limited to the forecourts within the two imposing hornworks (Figure
5.7). These façades now represent the end of the pathway which may have
already existed before monumentalisation occurred. For instance, below the
mound at Camster Long, a series of post-holes ran directly along the line of
the spine of the later cairn in a south-westerly direction towards the south
chamber (Masters personal communication). Accompanying these were the
remains of large hearths and areas of burning. Hence a line of posts had
marked out a pathway to the tombs, and, along its length, just as with the
pathway enclosed within the tomb, fire had played a part in the activities
associated with its use.

In short, then, while the tomb was effectively becoming larger and more
visible in the world, the dead were becoming more restricted; they simply
could no longer be approached.

In Orkney, something quite different occurs within an apparently similar
move towards monumentality. Within the architecture of the Stalled cairns,
we see the lengthening of the pathway within the tomb. In contrast to the
Caithness and Sutherland tombs, the interior of the tomb becomes emphasised and the passage to the final goal is severely enlongated (Figure 5.5).
Consequently, the mound is expanded to accommodate this internal development and, as before, the final area within the tomb maintains its special
significance (Richards 1988, 53–4). The passage from the outside world to the

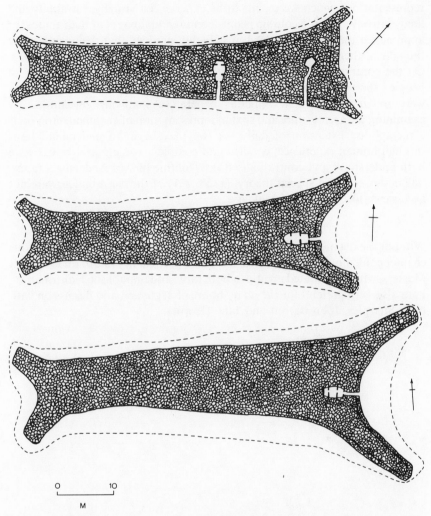

Figure 5.7: The horned cairns of north-east Scotland (top to bottom): Camster Long, South
          Yarrows, North and South Yarrows, South (after Henshall 1963).

sacred place of communication with the gods and ancestors is now a considerable journey. Significantly, it is a restricted pathway visible to none other
than those undertaking its dangerous passage.

CONCLUSION

In this chapter, I have attempted to show that not all chambered tombs are
the same and that broad generalisations of evolutionary nature, for instance
from simple to complex 'types', are inappropriate in understanding their
sophisticated architecture. Instead, they should be seen as they are: spatial

representations which were built to be experienced visually, physically and imaginatively. When Neolithic people conjured up images of their tombs, or approached them with the dead, it is highly unlikely that they would have thought of them as territorial markers or in terms of rights over resources. On the contrary, they would have felt the same fear that the majority of people experience when death and mortality are laid bare before them. They were moving towards a religious experience involving revelation. By examining the architecture and spatial representation of chambered tombs as a metaphoric extension of daily life, we may begin to understand how, through human experience, detailed and complex cosmological beliefs were both understood and contextualised in Neolithic life. In Anderson's terms, 'the design . . . and special theory' (1868, 481) of the cairn-builders are not necessarily lost to the archaeologist.

ACKNOWLEDGEMENTS

Without the detailed work of Audrey Henshall over the last thirty years, this chapter could not have been written. I would particularly like to thank Lionel Masters, who contributed greatly in both ideas and unpublished information. I am also very grateful for the many hours of argument and discussion with Niall Sharples, John Barrett and Jane Downes.

6

Are the Clava 'Passage Graves' Really Passage Graves?: A Reconsideration of the Nature and Associations of the Clava Passage Graves and Ring-Cairns

Gordon J. Barclay

There are two works of lasting value in the study of the Clava cairns – the report of Piggott's programme of research into the ring-cairns and passage graves (S. Piggott 1956) and, of course, Audrey Henshall's thorough, scholarly examination of the cairns in Volume One of her *magnum opus* (Henshall 1963).

It is one of the greatest ironies in Scottish archaeology that this well-known, geographically restricted group should still, almost forty years after Piggott's excavations, be no better dated and little better understood. The only excavation since then, of the Clava cairn at Newton of Petty, remains unpublished after almost twenty years. The passage graves in particular remain an isolated group, while the comparanda available for the Clava ring-cairns have expanded considerably.

Henshall eschewed the use of simple typological explanations for the origins of the Clava group (cf. Corcoran 1969a, 95). Graham and Anna Ritchie (1981) neatly paraphrased her argument: 'Audrey Henshall suggested that the Clava passage graves were a locally evolved group and has put forward an ancestry within henge monuments, stone circles and ring-cairns; she rightly points out the absence of any hint of multi-period construction, the presence of stones graded in height and of cup-markings – all features alien to the mainstream of passage grave tradition' (although it has been argued since (Barclay 1990) that the cairns may not have been single-period). Henshall drew particularly on the ring-cairns and recumbent stone circles of Grampian Region in her discussion; since then, the known distribution of ring-cairns has expanded and become more dense, particularly in Kincardineshire, Angus and Perthshire (e.g. RCAHMS 1990). Burl (1976), in his consideration of stone circles in the British Isles, took further the discussion of the relationship of the Clava ring-cairns, passage graves and stone circles with the ring-cairns and recumbent stone circles of north-east Scotland (cf. J.N.G. Ritchie and MacLaren 1972). Barnatt (1989) has described the Clava cairns and their stone circles as 'best viewed as an aberrant monument combination'.

Although the title of this chapter is, to a certain extent, tongue-in-cheek, there are aspects of the development of our understanding of the nature of ceremonial/burial monuments of the fourth and third millennia BC which make worthwhile a reconsideration of the relationship between the Clava cairns and other monuments of that period in eastern Scotland, allowing us, with the advantage of more data, to take further Henshall's arguments on the origin of the Clava group. The growing appreciation of the complex constructional sequences which were involved in the development and use of burial/ceremonial sites of the third and second millennium BC, in particular the appearance of ring-cairn/ring-bank features in such sequences, is of use here. In this area, the dangers of the simplistic comparison of individual features within the complex development of individual sites must be acknowledged – the nature of the development of sites, in the way the space defined by the monument is changed over time, may be compared only with caution (Barclay 1989a).

There are four sites, excavated since Henshall's survey, which are of particular relevance to a discussion of the Clava cairns: the Pitnacree mound (Figure 6.1a; J.M. Coles and D.D.A. Simpson 1965), the North Mains mound (Figure 6.1b; Barclay 1983a), the Sketewan cairn (Figure 6.1d; Mercer and Tipping 1989) and the ring-cairn sequence in the ceremonial and funerary complex at Balfarg (Figure 6.1e; Barclay and Russell-White forthcoming). At the first two sites, an upturned-bowl-shaped mound was found to be the product of a series of distinct structural phases. The most significant, in the context of this discussion, was the stage where an open space was surrounded and defined by a high ring-bank, but where provision was made for continued access to the area prior to a further alteration of the nature of the mound and its defined space. As in the Clava passage graves, the central space thus had a formal means of access (Figures 6.1a, 6.1b). Although the two sites were built about a thousand years apart, it is at some time within this thousand years that the Clava cairns, of both kinds, were probably in use.

If we are to reconsider the nature of the Clava passage graves in the light of the evidence from Pitnacree and North Mains, we must first examine the evidence for the structural development of the Clava cairns.

Henshall reviewed the early reports of the Clava cairns and lucidly presented the development of antiquarian understanding. From early days, the cairns with passages had been identified as roofed structures, compared with early Boyne-type tombs. What is the evidence that the Clava cairns with passages were ever roofed? Henshall identified eleven sites as passage graves; Corrimony, excavated by Stuart Piggott in 1952 and generally reckoned to be the most complete (Figure 6.1c), is the only one to have a slab (c. $2 \cdot 5 \times 1 \cdot 5$ m) considered suitable for roofing; a reconstruction of the roofing

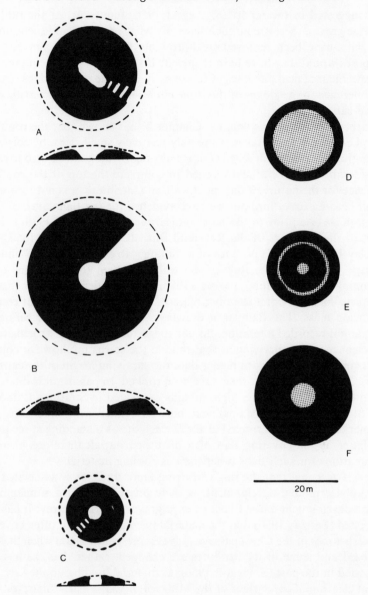

Figure 6.1: Plans of: a. Pitnacree, Perthshire; b. North Mains, Perthshire; c. Corrimony, Inverness-shire; d. Sketewan, Perthshire; e. Balfarg, Fife; f. Culdoich, Inverness-shire. Note that in a–c, the black areas are the primary mounds; the dashed lines indicate the shape and size of the completed mounds. Access to the central spaces as follows: a and c – through roofed passage; b – through empty work-bay of the mound. In d–f, the black areas indicate the extent of the primary ring-cairns; the toned areas show the completed cairns.

was suggested in the report (S. Piggott 1956, Figure 4). At the other ten passage graves, there are no such slabs. By what process could such substantial slabs have been removed so thoroughly from the sites, and for what purposes would they have been removed? If large slabs were being removed for specific practical purposes of re-use, why were the roofing slabs removed in preference to the stones of the stone circles which are characteristic of the Clava cairns?

Barber (1988 and this volume, Chapter 2) has shown that the roofing of chambers can be undertaken using only relatively small slabs, by corbelling: either the roof can be corbelled completely or corbelling can be used to reduce considerably the size of slab needed to complete the top of the roof. The evidence for the nature of the upper walls at Corrimony was not recorded in detail before excavation, but we have evidence for the Balnuaran of Clava cairn, in a state prior to the most radical reconstruction of 1930–1, in the form of the drawings of the Reverend Burnett Stewart (Innes 1860, 48–9; Barclay 1990). There is no trace of a roofing slab at either of the Balnuaran passage graves, but the tops of the walls do seem to show signs of the beginnings of corbelling. Barber (1988, 58) has demonstrated that the complete corbelling of a chamber requires a substantial amount of counter-balancing mass. The Balnuaran drawings, showing the cairns before any substantial recorded alteration, do not suggest to this author that there was sufficient material surviving at that time in the cairns to allow for counter-balancing a structure much higher than the surviving height of the cairns; of course, material might by then have been robbed. In passing, it is interesting to note that the two large, high mounds excavated in Strathtay (Pitnacree) and Strathearn (North Mains) were both associated with large slabs, both cupmarked stones, interpreted at the former site as a standing stone and at the latter as the covering slab of a disturbed burial; therefore, there are explanations for such slabs other than as roofing material.

If it is accepted that the ring-cairn/ring-bank tradition is associated with multi-phase mound-development, is there any evidence for similar multi-period development in the Clava passage graves and ring-cairns? It has been suggested (Barclay 1990) that the material piled against (and often covering) the kerbstones of the Clava passage graves represents a phase when the cairn is closed and some of its attributes are changed, rather than, as has been suggested in the past (S. Piggott 1956), as material holding up the kerb. The recent clearing of the surface of the Miltown of Clava cairn (Sharples 1990) has suggested that the shape of the cairn was changed over time. The discovery of two apparently earthen barrows near passage graves, one at Miltown of Clava (Barclay 1989b), the other at Corrimony (Harden 1989), may be of interest here. The round mound at Miltown of Clava, when ploughed recently, produced quantities of stone (Harden personal communication). It may be suggested that, as in the case of other complex stone monuments, a phase of use of the mound, or a space defined within it, might have ended with the mounding-over of that phase, to produce the typical upturned-bowl-shaped barrow. Are the earthen mounds at Miltown and Corrimony turf-covered Clava mounds, or earth and timber equivalents of the Clava cairns? Could it be that the Clava passage graves, at the end of the use of the chambers, were in some cases 'completed' in this way, taking even further the closure of cairns as evinced at Balnuaran (with the hiding of the kerb and the sealing of the entrance (Barclay 1990))? If the chambers of the Clava cairns were in use perhaps only for a limited period, and given that there is no absolute evidence for the roofing of the chambers, it might be suggested that they were either never roofed or roofed only for a limited time (perhaps in wood), and were closer in nature to the Pitnacree and North Mains mounds, in their ring-bank phases, than to the passage grave tradition with which they have been associated. It is worthwhile here to look at Piggott's results from Corrimony. He describes in some detail the filling of the passage and the chamber with boulders and soil. He suggests that most of the fill was nineteenth-century in origin but that some of the fill (the slabs in the chamber over the body stain in particular) was original. At North Mains, this author also noted clear evidence of nineteenth-century distur-bance within a stone deposit, filling the central space (Barclay 1983a). Could it be that the Corrimony deposit was similarly largely original, but disturbed during the antiquarian investigation of the mound?

If we assume for a moment that the sequence is as suggested here, let us take the parallel between North Mains and Corrimony further: we can see that in both cases there was perhaps only a single burial event, in a clearly-defined circular space, into which a formal access was available until a late stage in the mound construction, followed by the deliberate sealing of the burial area.

Let us turn briefly to the Clava ring-cairns. The parallels for these monuments have become more numerous since Henshall's survey. In par-ticular, ring-cairns have been excavated and have revealed complex construc-tional sequences. In the Balfarg cairn complex and at Sketewan, round mounds/cairns visible before excavation were found to conceal an earlier structural phase as ring-cairns. As in the Clava ring-cairns, and by definition most other ring-cairns, a central space was preserved for part of the life of the monument; however, in contrast to the passage graves and the mounds at Pitnacree and North Mains, there was no formal means of access through the surrounding cairn material. As in the excavated Clava-type ring-cairn at Culdoich (Figure 6.1f), the central open spaces at Balfarg and Sketewan were filled in; at Balfarg, this was done with a second ring-cairn and then an earthen mound covering the whole cairn; at Sketewan, the central space was filled in to form a platform cairn (Figures 6.1d, 6.1e). The pattern of filled central spaces of ring-cairns/ring-banks is widespread, but the appearance of the phenomenon in the lowland strip from Perthshire round the coast of north-east Scotland to the area around Inverness is of particular interest in discussing the relationships of the Clava passage graves and ring-cairns. In passing, it is interesting to note that Mercer has suggested a link between another element of the Balfarg complex with the recumbent stone circles and the Clava stone circles; he has argued (1981) that the main timber ring within the henge monument was graded in height towards the south-west, as in the Clava stone circles and the recumbent stone circles.

In summary, we can take further the suggestions made by Henshall, Burl and Barnatt, that the Clava ring-cairns, passage graves and stone circles are hybrid monuments combining characteristics and traditions of the monuments to the north and west with those to the east and south. We can demonstrate more clearly than was possible at the time of Henshall's survey (1963) that the Clava passage graves and ring-cairns have strong links with traditions of development and use of complex burial/ceremonial monuments in eastern Scotland. Recent work in the Lowlands has begun to reveal a more mainstream eastern British, but regionally distinct, suite of fourth- to third-millennium BC monuments. Excavation of two crop-mark enclosures has demonstrated a possibility of an enclosed settlement tradition in the third and second millennia BC (Barber 1982; Barclay and Tolan 1990), and work at Inchtuthil has dated to c. 3800 BC a long mortuary enclosure which would not be out of place in Yorkshire or Wessex (Barclay and Maxwell 1991). The long barrows of eastern Scotland (S. Piggott 1972) are beginning to seem less isolated (see also Kinnes this volume, Chapter 7).

The Clava passage graves, ring-cairns and stone circles have long been seen as a hybrid group. Perhaps, rather than being seen as a south-eastern oddity in the passage grave tradition, our increasing understanding of the Neolithic of the eastern coastal plain allows us to consider the Clava phenomenon more as a north-western element of that eastern tradition. Perhaps the excavation of one of the recently discovered, apparently earthen mounds at Clava or Corrimony would cast further light on the subject.

ACKNOWLEDGEMENTS

I am most grateful to Roger Mercer for information on the site at Sketewan in advance of the publication of the final report, and to Lesley Macinnes, David Breeze and Trevor Cowie for reading and commenting on this chapter.

7

Balnagowan and After: The Context of Non-Megalithic Mortuary Sites in Scotland

Ian Kinnes

and wondered how anyone could ever imagine unquiet slumbers, for the sleepers in that quiet earth. (Emily Brontë, *Wuthering Heights*)

A PROVISIONAL CORPUS OF NON-MEGALITHIC MORTUARY SITES

Compiled December 1990. Corpus numbers refer to OS 100 km Grid square with site number that of Kinnes 1991 and forthcoming. Dimensions given in metres. Note: DES = *Discovery and Excavation in Scotland.*

1: Excavated long barrows

No.	NGR	Site	L	W	H	Or	Exc	Ref
NJ5	453414	Cairnborrow	35	15	1·8	E	1957	Henshall 1963, 392
NO2	627073	Dalladies	69	24	2·5	ENE	1970	S. Piggott 1972
NT1	813014	Bellshiel Law	112	18	1·2	E	1935	Newbigin 1936
NT8	622590	Mutiny Stones	82	21	1·8	ENE	1871	
							1934	Henshall 1972, 404
NT9	003388	Biggar Common	16	6	2	E	1988	inf. Sheridan
							1990	inf. Johnston
NX5	854873	Fleuchlarg	45	25	3·6	SSW	1937	Henshall 1972, 418
NX6	924614	Slewcairn	22	13	2	N	1973	inf. Masters
NX7	968651	Lochhill	22	11	1·7	NE	1969	Masters 1973

2: Unexcavated long barrows

NC1	586071	Lairg	57	15	1	NE	DES 1973, 55
NH1	729798	Cairn Liath	36	14	1·8	ESE	Henshall 1972, 568
NH2	756973	Craig an Amalaidh	23	14	1·8	SE	ibid., 581
NH3	734834	Edderton Hill	61	14	?	NE	RCAHMS 1979
NJ1	479008	Balnacraig	35	15	2·5	E	DES 1974, 6
NJ2	490005	Blue Cairn	43	24	1·8	ESE	Henshall 1963, 392
NJ3	851070	Long Cairn	48	16	2·7	ESE	Henshall 1972, 544
NJ4	795151	Midmill	65	29	3·5	ESE	DES 1975, 6
NJ6	149670	Duffus	49	20	1·8	E	DES 1972, 51
NJ7	447647	Tarrieclerack	37	10	1·2	E	Henshall 1963, 391
NJ8	737620	Longman Hill	63	21	4·2	NNE	Henshall 1972, 546
NJ9	723596	Hill of Foulzie	33	18	1·5	E	Henshall 1963, 394

No.	NGR	Site	L	W	H	Or	Exc	Ref
NJ10	946503	Knapperty Hillock	90	20	1·8	ESE		ibid., 395
NK1	024336	Pol Hill	21	9	1·8	N		ibid., 396
NK2	074421	Cairn Catto	47	22	1·8	SE		Henshall 1972, 544
NN1	034034	Auchindrain	46	9	1·5	NE		ibid., 358
NN2	008170	Loch Aweside	31	9	1	SE		ibid., 364
NN3	086147	Drimfern	45	9	0·6	NNE		ibid., 319
NN4	830120	Cairn Wochel	?54	?14	?	N		ibid., 478
NN5	729466	Fortingall	32	9	1·5	ENE		ibid., 478
NN6	678944	Glenbanchor	29	12	1·5	S		ibid., 378
NO1	633664	Capo	73	22	2·5	ENE		ibid., 562
NO3	818076	Gourdon	46	14	2·5	ENE		ibid., 560
NO4	795768	Hillhead	52	22	2·7	ENE		ibid., 560
NO5	796817	Blackhill Wood	48	16	1·2	E		inf. RCAHMS
NO6	823805	Bruxie Hill	35	20	0·8	E		DES 1978, 11
NS1	864136	Meadowfoot	66	18	2	SE		DES 1975, 19
NT2	792021	Dour Hill	50	9	1·8	E		Jobey 1977, 204
NT3	732274	Caverton Hillhead	?104	?13	?	E		Henshall 1972, 480
NT4	987206	Dod Hill	24	13	1·5	NNW		Gates 1982
NT5	022495	Greensmoor	83	15	0·9	N		Henshall 1972, 459
NT6	082496	Dunsyre	15	13	0·6	SE		DES 1972, 51
NT7	179546	Harlaw Muir	60	18	0·9	ENE		Henshall 1972, 468
NX1	212674	Cairn na Gath	30	19	2·7	S		ibid., 538
NX2	393688	Drumwhirn	41	22	3·6	E		ibid., 452
NX3	559924	Cairn Avel	36	22	3	E		ibid., 447
NX4	838926	Capenoch Moor	34	17	2·7	SSW		ibid., 417
NY5	537827	The Currick	43	23	1·7	E		Masters 1984, 57
NY6	527862	Langknowe	52	14	1·5	N		Henshall 1972, 479
NY7	638922	Devil's Lapful	58	14	1·5	NE		Masters 1984, 59
NY8	041987	Stiddrig	32	19	2·4	SE		Henshall 1972, 420

3: Long mortuary enclosures

No.	NGR	Site	L	W	H	Or	Exc	Ref
NOa	616480	Douglasmuir	65	19	–		N	1980 Kendrick 1980
NOb	125395	Inchtuthil	54	10	–		E	1960 Pitts and St Joseph 1989 1985; DES 1989, 64

4: Round barrows

No.	NGR	Site	D	H	Exc	Ref
NJ R1	766043	East Finnercy	?	1·5	1952	Atkinson 1962
NJ R2	702435	Midtown of Pitglassie			1955	
			10	?	1978	inf. Shepherd
NJ R3	929497	Atherb	?	0·9	1890	Milne 1892
NJ R4	360592	Boghead	15	1·5	1972	Burl 1984
NM R1	929363	Achnacreebeag	18	1·2	1968	J.N.G. Ritchie 1970
NN R1	928523	Pitnacree	28	2·7	1964	J.M. Coles and D.D.A. Simpson 1965
NS R1	067685	Hilton	12	0·7	1972	Marshall 1976
NS M1	292495	Courthill	27	6	1872	Patrick 1872
NT R1	977371	Broomridge	5	1	1858	Greenwell and Rolleston 1877, 410

| NT R2 | 520850 | Gullane | 2 | 0·5 | 1902 | Richardson and Richardson 1902 |
| NX R1 | 187609 | Mid Gleniron B | 6 | 0·6 | 1966 | Corcoran 1969b |

Note that this list excludes some sites variously claimed as of Neolithic date, namely:

— North Mains 2 [NN Ra; Barclay 1983a] flat grave NN F1 (6 below) cut by ring-ditch of unknown date.
— Chatton Sandyford [NU Ra; Jobey 1968] charcoal on old surface and in ?grave fill dated at 3720–3515 CAL-BC (GaK 1507); no other confirmation.
— Bamborough 194 [NU Rb; Greenwell and Rolleston 1877, 414] ?grave format as NU Ra with basal socket; no other confirmation.
— Glenquicken [NX Ra; Yates 1984b, 182] 'greenstone axe fragment, polished flint ball, arrowhead with skeleton in cist'; finds lost, no other confirmation.

5: Burials in henges and related monuments

F = features, D ditch, PC pit circle, SC stone circle

No.	NGR	Site	Diam	F	Exc	Ref
HY H1	386125	Stones of Stenness	45	D/SC	1975	J.N.G. Ritchie 1976
NO H2	282031	Balbirnie	15	SC	1970	J.N.G. Ritchie 1974
NS H1	987717	Cairnpapple	40	D/PC	1947	S. Piggott 1948
NT H1	933346	Whitton Hill 1	10	D/PC	1983	Miket 1985
NT H1e	934352	Whitton Hill 2	8	D/PC	1983	ibid.

6: Flat graves

Bur = burials, C cremation, I inhumation, M multiple; Ass = associations, Axe diagnostic flint axe, Bowl pottery, C14 radiocarbon result, GW Grooved Ware pottery, Unst Unstan pottery.

No.	NGR	Site	Bur	Ass	Ref
HU F1	401099	Sumburgh	MI	C14	Hedges and Parry 1980
NJ F1	144650	Easterton of Roseisle	MC	Bowl	Walker 1968; Henshall 1983c
NK F1	054370	Greenbrae	?	Axe	Kenworthy 1977a
NN F1	928163	North Mains A	C	Bowl	Barclay 1983a
NN F2	928163	North Mains B	C	–	ibid.
NS F1	585175	Borland Castle	MC	–	M'Leod 1940
NS F2	505713	Knappers 1	?	Axe	J.N.G. Ritchie and Adamson 1981
NS F3	505713	Knappers 53	C	Bowl	ibid.
NT F1	925305	Yeavering	C	GW	Hope-Taylor 1977
NT F2	925305	Yeavering 29	C	Bowl	ibid.

7: Burials in domestic contexts

Bur = burial, I inhumation; Ass = site association, GW Grooved Ware, Unst Unstan/Hebridean Ware.

No.	NGR	Site	Bur	Ass	Ref
HY D1	230187	Skara Brae	2I	(GW)	Childe 1931a
NF D1	676913	Northton	I	(Unst)	D.D.A. Simpson 1976

Table 7.1: Regional distribution of non-megalithic sites (regions as Kinnes 1985, Figure 1. Cf. overall density – essentially megalithic – ibid., Figure 5; simple tabulation neatly expresses both actual and imposed variability in the record).

Region	NMLB	LME	RB	H	F	D
Ork-Zet	–	–	–	1	1	1
NW	–	–	–	–	–	1
N	7	–	–	–	–	–
NE	18	2	4	–	2	–
W	3	–	3	–	2	–
SE	12	–	3	4	2	–
SW	9	–	1	–	1	–

NMLB = Non-megalithic long barrow; LME = long mortuary enclosure; RB = round barrow; H = henge; F = flat grave; D = burial in domestic context.

INTRODUCTION

It seems these days that the purpose of a paper should be explicit, so I shall begin accordingly, because context is all (Barrett and Kinnes 1988). Ancestral vices incline me towards an interest in the Scottish Neolithic, personal preoccupations to the dead and their commemoration, especially non-megalithic, and scholarly tradition in favour of Audrey Henshall.

One of the more extraordinary episodes in the history of Western Europe was the systematic construction of the great mortuary monuments by the first farmers. This transcendence of the mundane realities of the agricultural calendar and technological limitation rightly remains a major concern of those who seek to recreate a vital past.

The Scottish record is unmatched elsewhere in the quality of monumental survival (Henshall 1963, 1972; J.L. Davidson and Henshall 1989). These notes take advantage of this and attempt some extension to interpretations dominated by the more evident visibility of stone structures.

Other than as some archaeological folk-memory of *ex oriente lux*, perhaps a legacy of the first and Antipodean Abercromby Professor, there is no particular reason to see the Scottish Neolithic as secondary or derivative (Kinnes 1985), even though that colonising view seems to have been pre-eminent. Stuart Piggott (1954) could only derive a few possible long barrows from southern Britain, yet his colonisation model was followed, albeit in increasingly complex ways, by the next generation (Corcoran 1969a; J.G. Scott 1969; Henshall 1963, 1972).

LONG BARROWS

From the Cheviots northwards, forty-nine probable non-megalithic (NM) long barrows are known to the author (see Corpus; for an extended discussion, see Kinnes 1991). The record has roughly doubled within the last forty years, and there is no particular reason to doubt that more will be added as fieldwork intensifies and known sites are reassessed. Some groups must be regarded as doubtful in attribution, being in areas of predominantly stone-chambered tradition (Loch Fyne, Grampian, Dornoch), but the Solway region shows that this does not preclude NM presence.

In terms of length and orientation, there is no reason to distinguish the northern and southern British mounds: both show a comparable length range, from 20–120 m, averaging around 45 m, and a preponderance of easterly alignment. Cairns tend to reflect original appearance more closely than earthen mounds, and the only size correlate here is that width-height shows greater consistency than length-height, the factor of length-variation having no current explanation except that most regional groups have a considerable range. Orientation must be reconciled with siting: the overall preference would be east to south-east along the contour of a valley side, alignment perhaps signalling the solar-lunar cycles of the agricultural calendar and location separating lowland arable from upland pasture. This, it must be stressed, is preference, not Platonic ideal, and extreme variations, such as Slewcairn facing north and uphill at 200 m OD, should not be seen as enforced by marginality or degeneration.

One striking north-south differentiation lies in the absence of quarry ditches north of the Yorkshire Wolds. While geology lends itself to cairns of collected surface or outcrop stone, there are other factors. Several of the eastern sites lie on easily-dug gravel or till, and Dalladies had initial defining slots. Throughout Scotland, ditches are not uncommon as enclosing features from henges onwards. In the south, the quarry ditches are not simply expedient sources but retain formalities of plan, profile and deposition practices which make them integral to the overall monument. Why then should they be absent? Further excavation may alter this, and the likely long mortuary enclosure at Inchtuthil certainly conforms to the southern ditched analogues. It is interesting, however, that enclosure and incorporation/exclusion principles do not appear to be integral to the northern earlier Neolithic.

To this regional differentiation might be added another, although the boundary lies somewhere around the Trent. Forecourts are unknown in the southern NM series but recurrent elsewhere. In essence, the ditched and internalised southern sites are exclusive, the northern forecourts allowing some greater participation even if chamber access is selective and mortuary houses are tucked away behind. Forecourts tend to have signs of activity – pits, hearths etc. – and rather more by way of finds than the chambers. There is a strong temptation to explicate these observed elements in processual terms, contrasting the highland and lowland zones thus: highland zone – more economically diversified; population dispersed, possibly clan-based, ?more 'Mesolithic'; monuments integrating rather than excluding (see above); no mortuary enclosures; vs lowland zone – strongly agricultural economy; population denser, ?tribal, ?less 'Mesolithic'; monuments excluding; enclosures.

EXCAVATED LONG BARROWS (SEE FIGURES 7.1 TO 7.3)

Few long barrows have been examined, and, of these, some in such a limited way that little information accrues. Fleuchlarg and the Mutiny Stones had probable stone revetment walls, Cairnborrow no trace of forecourt lining or terminal structure. Bellshiel Law had a rough boulder kerb and internally an axial ?grave. The small and composite turf-earth-rubble mound at Biggar Common apparently covered earlier occupation but had no structural components, although one of the secondary graves is of some interest (see below).

Three sites have been much more informative, with comparable mortuary structures. The nearby chambers at Slewcairn and Lochhill began as linear zones (Kinnes 1979) defined and subdivided by sizeable posts, and an elaborated version existed at Dalladies on the other side of the country. That at Lochhill had an impressive post façade and stone forestructure embellishment, and a paved offertory or 'mortuary house' was set at the rear at Slewcairn. Dalladies lay transversely within a trapezoidal area defined by slight flanking ditches. It is worth noting that the orientation and dimensions of the final monument are predicated from such modest beginnings.

Each chamber was rebuilt to a standard format, the posts being burnt or withdrawn and a ?plank-lined, coursed boulder wall now providing definition. At Slewcairn and Dalladies, revetted trapezoidal mounds with well-defined forecourts were built at this stage, with continued access to chambers in a fashion strongly reminiscent of megalithic practice. That at Slewcairn had a lateral slab and drystone chamber of unknown function. The Dalladies mound was substantially earthen, with some internal structuring of accumulating dumps, and involved the deturfing of some 7,300 sq m of grassland.

Closure was again uniform, the wooden components being burnt (including the façade at Lochhill) and the chambers stone-filled. At Lochhill, the forestructure was now developed into a simple megalithic chamber terminal to a trapezoidal cairn with forecourt. Finally, an envelope of added material concealed the original mounds and forecourts. The uniformity of both structures and sequences is striking but, on analogy elsewhere, especially in southern Britain, is unlikely to be recurrent in all future investigations. Certainly, records of the partial destruction of Knapperty Hillock strongly suggest a crematorium.

Mortuary deposits – a cranial fragment at Dalladies and some cremated bones at Lochhill and Slewcairn – are not informative. Radiocarbon dates are too few for phasing, and all apparently date monument closure: Lochhill 4005–3770 CAL-BC (I-6409); Dalladies 4190–3940 CAL-BC (I-6113), 3490–

Dalladies NO 2

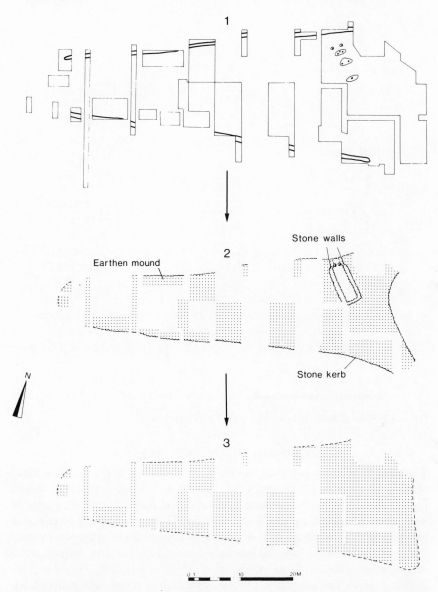

Figure 7.1: Plans of Dalladies NM long barrow, Phase 1–3 structures (illustration by P. Dean).

3355 CAL-BC (SRR-289) and 3375–3185 CAL-BC (SRR-290). The forecourts at Slewcairn and Lochhill were rich in Bowl sherds and flintwork, but there was little in the chambers: knives and a leaf-shaped arrowhead at Slewcairn, and a knife and cup-marked slab at Dalladies.

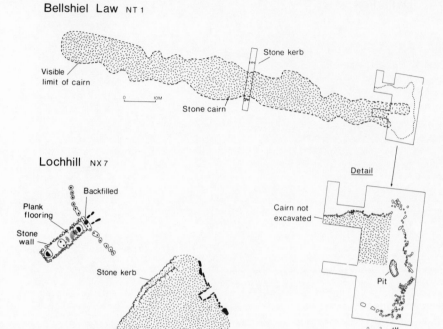

Figure 7.2: Plans of Bellshiel Law and Lochhill NM long barrows.

LONG MORTUARY ENCLOSURES

The term 'long mortuary enclosure' is tendentious but unproven: first identified at Dorchester (Atkinson, C.M. Piggott and Sandars 1951), in classic
form, some eight have now been excavated and many cropmark examples
have been identified in southern England. Dating is usually vague and
function unestablished: all rests on perceived links to the long barrow format.
These sites may fill the lowland lacunae of mound-distribution; indeed, some
might be denuded barrows: while of no clear practicality, they have no
proven role in the mortuary process, rare human bone fragments (from
Dorchester and Normanton Down) being no more significant than on any
other Neolithic site.

Inchtuthil conforms closely to the usual narrow rectangular enclosed plan
and, as elsewhere, is lacking in cultural material. The solid fence established
as a secondary ditch feature is unique, but its deliberate burning echoes
common Neolithic ritual practice. Attention has already been drawn to its

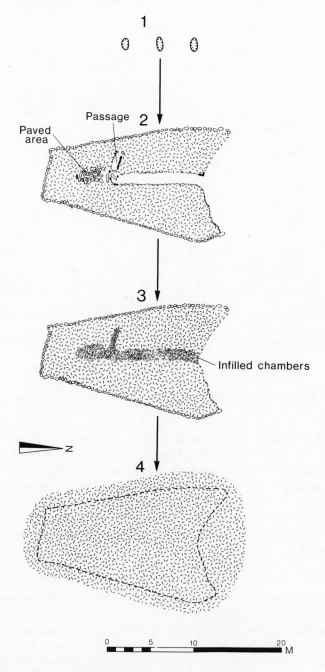

Figure 7.3: Plans of Slewcairn NM long barrow, Phase 1–4 structures.

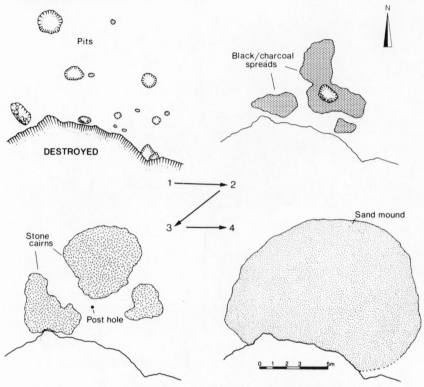

Figure 7.4: Plans of Boghead Mound NM round barrow, Phase 1–4 structures.

anomalous nature within known Scottish monuments, but real assessment must be reserved. The other candidate, Douglasmuir, is more contentious, being placed here by default with its odd palisade definition. It is certainly early, judging from its pottery and radiocarbon date, and parts at least had been burnt down; some local congeners have been suggested but remain unexcavated (Kinnes 1985, 40). In essence, this category, as with most of this chapter, simply not only begs questions but also pleads for even the simplest of answers.

ROUND BARROWS (SEE FIGURES 7.4 TO 7.9)

Although one faction continues to preserve the native residual/Beaker impact explanation for the existence of nominally pre-Bronze Age round barrows (S. Piggott 1954; Atkinson 1972; Grinsell 1982), proselytisation (Kinnes 1979) has won some following, even if uncritical (as Thomas 1984). The north British circumstance exemplifies the two crucial problems: acceptance of the NM round barrow format and the eclectic nature of the largely randomly-

Achnacreebeag NM R1

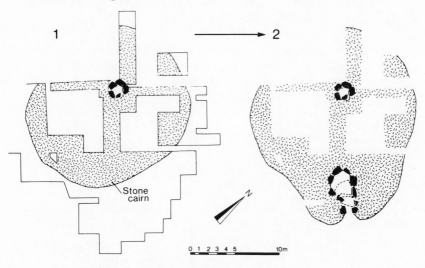

Mid Gleniron B NX R1

Figure 7.5: Plans of Achnacreebeag NM round barrow, Phase 1-2 structures, and of Mid
Gleniron B NM round barrow.

accumulated evidence. There is insufficient for patterning but enough for
security, allowing for reasonable speculation. Burial practice is commonly
confused with architectural style but can be coincident, and an argument can
be made for distinctive regional/cultural traditions.

Internal structures

It should no longer be surprising that the format of round barrow internal
structures is highly variable: a period lasting at least 1,500 calendar years
ought to have had considerable capacity for change and development, and
Scottish geography lends itself to regionalism (Kinnes 1985). An earlier
attempt at classification married changing formats broadly to the temporal
trajectory (Kinnes 1979), although Stages 1-6 were not envisaged as the strict
phasing familiar to the European scene, denied offshore by the limited nature
of the material record.

The linear zone, originally a two-poster and redefined by a low kerb, at

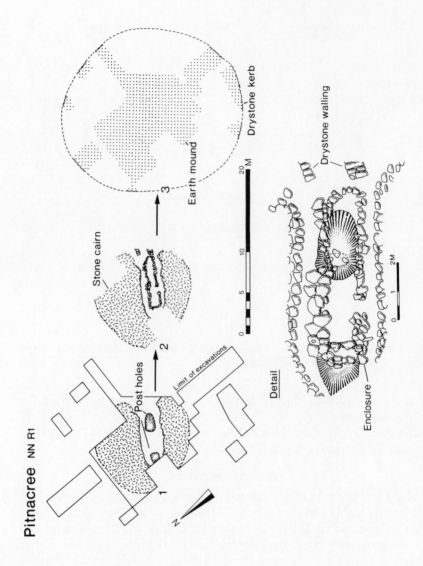

Figure 7.6: Plans of Pitnacree NM round barrow, Phase 1–3 structures.

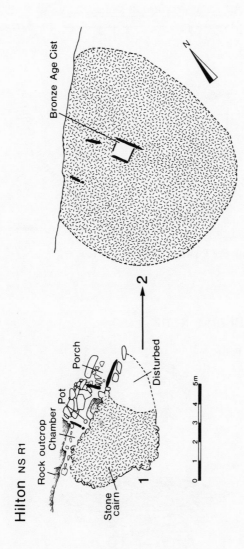

Figure 7.7: Plans of Hilton NM round barrow, Phase 1–2 structures.

Courthill NS M1

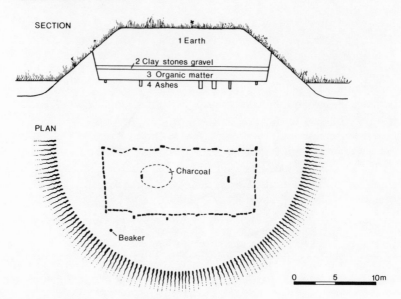

SECTION

1 Earth

2 Clay stones gravel

3 Organic matter

4 Ashes

PLAN

Charcoal

Beaker

0   5   10m

Figure 7.8: Plan and section of Courthill NM round barrow.

Gullane NT R2

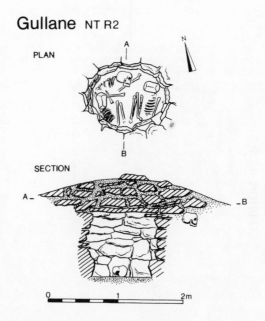

PLAN

A

N

B

SECTION

A

B

0   1   2m

Figure 7.9: Plan and section of Gullane NM round barrow.

Pitnacree links easily to many others throughout Britain beneath round and long barrows (Kinnes 1991), and a segmented slab and dry-stone version occurs at Hilton. Courthill, if Neolithic (see below), might be a two-poster within an enclosure. The indifferent record at Atherb, while uncertain as to mound form, must describe a crematorium, most familiar in East Yorkshire (Manby 1963) but probably represented locally at the Knapperty Hillock long cairn. The ring-bank enclosure(s) at Midtown of Pitglassie, early by ceramic and radiocarbon association, are unmatched at this date, providing an interesting addition to the repertoire. The minimal mound at Broomridge covered a communal pyre with cremated bone, sherds and flintwork, a context closely matched in Suffolk at Swale's Tumulus (Briscoe 1957). Although no certain species identification could be made for bone from Boghead, overall circumstance argues for comparable interpretation: Burl's argument (1984) for two-poster presence, although tempting for linkage elsewhere, carries no conviction. The little information available for East Finnercy might just provide attribution here, but this cannot be affirmed yet.

Little information exists for subsidiary or attendant structures, although extensive excavation of south British sites almost invariably demonstrates complex layouts. The horseshoe cairn at Pitnacree invokes two recurrent themes: embankment of linear zones and interim phasing of mound construction. U-plan or flanking banks commonly define NM chambers, and in the remarkably well-preserved example at Haddenham these are now understandable as vital structural support for the plank-built box. The scale at Pitnacree is exceptional to the point of ranking as a Phase 1 mound: although most NM monuments seem to seal open-air complexes, examples as varied as Aldwincle and Kilham (Jackson 1976; Manby 1976) provide analogy for interim monumental markers. This circumstance also existed at Hilton. The three or four cairns at Boghead might similarly have defined a mortuary or ritual focus. The status and function of the Pitnacree 'passage' remains unknown by reason of incomplete excavation; it is not matched elsewhere.

The final category here is less certain: sub-circular slab- or dry-stone cists have more in common with NM practice than with megaliths, since continued access was not architecturally contrived. None is securely dated, but a Hebridean chamber was secondary to one at Achnacreebeag, and organised deposits of crania and longbones lay against the cist at Gullane. The latter are not certainly Neolithic, given the Bronze Age contexts documented by Peterson (1972) and the Iron Age contexts documented by Whimster (1981). Mid Gleniron B, adjacent to a long cairn of Clyde affinity, could belong here by structural affinity. Elsewhere, a round cairn with large closed cist preceded the Severn-Cotswold long cairn at Notgrove (Clifford 1936), and, less certainly, a comparable sequence has been suggested at Sale's Lot (Darvill 1987. It should be noted that an unpublished drawing of Winterbotham's excavation of Belas Knap in the archive of the British Museum's Prehistoric and Romano-British Department refutes Darvill's claim for the same circumstance there.)

Other than in the examples cited above, mound structure is little-known. By and large, easily-available surface materials are used, although deliberate selection can be shown in the essentially stone-earthen sequences at Pitnacree, Pitglassie and Boghead.

Finally, return must be made to Courthill. Largely forgotten in the literature, this site was restored to some prominence by its suggested affinities with Pitnacree (J.M. Coles and D.D.A. Simpson 1965). More recently, it has been ranked both as a Beaker monument (J.N.G. Ritchie 1970b) and as an early medieval house below a motte (most recently by Scott 1989). The evidence remains ambiguous, but Linge's calm appraisal (1987) documents as many as twenty large mounds of likely prehistoric date in Ayrshire. This is an outstanding problem for resolution; perceptions have almost certainly been hindered by the relative prominence of chambered cairns and cists in the Scottish record. That size and regional affinity are not a reliable guide to attribution was shown by North Mains, where the mound, originally seen as a Pitnacree congener, is certainly of Early Bronze Age date (Barclay 1983a).

Mortuary practice

Nothing survived at Hilton, Achnacreebeag and Mid Gleniron B, probably through acid soil effect, but local context suggests that burnt bone should survive; perhaps, therefore, lost inhumations are suggested, although skeletal absence at this period does not preclude original mortuary function (Kinnes 1975; 1981). Gullane had three primary crouched adults and the crania and longbones of four more placed outside, an overall disposition recalling cumulative or selective chamber practice.

Elsewhere, cremation is universal, either by selective survival (a still unpredictable circumstance) or by invariable practice. Courthill had a deposit of burnt bones, not certain to be human but likely so; some reservation on Boghead has already been expressed. An argument has been made for integrated process (Kinnes 1985) and remains plausible, given the Broomridge and Boghead pyre residues, Atherb crematorium and cremations at Pitnacree and Pitglassie. No worthwhile palaeodemography can be deduced.

Associations and dating

Four sites – Courthill and the three closed-cist sites – have no useful associations, although that at Achnacreebeag preceded a Hebridean-style chamber with Bowl and Beacharra material. Pitnacree had Bowl sherds on the old land-surface, and the mortuary episode was bracketed by charcoal dates of 3705–3510 CAL-BC (GaK-601) and 2930–2730 CAL-BC (GaK-602).

The remaining sites all have direct associations with Bowl sherds and flintwork (Henshall 1983), supplemented by charcoal dates for Pitglassie (3850–3620 CAL-BC (GU-2014) and 3490–3355 CAL-BC (GU-2049)) and Boghead (five between c. 4000–3500 CAL-BC and two outliers at c. 5000–4800 CAL-BC and c. 2900–2500 CAL-BC (SRR-683-6, 688-90).

HENGES AND ALLIED SITES

It is not intended here to review the overall henge evidence (Harding and Lee 1987) but simply to assess known mortuary use. Cremation cemeteries are known from Cairnpapple, Whitton Hill 1–2 and Balbirnie, and a single deposit from Stenness. The first three are linked to pit-circles within enclosures, a familiar circumstance in southern England as seen in the Dorchester cluster (Atkinson, C.M. Piggott and Sandars 1951). At Whitton Hill 1, the cremations were certainly an addition to the original layout, post-dating the burning of the timber structure. Elsewhere, this has not been established. Those at Balbirnie were in the circle stone-holes but not certainly primary, and that at Stenness was in the central 'hearth' which cannot be directly linked to the enclosure or circle. A primary mortuary component seems likely for Whitton Hill 1, with an urned cremation in a central grave. Two unburnt human bones were recovered from the ditch base at Stenness.

Grooved Ware sherds were associated with some cremations at Balbirnie and Whitton Hill 1, and were found in primary ditch-fill at Stenness. The ?primary grave at Whitton had a badly-preserved inverted vessel whose best affinities seem to lie with the Meldon Bridge style. Other links to the Dorchester series are shown by skewer-pins from Cairnpapple and a flint fabricator from Whitton.

Radiocarbon dates, all on charcoal, broadly confirm a Late Neolithic attribution: Whitton 1 grave 2660–2285 CAL-BC (BM-2266R), Stenness cremation 2925–2740 CAL-BC (SRR-351), Whitton 2 cremation 2470–2135 CAL-BC (BM-2205R).

FLAT GRAVES AND DOMESTIC CONTEXTS

These categories do not comprise a single phenomenon but must be seen as the largely fortuitous recovery of practices outside monumental traditions and of unknown relative importance at any time during the period.

At Sumburgh, a stone-lined pit held at least ten inhumations with sherds and flintwork, the whole strongly reminiscent of chamber practice, and with bone dated at 3065–2910 CAL-BC (GU-1075). This is a valuable reminder of the variability of deposition or process, even in an area with a major monumental tradition (Henshall 1963: Zetland group). Southern parallels include sizeable pits at Cats Water (Pryor 1984) and several Thames Valley sites (Kinnes forthcoming).

The mortuary status of Greenbrae and Knappers 1 is unknown; both were possibly inhumations. Each had a high-quality edge-polished flint adze, accompanied at Greenbrae by massive jet and amber beads. The Biggar Common association features an edge-polished axehead and a bifacially-worked object, both flint, and its context as a grave inserted into an existing monument echoes those such as Whitegrounds and Ayton East Field. These are clearly linked to a number of northern English round barrow single graves which represent a novel individual prestige mode around 3000 BC (Kinnes 1979; Kinnes et al. 1981).

Cist inhumations were associated with Unstan and Grooved Ware occupation at Northton and Skara Brae respectively, but their actual relation to the domestic activities is unknown. Scattered bones are also recorded at Skara Brae and are a familiar feature of several southern sites.

The remaining examples are all cremations. It can be suggested that the stone-lined pits with burnt fills and ash or burnt bone residues at Easterton of Roseisle and Borland Castle, the former with Bowl sherds, are crematorium pits of a form attested in East Yorkshire at Bridlington and Garton Slack (Earnshaw 1973; Brewster 1980) and in Antrim at Killaghy (E.E. Evans 1940). Simple pits with cremations and Bowl sherds are known at North Mains and Yeavering, and at Knappers 53, which has a complete vessel and a flint knife comparable to that from Dalladies. North Mains had charcoal dated at 3490–3345 CAL-BC (GU-1546). Comparable associations are known at Garton Slack 137 and Roughridge Hill (Mortimer 1905, 346; Proudfoot 1965). Grooved Ware sherds were with burnt bones at Yeavering, and this can be matched at Tebb's Pits (I.F. Smith 1956) as well as various henge contexts already mentioned. Likely urns in this tradition are known from Eddisbury and Winhill (Wainwright and Longworth 1971, 201; Bateman 1861, 255).

CAVE BURIALS

Throughout southern Britain, any area with caves has produced evidence for Neolithic mortuary deposits, varying from ill-defined bone presence to complex structuring (Kinnes forthcoming). Scotland has no proven examples, but possibilities exist as distant as Inchnadamph (Lawson 1981). Even more likely are those around Oban, where there is intriguing potential for mortuary variation on an economic, perhaps chronologic or behavioural, interface (Pollard 1990). Radiocarbon-dating the bones would seem an obvious first step in the dialogue.

A NOTE ON IRISH PARALLELS

Although familiar in the literature, Hiberno-Scottish contacts or shared characteristics have received little detailed attention of late. Generalised statements tend to revolve around the western seaways with the distribution of Antrim flint and stone, Court and Clyde tomb parallels, 'Grimston-Lyles Hill' bowls, Boyne-Hebridean-Orkney passage tombs and so on, usually with implicit assumptions of the *spread* of traditions and the *movement* of people.

The model is easy to criticise (Kinnes 1985), but creative evaluation of the components must await detailed reassessment on both sides of St George's Channel.

For present purposes, two allied points are made by a rapid overview of NM sites in Ireland: firstly, megalithic structures so dominate the record that other formats occupy only a minor, if any, part of synthesis and interpretation; secondly, their variety echoes that of other parts of the Atlantic fringe where account has been taken of NM traditions.

The cremation processes of eastern and northern Britain are present in Ireland. Crematoria exist with long and round cairns at Dooey's Cairn and Fourknocks II (Collins 1976; Hartnett 1971), the former curiously regarded as an eccentric version of a court chamber. The crematorium long cairn at Ballafayle, Isle of Man (Henshall 1978), is also worth recall, so that current absence of this format in the southern Celtic Sea province is not without significance.

A crematorium pit has been recorded at Killaghy (E.E. Evans 1940). Likely pyres with burnt bone residues, sherds and flintwork underlay a wide variety of monuments. Examples of the dozen or so known can be cited below court tombs (Carnanbane: Evans 1939), passage tombs (Townleyhall: Eogan 1963) and Bronze Age cairns (Moneen: M.J. O'Kelly 1952) and within enclosures (Dun Ruadh: Davies 1936). Urned cremation is known at Monknewton (Sweetman 1976) in a vessel of familiar passage tomb association.

Enclosure of ambiguous function (Goodland: Case 1973) and ring-ditches or round mounds (Rathjordan: Ó Ríordáin 1947; 1948) provide further possibilities. Inhumation graves occur separately (Clane: Ryan 1980) and on domestic sites (Lough Gur: Ó Ríordáin 1954). A timber structure beneath the main mound at Knowth (Eogan 1984) might be a mortuary house rather than a dwelling.

Best-known is the single-grave, round cairn tradition named after the Linkardstown example (Ryan 1981) and associated with distinctive ornate vessels. Interpretation of these as a residual Neolithic reaction to new Bronze Age fashion (Herity 1982) can be discounted by a suite of radiocarbon dates (Brindley, Lanting and Mook 1983; inf. Lanting) more or less coeval with the prestige graves of Britain.

It is not suggested that the resistance of some Irish scholars to acceptance of NM practices as part of the explanatory process is echoed in Scotland, but the common experience of two adjacent 'megalithic' provinces invokes both shared problems and possibilities. In parallel, the critical testing of the approved England-Antrim-south-and-west sequence of Neolithicisation by Green and Zvelebil (1990) should at least arouse some uneasy echoes in Scotland.

SYNTHESIS

The foregoing should at least affirm that the well-attested stone chambered monuments of Scotland, while varied and long-enduring, represent only one part of the spectrum of Neolithic mortuary practice. It remains to be established how this operated at any given chronological horizon or regional/ local level. Certainly, in the earlier period, we can document the archaeological contemporaneity of NM and megalithic long and round cairns, flat graves, 'processing' sites, and cremation and inhumation as deposition.

Throughout Britain, no NM long barrow, either by association or by radiocarbon dating, certainly post-dates 3000 BC, and this is likely to hold in Scotland. This fact has engendered much literature following Corcoran's demonstration of some megalithic sequences (1972), strongly influencing the explanatory synthesis of Henshall (1972).

While it is true that such classic sites at Dyffryn Ardudwy, Mid Gleniron I–II and Tulach an t-Sionnaich have a round-long succession, this is not enough to impose the same on other sites where limited excavation or field observation suggest internal complexity (*pace* Henshall). Such arguments impose unproven and essentially Darwinian evolutionary systems on an observed record whose variability demands much more complex assessment of social dynamics. The unfortunate use of the term 'proto-megalith' is a prime demonstration of the incipient dangers (J.G. Scott 1969). One further example should suffice: the round cairn chambers at Mid Gleniron are no more than open-fronted boxes, simple in form and easy of access. How do they relate to the closed, high-septalled format as seen at Cairnholy I, whose contrived difficulty of access varies a common and apparently early theme seen in structures as nominally disparate as portal tomb and NM linear zones (Kinnes 1981, Figure 6.1)? Without wholly subscribing to the Gallic logic of nomenclature-taxonomy which identifies the remarkably-preserved chamber at Haddenham as a *dolmen en bois* (Joussaume 1990), it does at least invoke appropriate questions on the interplay of descriptor-label-function which is only the first level of analysis for any archaeological circumstance, let alone those which transcend the predictably-functional.

Setting aside for the moment the certain complexities of monuments in action, the practical record of the NM-megalithic relationship as seen in excavation should be reviewed. At Wayland's Smithy (Atkinson 1965), successive long barrows had a linear zone and transepted chamber; at Lochhill (Masters 1973), a slab box replaced or commemorated the forestructure; at Gwernvale (Britnell and Savory 1984), timber structures likely to be ritual preceded a Severn-Cotswold cairn. To compound the circumstance, recent work at Whitwell (inf. Wall), where limestone slabs were available and used for passage and revetment, revealed a succession of post-bracketed linear zones with round and long cairns. This combination recalls those in Scotland where stone kerbs, forecourts and subsidiary structures show that 'megalithic' chambers could have been built and would have been more enduring than the chosen NM method. Compounded to this are sites such as Hilton, a stone-built linear zone on the 30-sq-km island of Bute with five standard

Clyde cairns, or Sumburgh, known only from salvage records but strongly reminiscent of Nordic *Totenhütten* (Feustel and Ulrich 1965; naturally, no cultural link suggested), in a small archipelago with 100+ chambered cairns. It would be easy if not facile to declare a precocious NM phase, more or less important by region, but this would only deny the essential complexity of embedded and manipulated traditions. Whatever, neither expediency nor mechanistic evolution will serve as motive force or explanatory means.

Much of this chapter has been devoted to stressing problems which are universal. The archaeological record is partial and its perception both dependent and opportunistic. For example, Henshall's megalithic corpus derives both from the best-preserved context in western Europe (where else is there such a combination of the monumental landscapes of Caithness-Sutherland-Orkney, the assiduous work of Bryce in the West and the steady, if overdue, emergence of the lowland record?) and personal devotion. While the NM component remains undervalued to the detriment of understanding, it has to be accepted that the record is unguided and accidental and likely to remain so since, apart from 'unchambered' long barrows and henges (where mortuary role is seen as incidental), round barrows depend on excavation and are anyway seen as odd in short-cist country, just as they are regarded as Bronze Age in southern Sites and Monuments Records. The relative role of flat graves, as tendentious and negative a term as NM, remains dependent on chance discovery. Mortuary practice is not easily analysed (Barrett 1988), but possibilities exist, both for reworking of established archives (J.L. Davidson and Henshall 1989; Richards 1988) and active testing of hypotheses (Barber 1988); Scotland remains, if the will is there, the best of laboratories.

I have attempted both state of record and state of research for Scotland. Megaliths, I am sure, will continue, and perhaps rightly, to predominate in synthesis, but they were not, and this should no longer surprise, the sole commemoration of the most expressive and diversified period of Scotland's past.

The opening words by Brontë were preceded by others appropriate in tribute to a devotion to proper archaeology and those remarkable Scottish monuments:

> I lingered around them, under that benign sky, watched the moths fluttering among the heath and hare-bells, listened to the soft wind breathing through the grass . . .

8
Mortuary Structures and Megaliths

J.G. Scott

INTRODUCTION

Perhaps the most unexpected outcome of the study of Neolithic cairns and barrows over the past forty years is the proof that the barrow or cairn still visible today may mark only the final stage in a succession of structures connected with the disposal of the dead: even the cairn or barrow itself may have been of multi-phase construction (Vyner 1986, 11). This view is far removed from that once held, that the long chambered cairn was already completely developed when introduced into these islands, arriving like Aphrodite, fully formed, from the (western) sea. A further surprising revelation is that the various elements of this succession of structures may be found in recognisable combinations beneath both cairns and barrows, long and round, from Wiltshire to Perthshire and from Yorkshire to Ulster. Problems of interpretation remain, despite much useful discussion. It would appear that the dead were exposed before burial, but how this was done has not received great consideration. What follows might be described as an armchair re-excavation of excavation reports in search of evidence, in particular of raised mortuary platforms, for the exposure of the dead.

MORTUARY STRUCTURES AND MEGALITHS

A start may be made with the Neolithic mortuary enclosure, Aldwincle 1, Northamptonshire (Jackson 1976). Within intermittent lengths of ditch were two post-holes 1·68 m apart (Figure 8.1, 1). Jackson considered these to represent a mortuary structure, approximately axial to the ditched enclosure, and so to be associated with it (ibid., 24–5). Two further, similar but later post-holes, about 2·24 m apart, were better preserved (Figure 8.1, 2). The D-shaped impression in one, 0·86 m below the old ground surface, may mark a segment of a massive tree trunk. Its partner had been at least as deeply set into the old surface. Between these posts were two adult male inhumations, one deposited as a pile of bones, the other on its back in a fully crouched (perhaps trussed) position. Both skeletons were incomplete (ibid., 65–6).

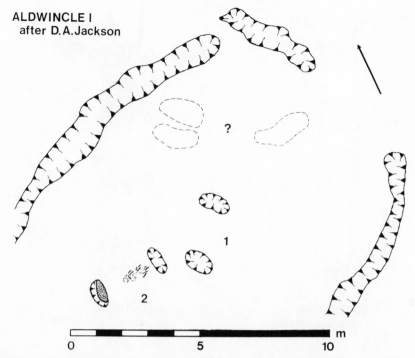

ALDWINCLE I
after D.A.Jackson

Figure 8.1: Plan of mortuary structure at Aldwincle I, Northamptonshire (after Jackson 1976).

Many of the small bones of the hands and feet were missing, while both skulls were fragmented.

The posts could have stood some three metres high, stable enough to support a raised platform from which the decayed bodies, and bones not removed by predators, had fallen to the ground between. Features to note at Aldwincle 1, therefore, are two-point support mortuary structures, probably at least three in succession, built within a mortuary enclosure. The structures seem to have decayed *in situ* or to have been dismantled: none was burnt. The use of structure 2 may have ceased through collapse when one of the two bodies had not been long exposed.

Possibly the closest parallels for the Aldwincle 1 mortuary structures – especially for their small size – are to be sought in Yorkshire, but unfortunately in the nineteenth-century explorations of Greenwell (Greenwell and Rolleston 1877) and Mortimer (1905). Kinnes (1979) has made valiant attempts to extract and classify information derived from their excavations of Neolithic round barrows. It may with all reserve be deduced from his drawings that small, two-point support mortuary structures existed at Langton II (ibid., 11, Figure 10.4) and at Heslerton (ibid., 13, Figure 11.2). At Heslerton, remains of at least fourteen individuals were found in

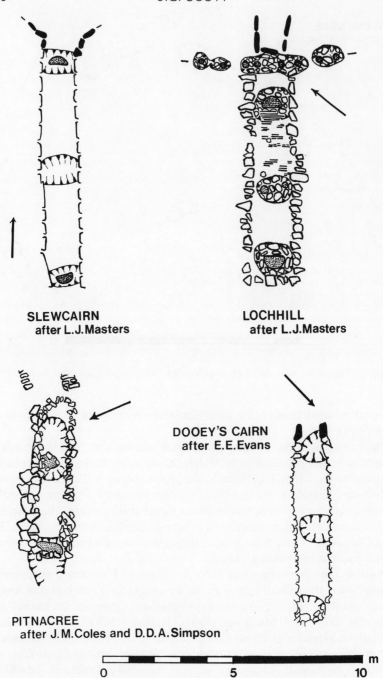

Figure 8.2: Plans of mortuary structures at Slewcairn, Kirkcudbrightshire (after Masters 1981b), Lochhill, Kirkcudbrightshire (after Masters 1973), Pitnacree, Perthshire (after J.M. Coles and D.D.A. Simpson 1965) and Dooey's Cairn, Co. Antrim (after E.E. Evans 1938).

confusion between the post-holes, suggesting the collapse of an exposure platform rather than a burial chamber used for presumably successive interments. Kinnes' drawing suggests that a larger two-point support mortuary structure existed at Aldro 94 (ibid., 14, Figure 12.1). All these burials were unburnt, and found beneath round barrows.

A more elaborate Yorkshire mortuary structure was found by Mortimer in 1892 at Callis Wold, Humberside. A slab pavement, 3·66 m long and 0·91 m wide, lay between post-holes large enough to have held massive upright timbers. Only one post-hole had been detected by Mortimer, but re-excavation by Coombs (1976) revealed the other. Mortimer (1905, 162) states that the west post-hole filling contained numerous portions of adults' and children's bones. Coombs (1976, 130) found that the opposite post-hole also contained human bones, including a skull, and that one of the pavement slabs had tipped into the hole. This feature is exactly that observed by Ashbee (1966, 8) at Fussell's Lodge (discussed below, and see Figure 8.3) – 'apparent partial infill with bones could result from "replacement" of a post by fall-in and settlement as in Pit A'. Upon the pavement, according to Mortimer, were ten adult skeletons and an infant burial. The skeleton nearest the west post-hole he confirms in detail as crouched, but the other bones he describes as in greatly crushed and broken condition. It would have been quite impossible to lay out eleven crouched burials on a pavement only 3·66 × 0·91 m in size. Mortimer is compelled to argue that all the bodies had been interred at the same time (1905, 163), which seems innately unlikely. It is far more probable that the one arguably crouched burial was the most recent of a series placed upon a raised platform which had collapsed, depositing the previously exposed bodies in a crushed and broken condition. The descriptions of the post-hole fillings show that the posts had decayed *in situ*. There was no sign of burning.

A similar pavement, described by Greenwell (Greenwell and Rolleston 1877, 216) as of chalk slabs, 2·90 × 1·07 m in size, was found in Cowlam round barrow 57 (Kinnes 1979, 13, Figure 11.3a). The incomplete remains of five bodies lay upon it. Greenwell's explanation (Greenwell and Rolleston 1877, 221) was that 'the bodies may have been previously deposited, either under or above ground, at some other place, and may afterwards have been removed to where they were discovered, for none seemed to be complete or to have all their bones in proper order'. He further (ibid., 215–16) describes a 'hollow', 0·91 m in diameter by 0·31 m deep, as 0·61 m away from one end of the pavement. The inference is that the 'hollow' was a hole for one of the two posts of a mortuary structure which had decayed *in situ*. Again, the condition of the bones suggests that they had fallen from a raised platform.

Implied Yorkshire links are to be found in the Grimston-style pottery found in a slightly oval barrow at Pitnacree, Perthshire (J.M. Coles and D.D.A. Simpson 1965). The earliest feature beneath the barrow was a mortuary structure (Figure 8.2) marked by two ramped post-holes. The shapes of the holes suggest that they had held segments of massive tree trunks which might have stood to a considerable height. They were 2·74 m apart, and had decayed *in situ* (ibid., 41). No relics could be directly associated with the structure, but it could have been a two-point support raised mortuary platform.

The clearest evidence for the exposure of the dead comes from a two-point support mortuary structure found by Professors Atkinson and Piggott at Wayland's Smithy, Berkshire (Atkinson 1965). The structure (Figure 8.3), in its final phase, had been enclosed in a stone-kerbed oval barrow, the whole of which in turn had been incorporated into the mound of a chambered cairn (ibid., 129, Figure 2). The structure's D-shaped post-holes, 0·91 m deep, had contained split tree trunks, 1·22 m in diameter. Between them was a sarsen pavement, 4·88 m long and 1·52 m wide, on which lay the skeletal remains of at least fourteen individuals, only one of which had been laid separately (ibid., 127). After a preliminary examination of the bones, Atkinson concluded that the condition of the bodies had varied from nearly complete articulation to complete disintegration, that they had not been disinterred after inhumation, that they had not been attacked by rodents, but that they could have been exposed to attack by carrion-eating birds, which would account for the large missing proportion of the bones of the hands and feet and of other small bones such as knee-caps and lower jaws (ibid., 129–30).

Atkinson was able to show that the mortuary structure in its final phase resembled a low ridge-tent, with sides presumed to have been of timbers resting at their upper ends against a ridgepole, to give a 'pitched' mortuary structure, which had evidently decayed *in situ*. He suggested that the two posts might well have projected above the final covering mound (ibid., 130–1).

Associated with the mortuary structure were two lines of post-holes forming a funnelled approach to the north end of the structure and evidently associated with it (Figure 8.3). An exposure platform may have been originally supported by the two large posts, which in a final stage were still serviceable enough to be converted for use in a ridged burial chamber. The body laid separately may have been exposed only shortly before the chamber was sealed and buried beneath the barrow.

The Wayland's Smithy mortuary structure and its funnelled approach lay beneath what Atkinson described as 'the smallest "unchambered" long barrow hitherto discovered in Britain' (ibid., 127). Probably the same basic elements mark a primary phase in the long barrow at Kilham, Yorkshire, originally dug by Greenwell (Greenwell and Rolleston 1877, 553–6) and re-excavated by Manby almost a century later. At the east end were two pits, 1·20 m apart, large and deep enough to have held the supporting timber uprights of a raised mortuary platform (Figure 8.4,1). Manby (1976, 148) reluctantly concedes that these pits might have been post-holes: one had been dug out by Greenwell and the filling of the other was ambiguous.

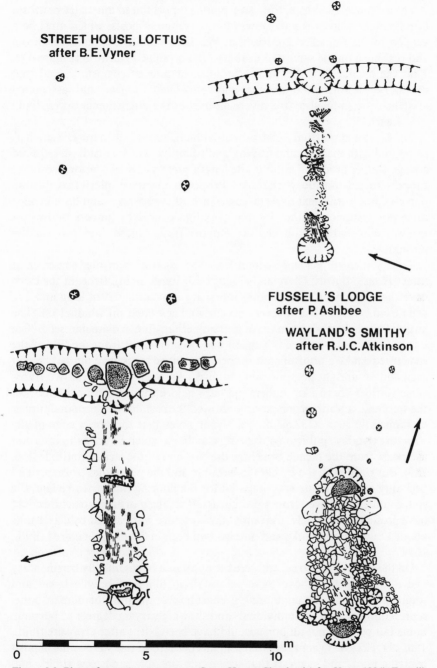

Figure 8.3: Plans of mortuary structures at Street House, Cleveland (after Vyner 1984), Fussell's Lodge, Wiltshire (after Ashbee 1966) and Wayland's Smithy, Wiltshire (after Atkinson 1965).

The evidence, therefore, for a two-point support raised mortuary platform at Kilham is in itself slight. However, an avenue of posts, which must be a version of the funnelled approach at Wayland's Smithy, extends east from and is aligned on the same axis as that of the presumed platform (Figure 8.4). That the avenue is earlier than the adjacent ditched enclosures, and that mortuary platform and avenue may have had a prior and associated existence, are implied by the divergent axis of the ditched enclosures (ibid., 116, Figure 3).

The proposed mortuary platform at Kilham, about 1·20 m long, is small as compared with the structure at Wayland's Smithy, which must have required a ridge-timber at least 5 m long, the length presumably of a prior two-point support raised mortuary platform. Proposed mortuary platforms in long barrows and cairns next to be discussed are all even longer, and have at least three-point support, either by massive aligned upright timbers or by two massive end-timbers with central support from spaced twin but smaller uprights.

The most recent evidence comes from the excavation of the long cairn at Street House, Loftus, Cleveland (Figure 8.3; Vyner 1984). Beneath the cairn were the remains of a three-point mortuary structure, 7·20 m long and 1 m wide (ibid., 159), which overlay an earlier back-filled pit (ibid., 153). The largest feature had been a massive timber, perhaps 1 m in diameter, set 1·80 m into subsoil at the east end. Topsoil had been stripped from the line of the structure to take a floor of split timbers. A central transverse pit had held at each end an upright post, possibly squared. Between these stood two transverse vertical board-like timbers, perhaps held upright by floor timbers. At the west end, a transverse post-hole showed the remains of a terminal timber or timbers, 0·80 × 0·32 m in size. Vyner notes that the north edge of the structure overlay spill from a flanking clay bank which he seems to interpret as upcast from the façade trench at the east end of the structure (ibid., 156, 159). But since both the earlier pit certainly and the post-holes probably had been dug before the site was prepared for the flooring timbers to be laid, the spill could have derived from prior upcast. If so, the mortuary structure could have preceded the façade. Certainly, the structure was flanked by clay banks about 1 m wide, for banks and timbers had been in contact when fired (ibid., 161).

On the floor of the structure were burnt human bones, mostly fragmentary and disarticulated. Above these was a 10 cm filling of heavily burnt and fragmented sandstone containing a considerable quantity of human bone, representing at least five individuals and showing varying degrees of burning. Some but perhaps not all bones could have been burnt after exposure (ibid., 156, 159, 182–3). Vyner notes that remains perhaps of turf were in the deposit over the floor, and suggests that turves and possibly sandstone rubble had been piled on the roof to weight it down against storms.

Pace Vyner, it is suggested here that the remains are those of a raised

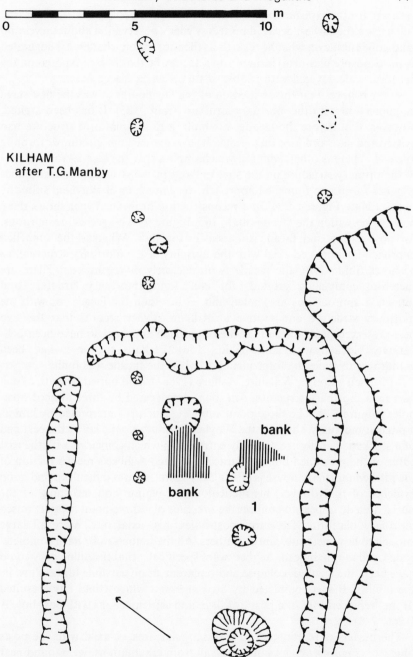

KILHAM
after T.G.Manby

bank

bank

1

Figure 8.4: Plan of mortuary structure at Kilham, Yorkshire (after Manby 1976).

platform for the exposure of the dead, the scattered bones on the floor having fallen from the earliest decayed burials. Vyner's observation about turves and sandstone rubble on what he regards as the roof (or on what here is suggested as the exposure platform) is interesting. It may be that bodies exposed on the platform were covered with rubble or turves when placed there.

Vyner believes that the excavation of the façade trench was the first stage in connection with the mortuary structure (ibid., 185). It has been argued, however, that before the façade was built, a raised platform structure had existed and had been used on the site, the massive east upright timber forming one end. There is other evidence which implies that the façade was not part of the primary structure on the site. In front of the structure were two lines of posts forming a funnelled approach, very much as at Wayland's Smithy (ibid., 154–5, Figures 2–3). In a reconstruction drawing, Vyner shows these posts as set within the façade (ibid., 165, Figure 9). This seems incongruous, for post-setting and façade sit uneasily together. Whereas the funnelled approach is almost co-axial with the uprights of the mortuary structure, as he notes (ibid., 190), the façade is on a clearly divergent axis. There are therefore compelling grounds for considering mortuary structure and funnelled approach as associated and earlier than the façade, as with the mortuary structure and avenue at Kilham. Vyner records that the two best-preserved posts of the funnelled approach appeared to have been deliberately blocked with stone (ibid., 156). Perhaps the posts had been withdrawn to leave the forecourt clear when the façade was built.

At Fussell's Lodge, Wiltshire, Ashbee (1966) found buried beneath a long barrow a mortuary structure, 6 m long, demarcated by three aligned post-holes (Figure 8.3). The three-point support structure, interpreted by him as a pitched mortuary house of the Wayland's Smithy type, lay at the east end of a stockaded enclosure, the only entrance to which coincided with the east gable of the presumed house. Attractive though Ashbee's reconstruction of the pitched mortuary house is (1970, 52, Figure 34), it is difficult to find good evidence of it. However, his meticulous excavation and recording of the burial area do appear to confirm the presence of a three-point support raised mortuary platform. The three post-holes, his 'axial pits', were all large enough to have held substantial timbers. All the timbers must have completely decayed *in situ*: indeed, Ashbee notes specifically that the filling of A could have been 'the result of collapse and replacement of erstwhile timbers', while the infill of B was completed by broken bones which could have resulted 'from "replacement" of a post by fall-in and settlement', as with post-hole A (1966, 7–8).

The burials were confined to a rectangular area co-axial with the posts (ibid., 13, Figure 4). Stacks of bones, all from inhumations, were found near and partially overlying post-hole A, near and overlying B, and between B and C. Nowhere were the bones in articulation, though perhaps between fifty-three and fifty-seven individuals were represented.

Ashbee remarks that between the bone stacks next to post-holes A and B, there 'were scattered bones, mainly those of young persons, all much eroded and decayed' (ibid., 8). 'These merged with the more decayed pieces beneath the two main groups A1 and A2 and B. Most of the decayed bone was in small pieces. Decayed larger bones were rare and were normally lowermost in the stacks'. He shows these decayed bones as a continuous scatter between post-holes A and B (ibid., 13, Figure 4). They are most probably bones which had fallen from early burials on an exposure platform, while the better-preserved bones in the stacks were from later burials: stratification and bone conditions agree.

Beyond the east end of the mortuary structure was a funnelled approach of four posts which evidence from other sites would suggest should be associated with the structure. It appears to the writer that the mortuary structure was in an advanced state of collapse and decay when the stockaded enclosure was built, and that this could explain why some bones had been attacked by rodents (ibid., 9).

In Scotland, mortuary structures have been recognised at Neolithic sites other than Pitnacree, Perthshire, already discussed, and it has become apparent that such structures have played their part in the development of megalithic burial chambers. In the South-West, two excavations by Masters, of cairns at Lochhill and Slewcairn, both in Kirkcudbright, have produced a mass of evidence which has solved – and posed – several problems. At Lochhill (Masters 1973), the earliest feature was a three-point support mortuary structure, 7·50 m long and with an average width of 1·40 m (Figure 8.2). The post-holes were all about 0·75 m deep; each of the outer two had held a D-shaped timber about 0·90 m across. The central hole had held two posts. In the north-east section were the remains of a burnt oak plank floor. Further to the north-east, the mortuary structure had been fronted by a shallow concave façade of vertical posts (Figure 8.2). Set centrally into the upcast from the façade trench were four stone orthostats which, as Masters points out (ibid., 99), recall the funnelled approaches at Wayland's Smithy and Fussell's Lodge.

Masters had estimated that the upright timbers of the mortuary structure might originally have stood to a considerable height. If so, they could have served well as the supports of an exposure platform. His further opinion that the D-shaped timbers had rotted away before the cairn was built supports the suggestion that the first period on the site saw the construction and use of a three-point support exposure platform.

The subsequent development of the site is important for its megalithic connotations. After a time, what was left of façade and mortuary structure was burnt down. A stone cairn was built, perhaps in two phases, the first intended to cover only the area of the wooden structures (ibid., 99). The next phase was the concealment of the entire monument within a long trapezoidal cairn with a shallow concave façade; an entrance to the original funnelled approach was retained. Finally, entrance and façade were concealed by blocking, so that externally the site assumed the appearance of a Clyde cairn.

Masters' second excavation, at Slewcairn, revealed a trapezoidal cairn with a slightly funnel-shaped façade (1981b, 167–8). A mortuary structure, defined by slab and boulder walling, had superseded and overlay three post-holes (ibid., 168, Figure 3). The two outer holes had held massive split tree trunks. The filling of the central hole was ambiguous, but it might originally have held two posts, as at Lochhill (Figure 8.2). The south post at least had been removed prior to the construction of the later stone mortuary structure and cairn. Again it may be argued that at Slewcairn, as at Lochhill, a three-point exposure platform, about 8 m long, had been the primary structure on the site. The final trapezoidal cairn, with blocking placed in front of the façade, as at Lochhill, resembled a cairn of Clyde type in superficial appearance.

At Lochhill and Slewcairn, there is a transition from the use of timber to the use of stone. A stone structure, because of its permanent materials, invites re-use, even though re-use may have been far from the minds of the original builders. Furthermore, structures in stone may fossilise details of earlier structural practice in timber which have little relevance in stone. One Clyde cairn illustrates the process – Cairnholy I (KRK 2), originally excavated by Stuart Piggott and Terence Powell (1949), and later interpreted by the writer as of more than one period of construction. The argument (J.G. Scott 1969, 192–5) was that the rear compartment of the burial chamber was originally an independent monument, with exceptionally tall slabs at front and rear, and with a pair of tall slabs forming a portal (Figures 8.5 and 8.6). It was later suggested (J.G. Scott 1976) that this structure was a skeuomorph in stone of a raised platform mortuary structure, the tall end slabs representing the two-point support timbers. Of course, the Cairnholy chamber is too small to have itself functioned as an exposure platform. It is a burial chamber, and was probably never intended by its builders to be anything else. It may also be suggested that the tall, slender orthostats selected for the entrance portals and façade at Cairnholy I are skeuomorphs of the wooden timbers used in a façade such as that at Lochhill. Cairnholy I thus appears to embody in stone several elements of timber construction, yet may have functioned without any actual timber structure at all (Figure 8.6).

That the concept of the mortuary structure – and indeed it may be suggested, of the raised exposure platform – reached Northern Ireland can be shown at Dooey's Cairn, Ballymacaldrack (Figure 8.2), originally excavated by Estyn Evans (1938) and re-excavated by Collins (1976). Evans (1938, 68) showed that the three 'pits' which underlay a stone mortuary structure were the earliest features on the site. Collins (1976, 3) was satisfied that all three 'pits' were likely to have been post-holes. If, as seems possible, they had held the upright timbers supporting a raised exposure platform, then probably this and its supports were burnt to the ground to enable a later paved mortuary structure to be built.

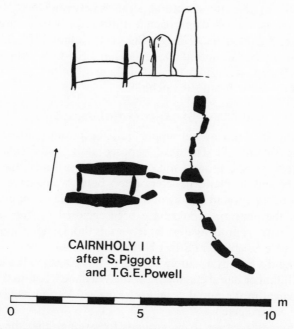

CAIRNHOLY I
after S. Piggott
and T.G.E. Powell

Figure 8.5: Plan of the Clyde chambered cairn, Cairnholy I, Kirkcudbright (after S. Piggott and Powell 1949).

Figure 8.6: The forecourt of the Clyde chambered cairn, Cairnholy I, Kirkcudbright. The standing stones of the façade appear to have been selected to imitate standing timbers.

Collins (ibid., 6) notes the structural parallels between Dooey's Cairn and Lochhill. The stone-funnelled approach features at the two sites are strikingly similar (Figure 8.2; Masters 1973, 98, Figure 1; Collins 1976, 2, Figure 1). There was no timber façade at Dooey's Cairn (ibid., 3), but the deeply concave stone façade seems to mark a final phase of construction in much the same way as the stone façade at Lochhill.

DISCUSSION AND CONCLUSIONS

A reconstruction of a three-point support raised exposure platform may now be attempted (Figure 8.7). The dead, exposed aloft, would have been safe from predatory beasts, though not from predatory birds. Inevitably, as bodies decayed and the platform deteriorated, bones would have fallen from the platform to the ground below, and it is reasonable to suppose that the area beneath the platform would have been enclosed by hurdles or some other form of barrier, proof against larger beasts though not against rodents. With the possible exception of Street House, there is no trace of timber sides save at Wayland's Smithy 1, surely strong evidence against the assumption that well built timber burial chambers, of the Wayland's Smithy 1 type, were a normal element in the burial structure sequence. Various stages of decay and collapse are indicated.

There seem to the writer to be grounds for arguing that the first raised platform structures are likely to have been small, as at Aldwincle 1, simply abandoned to decay and then replaced by similar structures abandoned in turn. Increase in size and the use of stone pavements and timber floors imply an intention to continue use over a period of time. Even such structures, however, appear likewise to have been abandoned to decay. It should by no means be assumed that concealment beneath a barrow or cairn necessarily followed. From the evidence which we have, it may be noted that the smaller structures tend to be found under round barrows or cairns and the larger (and later?) under long barrows or cairns.

It has been impossible to discuss, or even to mention, many aspects of a complex subject. It has been suggested that the final cairns at Lochhill and Slewcairn are of Clyde type, but quite clearly their earlier phases represent a totally different tradition, perhaps stemming from north-east England. Are Lochhill and Slewcairn therefore to be classified as Clyde cairns? The answer would appear to be not, though their final Clyde appearance may imply that local control had passed to builders and users of Clyde cairns (cf. Kinnes 1975, 27).

Cairnholy I is probably still best regarded as a Clyde cairn, but is it right to assume that because it imitates wooden prototypes it is therefore chronologically later than those prototypes? The outer compartment of the burial chamber had a roughly paved floor, upon which was found a much-abraded fragment of a jadeite axehead, which S. Piggott and Powell suggest is likely to belong to an earlier phase of the tomb's use (1949, 117, 121–2,

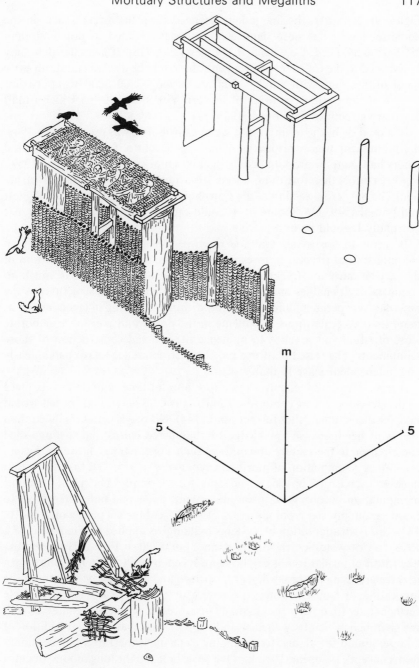

Figure 8.7: Suggested structure, use and two phases of decay of a three-point support raised
mortuary platform.

Figure 9). Recently, the fine jadeite axehead from the Sweet Track, in the Somerset levels, has been dendrochronologically dated to not later than 3807–3806 BC (J.M. Coles and B.J. Coles 1990, 218). If a similar date may be ascribed to the Cairnholy I fragment, this could be used to equate an early phase of that cairn with Manby's Mature Period – 3900–3000 BC approximately – of the Earlier Neolithic of Eastern Yorkshire, during which ritual/mortuary structures developed (1988, 37).

It should be borne in mind that when Cairnholy I was excavated in 1949, the monument was regarded as a unitary structure, for the multi-period theory had yet to be propounded by the Liverpool school (Powell et al. 1969). The excavators therefore did not look for evidence of multi-period construction. The only cross-section of the Cairnholy I cairn is ambiguous (S. Piggott and Powell 1949, 114, Figure 6). It could thus be that further excavation at Cairnholy I would be informative.

It seems to the writer that the multi-period approach to the study of Neolithic burial structures, foreshadowed in the report of the excavation of the Clyde cairn at Brackley (ARG 28; J.G. Scott 1956), has much to commend it. It enables one to visualise the more elaborate structures as the outcome of experiment and interaction within and among independent communities over generations, producing in the process an ever more elaborate store of ritual and practice to influence the use and construction of those monuments. The raised platform mortuary structure may have had an early and independent place in that process.

Audrey Henshall recognises the importance of time-span and of its place in the development of composite tombs (1974, 139–41), and indeed would take the dissection of sites further (ibid., 144). No-one is better qualified than she, with her immense knowledge of chambered cairns and distinguished contribution to their study, to continue such work. Kinnes, however, has no time for 'a re-animation of moribund typologies' (1975, 17). Instead, with a massive exercise of hindsight, he opts for 'a simple scheme of modular manipulation according to need and intent' as 'a plausible alternative to linear taxonomy *qua* typology' (ibid., 19–20). As Masters points out (1981b, 164), this is an adaptation of 'systems building' as applied by Fleming (1972, 1973) to Cotswold-Severn tombs. Kinnes (1975, 20–1, Figure 7) argues that 'the forms of insular tombs can be reproduced' by utilising 'a basic box form in three grouping patterns – linear, dispersed and agglomerate' – without the invocation of 'sub-Darwinian principles of evolution and reversion'. He further states (ibid., 25) 'that in many instances, long cairns are integral with the chambers which they enclose and support' and that the final addition of a large mound to original free-standing elements is 'part of a planned long-term concept'. It appears then that the basic box and the long mound or cairn are all part of 'systems building'. But what does this imply in terms of time and origin? At the beginning of this chapter, reference was made to the long chambered cairn arriving, like Aphrodite, fully formed, from the (western) sea. Are we now to see the cairn arriving not so much fully formed as in kit form?

EDITORS' NOTE

This paper was written before the final publication of excavations at the key site at Haddenham, Cambridgeshire. Consequently, it has not been possible to incorporate this site into the discussion here.

9

Scottish and Irish Passage Tombs: Some Comparisons and Contrasts

George Eogan

INTRODUCTION

From the point of view of early settlement Scotland and Ireland share many features in common: both occupy approximately the same land area, both have long coastlines and both can be divided, very roughly, into a highland zone to the west and a lowland zone to the east. Furthermore, in both cases, ritual was a prominent feature of Neolithic life and in some areas this was expressed in the building of megalithic tombs. For Scotland our knowledge of these tombs has been amplified by the remarkable studies of Audrey Henshall – not only in her two great volumes (1963 and 1972) and her subsequent (and joint) reworking of the Orcadian and Caithness tomb evidence (J.L. Davidson and Henshall 1989; 1991), but also in a series of excavations. In doing all of this Henshall has put the Scottish tombs on a footing hardly equalled in any other part of Europe, and as a result other workers can evaluate the evidence not only in its national but also its international setting.

One area that has for long been considered as having connections with Scotland during the Neolithic is Ireland, and it is therefore considered appropriate to offer Audrey Henshall this brief chapter on one aspect of megalithic tombs, namely passage tombs.

MEGALITHIC TOMBS IN IRELAND AND SCOTLAND

From Henshall's abovementioned work we know that Scotland has close to six hundred megalithic tombs and that these can be grouped, very broadly, into two main traditions, namely Clyde tombs (which have close links with Irish court tombs) and passage tombs. The former, represented by about a hundred and thirty sites, have a restricted south-westerly distribution with the heaviest concentrations mainly in western Argyll, between the Firths of Clyde and Lorn, and on the island of Arran. Passage tombs are much more common, represented by approximately four hundred and fifty examples, and have a much wider distribution. Henshall has isolated six main passage tomb groups, namely Bargrennan, Hebridean, Orkney-Cromarty, Zetland, Clava and Maes Howe.

Comparing megalithic tomb forms in Ireland the situation is somewhat different: first, there are approximately one thousand six hundred known examples, some thousand more than in Scotland, and these can be classified and enumerated as follows:

- long barrow (court and portal) tombs: around six hundred
- passage tombs: around three hundred
- central chamber without passage – 'Linkardstown-type burials': currently around a dozen known or suspected;
- wedge tombs: around five hundred.

There are also nearly two hundred unclassifiable tombs.

Second, although court tombs are clearly related to the Clyde tomb tradition (in ways which need not be discussed here), three main classes of Irish tomb – namely the portal tomb, the Linkardstown-type burial and the wedge tomb – are absent from Scotland. Furthermore, although Scotland and Ireland share the presence of passage tombs (whose points of similarity will be discussed below), these tombs differ in some important respects, not least in the fact that clear regional groupings can be defined for Scotland but not for Ireland.

IRISH AND SCOTTISH PASSAGE TOMBS

The figure of approximately three hundred Irish passage tombs cited above can only be taken as a rough estimate, since many largish round mounds, especially those with a hilltop setting, are potential examples. Detailed structural information is sparse, but sufficient to demonstrate diversity in tomb design. Chamber shape varies from circular or near-circular to rectangular and square, with other variants comprising the polygonal and figure-of-eight chambers as seen at Carrowkeel and Carrowmore (whose form may have been influenced by local geology), and chambers with recesses, those with cruciform plans being the commonest. Tombs with undifferentiated chambers are a small but possibly significant group in view of the fact that two are earlier than the large mound at Knowth (Eogan 1986) and another constitutes one of the tombs in site 1. Such tombs are rare outside the Boyne Valley, where ten definite examples are known, eight at Knowth and two at Newgrange.

Despite these and other differences in tomb form, practically all Irish passage tombs share other features such as hill-top setting, round mound and kerb of individual stones, cemetery grouping, grave goods and, in some regions, megalithic art. They therefore constitute a group without clear regionalism except for one feature, that is the concentration of megalithic art in County Meath in the east of the country.

In comparing Irish and Scottish passage tombs, the closest and most obvious links are those between the major monuments of the Boyne Valley and Henshall's Maes Howe group. Before considering these, however, certain other points of similarity should be noted.

First, the Bargrennan group of tombs (which are discussed at length by Jane Murray in Chapter 3) have some morphological features in common with the Irish undifferentiated passage tombs, not only in chamber shape but also in the kerbed round cairn. Undifferentiated passage tombs are an international type but the nearest group to Bargrennan is in Ireland; indeed their geographical location at the head of the Irish Sea in south-west Scotland may suggest limited but positive influence from Ireland, possibly from the Boyne Valley, as it is there that the largest number occur.

Second, the simple chambers of the Hebridean group display some similarities with the simple Irish passage tombs: compare, for example, Unival, North Uist (UST 34: Henshall 1972) with Fenagh Beg, Co. Leitrim (Herity 1974, Figure 66.1). The concentration of tombs in the relatively remote Hebridean Islands has been remarked upon in the past, and Piggott (1954, 224) advocated a model of seaborne colonisation from the south to explain this. Since the Uists are but a hundred miles north of Malin Head, and reachable directly by sea, it may be, then, that the similarity in chamber shape with simple Irish passage tombs is not merely fortuitous. (However, three complicating factors must be borne in mind: first, as Frances Lynch (1975, Figure 7) has shown, the simple chamber is a most basic and widespread form, being found right along the Atlantic façade – one could argue that the choice of this shape merely reflects local enterprise, or lack of it. Secondly, the simple round chamber with passage as found in the Hebrides is rare in Ireland, as is the larger rounded chamber. Furthermore, despite Childe's (1935b) arguments for ceramic similarity, the grave goods in the two areas differ considerably.)

Third, despite their markedly circular chambers, passage tombs of the Clava type (see Barclay this volume, Chapter 6) also appear to reflect some contacts with Ireland. This is indicated by roof corbelling, the presence of a cairn kerb, cemetery grouping (at Clava) and some art.

Finally, as far as the Orkney-Cromarty and Zetland groups are concerned, might an origin for the presumed prototype of the series, the tripartite 'Camster' type chamber in a round cairn, be sought in the west, perhaps in Ireland? The tripartite chamber might suggest an Irish cruciform tomb background, and further points of similarity are present in the round kerbed cairn, the use of the corbelled roof, and the clustering of tombs (admittedly infrequent), particularly in Caithness. One could instance the group of nine tombs centred on Ben Freiceadain, the Sordale Hill group of eleven, the nine just inland from Dunbeath and two in the neighbourhood of the Loch of Yarrows (Henshall 1963, 54–6).

Maes Howe tombs

This group shares with Irish passage tombs similarities in tomb design, significant orientation, architecture and megalithic art (Bradley and Chapman 1984). The splendid chamber architecture is a feature of these tombs, especially the skilled use of slabs and corbelling producing barrel vaulting. However it is the art which, although previously recognised, now deserves detailed comment in this discussion of possible Irish-Scottish links.

Megalithic art is found at five sites, namely: Holm of Papa Westray South, Eday Manse, Pickaquoy, Pierowall and Maes Howe (Twohig 1981, Sharples 1984, Ashmore 1986). At the first four it consists of shaped motifs, all formed by picking. When first opened up it appears that the Holm of Papa Westray South had up to eleven decorated stones. Today there are but five definite examples (Twohig 1981, 227). The largest, a lintel over cell 2, has arcs and dots resembling eyebrows and eyes, other dots, a T-shaped and a crooked motif. Another stone has a short zigzag and to its immediate left is a lozenge and other lines. One of the two remaining stones has a circle, the other dots.

At the next three sites linked spirals and concentric circles are a feature. At Pierowall, one of the three decorated stones (Sharples 1984, Figure 28) is the most notable example of its class in Scotland.

The art at Maes Howe is different and hitherto has not been considered as art, but rather as dressing (Ashmore 1986). It consists of marks made by picking over portions of certain stones (Figure 9.1). This is close picking and at least two types of tools were used, a punch with a fairly fine point and a chisel (cf. Henshall 1963, plate 24A). Such picking is found on several stones and these are in key positions. As one enters the passage there is a panel on the upper part of the blocking stone. The entrance to the chamber on the inside is framed by this art as it occurs on the two jamb stones and the capstone. On the jambs it is found over the left half of each (as one looks outwards from the chamber) and on the upper part of the roof stone above where it resembles edge dressing. This work is also found at the entrance to all three cells; in part these are also framed. On the right hand recess it occurs on the faces of the bottom course flanking the entrance. On the left recess the bottom stone of the course has picking, again on the entrance face but also as a patch on the outer face; while on the opposite side the chamber face of the single stone forming this side has dressing on the right hand half. There is also some picking on the lower edge of the wall stone which forms a floor to the entrance. Inside the cell, to the left, is a patch on the second stone from the top. The left bottom stone of the end cell has picking on the face parallel to the entrance, while on the opposite stone the picking is on the chamber side and is confined to the third of the surface that adjoins the entrance. There are some other patches of picking here and there on other chamber stones. In addition, the long edges of some corbels have been dressed. Whilst the latter might have been an architectural feature, the other picking was hardly used

Figure 9.1: Maes Howe, Orkney: view from the chamber. Picked decoration occurs on the
stones framing the passage entrance (photograph by M. Brooks, reproduced
courtesy of Historic Scotland).

to modify surface irregularities or blunt edges, being mainly used to frame
entrances and therefore occupying key locations. It can best be compared to
the close variety of diffuse picking that occurs on the great sites of the Boyne
Valley (Dowth, Ballincrad, Knowth and Newgrange). Here diffuse picking is
only found in profusion at these sites and therefore must have had special
significance (Eogan 1990).

There is also some incised art in the Maes Howe tomb (Ashmore 1986)
which can be compared to what one finds on Boyne tombs; similar art is also
found at Skara Brae (Twohig 1981, 238–9).

DISCUSSION AND CONCLUSIONS

Over Neolithic and Eneolithic Europe chambered tombs have a wide distribution, over wide geographical areas. Many share features in common but
these are usually limited: chamber form, for example, may be shared but not
burial rite or grave goods. The definition of regional groups or tomb types
can be influenced by local geological conditions – unlike the Cotswold area,
for instance, the Wessex Downs did not have a supply of suitable building
stone for mound construction, so 'earth' was resorted to. Furthermore,

within a regional group or tomb type there can be considerable variation. This is especially so in the case of the four hundred and fifty or so Scottish passage tombs, causing the late John Corcoran to comment that 'the fertility of megalithic invention' is a feature of Scottlish megalithic tomb architecture (1966, 51).

It is clear that what we conventionally term a passage tomb is common to both Scotland and Ireland and, interestingly enough, largely confined to the northern area of both countries. Despite Piggott's observation (1954, 224, 231–2) of the apparent combination of Clyde and passage tomb features in the tombs at Nether Largie, Argyll (a segmented chamber under a round cairn) and Clettraval, North Uist (a passage segmented by sills and a trapezoidal chamber under a similarly-shaped cairn, with straight façade), there is no clear-cut development from Clyde tombs to passage tombs. Therefore the Scottish passage tombs have to be the result of a new invention, introduction, or stimulation from outside. Whilst differing in some respects from other passage tomb groups in Europe, they nevertheless have features that can be compared externally, such as cairn and chamber form. In view of the apparently earlier history of collective tomb building in other parts of Atlantic Europe to the south the Scottish tombs could then represent a northern extension. However, it is difficult to prove this as none of the tombs possesses a combination of externally-shared traits, since the grave goods are of local origin and there is considerable morphological variability amongst the tombs. On the whole, however, it does appear that the first passage tombs in Scotland (wherever they may be) owe their origin to outside influence; and the nearest region from where such influence could come is Ireland. Furthermore, as far as one relatively late group (the Maes Howe tombs) is concerned, one can also argue for Irish influence in tomb design and ritual practice.

Considering the points of similarity between Irish and Scottish passage tombs as discussed above, one could suggest that Irish undifferentiated passage tombs may have been introduced into south-west Scotland where a local group (Bargrennan) emerged. The main thrust, however, was arguably northwards, following two routes: one directly to the Hebrides (resulting in the Hebridean group) and the other up the Great Glen (resulting in the Orkney-Cromarty group and, more tentatively, the Clava group). Following local development of passage tomb forms in Orkney, the emergence of Maes Howe type passage tombs may again show evidence for influence from Ireland.

What needs to be discussed here are the implications of these arguments. First, regarding Ireland as the possible point of origin of the entire Scottish passage tombs series: it is important to remember that passage tombs are not merely the material manifestation of ritual practices, but are part of a wider complex that involved the spread of farming into areas which previously lacked it. Perhaps the tombs are an aspect of the infilling of the landscape by people expanding into empty areas. If tomb-building can thus be understood as part of this process of population spread, then the complementary distribution of Clyde tombs and Scottish passage tombs, noted by Piggott (1954, 254), might be explained in terms of the avoidance of already-occupied areas by passage tomb builders. It is possible that Neolithic Ireland was more populous than Scotland before passage tomb building took place there and this may have been a factor which occasioned an extension of settlement. This would have consequential social implications: architecture, ritual and successful economics are mutually interdependent factors. To build the larger passage tombs would have required more planning: an apparatus had to be organised, communities had to be marshalled and a body of knowledge built up, firstly to initiate and then to maintain a building programme. It has been argued that passage tombs in Scotland were communal burial places (Renfrew 1979, 162–6). Some, however, are clearly also examples of monumental architecture, a feature of which is permanency and perfection (Trigger 1990). Such architectural accomplishments usually correlate with increasing stratification in society. At least they represent a maximisation of both ritual and economic returns and can be considered as symbols of both.

Second, regarding the Maes Howe group of passage tombs: despite some doubts by Henshall it can be argued that these tombs reflect Irish influence, more specifically from the Boyne Valley. I consider the group to be late, as Colin Renfrew has already done, but for different reasons. Regarding the group I, like Piggott (1954, 343–5), would place Maes Howe at its head, for morphologically it stands closest to its presumed Boyne prototypes – a fact that is supported by the close diffuse picking seen at Maes Howe and in the Boyne Valley.

Regarding the megalithic art on the Maes Howe tombs, only the above mentioned diffuse picking has any identical parallels in Ireland, despite the generalised similarities between the Irish and Orcadian examples in terms of shared use of the spiral motif, etc. This fact raises the wider issue of the relationship between the Maes Howe tombs and the Grooved Ware complex. Renfrew's view that the tombs are part of this complex has been accepted by Henshall and others; this is largely based on the finds of Grooved Ware from Quanterness and supplemented by radiocarbon dates. If so, this has a fundamental bearing on the wider appreciation of the Maes Howe group. Derek Simpson (1988, 34), however, considers these sherds as probably having been amongst the final objects to be placed in the chamber, their presence at different levels and locations being due to a late burial disturbing earlier deposits (see also MacSween this volume, Chapter 19). Apart from the Quanterness pottery, the double spiral on the Skara Brae pottery sherd (Piggott 1954, plate 12) and the incised decoration at that site may recall Irish passage tomb art. But the whole question of relationships between passage tombs and the Grooved Ware complex in my view remains a puzzle. Certainly there appears to be some connection, the stone maceheads being a case in point (Eogan and Richardson 1982), but the problem remains. Could a new complex, in the main post-dating the Maes Howe tombs, have emerged? This complex is characterised by a rich and prolific material culture, settlements (Skara Brae etc.) and ritual monuments (henges), but it need not necessarily have been home-grown and it could have overlapped with the passage tombs before supplanting them. In the region of the Lochs of Harray and Stenness one may speculate that a complex which succeeded the tombs emerged, something which is analogous to the Beaker complex in the Boyne Valley (Eogan 1986, 221) and to the stone rows and related monuments at Carnac, Brittany (Giot, L'Helgouac'h and Monnier 1979, 417–23). Somewhat parallel development may have taken place in the Clava region leading to the emergence of the ring cairns and the circles of free-standing stones around tombs, and at Callanish by the addition of an alignment.

While scholars might disagree about the extent and nature of Irish influence on Scottish passage tombs, one cannot but argue that it was the passage tomb builders who, to use the words of the famous prehistorian Gordon Childe who for so long worked in Scotland, ushered in the 'dawn of civilization'.

10

Body Politics and Grave Messages: Irish Neolithic Mortuary Practices

Gabriel Cooney

INTRODUCTION

Major themes of recent British and European work on Neolithic mortuary practice have included the recognition of the significance of patterning in the human deposits (Shanks and Tilley 1982; Thomas and Whittle 1986), the relationship between the burial deposits and defined architectural spaces (e.g. Thomas 1988) and the importance of individual sequences of events at different sites. This work has been concerned not only with examining these characteristics but also with trying to understand the relationships between mortuary practices and contemporary social practices and relations (e.g. Barrett 1988a; Richards 1988; Whittle 1988). It has recognised the significance, as Shanks and Tilley put it, of 'the cultural use of the body as part of any society's social construction of reality' (1982, 134). An important distinction stressed by Barrett (1988a, 31–2) is that mortuary rituals comprise not only those of a funerary nature, to do with the disposal of the corpse, but also those involving ancestors, which may include the use of funerary architecture and the bones of the dead.

In Ireland, by contrast, most concern in the study of the human remains recovered in Neolithic contexts has been at a functional level, identifying the rite of burial involved, the number and sex of individuals (where possible) and the presence or absence of grave goods. There has been a concern with treating the evidence from particular contexts such as individual tomb types together, and noting differences between them (e.g. Eogan 1986; Herity 1987; Twohig 1990). But little consideration has been given to the possibility of comparisons across archaeologically constructed typological boundaries. The presence of different practices within the same monument type has been interpreted as representing chronological change rather than potentially offering insights into the differential treatment of the dead (e.g. Herity 1987). While in some cases significant patterning has been noted in the burial evidence, as in the occurrence of unburnt skulls and long bones in the cremation deposits in passage tombs (Hartnett 1957; Eogan 1986), this has not been explored further.

It is somewhat ironic that this functional approach to prehistoric burial should be so prominent when there is clear archaeological and historical evidence from the Early Christian period in Ireland that the bodies of certain individuals in society, notably saints, were treated as artefacts. Both their corporal and associated relics were circulated and looked upon as commodities. As Lucas (1986) has shown relics and reliquaries played a multivalent role in Early Historic Ireland, being employed for example as insignia of office, in collecting tribute, as battle talismans and for sealing compacts and oaths. That this practice centred round the exhumation of the saint's bones and associated objects is indicated by the fact that the Irish term *reilic* (now *roilig*) usually refers to a cemetery (Lucas 1986, 6).

The aim of this chapter is to examine the burial record of Neolithic Ireland to see whether the patterns, contrasts and variability in mortuary practice noted elsewhere might not be present here also. Particular attention will be paid to the following oppositions: cremation and inhumation, articulated and disarticulated skeletal remains, adults and children/adolescents, males and females, individual and collective/communal identity and presence or absence of grave goods.

Having outlined the overall burial record from the Irish Neolithic and the range of contexts in which it occurs, the evidence from four excavated and published megalithic tomb sites with relatively well-recorded osteological records will be discussed in some detail. This will be placed in the context of other aspects of the archaeological record such as the associated artefactual material.

THE IRISH NEOLITHIC BURIAL RECORD

What is clear from a recent overview by Grogan (1989), on which the outline given here is based, is that the extant burial record is not only restricted to excavated sites but also appears to represent only a segment of the Neolithic population in Ireland. The figures from all contexts add up to between 400 and 500 individuals, with the majority, almost 400, coming from megalithic tombs. The adult:adolescent/child ratio in the tombs is in the order of sixty-eight per cent to thirty-two per cent, which is not what would be expected if the death population represented the demographic pattern of the contemporary groups. The number of children, for example, is significantly lower than would be expected in the type of traditional agricultural societies with a high infant mortality rate that we can suggest would have been characteristic of this period (Weiss 1973). In general, there do not appear to be strong, identifiable differences between the representation of adult males and females. However, the difficulty of sexing cremated remains must be kept in mind. A major exception to the trend of non-differentiation of males/ females and an emphasis on males can be seen in the individual burials, particularly in the Linkardstown type burials, where the emphasis is on the deposition of the inhumed skeletal remains of adult males within a cist, normally singly, either in an articulated or disarticulated form (e.g. Herity 1982; Manning 1985).

Looking at the record for mortuary rite, cremation is apparently more common than inhumation. (It must be remembered that many of the tomb sites are on acid soils which cause a taphonomic bias against the preservation of inhumed remains.) In the megalithic tombs, for example, some sixty-two per cent of the deposits were cremated and thirty-eight per cent inhumed. Again, the mortuary rite varies depending on context, with inhumation more prominent than cremation in portal tombs, Linkardstown-type burials and individual burials generally. Barrett (1988a, 32) has pointed out that there are problems in comparing inhumation and cremation assemblages, as they may represent different and successive stages in the tripartite structure of the death rite of passage. However, inhumations are not only the primary stage in the burial practice but may also represent a secondary burial. An important point which will be developed below is that, in the archaeological record, cremation and inhumation can occur in the same burial assemblage. Mention of portal tombs is a reminder of the significance of individual sites in the overall burial pattern. The portal tomb evidence is dominated by that found during the recent excavation of Poulnabrone on the Burren in Co. Clare (A. Lynch 1988), where there were the remains of twenty-two disarticulated individuals. The average number of known burials in court tombs is two to three, with twenty-nine sites producing evidence for the remains of approximately ninety-six individuals (Herity 1987). However, within these figures, the site of Audleystown, Co. Down (Collins 1954) is significant, as it alone produced one third of the court tomb total, with a minimum number of thirty to thirty-three individuals (nine to eleven cremations and twenty-one or twenty-two inhumations). Similarly, in the passage tomb total of c. 200 individuals, sixty-five come from the single site at Fourknocks I (Hartnett 1957). The passage tomb figures will of course be substantially increased by the addition of the analyses of the material from the tombs under the main mound at Knowth in the Boyne Valley (see Eogan 1986) and from the Mound of the Hostages, Tara (see de Valéra 1960), when published.

The four sites chosen for examination are the dual court tomb at Audleystown, Co. Down (Collins 1954; 1959), the passage tomb of Fourknocks I, Co. Meath (Hartnett 1957), the nearby complex but clearly passage tomb-related site at Fourknocks II, Co. Meath (Hartnett 1971) and the anomalous but again passage tomb-related site at Millin Bay, Co. Down (Collins and Waterman 1955). The reader is referred to the excavation reports for detailed descriptions of the sites.

AUDLEYSTOWN COURT TOMB, CO. DOWN

This is a dual court tomb close to the southern shore of Strangford Lough,

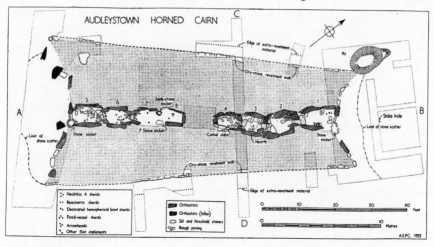

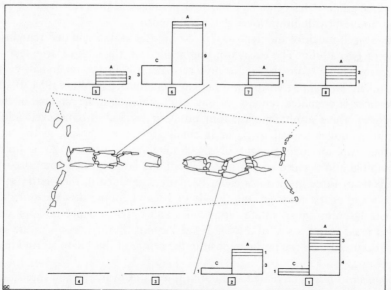

Figure 10.1: a. Plan of Audleystown, Co. Down (after Collins 1954); b. Interpretation of burial evidence from Audleystown. Key: A = adult, C = child; shaded part of column = cremations, rest = inhumations; Nos. beside columns = Nos. of individuals; Nos, in squares = chamber Nos.

comprising two four-chambered galleries with shallow courts (east gallery – chambers 1–4; west gallery – chambers 5–8) set back-to-back under a wedge-shaped cairn with the wider end facing south-west (Figure 10.1a). In several of the chambers, there was evidence of burning *in situ* and there was a circular patch of burnt material (a hearth?) in chamber 3. Chambers 3 and 4 apparently lacked burial deposits, but in the other chambers there was a 23–30 cm deep deposit of burnt human bone, fire-reddened stones, burnt soil, broken and burnt flint objects (particularly leaf arrowheads) and pottery sherds, packed down with stones. The cremated remains were spread through the deposit, but unburnt bones were more common, occurring in pockets and in neatly-arranged groups at all levels. Unfortunately, it is not always possible to link these bone-groups with the skeletal material described in Morton and Scott's report on the skeletal remains (1954), but the available evidence can be summarised as follows (see also Figure 10.16):

Chamber 1: cremated remains of one child, one adult female, two adult males; unburnt remains of one adult female and three males. Two of the unburnt males possibly represented by a group of ten small longbones and ribs laid in parallel rows on a slab close to the chamber's south side and covered by another slab. Associated artefacts with this bone group: one flint javelin-head, one flint flake, one worked quartz crystal.

Chamber 2: cremated remains of one adult; unburnt bones of a child and two or three adults. McCormick (1986, 38) has suggested the presence of a 'head and hooves' cattle burial over the main deposit.

Chamber 5: much of the deposit removed in the past. Cremated remains of one or two adults. The excavator commented on the lack of artefacts and cremated bone from the better-preserved deposit in the inner half of the chamber. This appeared to continue into chamber 6 (Collins 1954, 19–20).

Chamber 6: cremated remains of one adult male; unburnt remains of three children, three adult females, four adult males and two unsexed adults. Unburnt bones tended to occur in small groups and heaps; in the north corner was an arrangement of small longbones, adjacent to a human mandible and a piece of pig jaw. Two of the bone groups comprised the remains of three individuals each. Partially embedded in the matrix at the north end of the chamber, but mostly under and among thin slabs of shale, was a large group of human longbones and parts of a pelvis, apparently associated with a sherd of a Bowl Food Vessel, although sherds of the same pot occurred over the burial deposit in the centre of this chamber and in the next one, 7.

Chambers 7 and 8: cremated and unburnt remains of two(?) and three adults respectively.

There would appear to have been a complex sequence of events represented here: possible burning of the site before tomb construction; burning activity within some of the chambers; deposition of the burial deposit which the excavator argued took place as a single event; placing of packing stones over the deposit; and finally Early Bronze Age secondary activity in the form of the deposition of a Bowl Food Vessel with a possible human burial.

In terms of pattern or structure in the burial record (Figure 10.1b) the most notable feature is the mixture of cremation and inhumation and the dominance of the latter, comprising two-thirds of the individuals represented. Clearly, there are internal differences within the deposit, with for example chamber 5 containing only cremated bone irregularly spread through the deposit. There is a general association between the number of artefacts and the number of burials where bone-groups do occur (cf. Herity 1987, 118). One can also suggest a tendency for a greater proportion of the children and adult females, when identified as such, to be inhumed.

FOURKNOCKS I, CO. MEATH

In this unusual passage tomb, excavated by Hartnett in 1950 (1957), a much more distinct patterning can be discerned in the burial record. Here, a passage (which may or may not have been roofed: see F.M. Lynch 1973) leads into an unusually large roofed central area off which are set three chambers, two of which (the west and south) have decorated lintel stones (Figure 10.2a). Some human remains had been placed on top of the mound over the roof, but the main deposits occurred in the three chambers and the entrance passage.

The chamber deposits, some 10–20 cm thick, consisted of cleaned cremated bone mixed with unburnt bones (predominantly skulls and longbones) and a little charcoal. They were placed on flagged floors and sealed by a paving of thin slabs. Within the deposits were a number of artefacts of types usually associated with passage tomb burials, all burnt or heat-cracked.

The burial deposits in the passage are all in its outermost walled section, which stops some 2·5 m from the edge of the mound. At the point nearest the mound edge, underneath paving flags and beside the second upright on the east side, were the skeletal remains of a child in its first year, set within a deposit of cremated human bone. Above the passage pavement, the burial deposits appeared to consist of cremated and unburnt bones interspersed with several layers of rough paving. Unburnt bones predominated in the upper third of the fill, but in the lower two-thirds, cremated bone predominated, although unburnt skulls and other skeletal remains were plentiful. Little piles of cremated bone were found jammed into the interstices at the base of the uprights, sealed by thin flags or patches of dry-stone flush with the wall. An unburnt skull, set within a large spread of cremated bone, was found at pavement level beside the second upright on the east side, partly protected by a stone setting. At a depth of 50 cm in the fill, between the second upright on the east side and the fourth upright on the west side, were two crushed unburnt adult skulls facing outwards, with associated longbones lying nearby and cremated bone around them. A large, water-worn pebble was associated with each skull.

Looking at the patterning in the burial deposits, there are interesting concordances between the design of the monument, the placement of the art on the stones, the nature of the burials and the objects deposited with them (Figure 10.2b). Because of the integration of cremated and inhumed remains and the poor preservation of some of the material, the report on the human bones could not go much beyond differentiating them on the basis of age and

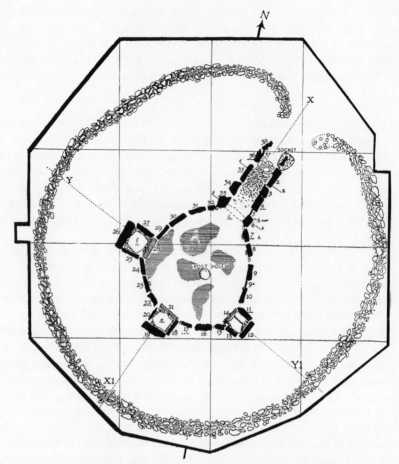

Figure 10.2: a. Plan of Fourknocks I, Co. Meath (after Hartnett 1957). See next page for
Figure 10.2b.

estimating the minimum number of individuals present. But even from this,
as Hartnett pointed out (1957, 270), clear patterns emerge. The proportion
of adult to child remains is sixty to forty per cent, but the rites differ
significantly. Only three out of the twenty-one child burials are cremated,
while the majority of the adult burials are (twenty-eight out of forty-four).
There are very few – only six – children in the chambers. The only place where
the proportion of children approaches that of adults is in the passage where
inhumation becomes the more prominent burial rite. There is also clear
differentiation between the chambers. The south chamber, facing ·the
passage, has not only the largest quantity of burial remains and burnt
artefactual material (including a decorated antler pin), but also a decorated
lintel. By contrast, the east chamber has the lowest quantity of burial deposit,

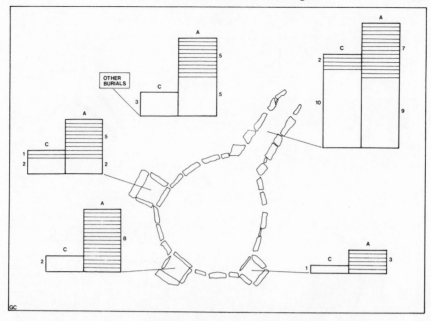

Figure 10.2: b. Interpretation of burial evidence from Fourknocks I. Key as in Figure 10.1b.

few objects (Hartnett 1957, 217) and no decorated lintel. The distinction between the central area and the passage is heightened by the fact that the decorated lintel now at the west inner end of the passage was thought by Hartnett (1957, 226) to have faced inwards towards the central area. As for the passage, the formality of deposition of bone here is emphasised by the continued focus on the area between the second upright on the east side and the fourth upright on the west side.

FOURKNOCKS II, CO. MEATH

Fourknocks II lies about 100 m to the east of Fourknocks I. This complex monument was excavated in 1951–2 by Hartnett (1971) and consisted of a mound erected over a small circular cairn with encircling ditch and, near this, a megalithic passage leading to a transverse, partly rock-cut trench. The mound was surrounded by a rock-cut ditch with an entrance gap at the outer end of the megalithic passage (Figure 10.3a). The cairn covered a small pit containing a small amount of cremated bone mixed with charcoal, and on the original ground surface nearby lay a few fragments of unburnt bone. On this surface between the pit and the edge of the cairn were some stone settings.

The megalithic passage was definitely roofed for most of its length, and cut into its floor, running the full length, was a central channel. The outer part of the passage was found to be filled with earth, and the roofed portion was filled to within 20 cm of the 80 cm-high capstones. The exact nature of the

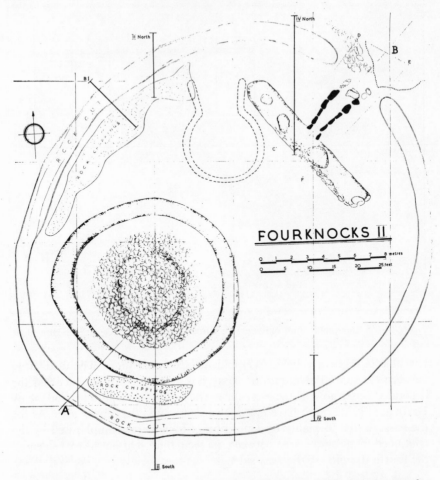

Figure 10.3: a. Plan of Fourknocks II, Co. Meath (after Hartnett 1971). See next page for Figure 10.3b.

fill's stratification was unclear, but three separate deposits of human remains were discernible. The largest, lying over the floor of the central channel in the inner third of the passage, consisted of the cremated bones of at least four adults with the inhumed remains of at least eight children scattered through them. A pin and parts of two others were associated with it. Above this deposit was a quantity of cremated bone, representing one adult and at least two children. High in the fill of the outer part of the passage was a deposit comprising the cremated bones of one adult and one child plus an unburnt adult tooth.

The transverse trench, which showed evidence of having been subjected to intense heat, had four hollows or pits. On the side opposite the passage, the

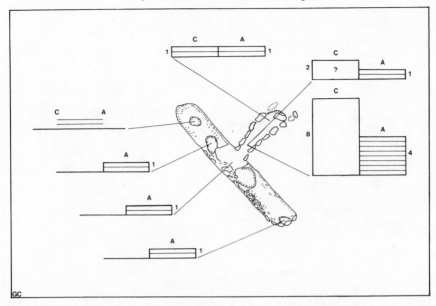

Figure 10.3: b. Interpretation of burial evidence from Fourknocks II. Key as in Figure 10.1b.

lip and sides of the trench were faced with large stones, some set upright. In or close to the four pits were cremations, three of which appeared to represent single adults whose corpses had been burnt *in situ*. There were pieces of worked antler with the two deposits in the west part of the trench. Part of an unburnt skull was found south-west of the trench in the body of the mound.

There is a marked distinction between the single burials in the trench and the collective deposit in the passage (Figure 10.3b). As at Fourknocks I, cremation is predominantly an adult rite, and the children were deposited in the passage. One striking difference between the two sites is the occurrence of deliberate, single cremations at Fourknocks II. The relationship between the two sites is discussed below.

MILLIN BAY, CO. DOWN

This anomalous site (Figure 10.4a) lies on a raised beach 100 m from the shore at the southern tip of the Ards Peninsula, across Strangford Lough from Audleystown. Before its excavation in 1953 by Collins and Waterman (1955), it appeared as an oval mound outlined by a kerb of standing stones. Upon excavation, it was found to be pre-dated by a dry-stone wall which continued outside the excavated area to the south. The tomb, consisting of a long, roughly rectangular, lintel-roofed and paved 'cist' set in a trench, lay to the west of this wall. The northern, slightly wider end of the cist was unroofed and had been deliberately filled in with slabs. At the other end were the remains of at least fifteen inhumed individuals (seven children, four

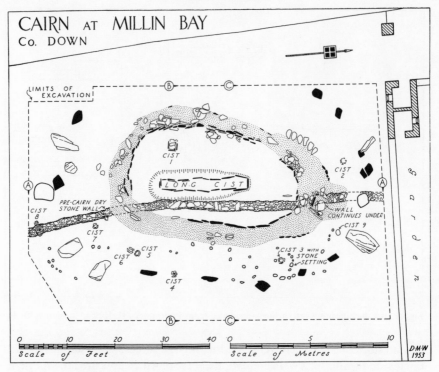

Figure 10.4: a. Plan of Millin Bay, Co. Down (after Collins and Waterman 1955). See next page for Figure 10.4b.

adolescents and four adults) and the scattered cremated remains of one adult male. The deposit was dominated by groups of selected bones, particularly skulls and longbones. No artefacts were present.

A small, rectangular, slab-filled cist was found to the south-west of the long cist. Surrounding both was a roughly oval setting of flagstones set end-to-end in the ground, buttressed by a low bank of shingle and stones. Most of these flagstones had incised and pecked decoration on the side facing the cists; similarly-decorated flagstones had been found in the long cist. Others were found in the bank behind the oval setting and in the cairn material which had covered the site. Some two to three metres further out were the remains of a second roughly oval arrangement of individually-set standing stones, together with three orthostats set along the long axis of the oval (with decoration present on two of the oval stones and one of the axials). Between the inner and outer oval settings were seven small cists set into the old ground surface. An eighth lay just outside the outer oval. Four of these cists contained unaccompanied cremation deposits, and there was also one uncisted cremation deposit. The cremations were of single adults, with one exception consisting of an adult male and female together. Between and

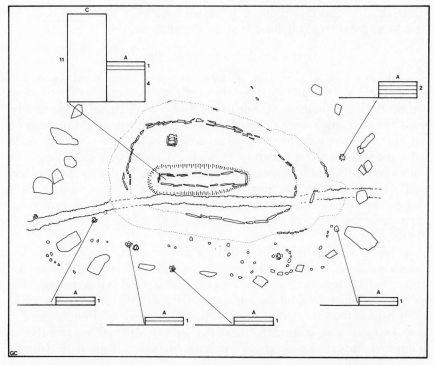

Figure 10.4: b. Interpretation of burial evidence from Millin Bay. Key as in Figure 10.1b.

around the cists were several large oval beach stones ('baetyls'), set singly or in small groups. The site had been covered by a low oval mound; the area encompassed by the inner setting by shingle and flagstones sealed with clay, the outer part by sand. The excavators interpreted the evidence as suggesting that the eight small cists and outer sand mound were added after completion of the inner feature, but not necessarily a long time later (Collins and Waterman 1955, 24–6).

The only artefactual material associated with the site was the crushed remains of a 'Carrowkeel ware' bowl, found on the old land surface, plus some worked flints including a fragment of a polished flint axehead (found in the filling of the central oval feature).

A marked distinction can be seen between the collective skeletal deposit in the southern end of the long cist and the predominance of single, individual cremations in the small cists (Figure 10.4b). In the collective deposit, the bones of children and adolescents predominate, whereas the cremated deposits in the small cists are all of adults. Thus there is a very clear spatial and contextual separation of the two sets of burial deposits. There are aspects of the evidence which parallel that from the sites already discussed, such as the occurrence of cremation as largely an adult rite of burial. On the other hand, the contrasts in deposition of human remains at Millin Bay could be said to be more clearly defined than on the other sites.

If we follow Whittle (1988) in defining ritual as formal, repetitive action taking place at a specific location, then certainly the practices surrounding the deposition of human remains in the four sites discussed above can be classified as ritual. Turner (1969) has shown how the ritual process can be used to reaffirm or renegotiate the social order. Mortuary rituals in particular offer the opportunity to portray an idealised image of social reality. As Ramsden (1991) has discussed, the structure of death is a mirror image of life, and, while deposition and burial form only part of funerary and ancestor rituals, they offer an insight into the way in which the living used these ceremonies and practices to reproduce their social system (I. Morris 1987, 8; Barrett 1988a, 31).

At the four sites, despite their striking differences in form and histories, there are indications of a similar general sequence of events. First, activities appear to have been carried out to make the sites special and sacred, whether by burning the ground, by the construction of a defined architectural space, or by placing foundation or dedicatory burials. In terms of defining space, it may be more than coincidence that the wall at Millin Bay has its most impressive appearance alongside the long cist which it pre-dates (Figure 10.4a). Second, the main use of the sites revolved around the processing and/or deposition of human remains. In all four cases, we are only looking at what may be the latest in a series of episodes of use. For example, at Fourknocks II, it would appear that the transverse trench had previously been used for burning, probably cremation. The dominance of disarticulation and the occurrence of bone-groups among the inhumed bones indicates the likelihood that the first, temporary burial took place elsewhere. The prominence of collective deposits, albeit of differing form at the four sites, indicates the concept of a communal, final grave or ossuary. The juxtaposition of different types of deposit together, cremated and inhumed, discrete individuals and mingled bones indicate that funerary ritual involved the use of bone from other contexts. The third and final general act in the sequence was the blocking of access to the burial deposits. Again, the method varied from site to site: at the Fourknocks sites, it consisted of closing access passages and placing final deposits of human bone; at Audleystown, slabs were placed over the burials; and at Millin Bay, the sacred space was covered with a mound.

Bearing in mind that we can document only part of the complex sequence of actions at these sites, a number of interesting comparative features do occur (see Figures 10.1b, 10.2b, 10.3b and 10.4b). First, there is a basic distinction between the way adults and children were treated in death. As with the general Irish Neolithic burial record, there are far fewer children than would be expected if we were looking at the burial record of the whole population. The remains of children and adolescents are predominant in the passage areas of the Fourknocks sites and at Millin Bay, and here they occur largely as collective deposits of inhumed bone. By contrast, adult remains predominate in the formal, defined burial areas such as the chambers at Audleystown and Fourknocks I, the transverse trench at Fourknocks II and the small cists at Millin Bay. The adult remains consist of both cremated and inhumed bone, the latter dominated by skulls and longbones. The evidence suggests a pattern of activity that linked children, peripheral location and inhumation on the one hand and adults, central position, greater emphasis on cremation and the provision of accompanying artefacts on the other. This implies a practice of excluding children from the full social process of death.

The idea of a communal ossuary may be represented in the burial chambers at both Audleystown and Fourknocks I. Here, the mingling of bones together may have idealised the concept of community (e.g. Ramsden forthcoming) in which children would not have figured in a major way. In each case, the excavator argued that the deposits were best interpreted as the result of single episodes of deposition (Collins 1954; Hartnett 1957). The emphasis on unburnt skulls and longbones and their arrangement within the structures may indicate that these parts of the body were treated in a special way and may have remained in circulation (e.g. Kinnes 1975), to play a role in rites requiring the presence of the ancestors. Particularly interesting is the contrasting pattern of depositional events seen at Fourknocks II and Millin Bay, where the formal adult burials take the form of individual (or exceptionally, a double) cremation. One can suggest that at Millin Bay this represents a different practice, where individual status is emphasised in the final deposition. If the ritual process was a way of reaffirming or altering the social order through practice, then what we see here is an emphasis on maintaining individual identity throughout the burial process: communal burial is now reduced in importance and associated with children and adolescents.

This difference in the burial process can be seen as either a chronological development or a reflection of different practices at different sites and by different groups. It can tentatively be argued that activity at Fourknocks II may be later than Fourknocks I on the supposition that the transverse trench at the former site was the location where the cremated bones in Fourknocks I were burnt. Millin Bay would appear to fit in with the developed passage tomb tradition. This assessment is based particularly on the art style (O'Sullivan 1986 and personal communication). The passage concept, although retained in the long cist, has become functionally redundant. So two sites showing a concern with single burial may be the later of the four discussed and may indicate a growing trend to recognise the role of individuals in both death and life. This is reflective of a trend seen in other aspects of the Irish Neolithic burial record, as in the use of the Linkardstown type burial and the provision of more elaborate prestige items for use in burial ritual than hitherto (e.g. Eogan and Richardson 1982). However, the Linkardstown burials illustrate that the trend may in some areas have developed early in the Neolithic. Multiple deposition continues alongside the focus, in some communities, on formal, final individual burial. We see two different concepts of death and society: one where community can be defined by reference to the burial record from the past, and a second where the ancestors may have become more remote and less relevant to the present, and it is the achievements of the living that are increasingly celebrated in death.

ACKNOWLEDGEMENTS

I wish to thank firstly Eoin Grogan for much useful discussion, for his helpful comments and for permission to use as yet unpublished data. My thanks go to the editors, particularly Alison Sheridan, for greatly improving the draft paper. Finally, I thank the participants at seminars in the Departments of Archaeology in Lampeter and University College, Dublin and the Department of Anthropology in McMaster University, Hamilton, Canada for putting up with the development of this chapter. Any errors are of course those of the author.

11

Monuments, Movement, and the Context of Megalithic Art

Julian Thomas

INTRODUCTION

The sheer scale of many of the monuments of Neolithic Europe is doubtless one of the main factors which has drawn them to the attention of the archaeologist (Shennan 1983). However, this interest in the monumental as a phenomenon has often taken the form of a concern with quantification, in terms either of dimensions or of work effort. The effect of such an approach is to alienate the monument, removing it both from the landscape and from its experience by human beings (Thomas 1990). Elsewhere, I have attempted to offer an alternative approach by analysing British Neolithic monuments in terms of their interpretation by persons physically encountering them (Thomas 1991). The earliest tombs and other monuments are structurally relatively undifferentiated, and served to make certain ideas manifest in the landscape through their physical presence and other symbolism. However, one can arguably discern a change through time to more elaborate arrangements which served to influence perception through the actual control of movement into and around the monument. If we accept that a parallel can be drawn between constructed space and written text (H.L. Moore 1986), such that the way in which space is organised and physically encountered can be likened to the writing and reading of a text, it is clear that one can attempt to impose an 'approved reading' of a monument such as a chambered tomb by restricting the ways in which the tomb and its contents can be approached and accessed. Thus, linear monuments such as cursūs and bank barrows, often constructed over landscapes which had already accrued some significance, served to limit the way in which those spaces could be encountered, by the mere fact of their shape and the position of their entrances. This can be taken as an explanation for the frequent juxtaposition of such linear monuments and earlier causewayed enclosures and tombs. Equally, the increasingly lengthy approach to the chamber within the passage tomb tradition, and the enhanced separation between chamber and forecourt in various groups of tombs, effectively constrained the way in which the ancestral remains could be accessed and experienced. Finally, within the henge tradition, a proliferation of architectural devices both new and drawn from the past worked in a still more elaborate way to impose patterns of movement in space and to condition encounters with objects and materials of symbolic significance. Timber circles and façades, pits, ditches and hearths were taken from an existing cultural repertoire (Clare 1987) and used to create complex arrangements which would require linear and circular movements, and changes of direction, to move through.

The approach outlined above concentrates on the internal organisation of monuments. In this contribution, I should like to place these ideas in the broader context of movement *between* monuments and of the use of megalithic art, using the passage tomb cemetery of Loughcrew in Ireland as an example. It has long been recognised that groups of monuments exist which, from their configuration alone, suggest that they might have been visited in sequence by groups of people. An obvious example would be the henges of the Milfield Basin (Harding 1981). In other cases, the relationships between monuments are more subtle. In the Avebury district, for instance, there is a group of monuments which were constructed over a period of many centuries. While these sites are of several different kinds, one can assume some kind of relationship between them as parts of a single landscape. It is interesting, then, that as Alasdair Whittle points out, the two largest – Avebury itself and Silbury Hill – are barely intervisible (Whittle forthcoming). Despite the unparalleled cluster of monumental architecture in the area, it is very difficult to take it all in as a unified panorama without the benefit of aerial photography. On the contrary, it may be that the arrangement of monuments along the Kennet Valley, mutually screened by low chalk hills, was to some extent the result of a desire that they should be experienced in sequence. This might be supported by the eventual contruction of the Kennet and Beckhampton Avenues, linear arrangements of stone uprights which in effect prescribe a specific pattern of movement through the valley. Walking along the Avenues, each monument is disclosed in sequence and its connotations and meanings digested before moving on to the next. Obviously, this does not imply a grand design operating in the construction of a cultural landscape from the time of the West Kennet long barrow and Windmill Hill onwards, so much as a knitting-together of past and present into a unified conceptual scheme at a later point in the sequence.

'READING' THE PASSAGE TOMB CEMETERY AT LOUGHCREW, COUNTY MEATH

As a more detailed exposition of the relationship between bodily movement through space and the experience of monuments, we could consider the passage tomb cemetery of Loughcrew in Ireland. This is a grouping of Neolithic monuments which extends over some two miles of upland overlooking the surrounding plains of western Co. Meath. The dominating character of this location has frequently been remarked upon (Conwell 1866, 355). Recently, Gabriel Cooney has drawn attention to the similar spatial configuration of the four main passage tomb cemeteries in Ireland, at Carrowmore and Carrowkeel in Co. Sligo, in the Boyne Valley, Co. Meath, and at Loughcrew (Cooney 1990). All have an essentially linear structure, arranged on an east-to-west axis, with one or more particularly large tombs as a form of focus. However, as Cooney further demonstrates, the large 'focal' tombs may actually be the last element to be constructed, and he regards this as evidence for a planned development of these cemeteries (ibid.; cf. Sheridan 1986a, 25).

One can easily postulate that the overall linear arrangement of the cemeteries was connected with a particular pattern of spatial movement. If we assume that some ceremony existed which required participants to move from one tomb to another, perhaps visiting all the tombs in the cemetery, then the linear arrangement might provide one clue as to the 'correct' sequence. However, this may not have been the only guiding principle: there may have been a correct ritual formula as decided through additional criteria (such as the relative symbolic significance of individual tombs), and, if this were the case, then the 'correct reading' of the cemetery as a whole would depend on a formal and ritualised passage through space, probably involving a procession.

At Loughcrew, the individual tomb interiors could obviously not all be experienced at once. Equally, a simple intervisibility study indicated that not all of the tomb exteriors could be seen at the same time, even if one were to stand on top of the cairns, a procedure which might not necessarily have been judged appropriate in Neolithic times. As with the Avebury landscape, these monuments could only be encountered by moving between them, and this immediately leads to further implications. If we assume that the people who built and used the tombs did not actually live in the rather limited area on the summit of the Loughcrew Hills, then such events would involve a group of people ascending to an area which was widely visible, yet perhaps perceived as dangerous. This might involve not merely the removal of people from the context of daily life, but also direct contact with the remains of the dead. Such a spatial movement, from the familiar to the dangerous and liminal and then back, bears the classic structure of rites of passage (Van Gennep 1960). As Turner (1974, 182) suggests, ceremonies which involve temporary contact with influences perceived as hazardous may be a potent source of social integration. Equally, the sharing of meanings implicit in the highly symbolic activities undertaken in the region of the tombs might themselves be involved in the production of a form of moral consensus (Bourdieu 1979, 79).

However, processional movement through such a group of monuments has other implications. If ceremonial activities involved entering the tombs, then the internal space of the monuments, i.e. the passages and chambers, could only have held a certain number of people at a given time: it may be that not all those involved in the use of the tomb were intended to gain access to these places, at least at any one time. It follows that the precise experience of the monument would vary between individuals according to their degree of access to its inner space. This would particularly be the case with ritual performances acted out inside the monuments. Those inside the chambers would actually be in a position to gain direct contact with the remains of the dead, and might be engaged in the deposition of cremated human bones and items of material culture. Since the systems of symbols manipulated in ritual tend to gain their coherence through their practice and practical mastery (Bourdieu 1977, 109), engagement in these acts would produce or reproduce differentials in ritual knowledge within the community.

One of the most significant features of the Loughcrew cemetery is the presence of pecked or incised decoration on a great number of the stones of the passages and chambers (Figure 11.1; Twohig 1981). As much as the human remains and other portable elements deposited within the chambers, these symbols might be expected to be part of the system of signification embodied in the tomb. As very explicitly symbolic media, they would contribute to the production of a 'reading' of the tomb space, and, in their distribution about the walls of the tomb, might be expected to be drawn upon in various ways in the performance of ritual. These are exclusively non-representational symbols. The very ambiguity which makes them difficult for the archaeologist to interpret would make them supremely suitable as elements of ritual discourse: having no one fixed meaning, they might become caught up in the production of quite different meanings at different stages in the ritual process (Turner 1969). Equally, the ambivalence of their meaning might mean that they could have different significance in different contexts and associations, or to different people 'reading' them on the basis of their individual access to knowledge. These points demonstrate that although a series of rituals carried out in a number of these tombs might at one level be experienced as a reaffirmation of the communal spirit, at another their entire significance might be apprehended in a variety of different ways by those present.

The organisation of decorated stones within and between the tombs is revealing (Figure 11.2). There seems to be little similarity between the individual monuments as to which motifs are to be used or the ways in which they can be combined. This certainly does not mean that the symbols are random and without significance. What it may mean is that the subtleties of the decoration as a system of signification could only be grasped by gaining access to a number of separate tombs. Within this diversity, some more basic patterns can be demonstrated. Using a classification of motifs developed from that employed by Twohig (1981), the overall possibilities of association between symbols were investigated. A basic division emerged between comparatively simple designs such as dots, spirals and meanders, and more

Figure 11.1: Decorated kerbstone in Loughcrew Cairn H (author's photograph).

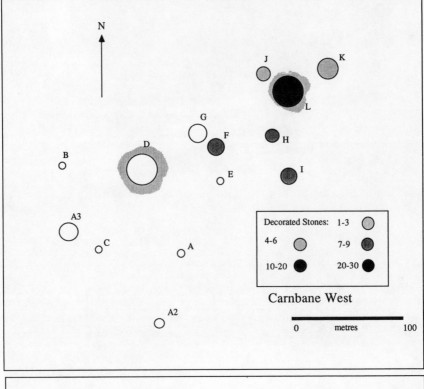

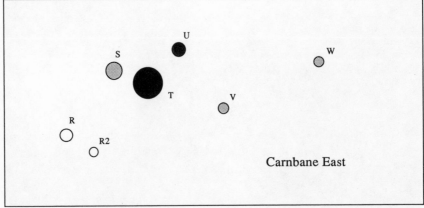

Figure 11.2: Plan of the Loughcrew passage tomb cemetery, showing numbers of decorated stones in each tomb. Ragged shading around D and L approximates to actual shape of cairns.

complex arrangements such as concentric circles and lattices composed of lozenges. The former group are primarily unbounded motifs, and are rarely found on the same stone as the more complicated bounded designs. These latter are frequently mixed together, and one might make the initial observation that these were more often found in the chambers than the passages of the tombs.

This suggestion can be corroborated by a second analysis which considers the number of separate motifs deployed on a given stone, giving a crude index of the complexity of design. For this purpose, the internal spaces of the tombs can be divided up according to the 'permeability' notation devised by Hillier and Hanson (1984). In this way, each individual stone and the designs it bears on its surface can be classified according to its 'depth' from the outside world into the monument, in terms of a number of separate units of conceptually differentiated space. Stones bearing seven or more separate motifs are only found three or four spaces into the tombs, and those with eight or more are found exclusively in those spaces four 'jumps' into the interior (Figure 11.3). This is well illustrated by Cairn T, where the two most complex designs are found in the western antechamber. The most complex design of all, comprising eleven separate motifs, is found on the underside of the capstone of this chamber (Figure 11.4). This pattern clearly indicates that only those people who had access to the deeper recesses of the tombs would be able to encounter these more complex combinations of motifs. In Cairns I and L, another aspect of this pattern can be recognised, where some of the more complex designs can only be seen if one enters the tomb, turns, and looks back toward the passage (Figure 11.5). If such a movement were carried out by one or two persons leading the procession into the tomb, they might then be facing others emerging from the passage. In such a configuration, the 'leading' individuals would have available to them a wider range of symbols, invisible to the others. If these symbols acted in some way as cues or prompts within ritual discourse, it is obvious that the individuals' bodily position would immediately have placed them in a position of advantage.

That access to the 'deeper' parts of the tomb might be limited to a small number of people suggests a reason for the spatial distribution of the decoration. Wherever one stood during tomb rituals, one would be able to see a certain amount of the decoration. However, only those who reached the innermost chambers would have at their disposal the full set of possibilities of combination and mutual association of motifs. One can easily imagine a situation where an individual might be allowed access to deeper and deeper areas of the tomb on successive visits, perhaps over a period of many years. Each new combination of symbols encountered might then make the individual more aware of the overall grammar, or indeed might contradict his or her previous understanding of the symbolic system as a whole (Barth 1975). Thus the various spaces occupied by different persons in the course of ritual performances would constitute a structured set of relationships with

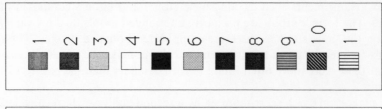

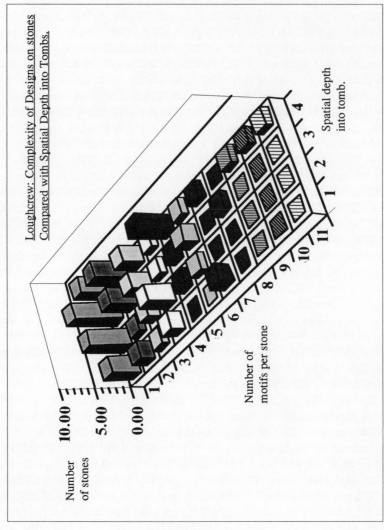

Figure 11.3: Graph showing the 'complexity' of designs on individual stones compared with spatial depth into the tomb.

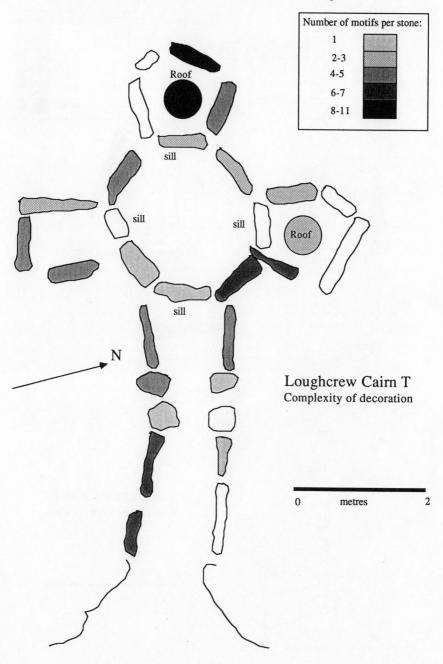

Number of motifs per stone:

1
2-3
4-5
6-7
8-11

Roof

sill

sill

sill

Roof

sill

N

Loughcrew Cairn T
Complexity of decoration

0   metres   2

Figure 11.4: Plan of the passage and chamber of Loughcrew Cairn T, showing complexity of
decoration on individual stones.

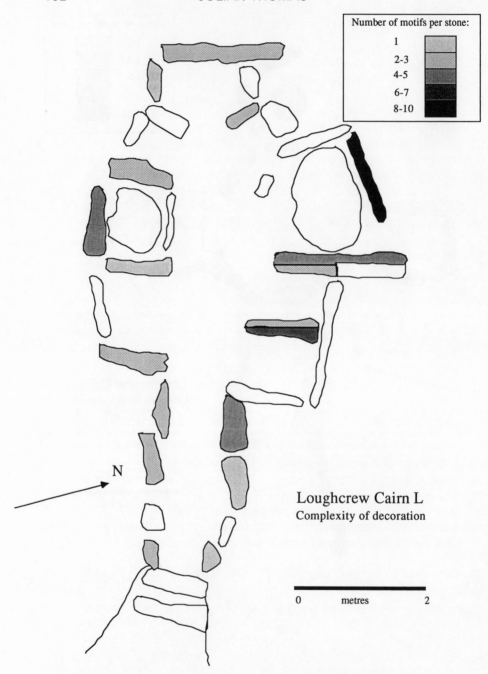

Figure 11.5: Plan of the passage and chamber of Loughcrew Cairn L, showing complexity of
decoration on individual stones.

regard to access to knowledge. At the same time, these differentials would be amplified by the different grasp which people would have of the acts and utterances carried out during such ceremonies. Incantations or chants uttered in the depths of the monument would be muffled and their meaning obscured to those outside in the forecourt. This recalls Frances Lynch's suggestion (1973) that one of the possible functions of the passage in passage tombs might be as a means of aural communication between interior and exterior, albeit in a reverse direction. If activities involving the deposition of human remains and material items were undertaken within the tombs, and still more so if the decorated stones were to be seen, some form of artificial light would have had to be introduced (Bradley 1989a). From outside, this would be experienced (if at all) as a mysterious flickering. In all, the chambers, passage and forecourt would create a spatial structure which graded access to the experiential elements of ritual on the part of the gathered participants, in which their location and posture implicated them in a series of relations of power and knowledge (Graves 1989). As Gilbert Lewis points out (1980, 8), ritual practice often uses and plays upon combinations of clarity and obscurity. Here, within the context of architectural space, the two are combined and skilfully manipulated.

DISCUSSION AND CONCLUSIONS

Megalithic tombs represent a stage for the performance of ritual practices within which gestures, bodily positions, deposition and the association of material items might result in radically different interpretations of the monument and its significance to the community. I have suggested elsewhere (Thomas 1990) that the gradual elaboration of tombs' architecture over time involved an attempt to influence the perception of persons entering their inner spaces. This still leaves unanswered the question of who precisely would enter the tombs. Spatial limitations would demand that this would not be the whole community at any one time, unless the actions and utterances of ritual were repeated a number of times. It seems more likely that the tombs were used for particular events, unrepeatable on any single occasion. Thus, access was limited not merely spatially but also temporally, a point which relates back to the sequencing of experience through procession and calendrical rites.

If not everyone were to be party to the ultimate and most explicit contents of performances, it is difficult to argue that the tombs functioned to maintain a particular dominant ideology through the presentation of unquestionable truths. Instead, they might be seen as a means of securing the reproduction of a tradition of 'reading' on the part of those granted access to the chamber space, while at the same time promoting a more general impression of awe and secrecy among those to a greater or lesser degree excluded. It is often the case that access to particular privileged locations can sanction particular utterances (Hirst 1985) or provide legitimacy for particular interpretations

(H.L. Moore 1986, 86): to speak from a certain position is to be 'in the true'. In this way, participation in the rituals of the inner tomb did not so much endlessly repeat standard formulae which would have to be accepted on face value by the population, as promote the understanding of the cardinal symbols of a minority, thereby privileging their position in the interpretation of the tomb in particular and the world in general. Significantly, the exclusion of the rest was graded rather than total.

The presence of pecked and incised symbols in the tombs of Loughcrew and the Boyne Valley can be seen as a further elaboration upon this same general theme, adding to the complexity of the symbolic system available to those permitted to enter the deepest spaces. As parts of the tomb itself, they were quite literally wrought in stone and fixed in their location, unlike other symbolic media which would be brought into varying configurations with them. Yet despite this, they were non-representational, and could mean one thing at one time and another at another. Drawing out the possible meanings of the art would require a skilled act of interpretation, which again would depend upon privileged access to knowledge. Such a position of enhanced knowledge as a familiarity with the more hidden designs provided would enable individuals to pronounce with authority on the inherently ambiguous symbolism of the tomb and its attendant practices. Only this familiarity would allow one to master the art, artefacts and other symbols as a complete and structured system in which each element had a particular relation with each other. Thus the tomb is less a machine for the reproduction of a uniform ideology than a weapon in the struggle to assert and maintain a sectional interpretation of reality. We are therefore entitled to think of Neolithic societies not as stagnant and bowed down by the dead hand of tradition, but as dynamic entities in which conflicts of interpretation and interest were endemic. Monumental architecture and art are far more concerned with attempts to insinuate interpretations than with imposing them by force, even if they effectively controlled the movement and vision of people entering them.

In such a context, the practice of moving between these tombs while engaged in a series of ritual performances could become one which was fraught with danger and ambiguity. Ritual can be seen as a field of struggles between interests for the maintenance and the subversion of the symbolic order (Bourdieu 1979, 82), and insofar as such a procession might be aimed at the maintenance of social cohesion and the reproduction of elite knowledge, we should recognise that even those excluded from these innermost secrets would be engaged actively in the communal production of interpretation. The privileged knowledge of those who undertook ritual activities within the chamber would have been meaningless if it were totally severed from the understanding of the community. Rather, as I have suggested, the tomb architecture served to grade knowledge, holding the participants in a kind of dynamic tension with respect to each other. In a sense, the production of meaning always depends upon the adoption of positions within a struggle (Macdonnall 1986, 47), and any ritual becomes sterile if it is not an arena for symbolic conflict. The architectural complexity of the tombs, and the dispersal of ritual knowledge within and between them, have the contradictory effects of privileging some people through their access to particular spaces while possibly creating different, apparently oppositional spheres of discourse. Thus it may be significant that the final acts carried out at many chambered tombs involve the blocking of the passage and/or the monumental elaboration of the exterior. The former strategy is widespread in Ireland and Britain (for instance at Fourknocks I, Co. Meath, or among the Cotswold-Severn tombs: Hartnett 1957; Thomas 1988), while the latter is a feature particularly of Orkney tombs (Sharples 1985, 72). In so doing, one renders inaccessible the inner space of restricted knowledge, privileging the 'front space' of more public and communal interaction with the monument.

Part 2
Decorated Stones

12

The Spiral-Decorated Stone
at Llanbedr, Meirionydd

Frances Lynch

The small stone with the carefully-executed single spiral which stands tucked away behind the font in the Church of St Peter, Llanbedr in coastal Meirionydd, excited a good deal of comment when it was first discovered in the 1860s, but it has since dropped out of archaeological discussion. This is undoubtedly because no satisfactory conclusions could be drawn about its date or context. Unfortunately this remains the case. There is no unequivocal answer to the outstanding questions regarding this stone and therefore this review is perhaps an inappropriate offering to Audrey Henshall who has done so much to order, clarify and solve problems of this kind.

The Llanbedr spiral-decorated stone was first noted in 1866 (*Archaeol Camb* 12 (1866), 537–8) when it was recorded that Dr Griffith Griffiths of Taltreuddyn had found the stone 'in Dyffryn Ardudwy, on the hills near some early stone remains' and had arranged for it to be brought down and set up next to the Standing Stones close to the village. The following year, it was illustrated rather inaccurately in an article on decorated stones in Wales by E.L. Barnwell (1867). In this article, Barnwell implies that the 'early stone remains' were hut circles which are very common in the hills above Llanbedr, but there is no positive evidence to support this supposition, which Gresham (Bowen and Gresham 1967, 14) finds very dubious. Barnwell links the Llanbedr stone with the cupmarked capstone of the probable portal tomb at Bachwen (F.M. Lynch 1969, 130) and with Newgrange. The following year (*Archaeol Camb* 14 (1868), 468), it was visited by the Cambrian Archaeological Association on their Summer Excursion and the story of its discovery was repeated. In 1903, it was visited by the Association again (*Archaeol Camb* 4 (1904), 149) and it was noted that the stone, 'in all probability belonging to the Bronze Age', had been mentioned in the context of Scottish cup and ring stones by the speaker to the Association that day, J. Romilly Allen (1882, 128), who had listed it as being associated with a 'fort', following Sir J.Y. Simpson (1865, 52).

In 1912, the Llanbedr stone featured in a wide-ranging article on spiral ornament in Wales (R.H. Morris 1912), prompted by an examination of a piece of spiral-decorated stone built into the modern porch of the church at Llanafan Fawr, Breconshire. This article (which ranges very widely, from Egypt to Brittany to Ireland to Scotland) is concerned primarily with the role and meaning of the spiral rather than with the date of the stones. It contains good photographs of the Llanafan stones and of the Llanbedr one which, at that date, was in the churchyard, having been moved from beside the Standing Stones in 1908. It was brought into the church itself in the 1960s (Bowen and Gresham 1967, 24).

This article by Morris is the last extended discussion of the stone; all subsequent references are brief and equivocal. In 1921, the Royal Commission (RCAM 1921, no. 145, 54–5) provided a description and a photograph on which the spiral had been incompletely blacked in, but did not proffer any opinion of their own about its date and origin. Ever since its inclusion in the bald and rather mixed lists of cup and ring stones of the 1880s, there has been uncertainty about the exact nature of its decoration. This is compounded by its duplicated appearance in the lists of 'Galician' art produced by MacWhite (1946). It is correctly shown as a spiral in Meirionydd on the map of 'Spirals in Bronze Age Rock Carvings' (Figure 7) and appears as such in the list (p. 79), but an unexplained dot on the map of 'Cup and Ring Scribings – Galician Group' (Figure 2) also appears near Llanbedr in the Conwy valley. No candidate for such a stone is known at Llanbedr, Caernarfonshire, and it is more than probable that the same Meirionydd stone is being referred to on both occasions – a confusion of geography and context which is repeated by D.D.A. Simpson and Thawley (1972, Figures 3 and 8).

In 1950, G.E. Daniel (1950, 197) mentions the Llanbedr stone as 'possibly the remains of a burial chamber' but admits that it is impossible to be certain. Presumably he would have considered it part of a passage tomb. However, it is not mentioned in the original publication of the decorated stones at Barclodiad y Gawres (Powell and Daniel 1956), perhaps because Terence Powell was particularly doubtful about its date.

Herity includes it in his lists of passage tombs and of decorated tombs (1974, 86, 102, 213) but does not comment further on the identification. However, it is not included, even as an uncertain site, in Elizabeth Shee Twohig's corpus of European megalithic art (Twohig 1981).

In Colin Gresham's comprehensive discussion of the prehistory of Meirionydd, the comments on the stone are surprisingly non-committal. He records (Bowen and Gresham 1967, 23–4) that the original site of discovery was believed to be in Cwm Nantcol (SH 6260 2570), and simply states that it is 'generally agreed' that it was part of a decorated tomb, without offering any further comment on his own, nor any illustration of the piece.

In 1967 and again in 1969, I failed to mention it at all, being at that time very doubtful indeed about whether it really was a Neolithic carving. Since then it has lain at the back of my mind, never completely dismissed, but never

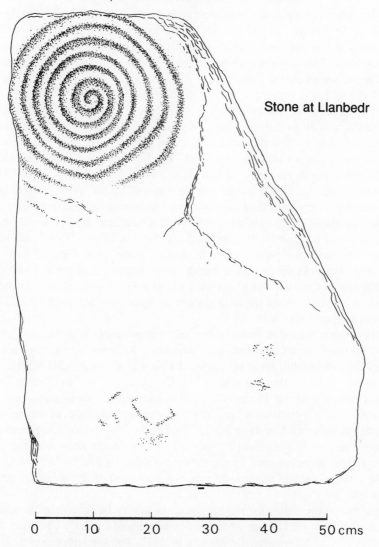

Stone at Llanbedr

0   10   20   30   40   50 cms

Figure 12.1: Spiral-decorated stone in Llanbedr church, Meirionydd.

integrated into any consistent view of the early history of Ardudwy. The invitation to contribute some small study of Welsh megalithic tombs to this volume has provided, therefore, the opportunity to look at this problem in greater detail.

The stone (Figure 12.1) is a small slab of medium-fine-grained rock described as andesite by the Royal Commission (RCAM 1921, 54). It is a pale grey/blue in colour and has a naturally smooth, flat face. It stands on a level base, and all the edges are rounded and appear to be unbroken, though the sloping side has been much battered along the arris. It stands at a maximum height of 0·77 m and is 0·57 m wide at the base and 0·35 m at the top. The thickness at the base varies from 0·40 m to 0·23 m, and at the flat top it is 0·30 m thick. The single neatly-pecked and tightly-coiled spiral is set right in the top corner where the outermost line has been cut on the top arris. On the left-hand side, the outer arc is lost on the edge, and stone may have been slightly damaged at that point.

The decoration is a single spiral of six-and-a-half coils, almost perfectly circular, 0·29 m in diameter and very evenly spaced. There is definitely no central dot, only a simple hooked end. The lines have been pecked with a medium/fine point, and are 15 mm wide and approximately 2 mm deep. They appear weathered, which should not be surprising since the stone has been exposed for a very long time, but is a notable point of contrast with pecked stones of Early Christian date. However, Neolithic stones which have remained within tombs look very fresh, so there is not much evidence to be gained from such comparisons. At the bottom of the spiral there is a gap, and the outer arc picks up again on the left side. Beneath it, there is a hint of a further arc, but the surface is uneven and the mark is not certainly artificial. Close to the bottom of the stone, there is some random pecking and the faintest suggestion of a broad V.

The original record is vague about the circumstances and the spot where the stone was found. Colin Gresham, who knew Ardudwy intimately, records a belief – presumably local hearsay – that it was at a spot (SH 6260 2570) 225 m up on the northern slopes of Moelfre overlooking Cwm Nantcol. He is very doubtful about Barnwell's assumption that the early stone remains were those of hut circles, and records no surviving structures of any kind at the site (Bowen and Gresham 1967, 24). The position is not one where one would expect to find a passage tomb; it is on a uniform slope without local prominence, overshadowed by the summit of Moelfre and tucked round the corner, out of sight of the coastal region where most of the Neolithic settlement lay.

Possible comparisons for the Llanbedr stone may be considered in reverse chronological order (Figure 12.2). The possibility of an Early Christian date was never explicitly stated by Morris in 1912, but the simple spiral from Llanafan Fawr that he illustrates does have some points in common. The technique of pecking, the thickness and closeness of the lines and the careful circularity of the spiral are all generally comparable; but, at three-and-a-half coils, the anti-clockwise spring is a good deal smaller, the carving is deeper (5 mm), and it is obvious that the stone is not complete (R.H. Morris 1912, 256). Unlike the Llanbedr stone, it is probable that the Llanafan spiral is part of a more complex piece, almost certainly a cross-slab or gravestone, which might be expected at this important early ecclesiastical centre.

The type of stone from which it might have come can be seen at Llanrhaedr yn Mochnant, where there is a very similar pecked spiral in the upper corner

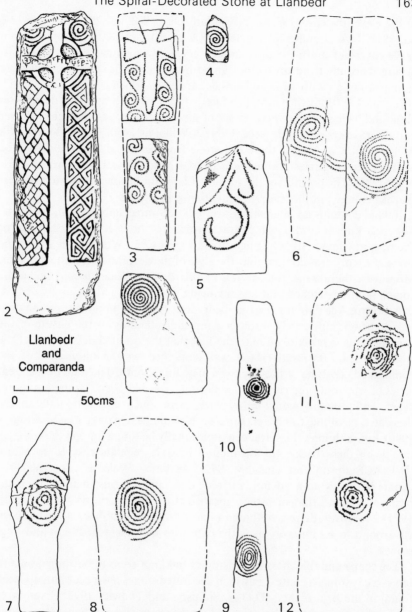

Figure 12.2: Llanbedr stone and comparable stones mentioned in the text. 1. Llanbedr; 2. Cross of Cwgan, Llanrhaedr yn Mochnant (after Nash Williams); 3. Llangeinwen, Anglesey (after RCAM); 4. Llanafan Fawr near Llandrindod Wells; 5. Clover Hill, Co. Sligo (after Twohig); 6. Templewood, Argyll (after RCAHMS); 7. and 8. Baltinglass Hill, Co. Wicklow (after Walshe in Twohig); 9. Loughcrew Cairn W (after du Noyer in Twohig); 10. Pickaquoy, Orkney (after Twohig); 11. and 12. Sess Kilgreen, Co. Tyrone (after Twohig). Outlines of some stones are approximate, but major dimensions are to scale.

of the eleventh-century Cross of Gwgan (Nash Williams 1950, Figure 134, no. 181). Two churches in Anglesey, Llangaffo and Llangeinwen, contain grave-covers of ninth- to eleventh-century date which carry pecked spirals arranged around the central cross. In both instances, the spirals form a loose S-shaped design with wide and rather carelessly-drawn coils (RCAM 1937, xcvi, 2 and 3). Both sites have produced stones which bear spiral decoration alone and have no cross, but they are of similar geology and may be the lower half of grave-covers (ibid., xcix, 1; Nash Williams 1950, Figure 24, no. 18). At Lankhill, Co. Meath, there is a stone from St Brendan's well decorated with concentric circles and without overt Christian symbols (Twohig 1981, Figure 283). The position of the spiral at Llanbedr, however, does not suggest that it belongs to this group of Christian gravestones.

Ireland contains an interesting group of decorated slabs of Iron Age date. The best-known and most characteristic are those forming the cist or chamber at Clover Hill, Co. Sligo (ibid., Figure 282). Whereas the size of the stone at Llanbedr is comparable, the style of the decoration is quite different. Moreover, the absence of carving of this date in Wales would make the comparison far-fetched and unconvincing.

A Bronze Age date for the Llanbedr stone has been implied on more than one occasion, but largely through a misunderstanding of the nature of the carving. This is probably due to the fact that the original description of the stone by E.L. Barnwell (1867) was combined with a discussion of the cupmarked capstone of the Bachwen megalithic tomb. The date of the great series of 'cup and ring' carvings on natural rocks has been disputed in recent years, and opinion would now place them much closer in date to the decorated Neolithic tombs (cf. Bradley this volume, Chapter 13, and Burgess 1990), but, although the spiral can occasionally be found among the complex motifs on these rocks, the distinction in style remains easy to recognise (D.D.A. Simpson and Thawley 1972). As far as Wales is concerned, the debate is somewhat academic, for only one 'cup and ring' marked rock has been found, and that in rather unsatisfactory circumstances (F.M. Lynch 1974). Moreover, there is nothing to suggest that the Llanbedr stone has been cut from a living outcrop, as is the case with most detached 'cup and ring' stones.

The shape and thickness of the stone would not seem to be appropriate to use as a capstone, a context in which decorated stones have occasionally been found in the Bronze Age (D.D.A. Simpson and Thawley 1972). Even rarer is the discovery of carving on standing stones or the components of stone circles. The best-known example of decoration in such a context is Long Meg in Cumbria, where a faint spiral occurs between two groups of concentric circles (Burl 1976, 90, Figure 14). At Templewood in Argyll, two stones of the south-west circle are decorated, one with a pair of concentric circles and the other with a meandering three-line spiral crossing two faces (RCAHMS 1988, no. 228). In all these cases, and in the rather more frequent ones where cupmarks occur on standing stones, the stones are very much taller and more impressive than the Llanbedr one, which is less than a metre high.

Comparisons with Newgrange and the decorated passage tombs of Ireland have been made since the stone was first discovered. Such comparisons may be considered under several heads – technique of carving, style of motif, placing of motif and suitability of the stone for use in a tomb.

The carving technique is in every way comparable to that found in the decorated passage tombs – pecking with a medium/fine point. This technique, as we have seen, is used in a lot of later carving where weathering and variation of rock prohibits distinction between a stone or metal pick. All one can say is that, in point of technique, the Llanbedr stone could well be Neolithic.

The spiral motif can be regularly found on passage tombs, but also occurs in later contexts, as mentioned above. The particular features of the Llanbedr one are its size (six-and-a-half coils, 0·29 m across) and the tightness and neatness of the coil. These features are rather less easy to parallel among the numerous Irish spirals, which tend to be smaller and more loosely and carelessly carved (Twohig 1981, passim). For instance, there are only two large, tightly-coiled spirals at Loughcrew (Cairn H, ibid., Figure 216), where concentric arcs and circles are preferred; but some do occur in the Boyne Valley. There is a large single spiral (to be distinguished from the 'double spirals' on the neighbouring stone) in the western side-chamber at Newgrange and on the roofstone of the eastern one (M.J. O'Kelly 1982, Figures 45 and 51), and they may occur among the obliterated motifs on passage stone L. 19 (ibid., Figure 41), though these may be double. At Knowth, tightly-wound spirals occasionally occur among the more characteristic open, 'broad-brush' style favoured at that monument (Eogan 1986), and at Dowth there is a damaged one in the cruciform chamber (C. 19, C. O'Kelly 1973, Figure 12). In Wales itself, the large spirals on Stone 8 at Barclodiad y Gawres (F.M. Lynch 1967, Figure 4) are comparable for size and neatness of execution, but they are not quite so tightly coiled.

All the spirals mentioned above form part of more complex designs. The occurrence of only a single motif on a stone is definitely unusual. Single motifs, like that at Llanbedr, can be found in Ireland at only three sites, all of them rather atypical in design. Two, Sess Kilgreen in Tyrone and Baltinglass in Co. Wicklow, are isolated monuments, while the third, Cairn W at Loughcrew, is an apparently non-cruciform chamber on the fringe of the cemetery (Twohig 1981, Figures 208, 251, 243). Outside Ireland, the surviving stone from the destroyed cruciform passage tomb at Pickaquoy, Orkney (ibid., Figure 260) and the tentative spiral on Stone 19 at Barclodiad y Gawres (F.M. Lynch 1967, 8) are the only examples.

It is interesting that the stones from Sess Kilgreen, Baltinglass, Loughcrew Cairn W and Pickaquoy are also approximately comparable to Llanbedr in size. At less than a metre high, the Llanbedr stone is not a very convincing component of a megalithic tomb, and there is no indication that it was broken from a larger piece, for all the edges are smooth and weathered. It had certainly not been smashed up when it was found in the 1860s. However, the existence of smaller decorated stones in the tombs of Ireland and Orkney does demonstrate that size need not preclude the identification of the Llanbedr stone as the last remnants of a megalithic tomb which – on the basis of the spiral which does not appear on any other type of monument – would have to have been a passage tomb of some kind.

Passage tombs do occur in Wales, both the earlier type with simple chamber and short passage (F.M. Lynch 1975) and the later ones, including the notable decorated cruciform chamber at Barclodiad y Gawres, Anglesey (Powell and Daniel 1956). However, none of these is in Meirionydd, where the tombs are predominantly portal tombs (F.M. Lynch 1969).

It would not be surprising to find a simple passage tomb in coastal Meirionydd (Ardudwy), for they have a scattered distribution up the Irish Sea coasts, and Ardudwy is arguably an area of early settlement. The presence of decoration on these early tombs, however, is not well-attested. It is certainly not present on those in Britain, and in Ireland the best examples of the type do not have it. There are some tentative marks on the kerb of Chamber I at Baltinglass, but they could have been added later, like the Christian symbol on its basin stone (Twohig 1981, 223). At Carnanmore, a member of the Antrim group, the decoration must pre-date the construction of the tomb (ibid., 202), but that construction is undated. Sess Kilgreen, Co. Tyrone (ibid., 202–3), which has several specific parallels to the Llanbedr stone, and its near neighbour Knockmany (Collins 1960) are large single chambers of rather unusual design extensively decorated in a style reminiscent of the cruciform chambers. Such decoration, together with complexity of structure and a preference for cemetery siting, is generally judged to belong to a later horizon, but ambiguous monuments such as these underline the fact that the detailed chronology is by no means certain or secure.

As well as the small, putatively early group, later passage tombs with a simple chamber but a long passage also exist in North Wales. The best-known of these, which must be one of the latest tombs to be built in these islands, is Bryn Celli Ddu in Anglesey (F.M. Lynch 1969, 111–12). The other, a much more obscure and dilapidated monument, is at Ystum Cegid Isaf, just across Porthmadog Bay from Ardudwy (ibid., Figure 34 and page 139). Neither of these tombs suggests any obvious Irish connection, where such simple polygonal chambers associated with a long passage are unknown. If distant comparisons are to be made, Brittany provides better parallels (L'Helgouac'h 1965, 21–79), not only for the plan but also for the decoration on the unusual stone from the pit behind Bryn Celli Ddu (F.M. Lynch 1970, 60). The presence of pecked decoration on a tomb of this group makes it easier to believe that the Llanbedr stone might have formed part of a monument of this kind. The existence of a Severn-Cotswold tomb amongst the portal tombs of Ardudwy shows that the long-established Neolithic community of this area remained open to new ceremonial and architectural ideas.

It is therefore not impossible that an isolated passage tomb might have been built on the slopes of Moelfre, just as one was built in comparable isolation at Ystum Cegid Isaf; but it would be easier to believe this if the stone were taller, if the reputed find spot were more prominent and if the decoration included a greater range of motifs. As it is, the case cannot be conclusively proved.

13

Turning the World – Rock-carvings and the Archaeology of Death

Richard Bradley

> The probable making of the cupmarks before the tomb was complete, the haphazard positioning of the stones in the tombs, and the very similar distribution of the cupmarked stones not associated with the structures, suggest that cupmarking was practised by the Clava tomb-builders on boulders near their settlements, and these stones, because of their size and accessibility, were often among those chosen for part of the tomb structure. (Henshall 1963, 32–3)

Landscape archaeologists have little time for burials. The dead are an inconvenience. Their intervention complicates the easy relationship between people and the distribution of resources; and their placing in the landscape must be put to use. So it is that the distribution of the dead comes to illuminate the life of the living. Burial mounds are plotted on soil maps as evidence for the distribution of settlements. The building of cairns becomes a side-effect of clearance, and the creation of mortuary monuments enshrines the territorial organisation of farmers.

Students of prehistoric ritual have equally restricted horizons, and, although they might resist the comparison, their work shares some of the same limitations. Neither group can command much evidence of earlier prehistoric settlements. While landscape historians seize on burial mounds as one indication of land-use, those who study monuments stress their geographical isolation. In doing so, they overlook the evidence of lithic artefacts found in and around these sites, and as a result they treat these extraordinary constructions as evidence of 'ritual landscapes' – specialised areas set apart from everyday activity.

Each school over-emphasises the distinction between landscapes and monuments, but it does so in its own way. What they share is a tendency to divide the archaeological record into foreground and background; and, in doing this, inevitably they promote their own specialist interests. A holistic study must be more even-handed. We must not put the dead before the living, nor the living before the dead. There are studies enough of the place of mortuary monuments in the landscape; I wish to show how the landscape itself played a part in funeral rites.

What we tend to speak of as landscape is really a system of *places*, each with its own significance (Tuan 1977). Some of those places were created or embellished as monuments, but others were unaltered features of the natural world. Rock art falls in between these two extremes, for in this case elements of the natural topography were enhanced by 'cultural' designs. In turn, those carved surfaces were to be deployed in the commemoration of the dead.

ROCK-CARVINGS

This chapter concerns the northern part of the British Isles (R.W.B. Morris 1989), and for the most part it ignores the evidence from Wales and western England, where rock-carvings are of a different character and have more in common with those in Atlantic France (Burgess 1990). Apart from occasional examples from Neolithic mortuary sites, such as Dalladies (S. Piggott 1972), the carvings in my study area are found in three contexts: on natural rock surfaces; more rarely on standing monuments; and inside mortuary monuments dating from the late third millennium BC. Here they may be found on cist slabs, on kerbstones or on loose stones within the body of the mound or cairn. Although the record is of poor quality, the finds in this last group have already been documented in detail (D.D.A. Simpson and Thawley 1972). But as so often happens, analysis stopped short at questions of style and chronology. I hope to extend the discussion to the mortuary ritual itself.

Before I do so, I must say something about the character of these carvings (R.W.B. Morris 1989; S. Johnston 1989). Those found in the open air vary in their size and complexity, although the basic element – the individual cupmark – could hardly be any simpler. Such features may be embellished by an array of curvilinear designs, of which the 'cup and ring' is the most widely distributed. These rings may be single or multiple and vary in their size and spacing across the rock surface. There are a number of less common design elements, some of them matched in the 'public' art of the Boyne Valley, but the geometric motifs found in that area are rarely seen on these sites. In some cases, a range of separate motifs may be joined by a network of lines. The visual impact of these designs varies considerably, but detailed study of the evidence from Northumberland and Mid Argyll shows that the larger and more complex motifs tend to be found together (Bradley 1991). At the same time, cupmarks and curvilinear motifs are at opposite extremes in the range of variation (ibid.).

Similar material comes from mortuary monuments, and here, at least, students of rock-carvings are agreed. Two observations are crucially important. First, the carvings do not seem to have been executed specifically for use on these sites, and often they were already old when the monuments

Figure 13.1: Certain and probable decorated cist slabs from Scotland (after J. Y. Simpson 1865).

were built (D.D.A. Simpson and Thawley 1972; R.W.B. Morris 1989, 49). Often, the carved slabs are broken and the designs are truncated (Figure 13.1). In some cases, this was clearly done in order to fit carved stones into the burial cist, but the same observation applies to pieces that are found on their own. Other carvings were worn or weathered before they were introduced to these monuments.

Second, there could be a discrepancy between the likely date of the carvings and the grave goods with which they occur (Burgess 1990). A number of the motifs found with Early Bronze Age burials are shared with the art in Neolithic passage tombs (S. Johnston 1989); some of the same designs appear on Late Neolithic pottery and on other portable artefacts (D.D.A. Simpson and Thawley 1972). This provides a further reason for arguing that some of the stones were brought to these sites *after* they had been carved. At the same time, a few of the carvings do depict metal artefacts, but these are not associated with the normal repertoire of rock art, and where axeheads are depicted on the same stone as simple cupmarks, there is evidence that the designs belong to separate phases (R.W.B. Morris 1977, 109–10). There may even be an exception to prove the rule. A decorated cist slab found at Knappers near Glasgow is unusual because the design is unweathered: the stone seems to have been decorated when the structure was built, and, more importantly, it shares design elements with passage tomb art, in the form of two-ring concentric circles. The only artefact in the cist was a flint adze of Neolithic date (J.N.G. Ritchie and Adamson 1981, 188–92 and 198–9).

This is the point at which analysis normally ends, but there are other observations to be made. A few of the stones had been carved on more than one surface, suggesting that they originally formed part of free-standing structures, probably menhirs. On the other hand, there is a contrast between the motifs found at mortuary monuments and those in other contexts. Simple cupmarked stones are very much under-represented among the cist slabs, while geometric motifs are more often found with the dead. Two design elements associated with passage-tomb art – concentric circles and spirals – are over-represented in comparison with the carvings at open-air sites (MacLaren in Henshall 1966, 211–12; D.D.A. Simpson and Thawley 1972).

The location of the carving in the cist can influence the position of the burial. The surviving records are of poor quality, but there are several sites, such as Alwinton, Northumberland, and Parkburn, Midlothian, where a cremation or a pot had been placed at the foot of the decorated stone (Greenwell and Rolleston 1877, 422–3; Henshall 1966). There are even instances in which the selection of motifs is reflected in the character of the grave – clearly, the process was carefully structured. In Northumberland, we can see something of the logic behind the re-use of rock carvings. Here, the contrast between cupmarked stones and curvi-linear designs is more than usually apparent. There are records of sixteen cists with carved designs: twelve of them incorporated circular design elements and only one was limited to cupmarks. On the other hand, where single slabs covered cremation burials, five of the stones were decorated with cupmarks and only one had more complex decoration (Beckensall 1983, 40–3).

It is one thing to identify a structure in the selection and re-use of carved stones and quite another to provide an interpretation, but it is precisely at this point that landscape archaeology should make its contribution. How had these designs been used in the world outside the tomb? And how were they transformed on their introduction to these monuments?

CHANGING CONTEXTS

The distinction between cupmarks and more complex designs is most important here. Rock art is commonly found at viewpoints, and there are areas in which circular motifs are found at a greater elevation than cupmarks. In turn, the cupmarked stones are sometimes on lowland soils capable of sustaining year-round occupation (Bradley 1991). At the same time, there are striking variations in the distribution of different motifs and in their articulation with one another. In Northumberland, it seems clear that the larger and more complex designs overlook the most productive soils, yet it is at sites with a view over the main group of henge monuments that this evidence is most apparent (ibid.).

The same is true in western Scotland, where some of the most complex panels of rock art are located close to the ceremonial monuments of Mid Argyll. Not only do the decorated rocks cluster around the main approaches to these sites; the most elaborately-carved surfaces overlook the points at which these different routes converge (ibid.). They command extensive views over the surrounding lowlands, and one group of rock-carvings at Achnabreck shares two unusual motifs with the monuments themselves. Other rare motifs are shared between rock surfaces around the edge of the same region (ibid.). One feature of special interest is the local concentration of design elements associated with passage tomb art (R.W.B. Morris 1977, 23).

These observations strengthen the argument that there was something special about the designs selected for re-use. They are among the more complex motifs found at open-air sites, and would generally have been located at prominent viewpoints in upland areas or (in north Northumberland, for example) close to major Neolithic monuments. The rare motifs shared with Irish passage tombs exemplify this tendency exactly, and in some instances, the carved pieces may actually have been taken from older monuments. As we have seen, there are fragments that had been carved on more than one surface, and these may have formed part of menhirs or even stone settings. Again, such constructions could have been conceived in relation to the wider topography, and some examples were aligned on natural features. Those same alignments could also point towards astronomical events (Ruggles 1984).

It seems likely that the elaborately-carved stones incorporated into mortuary monuments had originally been associated with special places in the landscape, both natural and artificial. Among these were prominent viewpoints. The carvings would originally have *looked out over* the terrain. By contrast, the simple cupmarked stones were sometimes in positions that commanded less extensive vistas. In some cases, already-carved rocks were removed from their parent geologies into lowland regions where the same visual effects could not have been achieved.

If the rock-carvings had originally been *turned outwards* – to lower-lying areas or to monument complexes – there can be no doubt that they could be reversed when they were deployed in mortuary ritual. During their secondary re-use, they were no longer directed towards the outer world; *now they were turned towards the corpse.*

We can see this in three different ways. Despite the relatively large number of carved stones found with Bronze Age cairns, there is remarkably little sign of decorated kerbstones. Only one barrow (Hutton Buscel, Yorkshire, cf. Lyles Hill, Co. Antrim) has been published where decoration could be viewed on the exterior of the monument, in contrast to the evidence of older passage tombs (Brewster 1984; E.E. Evans 1953). Unfortunately, details of this site are not available and the character of the carvings is not known. In any event, it contrasts with the evidence from two other cairns in northern England, where carvings were found on the *inner* surface of the kerbstones where they could not have been seen (Glassonby, Cumberland/Cumbria and Weetwood Moor, Northumberland: Collingwood 1901; Thornby 1902; Beckensall 1983, 119–21).

It seems less surprising that the carved stones used in cists were turned towards the burial. This applies to the wall-slabs and also to the covering stone, the underside of which was usually the side with the decoration. Where stones had already been carved on more than one surface, the most elaborate designs faced inwards towards the burial (Figure 13.2; cf. R.W.B. Morris 1989, 47). The same process is evidenced at Cairnholy I, where a megalithic tomb was reopened so that a decorated slab could be propped against the existing side wall, facing a deposit of Bronze Age pottery and cremated bone (S. Piggott and Powell 1949, 118 and 123). We have seen how the decorative motifs associated with burials could be among the more complex found in open-air art. A good demonstration of this point is provided by two Bronze Age cists at Balbirnie (J.N.G. Ritchie 1974). One of the fragments making up Cist 1 was decorated on the inner surface with a series of motifs including cup and ring marks; according to the excavator, it had been 'trimmed from a larger stone' (ibid., 21). Cist 3 nearby was entirely undecorated, but one of the structural elements had been held in place by a large packing-stone, which had also been broken. In contrast to the fragment from Cist 1, it was decorated with cupmarks (ibid., 39).

This last observation recalls the finding of carved fragments, often cupmarked stones, in the material of Bronze Age cairns. These are rarely recorded in detail, but there are instances in which they are known to occur in concentrations above the position of the grave. On two sites in north-east England, the published evidence is still more striking. A cairn on Weetwood Moor in Northumberland contained a series of cupmarked stones, almost all of which had been placed face downwards; it is also one of the sites with a

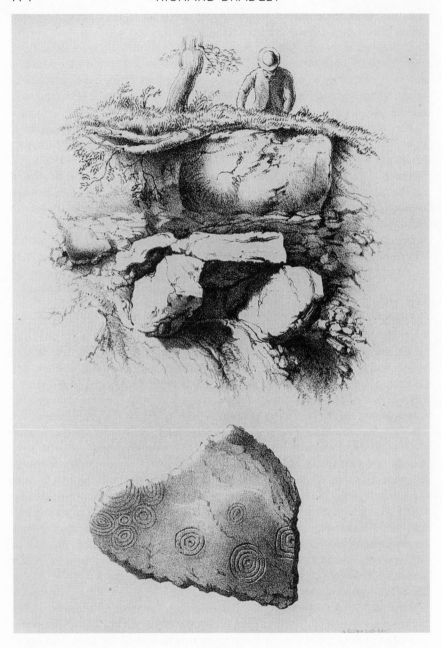

Figure 13.2: Cist with decorated capstone from Craigie Hill (after J. Y. Simpson 1865).

kerbstone decorated on the inside (Beckensall 1983, 119–21). This use of cupmarked stones finds a striking parallel at Brotton in Yorkshire. It is worth quoting the excavators' account: 'Eight of the stone heap above the grave had "cup" markings, one with a "cup" both on the upper and lower surface. The "cup" was usually but not invariably downwards. If there were cups on more than one surface, the larger had the lower position' (Hornsby and Stanton 1917, 267).

The same mound contained a decorated slab, lying on the old land surface in between two graves covered by cupmarked stones. This slab was decorated with cup and ring marks and had also been placed face downwards. This practice is known elsewhere, but has been overlooked because it is assumed that such isolated pieces were the cover-slabs of cists. Although a Beaker pot was found beneath a similar slab at Mount Pleasant in Yorkshire (Sockett 1971), these fragments can be isolated finds from the core of the cairn. In one case, such a slab was marked on both surfaces, but again the side with the more prominent designs faced downwards (Brydon 1870). In other cases, slabs which had been decorated on the underside were found in the material of the cairn *well above* the position of the stone covering the burial cist (e.g. Reid and Fraser, 1924). Although the decoration may have been directed towards the dead, these slabs were never part of the cist itself. Except in the most symbolic sense, they could not have been 'seen' from the tomb.

CONCLUSIONS

The incorporation of already-carved stones into Bronze Age mortuary monuments has been used as a source of chronological information, but until now it has never been treated as evidence of ritual practice. Yet the particular ritual indicated by these finds is one that makes a specific reference to *places*, both cultural and natural, in the wider landscape. These were places where earlier generations had left a mark, yet the careful selection of particular motifs for re-use implies that such carvings could still be 'read'. The apparent links with passage tomb art in one direction, and with the decoration of portable objects in another, suggest that this process may have been connected with the communication of ritual knowledge. That may be why some of the motifs employed in Bronze Age burials had been so closely associated with groups of specialised monuments, and even with the kinds of artefact deposited there during the Neolithic period.

The rock-carvings would have been easy to find, and many of these motifs might have been directed to a large audience. Their placing in the natural terrain suggests that they had occupied viewpoints commanding a wider landscape. The transfer of those fragments from their original context to the mortuary monument brought the landscape, and the past itself, into direct relationship with the dead. The careful reversal of these pieces in the building of mounds and cairns must have formed part of the ritual process: the outer world was changed by the fact of death. While the deceased might be placed with some care in a landscape inhabited by the survivors, elements of a very different landscape – one constructed around special places and specialised knowledge – were incorporated in the final monument. Symbols that may once have been addressed to the wider world were turned around and directed towards the dead person. Messages inscribed on a landscape that was already receding into myth were relayed exclusively to the ancestors.

Part 3
Artefact Studies

14

'Their Use is Wholly Unknown'

Mark Edmonds

For many years past, archaeologists have recognised the fact that within the Scottish area there are contained certain classes of objects which are of special interest to us because they belong exclusively to this limited area. (F.R. Coles 1908, 1)

INTRODUCTION

For more than a century, the carved stone balls of Scotland have inspired a considerable volume of research. Numerous studies have combined detailed descriptions with speculation concerning both the date of these objects and the significance which they might have held for the societies within which they were produced. To this can be added a considerable number of letters in the National Museums of Scotland (NMS) archive, which attest to a high level of interest in their function and origin on the part of individuals working outside the formal boundaries of the discipline.

Of these studies, the corpus compiled by Dorothy Marshall remains by far the most substantive statement of current knowledge on the distribution, date and physical characteristics of these distinctive artefacts (Marshall 1977; 1983). A total of 411 examples have been recorded – 406 within Scotland itself – with particularly high concentrations in the north and east. On the basis of a number of attributes and associations, Marshall argues that they were probably produced and circulated during the Later Neolithic and Early Bronze Age. Moreover, she proposes a classificatory scheme which distinguishes different 'types' of ball on the basis of the number and character of projections which they bear, and the presence, location or absence of incised decoration (Figure 14.1).

It is not the intention in this chapter to attempt any significant revision of the scheme offered in that paper. Rather, I want to begin where that discussion ended, by exploring some of the questions which have arisen in the face of varied attempts to move beyond the seemingly unproblematic process of physical description. As the literature suggests, these enigmatic objects have sustained a variety of different and often contradictory interpretations. For

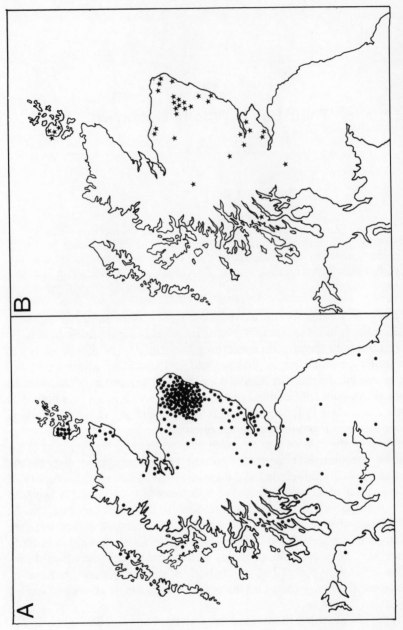

Figure 14.1: Distribution of carved stone balls (A) undecorated, (B) decorated (after Marshall 1977, with additions from Marshall 1983).

that reason, their history as objects of archaeological enquiry is interesting in its own right. Yet there is also a sense in which their interpretation throws up a series of issues which are of direct relevance to current debate about the roles played by material culture in the reproduction of past social life. In the light of this debate, it can be argued that despite the relative paucity of immediate contextual information, the study of carved stone balls can contribute to our understanding of the character of social life and the conditions of social change during the Neolithic.

THE INTERPRETATION OF CARVED STONE BALLS

In certain respects, F.R. Coles' correlation of interest with geography remains as valid today as it was in 1908. For many, the fascination of carved stone balls derives from the fact that they are more or less peculiar to Scotland. Indeed, the last few years have witnessed their deployment in a wide variety of settings, and their use, together with other media, to evoke a sense of national or regional identity. Most recently, this has taken the form of exhibitions and catalogue entries, in which they have been presented as expressions of a distinctive and persistent creative spirit. Yet in keeping with many earlier studies, interest has tended to focus upon the objects themselves. Questions of function and chronology have had pride of place, and there has been little direct concern with the broader social, material and historical conditions under which they were produced and used.

Chronology

Given the paucity of secure archaeological contexts noted by almost every author from Evans (1872) to Marshall (1977), arguments over the chronology of carved stone balls have played a central role in shaping broader narratives. For the most part, discussions have worked outwards from the objects themselves, with particular attention given to the character, and in some cases the quality of the decoration on a number of balls. Evans, for example, emphasises the high quality and precision of the working on a number of balls, drawing parallels with an Iron Age copper alloy ball bearing similar decorative motifs from Walston, Lanarkshire (Reg. No. NMS AS 39). On the basis of these stylistic comparisons, he suggests that:

> Whatever the purpose of these British balls of stone, they seem to belong to a recent period, as compared with that to which many other stone antiquities may be assigned. (J. Evans, 1872, 378)

Writing four years later, J.A. Smith sets the tone for many later discussions in his use of alternative stylistic parallels to argue that:

> instead of belonging to the Stone or Bronze Ages, or any such indefinite ancient period, it was much more likely that these curious stone balls might belong to the ancient, though comparatively historic periods of the sculptured stones, these silver chains and brooches, and Cufic and Anglo-Saxon coins. (Smith, 1879, 56)

Smith's arguments are further supported through references to historical
accounts of the Battle of Hastings and the reproduction of panels from the
Bayeux tapestry. On this basis, he advances the argument that carved stone
balls were the 'lignis imposita Saxa' – maceheads carried by the Saxons –
'when they flocked in early times into Scotland, and where they were
probably used by the people to a much later date than in England' (ibid., 61).

The suggestion that carved stone balls are of Iron Age or later date
continues for some time after Smith (e.g. F.R. Coles 1908, 15; Mann 1914).
Little credence is given to the possibility that reported associations with cists
or cairns might reflect an earlier date (J.A. Smith 1876, and see below).
Instead, the greater emphasis continues to be placed upon stylistic affinities
and the perceived quality of working. For a long time after Evans, authors
are reluctant to attribute these levels of skill to any 'indefinite ancient period'.
In a similar manner, the 1892 Catalogue of the (then-named) National
Museum of Antiquities of Scotland (NMAS) assigns an Iron Age date to the
balls on the basis of their decorative motifs, while Parkyn (1915, 328) talks
of the 'late Keltic' engraving on a number of examples. In both cases, specific
parallels are drawn with the metal ball from Walston, Parkyn suggesting that
this may have been a prototype for copies rendered in stone (ibid., 329).

By contrast, Childe's discussion of the balls recovered during excavations
at Skara Brae questions the use of similarities in ornament style as the basis
for determining their date, citing the presence of similar designs at
Loughcrew and Newgrange (Childe 1931a). Although superficially similar to
Smith's arguments, his use of parallels between the spatial patterning of balls
and of other classes of archaeological data marks a break with this earlier
interpretative tradition. Particularly interesting here is the shift implied by his
terminology. While he characterises the site as 'Neolithic' or 'Stone Age' on
technological grounds, citing material parallels from Copper Age and Magle-
mosian contexts in Central Europe and Scandinavia, he nevertheless remains
equivocal about its date in this publication. On the subject of carved stone
balls he observes that they share the same unusual distribution as objects with
Pictish symbols, a correspondence which is taken as a reflection of contemporaneity (ibid., 104).

The character and affinities of the decoration on a number of balls feature
prominently in more recent discussions. However, with the advent of
absolute dating, and in the wake of more detailed comparative studies, they
are used to reject rather than reaffirm the attribution of an Iron Age or Early
Historic date (e.g. Childe 1946; 1962; MacKie 1976; S. Piggott and Daniel
1951; Powell 1966). Inferring a Later Neolithic horizon from the context of
the balls at Skara Brae, Marshall (1977) postulates a number of more or less
direct parallels with designs in other media from Neolithic contexts. Specific
links are drawn between the spirals, concentric circles, chevrons and zigzags
on a number of balls and those found in passage tomb art, on Grooved Ware
pottery and on the Folkton drums (ibid., 61–3). She uses similar links and

associations to argue that the currency of carved stone balls may have extended into the Early Bronze Age (ibid., 62).

Function

Arguments over the practical roles played by carved stone balls have taken a similarly wide range of forms. However, one can identify broad trends through time in the character and content of interpretative models. The most persistent of these has been the use of broad morphological parallels culled from ethnographic and historical sources. From an early stage, discussions revolve around a small number of functional alternatives, most commonly the mace, the war club and the *bolas*, with arguments centred on the question of how individual examples might have been hafted (e.g. Anderson 1883; J. Evans 1872; J.A. Smith 1876):

> It seems more probable that they were intended for use in the chase or war when attached to a thong, which the recesses between the circles seem well adapted to receive. (J. Evans 1872, 377)

The source for these models lies in the encounter with contemporary non-Western cultures, and in historical documents. Thus J.A. Smith (1876) draws heavily upon Evans' argument (1872) that clues as to the function of these 'curious implements' are to be found through comparison with the material culture of the 'Esquimaux', 'the Chippeways', 'the Algonquins', or the indigenous inhabitants of Fiji (J.A. Smith 1876, 53, 61). These are then supplemented by the historical accounts described above. Similarly, Anderson (1883) refers to contemporary accounts of indigenous American groups in his argument that they were probably hafted as clubs or maces. In each case, these parallels are also used to support the idea that carved stone balls were but a single element in a rich and heavily-ornamented organic material repertoire, perhaps even with wooden precursors (J.A. Smith 1876). This remains a persistent theme in many later discussions (e.g. Childe 1931a, 107).

At first glance, this reliance upon broad ethnographic parallels does not seem altogether surprising, particularly given the lack of reliable contextual evidence. However, in the earliest studies it must also be understood as a reflection of the dominant idea that variability in the character and technological complexity of ethnographically-observed societies provided an appropriate model for succession or social evolution through time. It is debatable how far the use of ethnographic sources by later authors was informed by a similar set of ideas or concerns (Trigger 1990b). However, like many contemporary studies of prehistoric landscape monuments, this early reliance on broad 'top-down' analogies privileged questions of function, and directed attention away from the contexts of the objects themselves (C. Evans 1988). This tendency was exacerbated by the general consensus that the balls were of Iron Age or later date, a view which placed certain constraints upon the interpretation of evidence for their associations (J.A. Smith 1876).

The mace and the *bolas* dominate early accounts, evoking images of warfare and the hunt. Yet these discussions also contain suggestions that carved stone balls were used as gaming pieces, weights or stamps, or as 'equipment for the purposes of divination'. More often than not, these alternatives are only described in order to be rejected (e.g. J. Evans 1872, 377). Yet with the passage of time, it is possible to detect a subtle shift of emphasis. These and other suggestions are given a greater degree of credence, and for the first time the question of artefact symbolism is raised (e.g. Mann 1914; Parkyn 1915). What is interesting here is the fact that these ideas are only given serious attention after the emergence of the consensus that the balls were of Iron Age or later date. In keeping with the social evolutionary models of the day, it seems that authors were reluctant to attribute these more sophisticated or complex roles to objects from earlier periods (Mann 1914). Anticipating some of the themes which were to emerge in later accounts, F.R. Coles' review provides an early example of this shift:

> The suggestion has been hazarded that balls of this variety were the heads of maces, the plain undecorated disc being affixed to the top of the staff. This may be one explanation; but such balls may also have been used in a sort of game or competition, in which the various discs each had its own value and significance, or was emblematic of some idea or symbolism which to us is at present unintelligible. (1908, 14)

Letters sent to the NMS (hitherto NMAS) throughout this century reveal an increasing level of interest in this constellation of alternative hypotheses, but surprisingly little concern with the uncertainty surrounding their date. The comparison of carved stone balls with dice appears several times, as does the suggestion that they served as standard weights. References are also made to the manner in which similar items were used in the recent past, for example as solids around which string or fishing lines could have been stored. In other cases, it is argued that historic or contemporary associations of specific balls hold the key to understanding their original role. Mention is made of individual examples being placed beside the family Bible for evening prayers, or the association of rows of balls with church altars, and, in each case, a general sense of continuity is implied. Further letters develop this concern with symbolic associations, and in one case it is suggested that the decorative motifs served as 'maps' delineating patterns of movement for dances or processions.

Some twenty-five years later, Childe acknowledges the striking uniformity in the size of many balls, but finds no statistical basis for accepting their use as standard weights. (This remains the case despite more recent analysis.) Instead, he argues that while undecorated balls may have fulfilled an essentially utilitarian role, decorated examples were probably imbued with 'a ceremonial value and served perhaps as insignia of rank' (1931a, 108). In effect, he maintains an overly rigid distinction between function and symbol, a dichotomy which can still be found in a number of more recent artefact-based studies (e.g. Chappell 1987). He goes on to suggest that the distinction between plain and decorated balls reflects a trend through time, in which the ceremonial use of balls 'belongs to a time after the practical use of the weapon had been established' (ibid.). In subsequent discussions, and with the emergence of diffusion as a major explanatory device, this chronological trend acquires a spatial dimension, the distribution of balls across Scotland being read as evidence for the movement of the 'Rinyo Culture' (Childe 1962, 21).

Childe's discussion establishes a direct concern with the ceremonial and symbolic properties which might have been invested in carved stone balls. Despite important changes in conceptions of chronology, context and even function, these properties are addressed in all subsequent studies, often to the exclusion of other possibilities. MacKie, for example, discusses their significance through reference to a generalised notion of 'prestige goods', seeing them as the paraphernalia of elite groups (1976; cf. D.V. Clarke, Cowie and Foxon 1985). Marshall advances a broadly similar argument, questioning the idea that they ever served a clear practical role (1977). In addition, she makes the important point that because of the lack of secure associations with graves, these items may have been 'family or clan possessions rather than personal ones' (ibid., 63).

Once again, this shift in the archaeological consensus parallels a trend which can be detected in the letters sent to the NMAS/NMS over the last two decades. Here too, references to maces, warfare and hunting are conspicuous by their absence, and in their place we find an emphasis on the quantitative or symbolic qualities of individual balls. Yet, like those discussions, many of the letters take no account of the idea that the late fourth to early third millennium BC may have been a time of profound, and in certain areas violent, social change (e.g. Bradley 1984; Mercer 1980a). Little attention is given to the possibility that carved stone balls (like other material categories) were implicated in these changes.

Several letters focus on the extent to which specific examples reflect an attempt by the manufacturers to realise the five Platonic solids (i.e. tetrahedron, hexahedron, octahedron, dodecahedron and icosahedron), or explore the possibility that their form and size objectified a variety of abstract mathematical concepts. Others argue that carved stone balls embodied ideas associated with the movement of the stars and the passing of the seasons. There has even been the suggestion that they represent a standard division of the Megalithic Yard. Few would now deny that questions concerning the specific content and character of the knowledge which people may have had concerning the movement of the stars and the passing of the seasons represents a legitimate field of enquiry. But it is equally (if not more) important to establish the conditions under which those ideas were permitted to count as knowledge, and to explore the purposes served by that knowledge in reproducing the social world. In the context of this discussion, the point to stress is that these recent suggestions founder upon precisely the same problem faced by earlier studies. So long as the emphasis remains on the objects themselves, and not their broader context, it remains difficult to take our understanding any further.

The changing ideas about the date and function of carved stone balls illustrate the extent to which categories of archaeological data are constituted as much by the frameworks within which they are studied as by their inherent physical characteristics. Yet despite these changes, our understanding of the significance accorded to the balls remains somewhat limited. The traditional assumption that material categories arise from cultural norms is seldom questioned, and as a result it is difficult to ask why they take their particular form, or what purposes they served. This point is stressed by Marshall, and she acknowledges that her suggestion of 'ritual use' is to some extent derived from the rejection of any clear functional alternative (1977, 64). In that respect, her excellent study, like many others, adheres to the hierarchical structure of Hawkes' 'Ladder of Inference' (1954). As objects which have no direct analogues, and which resist clear practical or economic explanations, carved stone balls are effectively consigned to the margins of research, incapable of contributing in a substantive way to our understanding of the period.

From difference to reference

A concern with similar problems lies at the heart of current material culture studies. For some time, archaeologists have drawn an analogy with the structuralist conception of language as a basis for exploring the role played by material items in the process of social reproduction (Hodder 1982). More recently, attention has focused upon the way in which the production and manipulation of the material world can sustain or alter the categories and divisions obtaining within a particular society (cf. Bourdieu 1977). Rather than springing from a single cultural norm, material culture categories provide dispersed points of reference for the diverse networks of authority that are present in all social practices (Barrett 1988b). Several studies have also shown how ideas which are inculcated through the routine or habitual use of material culture in social practice may also be drawn upon at a more discursive or strategic level (Edmonds and Thomas 1987; Moore 1986).

Many of these issues have been addressed in a recent paper by Ian Hodder (1989), in which he draws attention to a series of long-standing problems with the language model, arguing that written texts provide a closer analogy for material culture (see also Moore 1986 and Tilley 1990). Drawing heavily upon the idea that a text is a work of discourse, whose interpretation is conditioned by context and reader (Ricoeur 1971), he argues that since the meanings of material items arise from the physical contexts and actions in which they are engaged, we need to move beyond the mere identification of structured systems of signs. He goes on to propose a relatively hierarchical model, whereby the primary (denotative) meanings of an object arise from the manner and context in which it is produced and used. This provides the source from which secondary (connotative) meanings can be drawn (ibid., 261).

This emphasis upon the relationship between material items, social practice, and broader historical structures is important, as is the analogical shift from language to text. At the very least, it offers a move away from the simplistic notion that people can transform the basic conditions of their existence through the simple manipulation of individual material categories. Equally important is Hodder's suggestion that the 'reading' of material culture 'texts' may be more constrained than the reading of their written counterparts. The examples that he uses to illustrate this point (notably axeheads and arrowheads) are well chosen, for in each case, it is possible to work from a general consensus about the practical roles that such items played. However, it is debatable how far the notion of primary and secondary meanings can accommodate the potential for artefacts to objectify a *constellation* of ideas, only some of which are related to their practical roles (Larick 1985; Miller 1985). Nowhere is this clearer than in the present case. Moreover, in the form developed by Hodder, the textual analogy cannot encompass the sense in which traditions of material culture production and use spanning several centuries can be sustained without direct reference to an original or (proto-)typical form.

Despite the uncertainty surrounding these questions, the general argument is of direct relevance to this discussion. At the very least, it necessitates a shift of focus. It directs our attention towards relations between objects and their contexts, and the broader conditions under which their meanings were sustained or transformed. This is of particular importance in the case of portable artefacts. The potential for objects to change their meanings as they move from one context to another has been well demonstrated in a number of studies of exchange (e.g. Barrett 1989). At the same time, objects may also serve as metaphors or metonyms, carrying ideas into a number of different contexts and conditioning their interpretation. Put simply, objects may 'presence' a variety of ideas and concepts. As such, they often play an important role in directing the interpretation of formal or ritual events (Lewis 1980; Turner 1967). They might refer to specific practices, persons or properties of people, to group affiliation or ethnicity, or even to more abstract concepts (Braithwaite 1982; Larick 1985). These arguments offer some potential for our understanding of the roles played by carved stone balls, and they will be discussed further below.

Towards a context for carved stone balls

Recent studies have drawn attention to the sense in which the onset of the Later Neolithic in Britain is marked by a series of changes in a number of different spheres of social life. For example, in southern Britain, the turn of the third millennium BC sees a shift from an emphasis upon the collective and the reaffirmation of generalised social categories, towards a greater concern with specific individuals in death (Bradley 1984; Kinnes et al. 1983; Thomas and Whittle 1986). Large corporate interments, comprising arrangements of disarticulated skeletal remains, gave way to smaller numbers of articulated skeletons, often accompanied by grave goods. Similarly, while references to established traditions of construction are suggested by the character of a number of oval barrows, the sequence witnesses the emergence of burials beneath round barrows, echoing the long-established practice noted for northern England (Kinnes 1979).

There can be no justification for the wholesale imposition of this scheme onto the Scottish data. There is relatively little evidence for the single-grave tradition in Scotland, and a number of studies have demonstrated the rich complexity of regional funerary practices (Henshall 1974; Kinnes 1985 and this volume, Chapter 7; Sharples this volume, Chapter 23). Limitations of space prevent a full rehearsal of these sequences here. However, as Kinnes points out (1985, 42), with the exception of Orkney, the turn of the third millennium BC does appear to witness a major restructuring of funerary traditions, manifest in the formal closure of many chambered tombs. Moreover, he suggests that these changes reflect a broad shift of emphasis, in which the living 'usurp' and transform elements of the roles traditionally associated with the ancestors.

Similar themes have been emphasised in studies dealing with the significance of henge monuments. Attention has been drawn to their association with communication routes, to evidence for feasting and to the fact that clusters of exotic artefacts and formal pit deposits are often found in their environs (e.g. Bradley 1984; Darvill 1987b). Further studies have emphasised their role in restructuring the interpretation of existing monuments. Henges would appear to represent a major transformation of the contexts in which a number of practices could be undertaken, providing locations in which new, more hierarchical relations of power and authority could be sustained (Kinnes 1985, 43; Richards and Thomas 1984; Thomas 1991).

Clearly, this general outline cannot do justice to the complexity of regional and local traditions. But in the present context, the point to stress is that parallel sequences of change can be detected at the level of portable artefacts. The early third millennium BC witnesses a marked increase in inter-assemblage variability and the movement of exotica over considerable distances (Bradley 1982). Elements of this trend may already have been established during the preceding centuries, and, in Scotland, the high densities of Cumbrian axeheads in the South-West and of Irish axeheads in the North-East provide a good case in point (P.R. Ritchie and J.G. Scott 1988). Yet it remains clear that the Later Neolithic is characterised by the proliferation of a wide range of highly distinctive portable artefacts. An increased emphasis appears to have been placed upon the use of easily recognisable raw materials, and many stone tools reflect an explicit concern with the realisation of specific styles (e.g. Manby 1979; D.D.A. Simpson and Ransom this volume, Chapter 17; cf. McInnes 1968). The circumstances in which many of these distinctive items have been recovered suggests that their production, use and deposition were mediated as much by their overt social significance as by their practical utility (D.V. Clarke, Cowie and Foxon 1985; J.N.G. Ritchie and Adamson 1981).

For several authors, this has been taken as evidence for the emergence of a series of regional elites around the turn of the third millennium BC, whose position was dependent on monopolising access to a variety of prestige goods (e.g. Bradley 1984; I.J. Thorpe and Richards 1984). As I have argued elsewhere, the movement of artefacts within and between regions does seem to have played an important part in sustaining a variety of networks of authority and obligation (Edmonds 1989). Yet our fascination with exotica has directed attention away from the sense in which many of these artefacts reflect an increased emphasis on local production, perhaps under some form of political control (Bradley and Edmonds in press). Moreover, the range and character of these items is such that they cannot all be subsumed within a single, generalised model of prestige goods, however one defines the term. Rather, they suggest that the Later Neolithic saw the overt deployment of portable artefacts in local contexts, as distinctive media through which to communicate and sustain a variety of ideas related to the social identity of individuals (cf. Edmonds and Thomas 1987).

Fragmentary evidence for the association of carved stone balls with other items suggests that they should be considered with similar themes in mind. Although their association with funerary contexts remains equivocal (see below), a ball and a boar's tusk were found close to a tumulus at Muckle Geddes, while the ball from Tomintoul was found in association with a perforated axehead (Marshall 1977, 58, 60). This latter example is particularly important, since it reaffirms Marshall's suggestion that the balls (along with maceheads) should be considered as part of a broader Late Neolithic/Early Bronze Age material complex (see also Roe 1968).

It remains difficult to assess the significance of variability between different balls. Marshall's categories effectively systematise the distinctions drawn between balls in earlier studies, yet these show no clear correlation with distribution or context. There is no reason to uphold Childe's argument (1931a, 108) that the balls originated in Orkney. Indeed, the data could support the opposite argument just as easily. Nor can one support the idea that the different types are chronologically discrete. The example from Towie (Figure 14.2) may just as easily have been worked with a flint tool as with a metal implement (cf. D.V. Clarke, Cowie and Foxon 1985). This could be tested via high-powered microscopy, but, in the absence of such data, the case for a later date remains unproven.

A further possibility is that the variability between balls reflects a process of emulation, in which different groups or individuals attempted to mimic the

Figure 14.2: Carved stone ball from Towie, Aberdeenshire (reproduced by courtesy of the Trustees of the National Museums of Scotland).

distinctive paraphernalia of other sections within society (Miller 1985). In this regard, the number and character of the projections on many balls is worthy of note, for out of a total of 411, 275 possess six knobs. The point to stress here is that the more complex designs require careful mapping and the maintenance of a high degree of control in working around the surface. By contrast, the creation of six projections is rather more straightforward, requiring only that the maker maintain a sense of opposing faces. It remains to be seen whether or not this distinction reflects the existence of producers working at different levels of specialisation, and, on the basis of present evidence, the concept of emulation should be treated with the same degree of caution as that applied in pottery studies (e.g. Bradley 1984, Thomas 1991).

Despite this uncertainty surrounding the significance of Marshall's categories, it is possible to work at a slightly broader level. The fact that locally available raw materials appear to have been used to manufacture at least some and probably most of the balls (Marshall 1977, 54–5) does not in itself rule out the possibility that they provided media for exchange. Indeed, the coincidence of their distribution with the products of the Group XXIV axe-head source at Killin suggests that lines of contact and communication clearly existed (Edmonds, Sheridan and Tipping in press). This is supported by the fact that some balls (such as Kirkton, Roxburghshire and Hillhead, Orkney: Hunterian Nos 145 and B 1914. 356) are clearly made of non-local stone. One could also argue that the character of the decoration on a number of balls suggests some movement of ideas, if not also objects (see below). However, the overall distribution would also accord with a locally-based model of production and perhaps circulation: there is no need to posit extensive, inter-regional networks.

It is with the character of the decoration on a number of balls that we can begin to establish a number of points of reference. The parallels with passage tomb art have already been noted, as have the broad similarities with some Grooved Ware designs. The specific meaning of these motifs remains obscure, and would probably have been open to different interpretations in the past. However, attention has been drawn to the highly structured ar- rangement of bounded and unbounded designs on Grooved Ware, and to the inter-relation of these patterns with specific contexts and practices (e.g. Richards and Thomas 1984; see also MacSween this volume, Chapter 19).

As with some Grooved Ware motifs, the designs on a number of balls might be said to have their source in passage tomb art (ibid.). The possibility that these designs have their origins in entoptic phenomena (i.e. images produced by the use of hallucinogenic drugs) does little to damage the argument (Bradley 1989b). The use of different motifs in specific locations within tombs may have played an important part in conditioning the reading or interpretation of the monument and its contents. But in the case of portable artefacts such as Grooved Ware and carved stone balls, those motifs are taken out of their frame. As such, they could have been redeployed in several different contexts, carrying with them the properties and associations accrued in the tombs. Alternatively, their meanings could have been trans- formed as they circulated in local contexts some distance from tombs, playing a rather different role in the establishment and maintenance of new sets of social categories. The distribution of carved stone balls adds a further element to this last point, for their designs have few parallels in mortuary contexts in north-east Scotland. For example, the art on Clava cairns and recumbent stone circles is largley restricted to more simple designs, often placed so as to face outwards (Henshall 1963; R.W.B. Morris 1989).

This raises a number of issues, not least the question of the nature of the links between different regional traditions in Scotland (see Sharples this volume, Chapter 23). However, it does suggest that, like Grooved Ware, carved stone balls were implicated in reproducing the new forms of authority and obligation which characterised the Later Neolithic. In the relatively small-scale, lineage-based societies with which we are likely to be dealing, divisions are commonly drawn on the basis of age, gender and the division of labour (Larick 1985; Meillassoux 1972). Further tensions may arise as lineages compete for dominance or control over particular material or symbolic resources.

In the present context, the apparent changes in a number of social practices, particularly those concerning the ancestors, suggest an increasing emphasis on drawing a wide range of distinctions within and between the communities of the living. As items which objectified ideas about the identity, status and affiliation of the individual, portable objects such as carved stone balls would have served to sustain those categories while at the same time offering the potential for their manipulation. Their deployment in different social practices would have conditioned the 'reading' of those practices and the relative position of those who could and could not participate.

This potential is suggested by the fact that specific balls may have been deposited in a number of different contexts. Domestic associations, albeit of a somewhat formal nature, are indicated by the examples from Skara Brae. Although they remain uncertain, funerary or votive contexts may also be inferred from the assocations which were disregarded during the nineteenth and early twentieth centuries. These patterns may reflect the essentially fluid nature of traditions of material culture use and deposition, but they also return us to Marshall's suggestion that carved stone balls were 'family or clan possessions' (1977, 63). Given the increased emphasis which appears to have been placed on the identification of particular lines of affiliation and descent, carved stone balls may also have served as hereditary emblems, sustaining those ideas across several generations.

CONCLUSION

While this chapter has attempted to explore aspects of the conditions under which carved stone balls were produced and used during the Later Neolithic, it inevitably provokes as many questions as it provides answers. At the most general level, I have tried to show how an emphasis on relations between objects and their broader contexts provides a starting point for a study of the specific roles which objects may have played in reproducing the social world (cf. Barrett and Kinnes 1988). These concerns also require us to relate those studies to issues raised in general social theory. Recent developments in material culture studies may reflect a greater concern with the relationship between human agency and social structure. But important problems remain, both with the textual analogy and with our understanding of the nature of material culture traditions.

At a more specific level, this discussion adds to the speculation surrounding the question of regional traditions during the Neolithic, a theme which is taken up at a number of points in this volume. Moreover, the period over which carved stone balls were produced and used remains unclear, as does the possibility that the passage of time saw a change in the manner of their deployment. For example, while the introduction of Beakers may have been associated with a variety of changes in the character and structure of social relations, there remains a clear emphasis upon the linking of people with specific practices through portable artefacts. At present, the lack of dating evidence and secure associations makes it difficult even to speculate upon the extent to which carved stone balls continued to play a part in this process. For that reason, it may be some time before we can refute completely Stuart Piggott and Glyn Daniel's statement (1951) that 'their use is wholly unknown'.

ACKNOWLEDGEMENTS

I am indebted to the editors for their patience during the writing of this chapter, and to Christopher Evans for his comments. Alison Sheridan deserves special thanks for her help in sorting through the NMR archive of letters.

15

Scottish Stone Axeheads:
Some New Work and Recent Discoveries

Alison Sheridan

> Major difficulties still attend the understanding of the role and occurrence
> of stone axes [in Scotland]. (Kinnes 1985, 24)

INTRODUCTION

Despite Ian Kinnes' gloomy pronouncement on the state of Scottish stone
axe studies in 1985, and despite the fact that much work still remains to be
done, significant advances and additions to the database since then can be
reported. This chapter aims to present a brief review of the current state of
Scottish stone axe studies, to discuss the recent fieldwork carried out at the
Creag na Caillich source of Group XXIV axehead rock, and to draw
attention to some of the recent (and not so recent but hitherto unpublished)
discoveries of importance, emphasising what they tell us about the social –
as well as utilitarian – significance of this class of object. ('Axehead' is here
used as a shorthand term to cover all unperforated axeheads, adzes, chisels
and axehead-shaped wedges, and 'stone' is used – unless specified otherwise
– to cover flint as well as other types of rock.)

This chapter is offered to Audrey Henshall in recognition of her long-
standing interest in Scottish stone axeheads (as revealed in her behind-the-
scenes contributions to the National Museums of Scotland files), and in
thanks for her encouragement with the Creag na Caillich project: she was one
of the few brave visitors to that bleak mountainside in spring 1989, and the
idea for this volume was conceived as a result of that visit.

STONE AXE STUDIES IN SCOTLAND

It is not intended to present a detailed history of Scottish stone axe studies
here, since Roy Ritchie and Jack Scott have already published an admirable
summary of the development of implement petrology (1988). Much of this
petrological work had been initiated by them in their capacity as the Scottish
members of the Council for British Archaeology Implement Petrology
Committee; another important aspect of this long-term project has been

Ritchie's systematic study of axehead morphology (following on from Robert Stevenson's work) and distribution (P.R. Ritchie 1987). Relatively few other studies have been undertaken, notable examples being John Howell's attempt at morphological classiciation of a sample of 1000 axeheads (1981), John McVicar's examination of the relationship between axehead size and distance from source for Scottish Group VI and IX specimens (1982), and James Kenworthy's essays on the edge-polished flint axehead from Greenbrae, Cruden, Aberdeenshire (1977a) and the 'Duggleby adze' from Knappers, Dunbartonshire (1981).

In their review of Scottish implement petrology, Ritchie and Scott (1988) presented the results of the 494 petrological examinations which had been carried out to date, underlined the numerical importance (and roughly 2:1 ratio) of the well-known Group VI and IX imports from Cumbria and Antrim respectively, and described the four Groups of Scottish axehead rock which had thus far been identified – Groups XXII, XXIV, XXXII and XXXIII. Brief mention was made of ungrouped rocks, with the comment that one identifiable series of axeheads from Aberdeenshire may have its source in the aureole of one of the 'granite' masses of the southern Uplands. The way forward was envisaged in terms of the continuing detailed documentation of museum collections and thin-sectioning of specimens, to iron out existing inconsistencies in the record.

While few would argue with such aspirations, nevertheless several key issues need to be addressed if Scottish stone axe studies are to be advanced much beyond their present state. First, the scope of the thin-sectioning programme needs careful definition, since blanket coverage is neither appropriate nor cost-effective, let alone feasible. (Other sourcing techniques, such as chemical analysis, have not yet received much attention in Scotland.) So far, fewer than ten per cent of the estimated 4000 + Scottish axeheads have been sourced in this manner, and thin-sectioning has been limited almost exclusively to specimens made of potentially groupable rock. Although further petrological groups almost certainly remain to be discovered, it would nevertheless be regrettable if 'ungroupable' axeheads were excluded from consideration, even if many of these cannot be sourced securely. What is needed is a balanced view of the relative significance of local and non-local axeheads in early prehistoric Scotland (cf. Kinnes 1985, 25).

Second, more attention needs to be paid to the flint axeheads of Scotland. In the absence of reliable quantitative information, it is difficult to estimate what proportion of Scottish axeheads are made of this material; superficial examination of the readily-available data reveals, however, that it may be as low as two to three per cent. The sourcing of the raw material remains a major problem: in addition to the general problems of characterising flint, there has been no systematic investigation of the numerous deposits of naturally-transported flint to determine whether they could have been used to manufacture the known Scottish axeheads (see also Wickham-Jones 1986;

Wickham-Jones and Collins 1978), although past and current work at the
Den of Boddam suggests that the Buchan deposits can be ruled out for all but
the smallest of specimens (Saville personal communication). While Wickham-Jones' statement that 'there is no definite evidence for any long-distance
movement of [flint]' (1986, 6) remains true, nevertheless there is good reason
to suggest that *some* of the Scottish flint axeheads are likely to have been
imported from north-east Ireland and England. The evidence for this is
discussed below.

Finally, the broader interpretative aspects of Scottish stone axes
require further consideration: that is, issues such as the nature and scale of
axehead manufacture, the methods of axehead distribution and the significance of exotic specimens (including the jadeite axeheads as discussed, for
example, by Woolley et al. 1979), and the various ways in which axes were
used during the fourth and third millennia and probably much of the second
millennium BC. (To what extent axes were used by Mesolithic communities
in Scotland remains unclear.) The following pages address some of these
problems.

FIELDWORK AT CREAG NA CAILLICH

The existence of a preferred source of axehead rock on the mountainside at
Creag na Caillich, overlooking Killin, Perthshire (NN 564369) has been
known since the early 1950s, thanks to the recognition of humanly-worked
flakes by a botanist, Dr Poore (Ritchie 1968; Ritchie and Scott 1988). Results
of an initial geological-cum-archaeological survey of the area by Roy Ritchie
were published in 1968 (after which the rock – a calc-silicate hornfels – was
named as 'Group XXIV'), and sampling of the archaeological deposits by
Euan MacKie in 1971 produced two radiocarbon dates suggesting exploitation during the late fourth to early third millennium BC (MacKie 1972).
Further geological examination of the area was undertaken by Dr Graham
Smith of the British Geological Survey in the late 1980s (cf. Harry 1952), and
a preliminary distribution map, showing the thirty confirmed Creag na
Caillich products, was published by Roy Ritchie and Jack Scott in their 1988
paper (map 19), with the comment that further suspected specimens are
known from various museums. In spring 1989, a five-week fieldwork project
was undertaken for the National Museums of Scotland by Mark Edmonds
and Alison Sheridan. This was designed to shed further light on the nature,
scale, date and circumstances of activities at this site. Full details of the
project and its results are presented in Edmonds, Sheridan and Tipping
(forthcoming).

Initial survey of the raw material source revealed that usable parts of the
calc-silicate hornfels exposure were limited in extent: the schists which had
been metamorphosed to create this rock were variable in composition, and
it appeared that all the usable areas had been exploited. Small-scale excavation at the rock-face, high on the slope, revealed that the material had been

prised and pounded from the deposit using hammerstones of local rock; the small amount of charcoal recovered did not suggest the use of fire-setting.

Beneath the base of the scree running down from the main deposit, on a peat-covered saddle of relatively flat ground, was evidence for the roughing-out of blocks transported from the rock-face. The main flaking area was small – less than 40 × 40 m, with a second, smaller concentration and a third scatter of debris to the east – but evidence for at least two distinct phases of activity was recovered from a 3 × 3 m trench which was excavated in the main area. Leaching by the acidic peat deposits had led to substantial decomposition, but it was possible to discern some discrete areas of flaking activity and to see that the apparently final-stage roughouts were considerably coarser than their counterparts at other 'axe factories' such as Tievebulliagh or Great Langdale. One possible reason for this is the relatively soft nature of the rock, which would have meant that less dressing was required prior to final grinding than was the case with porcellanite or tuff. No evidence was found for the final stages of axehead manufacture, and it is likely that these were carried out downhill at the nearby river or beside Loch Tay. Furthermore, no obvious evidence was found for the manufacture of anything other than axeheads, although subsequent thin-sectioning of a Cushion macehead suspected to be of the Creag na Caillich hornfels (see P.R. Ritchie this volume, Chapter 16), from Knock, Lewis, has confirmed the use of the rock for this artefact-type as well. (Roy Ritchie (personal communication) adds that further examples of Group XXIV Cushion maceheads may exist. Re-use of pre-existing axeheads cannot be ruled out, however, although the radiocarbon dates for the rock exploitation – cited below – accord with the suspected period of Cushion macehead use.)

The fieldwork results suggest small-scale, short-lived episodes of rock extraction and working on the mountainside, and the radiocarbon determinations indicate that the earliest dated manufacturing activity – represented by the lower flaking floor in the main working area – belongs to the Later Neolithic, at 2925–2878 CAL-BC (GU-2976, University of Washington calibration program used for this and other Creag na Caillich dates). This date tallies with the determinations obtained by Euan MacKie for the flaking activity which he noted nearby (3338–2950 CAL-BC and 2917–2655 CAL-BC, UB 371–2: MacKie 1972, calibrated 1991). The later of the two flaking floors noted in the 1989 main trench is dated to 2413–2170 CAL-BC (GU-2977).

The palaeoenvironmental record as reconstructed by Richard Tipping indicates that the activities took place close to the tree-line, in an area dominated by hazel and birch scrub (with elm) and spreading mire. By the time of the earliest flaking activity, some 20–30 cm of peat had already accumulated in the area. Some clearance of the elm and birch woodland (and of oak, regionally) may have been associated with this episode of activity, with subsequent possible light grazing of the area followed by rapid mire development (which may be contemporary with the later flaking floor). Tipping concludes that the episodes of rock extraction and working are unlikely to have been a concomitant of transhumant grazing, as had been suggested for the early phase activities at Great Langdale (Bradley and Edmonds 1988).

Much still needs to be discovered about the distribution and use of Group XXIV products and about the people responsible for their manufacture: Neolithic settlement evidence is markedly sparse in the area, and the nearest sites may well have been obliterated by Killin village. The biggest puzzle, however, remains, the thin but extensive distribution of the axeheads: outside Scotland, there is a scatter down the east side of England, with two specimens apparently being found nearly 600 km away in Buckinghamshire (Clough and Cummins 1988, 185). Given that Creag na Caillich axeheads do not appear to have been as durable as their Group VI or Group IX counterparts, and most certainly did not constitute Scotland's answer to jadeite, then no special property (other than perhaps their rarity value) can be suggested to account for their particularly extensive distribution. It may be, however, that as with many other grouped axeheads and with recent stone axeheads in New Guinea and Australia (MacBryde 1978), these objects moved substantial distances around extensive networks of contacts as a means of consolidating social and economic relationships as they passed from hand to hand.

RECENT DISCOVERIES

In this section, the introductory information on each specimen is summarised as follows: 1. Findspot location; 2. Nature of findspot; 3. Finder; 4. Date and circumstances of discovery; 5. Present location and Registration Number, if any (DCM = Dunrobin Castle Museum; GAGM = Glasgow Art Gallery and Museum; INVNG = Inverness Museum and Art Gallery; NMS = National Museums of Scotland); 6. Dimensions (in mm, length × maximum width × maximum thickness); 7. Shape, finish and condition; 8. Colour; 9. Material; 10. References.

Hafted stone axehead from Shulishader (Figure 15.1)

1. Shulishader, Point (Eye Peninsula), Lewis: NB 53203440; 70–80 m OD.
2. In peat, 15–25 cm above the mineral soil, 40–50 cm below the surface of the peat bank; an estimated 1–2 m of peat had previously been removed from the entire area. In a U-shaped, W/WSW-sloping depression surrounded on three sides by higher ground. The haft had been lying at virtually 90° to the peat-bank face, with the head slightly higher than the other end.
3. Mrs Macmillan and Miss Macleod.
4. April 1982, during peat-cutting. The lower end of the haft had unwittingly been truncated during 1981 peat-cutting; findspot area examined by Trevor Cowie and Niall Sharples, but missing part not found.

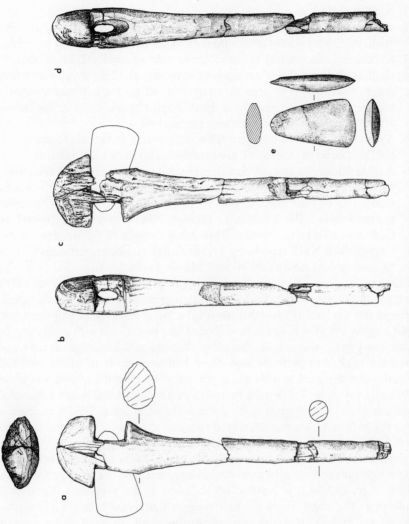

Figure 15.1: Stone axehead in its wooden haft from Shulishader, Lewis. Scale: 1:4. Illustration by Helen Jackson.

5. NMS AF 1097.
6. Axehead: 125 × 67 × 23; haft (surviving part) c. 480 × 101 (immediately above socket); minimum diameter 28; socket 60 mm from top.
7. Axehead: asymmetrical in plan; upper side squared off; blade slightly
   sinuous. A few flake scars remain unground; grinding striations clearly
   visible elsewhere. The area formerly covered by the haft has a slightly
   rougher surface than elsewhere. Haft: originally single piece, thickening
   at head; top rounded, socket area squared off.
8. Axehead: medium to dark grey (leached), with a lighter grey zone where
   haft had covered it; creamy grey speckles and dark grey banding.
9. Axehead: macroscopically consistent with porcellanite from Antrim (own
   judgment and P.R. Ritchie personal communication). Haft: rosaceous
   wood, one of four microscopically-indistinguishable species: Crataegus
   sp. (hawthorn), Pirus malus L. (apple), Pirus communis L. (pear) or
   Cydonia oblonga L. (quince). Hawthorn thought to be the most likely.
10. Unpublished NMS reports by Trevor Cowie (find circumstances), Theo
    Skinner (wood identification) and Maisie Taylor (haft).

Despite its recent damage, the haft is exceptionally well-preserved, with
fine tooling facets (which Taylor considers to be decorative) clearly visible
around the top half. It had been cut from a log at least 160 mm in diameter,
split lengthways. The hole for the axehead had been made with great care, in
such a way as to minimise the danger of shearing with use; larger at the front
than the back, and perfectly smooth, it had been made to fit the axehead
exactly, and designed so that the asymmetrically-bladed axehead would lie
obliquely within it. There were no traces of any additional binding material
(such as resin or thonging) to hold the axehead in place. Taylor concludes
that the haft had been manufactured using an axe similar to it, and that the
hole had been made by charring and abrasion.

Neither the axehead nor the haft shows any signs of having been used
(although the regrinding of a previously-used axehead cannot be ruled out).
How, then, did such a pristine object come to be preserved for several
millennia? The condition of the haft suggests that it had been quickly waterlogged and embedded in anaerobic conditions; only the head shows signs of
slight wet rot damage, suggesting that this part had not been buried immediately. Accidental loss of this carefully-made object cannot of course be
ruled out, but deliberate deposition (as a votive object?), perhaps in a shallow
pool or mire, is equally or more likely. Unfortunately, little is known about
the palaeoenvironmental history of, and early prehistoric activity in, the Eye
Peninsula: Newell's recent work at nearby Sheshader (1988) produced a
pollen record extending only to 2200 BC. Two chambered cairns are
known on the Peninsula, and several sub-peat features and finds have been
recorded (including a remarkable organic bag-like object from Sheshader);
the area would certainly repay further investigation.

The broader significance of the Shulishader axe is considerable. Only nine

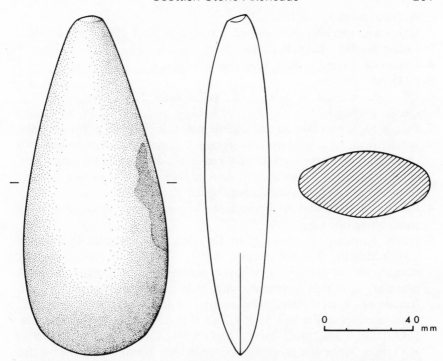

Figure 15.2: Jadeite axehead from Monzievaird, Perthshire. Illustration by Marion O'Neil.

other stone axe hafts are known to survive from Britain and Ireland; a few others have been reported, but are no longer extant. Three (from Coll, Lewis, Maguire's Bridge, Co. Fermanagh and Solway Moss) are of rosaceous wood, the others being of alder, ash, pine, birch and beech.

As for the possibility that the axehead (or its raw material) was imported from Antrim, this is not exceptional: twelve other porcellanite axeheads and axehead flakes are known from the Hebrides (P.R. Ritchie and J.G. Scott 1988; Sheridan, Cooney and Grogan in press), and it seems likely that the items (or raw material) were obtained directly by sailing to the source areas (Sheridan 1986b; McVicar 1982). A notable feature of some of these Hebridean specimens is their pristine, unused appearance (e.g. NMS AF 965, Loch na Craoibhe, Kershader, Lewis and NMS AF 1055, Boreray Island, N. Uist), suggesting that the 'votive deposit' hypothesis deserves further scrutiny.

Jadeite axehead from Monzievaird (Figure 15.2)

1. Monzievaird, Perthshire: exact findspot unknown (c. NN 8424).
2. Alleged to have been found 'in a cairn': clearly not the same site as the cairn at Monzievaird from which two 'blue stone' axeheads came (inf.

National Monuments Record).

3. Unknown; specimen had passed through at least three hands before joining the National collections.

4. Unknown; alleged to have been found 'long ago'.

5. NMS AF 1085.

6. 150 × 65 × 29; L/W ratio 2·3:1, W/Th ratio 2·24:1. Weight 414·8 g, specific gravity 3·23.

7. Pear-shaped, butt faceted and slightly pointed, blade deep, rounded and symmetrical; fat lentoid in cross-section. Polished all over, with only two small unground flake scars left. Broken into four pieces in the recent past, before joining the National collections in 1979; extensive surface cracking relates to this. No signs of damage or use in antiquity.

8. Pale green, with slightly deeper green veining and a 40 mm-long black patch along one edge.

9. Jadeite *sensu stricto*: examined by Dr Alan Woolley of the then-named British Museum (Natural History) in 1981. Thin-section results: the rock consists almost wholly of a coarse (grains up to 0·5 mm diameter), granular, colourless pyroxene, with little quartz and sphene present. Results of electron microprobe analysis of the pyroxene (19 analyses): average composition: SiO_2 58·7%, TiO_2 0·1%, Al_2O_3 22·1%, Cr_2O_3 trace, FeO (total) 1·8%, MnO 0·05%, MgO 0·9%, CaO 1·8%, Na_2O 13·9%, K_2O trace. Molecular proportions: jadeite 89·6, acmite 3·6, augite 6·8 (for a discussion of these terms see Woolley et al. 1979, 93 and Figures 4, 5)

10. Unpublished NMS report by Dr A. Woolley, and notes by Joanna Close-Brooks.

The axehead has been given the number 106 in the Catalogue of Jade Axes from Sites in the British Isles (see V. Jones, Bishop and Woolley 1977). Typologically, it belongs to W.C. Smith's (1963, 141) Type II 'plump' axeheads, with width:thickness ratios less than 3:1. Its thick lenticular section further categorises it as Type IIa, and thus as comparable in shape to the specimen allegedly found in a canoe in the Clyde at Glasgow in 1780 (ibid., no. 56: recently acquired by the Glasgow Art Gallery and Museum). If the width:thickness and length:width ratios are plotted on Woolley et al.'s Figure 2 (1979), it falls just above the area labelled 'dark', among axeheads which are very similar in shape to Monzievaird and which mostly come from southern England.

Despite its morphological similarity to other Type IIa axeheads, the Monzievaird axehead does not share their raw material: the latter are made of pyroxenite of widely varying composition, whereas the pure jadeite of the Monzievaird specimen is more characteristic of the large, flat, triangular axeheads which tend to concentrate in Scotland.

This find brings the number of Scottish prehistoric axeheads of jadeite and related materials to twenty-nine (for list, see V. Jones, Bishop and Woolley 1977, 291–2). In distributional terms, it can be considered in several ways: as a second specimen from the Loch Earn/Strathearn area, for example, or as the fourth axehead from Perthshire, the fifth axehead from the south Perthshire-Stirlingshire-Glasgow cluster, or indeed as one of the inland riverine (as opposed to coastal) Scottish specimens. It is only the fourth 'plump' axehead to be found in Scotland, the others being Type I thin triangular specimens (W.C. Smith 1963, Figure 3). Unfortunately, little can be said about its date or the origin of the raw material. Regarding the former, the sketchy findspot details do not offer any reliable clues, and the available chronological evidence from Britain and Europe indicates that jadeite was being used in Europe from the mid-fifth millennium BC to c. 2000 BC, and imported into Britain from the early fourth millennium BC until the mid- to late third millennium BC (Bishop et al. 1977; I.F. Smith 1979), thus covering a wide period. The Monzievaird specimen is not morphologically similar to the Type I axehead from the Sweet Track, Somerset, which is dendrochronologically dated to 3807/3806 BC (Hillam et al. 1990), or to the roughly-dated fragments from High Peak and Hambledon Hill (V. Jones, Bishop and Woolley 1977; I.F. Smith 1979), although the fact that the raw material resembles that used for the Sweet Track axe may be significant.

Regarding the source of the light green pure jadeite as used for the Monzievaird specimen, Woolley et al. commented that it 'is likely to prove very elusive' (1979, 95); preliminary work on European samples of jadeite-like materials by Essene and Fyfe (1967) had failed to find this material amongst the specimens from Alpine, Piedmont and Bavarian Fichtelgebirge source areas. However, recent work by Monique Ricq-de Bouard (personal communication) suggests that a Piedmontais source seems the most likely, with material possibly travelling north *via* the Rhine.

Whatever the source, the Monzievaird axehead is another important example of an imported exotic prestige item which, when added to the information from Creag na Caillich, makes a closer investigation of the early prehistory of Perthshire desirable (cf. Stewart 1959).

Recent finds of flint axeheads

A hoard of flint axeheads and flakes from near Campbeltown (Figure 15.3)

1. Auchenhoan, Argyll (NR 75651730; c. 110 m OD, c. 500 m from present shore).
2. Shallow pit (assumed) in east, seaward side of a knoll. Shape of pit and presence/absence of container for the hoard could not be determined, as site had been disturbed prior to inspection by Alan Saville and Alison Sheridan. Objects found spread over an area 3 × 3 m, but probably originally confined to an area smaller than 1 sq m; finder described the axeheads as having lain flat but at various angles to each other.
3. Arran Healer (then 12 years old).
4. December 1989; found while walking near home. First axehead spotted

Figure 15.3: Five flint axeheads from flint hoard from Auchenhoan, Argyll. (Photograph reproduced by courtesy of the Trustees of the National Museums of Scotland.)

amongst material eroding from the side of the knoll; further investigations
produced a further four axeheads and 173 other flint objects (comprising
two bifacial preforms/knives, three end scrapers, nine other retouched
flakes and 159 other flakes). Erosion had been initiated by previous

removal of loose surface stones by a farmer for a path.

5. NMS AFA 1-178.

6. i) $174 \times 71 \times 41$;   ii) $167 \times 53 \times 20$;   iii) $141 \times 51 \times 21$;   iv) $171 \times 51 \times 25$; v) $174 \times 53 \times 21$.

7. i) Roughly symmetrical in plan but asymmetric in profile: could be classed as an adze. Butt narrow, blade deeply curved and slightly splaying; bulbous D-shape in section; ii)–v) Very similar to each other: very slightly asymmetric in plan, symmetrical profile, thin; butt narrow; blade narrow (but broader than butt) and shallow. iii) differs from the others in having one curving lateral edge, and iv) has a narrow band of bifacial polish at its blade, with other traces further up one face. Otherwise i)–v) have unmodified flaked surfaces. All appear unused.

8. i) Predominantly dark grey but with ligher grey patches; ii)–v) light grey; iii) darker grey around blade, and iii)–v) speckled. In Saville's opinion, no two axeheads were made from the same nodule.

9. High quality flint: in quality, colour, texture and nature of cortex, matches Antrim coastal deposits.

10. Saville and Sheridan forthcoming.

Axeheads ii)–v) are so similar in shape and style of manufacture that the work of one person is suspected.

The similarity between the raw material of the hoard and Antrim flint, and the fact that exact parallels for the artefact types and the flintworking techniques can be found there (see Woodman in prèss, for example), strongly suggests that the material has been imported from across the North Channel. At least seventeen or eighteen nodules are represented, and several of the flakes can be refitted, but no complete nodule is present: this suggests that the material was knapped elsewhere, and only selected material incorported into the hoard.

The find is significant insofar as it is only the third such hoard of presumably imported Antrim flint in Scotland, the others (both from near Portpatrick, Wigtownshire) lacking axeheads. Other suspected Antrim flint imports (as well as plentiful other evidence for cross-Channel contacts) have been noted in the past (e.g. J.G. Scott 1969), and a fresh review of the evidence relating to local vs imported flint use in south-west Scotland would now be useful.

As for the reason for deposition, the unused appearance of all but a few of the objects, and the fact that some appear to be preforms, suggest that the hoard represents a cache of material newly arrived from Antrim (although a votive reason cannot be ruled out). Similar flint hoards – albeit rarely including axeheads – are not uncommon in north-east Ireland (Woodman personal communication). The date of the deposit remains debatable, but a fourth millennium BC – rather than later – date seems likely in the author's opinion.

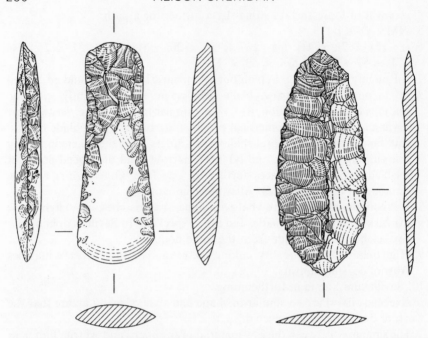

Figure 15.4: 'Seamer axe' and leaf point(?), both flint, from Biggar Common, Lanarkshire. Illustration by Sylvia Stevenson.

'Seamer axe' from Biggar Common (Figure 15.4)

1. Biggar Common, Lanarkshire (NT 00343883; c. 300 m OD).
2. Earlier of two secondary graves in non-megalithic long mound; in pit at W end. No trace of body, but adult extended inhumation assumed from pit shape.
3. Excavators working for the then-named Scottish Development Department (Archaeological Operations and Conservation team).
4. August 1990, during work on several sites on Biggar Common. Axehead associated wtih bifacially-flaked flint object resembling oversized and atypical leaf point.
5. Moat Park Heritage Centre, Biggar (awaiting formal disposal by Finds Disposal Panel).
6. 118 × 41 × 16.
7. Classic 'Seamer axe' shape: waisted – 'duck-billed'; butt broad and rounded, blade curved. Polished in the blade area and over parts of the lower two-thirds of the body. Appears unused: no trace of damage. (Same true of associated flint object.)
8. Mottled brown and light and dark grey (same as associated flint object).
9. High quality flint, comparable to that of the boulder clay deposits of the Yorkshire coast (cf. Manby 1979, 71).

10. D.A. Johnston 1990; Sheridan 1989. Detailed excavation report in preparation.

'Seamer axes' (and the closely-related 'Duggleby adzes') were recognised
by Manby (1974) as a distinctive subset of the Later Neolithic edge-polished
flint implements of Yorkshire, whose distribution concentrates in East
Yorkshire but extends southwards as far as Wessex, westwards to the
Pennines and northwards as far as Aberdeenshire. Five of the Scottish
'Duggleby adzes', from Aberdeenshire, Ayrshire, Dunbartonshire and Midlothian, were discussed by Kenworthy (1981); to these the present author can
add two further 'Duggleby adzes', from Kemback, Fife (NMS AF 981 and
Barbae, Stoneykirk, Wigtownshire (Wigtown District Museum 1988. 292)),
and two 'Seamer axes': the Biggar Common specimen and another from
Biggar (NMS AF 276). (A ninth 'duck-billed' specimen, from Kaeside,
Roxburghshire – NMS AF 879 – is excluded as being atypically small and
poorly-manufactured.)

These objects form part of a range of prestige items (the others including
jet sliders, polished flint knives and antler maceheads) which were in use
around 3000 BC. The Biggar Common association with an individual –
presumably high-status – burial is echoed elsewhere in Scotland (at
Knappers: boulder-built cist suggests possible single burial, despite absence
of human remains: J.N.G. Ritchie and Adamson 1981) and in Yorkshire (e.g.
at Duggleby: Manby 1974; 1988). One such burial, inserted into the Whitegrounds Earlier Neolithic barrow, is radiocarbon-dated to c. 3375–3085
CAL-BC (cited in Manby 1988, 59). It has been suggested (Pierpoint 1980,
187) that 'Seamer axes' and 'Duggleby adzes' were produced by specialists
working in the Eastern Wolds, and exported therefrom. As far as the Scottish
specimens are concerned, this view is supported by the uniformity of their
design and the size, quality and coloration of the flint (for which appropriate
local sources cannot convincingly be cited). Furthermore, in the Biggar
Common case, an additional Yorkshire link is suggested by the accompanying flint object: if this is indeed an anomalous laurel-leaf point, parallels for
its association with a 'Seamer axe' can be found in the hoards from York and
Seamer Moor (Manby 1988, 73).

Other evidence suggesting movement of artefacts between Yorkshire and
Scotland, not only at this time but also later (and possibly earlier) during the
Neolithic, has been discussed by Manby (1974; 1988) and Kenworthy (1977a;
1981). Briefly, this includes the following presumed Yorkshire imports to
Scotland: some non-'Seamer'-type edge-polished flint axeheads (e.g.
'Ardiffery', Cruden, Aberdeenshire: Kenworthy 1977a); all-over-polished
flint chisels, exemplified in Scotland by a specimen from Old Deer, Aberdeenshire (NMS AF 58); beads and sliders assumed to be of Whitby jet;
amber beads; edge- and all-over-polished flint knives; and ripple-flaked
transverse flint arrowheads. Reciprocal movement is thought to be represented by the 'Scottish' carved stone balls in Yorkshire.

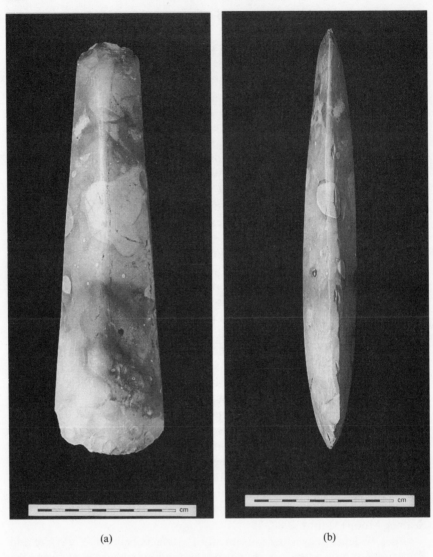

(a)   (b)

Figure 15.5: a + b Large all-over-polished flint axehead from Craggie, Nairn. (Photograph
reproduced by courtesy of the Trustees of the National Museums of Scotland).
a = front view, b = side view.

Polished flint axehead from Craggie (Figure 15.5)

1. Craggie Farm, Auldearn, Nairn (NG 90645370; c. 60 m OD).
2. 'Stray' find, presumably had been sub-surface: found in a row of stones
   cleared mechanically from a field; no other artefacts or surface features
   apparent upon site visit by Robert Gourlay.
3. Mr G. Allingham.

4. May 1989, during preparation of area for afforestation.
5. INVNG 1990.063.
6. 281 × 81 × 39.
7. Slender, butt thin, broad and rounded, blade shallow, sides gently con-
   vergent and squared off; cross-section a truncated, slightly angular
   ellipse. Polished all over, with polishing striations visible and a few
   remaining flake scars. Slight damage to blade, butt and surface, ancient
   in all but one case.
8. Variegated, with marbled effect: basically yellow-buff and light and dark
   grey, with creamy blotches.
9. Very high-quality flint, almost certainly imported (see below).
10. Unpublished report by Robert Gourlay.

This object belongs to a small, widely scattered but distinctive group of
all-over-polished flint axeheads. These are distinguished not only by their size
(most are over 200 mm long, some – including Craggie – considerably more),
but also by their shape (slender, tapering body, faceted sides), their exceptionally skilled manufacture, and their beautiful, often strikingly coloured
and/or marbled raw material.

In discussing the (three) East Midlands specimens, C.N. Moore
commented that examples are known from Wiltshire, Norfolk and Scotland,
but pointed out that no national inventory of these axeheads exists (1979, 86
and Figures 1 and 2 – his 'Class 7' type; cf. J. Evans 1872, 118–19). The
present author knows of the following ten Scottish examples: Folsetter,
Orkney (NMS AF 59), Brora, Sutherland (Dunrobin Castle Museum (DCM)
1831.1), Dunrobin, Sutherland (DCM 1869.2: sides slightly curving),
Invershin, Sutherland (butt only: DCM 1875.1), Smerrick, Banffshire (two
allegedly found together: NMS AF 61–2), Craggie, Nairn (discussed here),
Easter Auquharney, Aberdeenshire (NMS AF 498), Leuchars, Fife (in
private hands) and Gilmerton, East Lothian (NMS AF 60). There are four
further possible specimens which require closer inspection: these are from
Brownhill, Ayrshire (Macdonald 1882, 70–1 and Figure 1), Kirklauchline,
Wigtownshire (two specimens; sides not faceted; Wilson 1878, 13–14 and
Figure 3: note illustrated specimen is not in NMS as stated by C.N. Moore
1979), and Kirkmaiden, Wigtownshire (ibid., 14). A strong eastern and
coastal bias, both in Scotland and in Britain as a whole, is thus apparent.

Unfortunately, virtually nothing is known about the date of these objects
or the source of their distinctive raw material. While there is a general
tendency in Britain for all-over-polished flint axeheads to be of Earlier rather
than Later Neolithic date (e.g. Manby 1988), nevertheless no example of this
particular type has come from a datable context. The source (or sources) of
the raw material remains unclear, although it should be noted that axeheads
of similar shape and distinctive marbled flint have been found in Scandinavia,
manufactured from Danish raw material (Nielsen 1977, Figure 36). That they
were the product of highly-skilled flintworkers and were high-value prestige

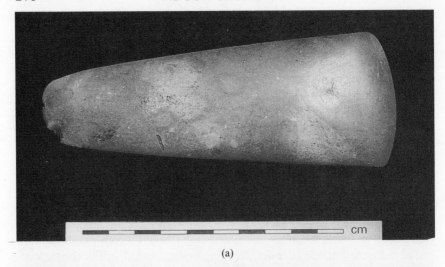

(a)

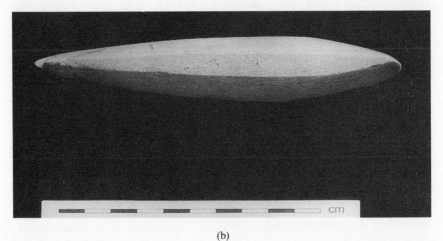

(b)

Figure 15.6: a + b All-over-polished flint axehead from Peattieshill Farm, Fife. (Photograph
reproduced by courtesy of the Trustees of the National Museums of Scotland.)

objects cannot, however, be doubted. The remarkable glassy polish seen in
particular on the Scottish specimens is similar to that noted on many Scottish
jadeite axeheads.

A few other flint axeheads with all-over polish are known from Scotland:
these differ from the aforementioned specimens in being smaller and, in most
cases, less slender. Two examples, hitherto unpublished, are shown in Figures
15.6 and 15.7. That from Peattieshill, New Gilston, Fife (Figure 15.6; NO
43580868; NMS AF 1099) resembles a smaller version of the type discussed
above: 133 mm long and made of fine orange flint with creamy grey patches,

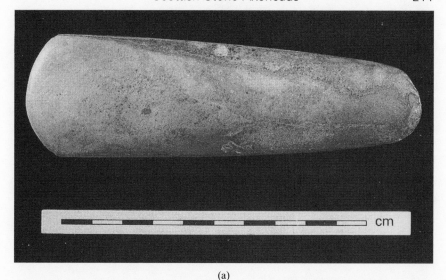

(a)

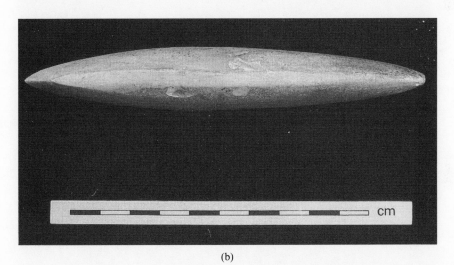

(b)

Figure 15.7: a + b All-over-polished flint axehead from Oykel Bridge, Sutherland. (Photograph reproduced by courtesy of the Trustees of the National Museums of Scotland.)

it was found in 1983 in soil churned up by cattle. The other (Figure 15.7) is from Oykel Bridge, Sutherland (NC 3800; INVNG 1990.071), found in 1989 during ploughing for afforestation: 128 mm long, it is less slender than the aforementioned specimens and made of creamy grey flint.

Superficial examination of these other all-over-polished flint axeheads reveals that they are unlikely to form a coherent group in morphological or flint terms, even though virtually all of them appear to be unused and of high quality flint. Closer investigation and comparison with similar axeheads elsewhere is clearly needed.

ACKNOWLEDGEMENTS

I am grateful to the following for permission to cite unpublished reports: Trevor Cowie, Theo Skinner, Maisie Taylor, Alan Woolley, Mark Edmonds, Richard Tipping, Alan Saville and Bob Gourlay. Thanks are also offered to Trevor, Alan, David Clarke, Terry Manby, Frances Healy, Alison Reid, Peter Woodman, Jill Harden, Monique Ricq-de Bouard and Edwina Proudfoot for their invaluable information and comments.

16

Stone Axeheads and Cushion Maceheads from Orkney and Shetland: Some Similarities and Contrasts

Roy Ritchie

INTRODUCTION

In the years when my study of stone axeheads had perforce to be a spare-time activity, little notes or messages in Audrey Henshall's distinctive hand would arrive from the (then-named) National Museum of Antiquities of Scotland. These would tell briefly but helpfully of stone axeheads which had come in for examination or accession and which she thought merited examination. They were quite typical of the help which she so readily extended to her many colleagues. This brief account of polished stone axeheads and Cushion maceheads in Orkney and Shetland is offered as some small complement to Audrey's magisterial work on the chambered cairns of the area and as an acknowledgement of help given and work shared throughout the years.

Orkney in particular has played a large part in the work on chambered tombs, not least because of the amount of excavation carried out on them. More recently, it has seen similar excavation work on Neolithic settlements which have added to the relatively small but growing number known from the United Kingdom as a whole. When the first volume of *Chambered Tombs* was published, there were fifty-five sites listed in each of Orkney and Shetland. With further work, the number for Orkney has now risen to eighty-one, and these figures could be taken to suggest population ratios in the range of 1:1 to 1·5:1 for the two island groups.

Among the possessions which have survived are polished stone axeheads and maceheads from both tombs and settlements. The relatively high number of maceheads found in Orkney has been a matter for comment for some time (see also D.D.A. Simpson and Ransom this volume, Chapter 17), while ordinary stone axeheads were seen to be few in number and small in size by comparison with Shetland (RCAMS 1946, Volume 1, 58). That has been the general picture until now, but new work in Shetland, while quantifying the differences between the two communities, also suggests points of similarity. An endeavour has been made to account for all finds of polished stone

axeheads from the two areas and to ascertain how far afield tools may have
been taken from the factory area already known from Shetland.

STONE AXEHEADS

The exact number of stone axeheads from Orkney has still to be quantified
– the excavations in Sanday and at Barnhouse have only just taken place and
are not yet fully published. If we add an allowance to the sixty-six finds
known from various museums and accounts, the current total is about eighty
items. A large proportion of these (thirty-six per cent) are from settlement
sites (twenty per cent from Skara Brae, nine per cent from Rinyo and seven
per cent from Sanday), while a further nine per cent are from chambered
cairns. This gives us a total figure of forty-five per cent for finds from
excavations, in striking contrast to Shetland and other parts of Scotland,
where the great bulk of discoveries rank as stray finds.

By contrast with this provisional total of eighty items from Orkney, we
have 298 from Shetland. There are, of course, other finds of polished stone
tools, such as knives and maceheads, from both areas.

Not only are there three-and-a-half times as many axeheads from
Shetland, but they are also noticeably larger. Using implement length as the
criterion, and omitting broken and fragmentary items from consideration, a
plot of numbers against length (Figure 16.1) shows the Shetland axeheads to
range in length mainly from 100 mm to over 300 mm, with quite substantial
numbers in the larger sizes. The Orcadian axeheads, on the other hand, range
in length from about 70 to 190 mm.

The peak at the lower end of the Orkney graph and the corresponding
subsidiary peak in that for Shetland are caused by the presence of miniature
axeheads, often well-made, with facetted sides and broad butts. In general,
the length of these is less than about 70 mm. This is a well-known type with
examples from the known axehead-factory sites in the Lake District, Killin
and Co. Antrim. The distinctive morphology and good-quality finish do not
suggest re-use of broken parts, and the generality that small axeheads are
reworked from larger originals and that they are necessarily later-stage
products must be resisted. Their purpose is not yet clear. Their weight is too
slight for them to have performed a chopping function, even when hafted:
their *raison d'être* may become clearer when notes on all of them can be
compared.

Indeed, the purpose of the Shetland axeheads in general poses questions.
Such information as is presently available shows that, during the period
which we are considering, both sets of islands were typified by birch-hazel
scrub, and one wonders why early Shetlanders needed such large axeheads.

Apart from being large, many of the Shetland axeheads are very well-
made, sometimes with splayed cutting edges. They show little or no sign of
use and give the impression of being ceremonial or prestige pieces.

A high proportion have concavo-convex long sections and have in the past

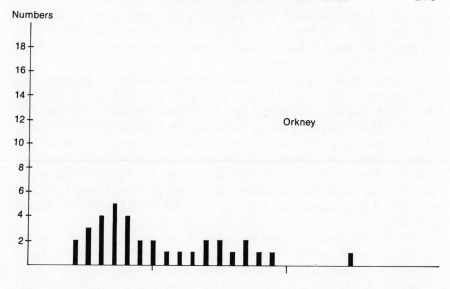

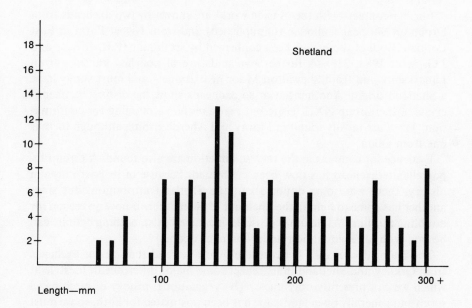

Figure 16.1: Numbers and lengths of Orkney and Shetland stone axeheads.

been termed adzes. However, the longitudinal asymmetry does not extend to the edge profiles, and here all are considered simply as axeheads. The reason for this asymmetry may lie in the way in which the parent rock splits, a factor which will be dealt with elsewhere.

The large size of Shetland axeheads is further emphasised by a comparison with specimens of Group VI (from the Lake District) and Group IX (from Antrim). A graph of comparative sizes for Scottish specimens of Groups VI and IX and for Shetland's Group XXII is given in Figure 16.2. The Group IX specimens fall into a relatively well-defined size pattern, from which the large 'Malone type' axeheads of Ulster are noticeably absent (Sheridan 1986b). The Lake District axeheads show a spread of longer items, while the Shetland specimens are larger still. They are also larger than the category of 'large stone axes' described by Shotton from south-west Wales (1972).

Among these large Shetland axeheads are a number with very fine to exceptional finish, excellent symmetry, extremely good polish and no signs of use. Two, from Daviot in Inverness-shire, come from outside Shetland (*Proc Soc Antiq Scotl* 6 (1864–6), 178–9). These have splayed blades and, although they have not been sectioned, the nature of the feldspar phenocrysts and the general appearance make their Northmavine origin reasonably certain.

Further contacts with the outside world are shown by two axeheads from Druim an Shi near Culloden (unpublished) and from Nisbet Farm in East Lothian. Both of these have been confirmed by sectioning (P.R. Ritchie and J.G. Scott 1988, 236). A further two finds are of polished knives – from Lanarkshire and from Shewalton Moor near Irvine – and must surely have a Shetland origin. Another ten or so axeheads show the distinctive phenocrysts of the Group XXII felsite but really require sectioning for confirmation. These are mostly found in Moray and Aberdeenshire, although there is one from Oban.

Evidence for contacts in the reverse direction are also found. A Group IX porcellanite axehead has now been confirmed. Because of its past museum history, there was some doubt about the Shetland attribution, but since another has come to light in the Shetland Museum there is now no reason for doubting this link. While other possible 'incomers' exist, nothing definite can be said without examination under the microscope.

The major discrepancy between the quantities and the sizes of axeheads from Orkney and Shetland must reflect some major difference in lifestyle at which we can presently only guess. The vegetational history of birch-hazel scrub and generally open landscape has been postulated for both, so we must look to some other factor for explanation. There is also the matter of size, since many Orcadian finds are distinctively miniature. Although these are also found in Shetland, there is a preponderance of large sizes in both utilitarian and ceremonial pieces.

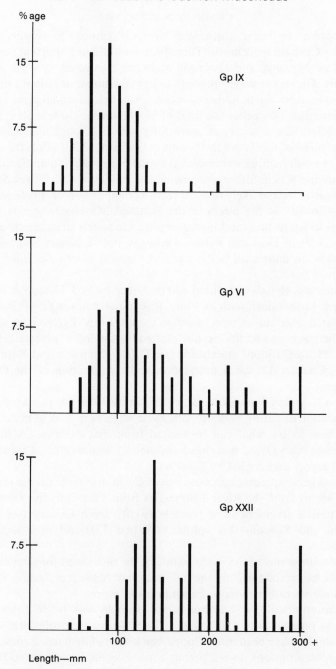

Figure 16.2: Relative lengths of Scottish axeheads of Groups IX, VI and XXII.

CUSHION MACEHEADS

The emphasis on items which were 'symbols' extends to another class of artefact – Cushion maceheads. These form a small but important part of the local Neolithic story and also raise problems connected with the origin of materials. The recent survey brought to light a number of hitherto unrecorded examples from Shetland Isles – no less than five, of which three are made of serpentinite. This raises the total of Shetland cases to seven.

Serpentinite as a source is something new. Although the majority of Shetland polished tools have their origin in the Group XXII felsite from Northmavine, a small number were isolated on the basis of their manufacture from a serpentinite which, although showing a certain amount of variation from piece to piece, looked likely to come from a common source. Professor Flinn, who has looked at the pieces in the Shetland Museum, suggests that the source is likely to be found in the serpentinite which stretches through the northern isles of Unst and Fetlar. Axeheads, both ordinary and miniature, maceheads, an unfinished battle-axe and Cushion maceheads have all been made from this.

Cushion maceheads were listed and described by W.J. Gibson in 1944 and have been further dealt with by Fiona Roe in two main papers (1968, 1979). An updated distribution map based on these sources is given here as Figure 16.3. There are also additions, not plotted, to the list of objects defined by Roe as 'Proto-Cushion' maceheads (see D.D.A. Simpson and Ransom this volume, Chapter 17, for a description and enumeration of the Orcadian specimens).

Only a fragment from Skara Brae (I.F. Smith 1979, 15) provides any sort of association or dating evidence: otherwise we have to look at materials and distribution to see what can be elicited from that evidence. A find from Stonehenge is an Ovoid macehead and not a Cushion-type as stated in the original report and copied by Gibson.

Curious geographical concentrations of Cushion maceheads are noticeable – there are six from the River Thames, six from Yorkshire, five from Lewis, eleven plus a fragment of a possible twelfth from Orkney (see D.D.A. Simpson and Ransom this volume, Chapter 17), and now seven from Shetland.

One common thread lies in the nature of the rocks used for their manufacture. Roe has noted this, and the publication of *Stone Axe Studies Volume 2* in 1988 allows rather more to be said on this score.

Not unexpectedly, a Northumbrian example was made from Group XVIII, as possibly was that found at Barr Beacon, Lincolnshire. Another four examples have been made from a black-and-white banded rock, but the published descriptions do not permit a more detailed comment to be made.

Group VI was the material for the finds from the Thames at Windsor and at Hammersmith, as well as the Great Hale (Lincs) specimen. That is

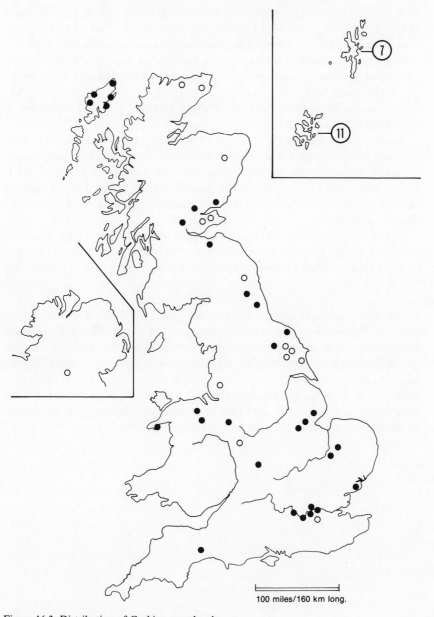

Figure 16.3: Distribution of Cushion maceheads.

described as being a banded variety (Cummins and Moore 1973, 252, no. 326) and there are others of fine-grained green banded material from Inveresk, Fife (unlocated – two specimens), Pitcairngreen, Fillaws, Evie, and Uig and Knock in Lewis. One of the Fife maceheads and the Knock specimen have been claimed to be of the riebeckite felsite from Northmavine (W.J. Gibson 1944, 20; P.R. Ritchie 1968, 132), but thin-sectioning of the latter has shown it to be of Group XXIV rock (see Sheridan this volume, Chapter 15).

With the exception of the Group VI and Knock maceheads, all of these comments are based on macroscopic study only. The other six green pieces are particularly intriguing: hand-lens scrutiny suggests either the Lake District or Killin as likely sources. Without sectioning, it is not possible to discriminate.

A recent re-scrutiny of the finds from Fife and comparison with waste from Shetland emphasises the difficulties of hand-lens examination. In some cases, it can be very difficult to distinguish between Groups XXIV and XXII on the one hand and Groups XXII and IX on the other. Only a suitable analysis will resolve this, but one is loath to sample such beautifully made and finished maceheads.

At any rate, it appears that Cushion maceheads are made from a relatively restricted range of rock-types, that they would certainly repay a more detailed study of their petrology, and that Shetland has a part to play in this.

CONCLUSIONS

Given these seven Cushion maceheads from Shetland and the eleven (possibly twelve) from Orkney, this brings us full circle. Where the axehead evidence points to some substantial difference between the two communities, the relatively high numbers of Cushion maceheads, the highest in the country, show a common emphasis on pomp or ceremony by the time these were in use. Whether the initiation of this community of purpose extended from north to south, or in the other direction, is something which can only be decided when more information becomes available.

17

Maceheads and the Orcadian Neolithic

Derek Simpson and Rachael Ransom

INTRODUCTION

The first publication of an Orkney macehead, and incidentally among the first maceheads to come from an archaeological context, was the extraordinary multiple-knobbed example recovered from Skara Brae (Catalogue No 9; Petrie 1868, plate 42, no. 5). Sir John Evans (1897, 221) mentions the finds from Firth and Lingro, and Graham Callander (1931) illustrated and commented upon a number of the maceheads and drew attention to the remarkably high incidence of broken examples. Maceheads of Cushion type were discussed by W.J. Gibson (1944) and their concentration in Orkney highlighted. The definitive studies of the British finds were by Roe (1968; 1979), who broadly divided maceheads into an Early Series, comprising artefacts of Ovoid, Pestle and Cushion types, and a Late Series subdivided into Bush Barrow and Largs types. A corpus of the Irish material was subsequently published by D.D.A. Simpson (1988; 1991). Although not specifically concerned with maceheads, Fenton's study of the manufacture and source of Scottish battle-axes (1984; 1988) has considerable relevance to the technology of maceheads.

Seventy-six maceheads of stone, bone and antler have been recorded from Orkney, and details of these are presented in the Catalogue (see also Figures 17.3 to 17.8). In terms of landmass, this represents the greatest concentration of such objects anywhere in Britain or Ireland. Apart from pottery, maceheads are the most consistently recurring diagnostic artefacts of the Later Neolithic period in the Orkney Islands. All of Roe's categories, except the Maesmawr Ovoid type occur, although their relative numbers vary, with Pestle and Cushion specimens far outnumbering Ovoid. Most significant is the concentration of Cushion maceheads. These are comparatively rare elsewhere in Britain and Ireland (W.J. Gibson 1944). Only one undoubted example has been recorded from Ireland, although the Pestle form is well-represented there and is, in fact, the commonest type in the Early series (D.D.A. Simpson 1988, 31). The Late groups of maceheads are represented by only four examples, three of Bush Barrow and one of Largs type. Similarly-shaped pebble hammers with hourglass perforations are unrepresented in Orkney, if one discounts a pebble with two opposed counter-sunk hollows of uncertain provenance, either from Orkney or Shetland, in the Hunterian Museum (Registration No 1914.1000). Roe (1979, 40, Figure 15) records only a single example from Shetland, and they are poorly represented on the Scottish mainland.

DISTRIBUTION

Maceheads are widely distributed within the Orkney Islands, with single examples coming from North and South Ronaldsay at the two geographical extremes, although by far the greatest concentration is in the Mainland (Figure 17.1). This is partly due to the much larger landmass of the principal island and the higher incidence of better-quality arable land, making chance discovery through ploughing more likely (J.L. Davidson and Henshall 1989, 16, Figure 7). As elsewhere, a high percentage of the maceheads are stray finds. For example, six maceheads are recorded from the adjacent farmsteads of Bookan and Bockan in Sandwick parish, but none has details of its discovery; other finds are assigned to parish only, and five are unlocalised examples. A small but significant number, however, have been recovered from settlement sites and chambered tombs. Curiously, the very large number of maceheads in the Mainland is not reflected in a similar concentration of tombs (Figure 17.2). Several of the much smaller islands to the north have a greater tomb-density for their landmass but a smaller proportion of maceheads, while Eday and the Calf of Eday have ten tombs in all and no corresponding maceheads. It is tempting to think that the Mainland concentration is linked to the occurrence there of the only two henge monuments in the islands. One unusual feature, first noted by Callander (1931), is the high incidence of broken maceheads, the fracture normally occurring across the perforation. He suggested that some may have been deliberately broken, and Roe (1979), taking up this idea, postulated a ritual significance for the practice; in this respect, the high incidence of such finds in proximity to the henges at Brodgar and Stenness may be significant. On the other hand, broken and fragmentary maceheads have also been recovered from the settlements of Rinyo, Skara Brae, Tofts Ness and Barnhouse, where they are less likely to have been ritually broken. But again, most show no traces of wear or abrasion to account for their fragmentary condition; perhaps here too, ritual activity is involved in an apparent 'domestic' situation.

PETROLOGY AND MANUFACTURE

None of the Orkney maceheads has been thin-sectioned; of the forty-two which have been macroscopically identified, all but two (Nos 11 and 37) are of igneous or metamorphic rocks. The structural geology of Orkney is comparatively simple, but many of the metamorphic and igneous blanks

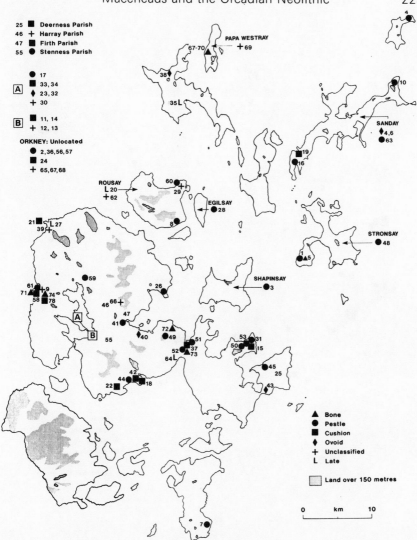

Figure 17.1: Distribution of Orkney maceheads by type.

could have been recovered from beaches or inland drift deposits. Here one must bear in mind Fenton's (1984; 1988) observation, in the case of Scottish battle-axes, that water-rolled or glacially-deposited cobbles were probably used rather than quarried material because of the suitability of their shape, which would reduce the amount of dressing and preparation. The same possibility clearly exists in the selection of suitable rocks for the manufacture of maceheads, and Dr Alex Livingstone has confirmed (personal communica-

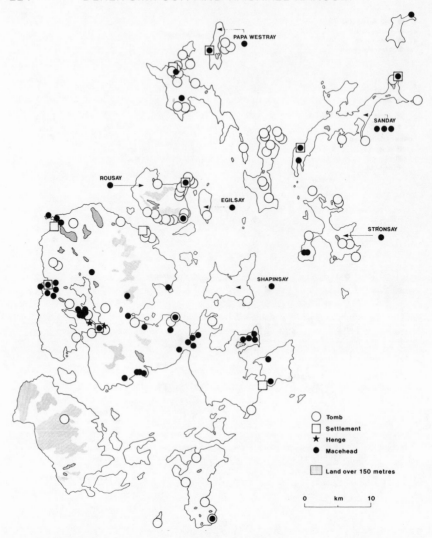

Figure 17.2: Distribution of maceheads, settlements, megalithic tombs and henges in Orkney.

tion) that many of the rocks could have been transported by natural means to Orkney from parent material in Shetland.

Support for the idea of local manufacture comes from the fact that six Orkney maceheads survive in an unfinished state (Nos 3, 4, 12, 39, 54 and 64). Of these, two are of Ovoid type, and there are one each of 'Orkney Pestle', '?Proto-Cushion', Cushion and Bush Barrow types. Only two examples have been geologically identified, and these are of camptonite (Nos 3 and 4). In some cases (e.g. Birsay, No 39), perforations have begun from opposed faces;

in others (e.g. Sanday, No 4), from one face only. The Birsay specimen is curious in that drilling had penetrated only about 5 mm from each face. By contrast, the perforation in the Sanday example extends almost two-thirds of the way through the object, and the intention may have been to complete the drilling process from one face only. In all cases, the bases of the partial perforations are smoothly concave in profile, suggesting that a solid rather than a tubular bit had been used.

BONE AND ANTLER MACEHEADS

Eight objects which might be considered maceheads are made from red deer antler or cetacean bone. Anna Ritchie describes the two examples which she recovered from the Knap of Howar as 'hammers' (1983, 77), implying a rather more utilitarian function, while others might be axehead or adze sleeves, as suggested by Piggott for the Skara Brae find (1954, 333), although this appearance could be the result of the more rapid erosion and decay of the softer cancellous tissue.

Other than in their hafting perforations, the three cetacean bone pieces show considerable variety in form, and the fragments of whalebone from which they have been manufactured are too small and too extensively worked to indicate which portions of the animals' skeletons had been utilised. The five antler specimens appear to have been made from tine and beam fragments, rather than from the crown, in contrast to most Late Neolithic English specimens. Few of the Orcadian examples resemble stone forms, with the possible exception of the antler and whalebone pieces from the Knap of Howar, which bear a superficial resemblance to the so-called Orkney type of Pestle maceheads. The remainder are of elongated form, similar to English examples from both Late Neolithic contexts (Mortimer 1905, 77, Figure 152), and Wessex Group graves (e.g. Lambourne, Berkshire: Greenwell 1980).

In Orkney, five of the maceheads are from domestic contexts in the settlements at the Knap of Howar and Skara Brae. The sixth came from an unspecified location within the Maes Howe-type passage tomb of Quanterness, and a mattock-like example was found in the lower compartment of a double-decker cist containing two cremations and a juvenile inhumation at Crantit, Kirkwall (Cursiter 1910). The final example, from the Skaill collection (No 74), has no archaeological association or specific findspot and, in publishing it, Callander was cautious in ascribing it to the Neolithic period, pointing out that similar objects had been recovered from brochs (1931, 96). Indeed, one cannot dismiss the possibility that it is a tool handle dating to the later prehistoric/Early Historic period.

The dating of these finds is loose and problematic. At the Knap of Howar, radiocarbon determinations obtained from samples thought to be contemporary with the whalebone objects were considered unreliable by the excavator (A. Ritchie 1983, 57), whilst at Skara Brae the antler macehead from Childe's House 9 (1931a, 60) has only the presumed *termini ante quos* date range of 3030–2775 CAL-BC (BIRM-788) to 2470–2135 CAL-BC (BIRM-433) (D.V. Clarke 1976a; 1976b; Renfrew and Buteux 1985). Furthermore, at Quanterness, where the find context is uncertain, there is a broad span of dates from 3515–3270 CAL-BC (Q-1294) to 2465–2290 CAL-BC (SRR-755) (Renfrew 1979; Renfrew and Buteux 1985).

OVOID MACEHEADS

Only ten definite and possible examples (six complete and four fragments, broken at the perforation) belong to this group. None has been recovered from an archaeological context, although two broken examples are among the stray finds from the Bockan/Bookan farms which also included Cushion and Pestle forms. The distribution is unremarkable, with seven recorded from the Mainland and the remainder from Sanday and Westray.

PESTLE MACEHEADS

These are the most numerous of the Orkney maceheads, represented by a total of twenty-seven examples. A high percentage (nineteen examples) are fragmentary, generally broken across the perforation, and their condition makes precise classification and in particular metrical grouping difficult in a number of cases, so that some may in fact belong to the Ovoid or Proto-Cushion types. In her study of Pestle maceheads, Roe (1968) divided them into Orkney and Thames types on the basis of the profile, the former being concave and the latter straight-sided. Ironically, using such criteria, the Thames type is the most frequent in Orkney, and in view of this the distinction has been abandoned in this chapter (although retained for descriptive convenience in the Catalogue).

Six specimens were recovered from archaeological sites: four from settlements and two from megalithic tombs. The complete macehead from the Bay of Stove, Sanday (No 16), came from a settlement site of uncertain character although including a substantial length of dry-stone walled structure (Lamb 1980, No 70). As for the Tofts Ness specimen (No 10), full details of its findspot will be presented in Hunter et al. forthcoming. The fragment from Rinyo (No 60), described by Roe (1968, 153) as an Ovoid, was found in the doorway of House 6 (i.e. 'K') belonging to Childe's third occupation phase. A fragmentary late Beaker came from the same horizon. The precise chronology of the Rinyo settlement is uncertain, with only a single uncontexted radiocarbon date of 2465–2220 CAL-BC (Q-1226) (Renfrew and Buteux 1985). The Skara Brae find (No 61) was recovered from the site prior to Childe's excavation, and its precise context is uncertain, although Piggott (1954, 331) saw no reason to dissociate it from some phase of the settlement.

The remaining two finds are of particular interest in that they are the only stone maceheads in Orkney to have come from chambered tombs; neither, however, was directly associated with the burial deposits, and both relate to episodes late in the tombs' use. At Isbister, the intact macehead (No 7) was part of a cache found in the scarcement of the tomb (Hedges 1983, 45) which included three axeheads, a knife and a jet V-perforated button, possibly contained in a bag (P.R. Ritchie 1959, 32). Morphologically, Isbister appears to include features of both cellular tomb and Stalled cairn, the link with the latter being reinforced by the occurrence of Unstan bowls, whereas the very large number of fragmentary human remains is paralleled in the Maes Howe-type tomb of Quanterness. The three broken but joining macehead fragments (No 8) from the lower Bookan type tomb at Taversoe Tuick were found just inside the kerbstone in the lower passage (Henshall 1963, 238). The only other Pestle macehead which has been recovered from an archaeological context is the broken example from the west tomb beneath the great mound of Knowth 1 in the Boyne Valley (Eogan and Richardson 1982). Like the Orkney examples, it too was not directly associated with the funerary deposits but was found outside the outermost sill-stone in the passage. Similarly, the Ovoid macehead from the Clyde tomb of Tormore 1, Arran (Henshall 1972, 372), did not apparently accompany human remains but was found with part of a Grooved Ware vessel, edge-polished knife and two plano-convex flint knives. A second Ovoid macehead from the Camster-type passage tomb of Ormiegill, Caithness, was again from a late context in an ash layer which also included an edge-polished knife (Henshall 1963, 284).

CUSHION MACEHEADS

Members of this group have been considered the most accomplished of the macehead series, and their characteristics were described by W.J. Gibson (1944). Roe (1979, 30) saw them as a development from the Ovoid group via increasingly elongated and narrow forms, 'Proto-Cushion' maceheads, which she believed not to be numerically important. Gibson drew attention to the concentration of finds in Orkney, and indeed, since he wrote, the numbers from the area have grown considerably. In all, twenty-one definite and possible Cushion and Proto-Cushion maceheads are known from Orkney. This number includes the recently-discovered broken example and fragment from the settlement at Barnhouse, Stenness (Nos 11, 14).

Gibson remarked upon the similarity in greatest breadth between several widely-scattered examples in Britain and raised the possibility of their manufacture by a single craftsman or workshop (1944, 18). However, in Orkney there are only five complete examples of the classic Cushion type, and although three of them share the same maximum width dimension, they vary in length from 135 mm (Grind, No 15) to 98 mm (Orphir, No 22). Such variability, and the very small sample, make inferences in terms of origin difficult even within Orkney. (See, however, P.R. Ritchie this volume, Chapter 16, for a discussion of the raw materials used for Cushion maceheads.)

Only three examples have come from archaeological contexts, and all, interestingly, are domestic. Least certain is the complete macehead from Smoogro, Orphir (No 18), said to have 'come from a kitchen midden'. A fragment was recovered from the midden behind House 6 at Barnhouse (No 11) and an even smaller fragment came from the uppermost midden at Skara Brae (Roe 1979, Figure 9l). Radiocarbon dates for this layer range from 2705–2370 CAL-BC (BIRM-434) to 2470–2135 CAL-BC (BIRM-433) (D.V. Clarke 1976a, 1976b; Renfrew and Buteux 1985). Outside Orkney, the only other Cushion macehead from an archaeological context is from Site 2 at Dorchester, Oxfordshire, with a cremation, bone skewer pin and a flint flake and fabricator (Atkinson, C.M. Piggott and Sandars 1951, 114 and Figure 31, 115–16).

THE KNOBBED MACEHEAD FROM SKARA BRAE

This was found by Petrie (1868) on the floor of House 3 in the second settlement. An almost identical object, but imperforate, came from St Thomas' Kirk, Rendall (Callander 1931, 96, Figure 19), and a second unperforated example came from Stenness. The Skara Brae specimen (No 9) bears no resemblance to any other macehead-type in Britain. Its extremely narrow and exaggerated hourglass-shaped perforation suggests that it was never intended to be mounted on a handle. Its links therefore are not with the mainstream macehead series, but rather with the imperforate spiked and knobbed objects from Skara Brae (e.g. Childe 1931a, plates 37.4, 39.1) and Quoyness (Henshall 1963, 247) and in the wider series of carved stone balls (Marshall 1977; see also Edmonds this volume, Chapter 14). As with these objects, the Skara Brae knobbled macehead is complete and undamaged, whereas the maceheads tend to be fragmentary. Might this have significance in terms of the iconography of the objects?

MACEHEAD ORIGINS

W.J. Gibson (1944) had suggested an origin for some at least of the Cushion maceheads in Orkney, an attribution based on metrical similarities rather than petrology. Indeed, as has been argued above, geological considerations throw little light on the specific origins of the source material, as the majority of Early maceheads in northern Britain appear to have been made from cobbles from drift or beach deposits. The idea that Orkney may be one of the centres of macehead production – at least as far as the Pestle and Cushion types are concerned – might receive some support from the very large number of examples of these types from the islands, very much higher for the land area than anywhere else in Britain. One must, however, distinguish between the location where the *concept* for a particular type arose and that where the examples of that product are most numerous; the two are not necessarily coincident. Indeed, if an origin for some types is to be seen in crown antler maceheads (as Roe suggested for Maesmawr-type Ovoid specimens: 1968, 162), then Orkney must be excluded on the present evidence. Until more maceheads are recovered from datable contexts and the techniques of high-precision radiocarbon dating are applied to suitable samples, the pinpointing of any one area in northern or southern Britain for the primacy of the type must remain entirely speculative.

MACEHEADS AND RITUAL

Maceheads, particularly those of the Cushion, Pestle and Maesmawr varieties in the Early series, appear to be ritual and/or high-status objects as reflected in the frequent use of relatively intractable materials such as igneous rock, quartz or flint for their manufacture, the choice of attractively-veined or coloured stone, the care and effort expended in their execution and their inclusion as grave goods with other prestige objects in Late Neolithic contexts (Kinnes 1979). Why then do they appear solely in Orkney (apart from the single example made of red deer antler from Northton, Harris: D.D.A. Simpson 1976), in domestic contexts on settlement sites?

The explanation may lie in the ambivalent function of these sites as both settlements and places for ritual or ceremonial acts. At Skara Brae this is suggested by the stone balls, the enigmatic spiked and multi-knobbed objects (including the 'macehead') and the peculiar use of midden material in the construction of the later 'village', echoing the ritual use of 'rubbish' elsewhere (cf. Case 1969; S. Piggott 1962; I.F. Smith 1971). Ritual elements are also apparent in the partially-excavated Links of Noltland on Westray, with the deposition of red deer carcasses, the deliberate back-filling of at least one structure, and the structured deposition of artefacts within this fill (D.V. Clarke and Sharples 1985). Furthermore at Barnhouse, Stenness, settlement and ceremonial centre appear to be as one, as expressed in the large building, Structure 8, standing within its own massive walled enclosure to the south of the main settlement (Richards 1989, 1990). Richards has suggested that its large central 'hearth' echoes the central feature of the Stenness henge (J.N.G. Ritchie 1976). A further possibility to be considered is the movement of 'ritual' objects such as maceheads and stone balls between tomb and settlements, in a manner analogous to the moving of human bones between tombs (Richards 1988), which could account for the presence of some of these in a domestic context which might otherwise be more at home in a funerary or ceremonial one.

MACEHEADS: ORKNEY AND IRELAND

Maesmawr-type maceheads are unrepresented in Orkney, but a link may exist in the source of decoration on the remarkable flint macehead from the east tomb beneath the great mound of Knowth 1, Co. Meath (Eogan and Richardson 1982). The facetting links it with the Maesmawr group, but the curvilinear ornament, in particular the conjoined spiral motif on face 1 (ibid., Figure 49), is difficult to parallel exactly among passage tomb carvings in Ireland. Comparisons were initially made with some of the designs on the Calderstones, Liverpool. The nature of the monument from which these stones came is uncertain, although it may have been a passage tomb, and the antiquity of some of the carvings is questionable (Twohig 1981, 228). The closest parallels, however, lie in Orkney in the possible lintel stone over the entrance to the damaged Maes Howe-type tomb at Pierowall on Westray (Sharples 1984; this volume, back cover), and on a second decorated stone from Eday Manse which may again have come from a destroyed passage tomb (D.V. Clarke, Cowie and Foxon 1985, 53, Figure 3.14).

From the west tomb at Knowth site 1 comes a broken Pestle macehead, the only Early type which is at all common in both Ireland and Orkney (D.D.A. Simpson 1988, 31). Their appearance in Ireland may very well reflect contact with Orkney, although the precise mechanics of such a link are difficult to determine (cf. Bradley and Chapman 1986). General architectural similarities between Irish and Orcadian passage tombs are apparent in such shared features as cruciform chamber plan, a larger cell to the right of the main chamber, and complex mound construction, in some cases involving near-vertical dry-stone-walled revetments (ibid., 35). Furthermore, one might perceive a parallel series of events towards the end of the tomb-building sequence in the two areas. The enclosing of the monument at Maes Howe by a possibly later earthwork (Sharples 1985) might be equated with the similar enclosure of Newgrange by a ring of standing stones, while the collapse of the revetment of the latter might be the result of deliberate slighting rather than of M.J. O'Kelly's (1982, 73) postulated earthquake activity, and therefore similar to the events associated with some Maes Howe tombs. Roe has argued (1968, 155) that Early series maceheads belong to a 'Macehead Complex', whose components include a range of artefacts most frequently associated with Grooved Ware. This pottery has only recently been recognised in Ireland, and the findspots are as yet few but perhaps significant as they include Knowth (Eogan 1984, 312), Newgrange (M.J. O'Kelly, F.M. Lynch and C. O'Kelly 1978, 111–31), and the Grange Circle at Lough Gur (Waddell 1974, 33). Radiocarbon dates suggest that the appearance of Grooved Ware in Orkney was not later than c. 3100 BC; it is probably later in Ireland, as may be the hengiform enclosures. Thus, one appears to have passage tombs earlier in the Boyne Valley and later in Orkney, but henges and settlements with Grooved Ware earlier in Orkney than in Ireland (and indeed perhaps earlier than in southern Britain). Maceheads, Grooved Ware and hengiform enclosures may be part of a 'package' similar to that suggested for the appearance of Beakers in Britain, but, perhaps significantly, the impact of the latter was slight in Orkney and of limited extent in Ireland.

LATE SERIES

Only four maceheads fall into this category, including the find from the Broch of Lingro, Kirkwall (No 64), which cannot be traced in the Hunterian Museum but, from the sketch on the record card, appears to belong to the Bush Barrow series. Similar specimens are from Birsay (No 27) and Heatherbank, Westray (No 35). The former's squat profile is unusual for a Bush

Barrow macehead, being more characteristic of the Ovoid series, although the central perforation suggests a late date. The only Orcadian member of the Largs group is the remarkable object from Rousay (No 20), polished at both ends but with the main body of the object covered with close pecking. None of these maceheads has been recovered from a dateable context in Orkney, but elsewhere they have been recovered from funerary contexts with Wessex and Cordoned and Collared Urn associations (Roe 1979). Battle axes are also rare in Orkney, only five examples including miniature forms being recorded by Fenton (1988, 121). The full-size versions are Northern Variants in the Late series and therefore broadly contemporary with the maceheads. Early battle axes tend to have Beaker associations, and their absence from Orkney would appear to equate with the slight Beaker presence there. Extensive Early Bronze Age activity in Orkney has yet to be recorded or recognised (Øvrevik 1985), but some material suggests the presence of high-status individuals, as are the battle axes and maceheads; notable among this material is the dagger from Wasbister and the amber and gold finds from the bell barrow in the Knowes of Trotty cemetery. The trace elements in the gold of the four discs link it with a series of ribbed sheet-gold dagger-pommel mounts (Taylor 1983), all but one of these from graves in Scotland (Henshall 1968). The exception is that from the Food Vessel cairn on Topped Mountain, Co. Fermanagh (Plunkett and Coffey 1898). A final Irish connection is suggested by the pecked Largs-type macehead from Rousay. The only known parallels for this peculiar treatment of a macehead are two Largs-type maceheads from Dunluce Castle, Co. Antrim, and Blessington, Co. Wicklow (D.D.A. Simpson 1991).

ACKNOWLEDGEMENTS

Grateful thanks are extended to Dr Euan MacKie, Dr Alison Sheridan, Mr Trevor Cowie and Mrs Anne Brundle for granting every facility to examine and draw maceheads in their collections. Information concerning unpublished material from recent excavations was generously provided by Ms Ann Clarke, Mr Steve Dockrill and Mr Colin Richards, and additional illustrations were provided by Ms Marion O'Neil and Ms Jane Downes. Macroscopic petrological identifications of a number of the maceheads were kindly undertaken by Dr Callum Firth (the Tankerness House material), Dr Graham Durant (the Hunterian Museum material) and Dr Alex Livingstone (the National Museums of Scotland material).

CATALOGUE

Note: the Catalogue numbers refer to the illustration numbers (Figures 17.3 to 17.9) and to those on the distribution map (Figure 17.1). All the illustrations were drawn from the originals except Nos 10 and 11, which were based on sketches kindly supplied by the excavators, and Nos 7, 9, 71, 73 and 74, which were based upon published illustrations. No 49 is drawn from a colour

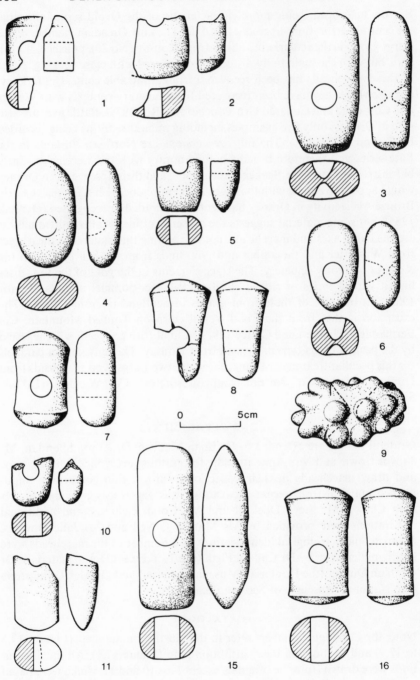

Figure 17.3: Orkney maceheads.

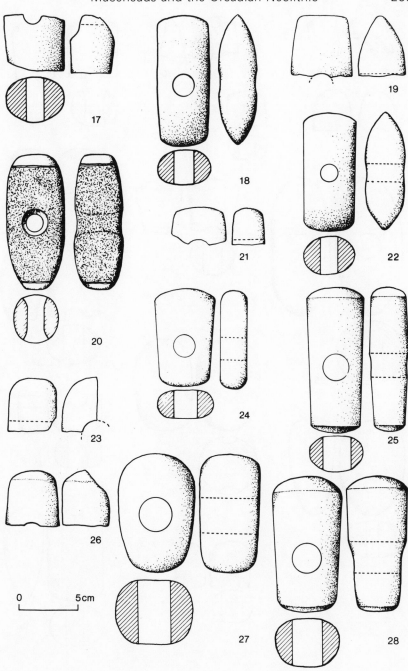

Figure 17.4: Orkney maceheads.

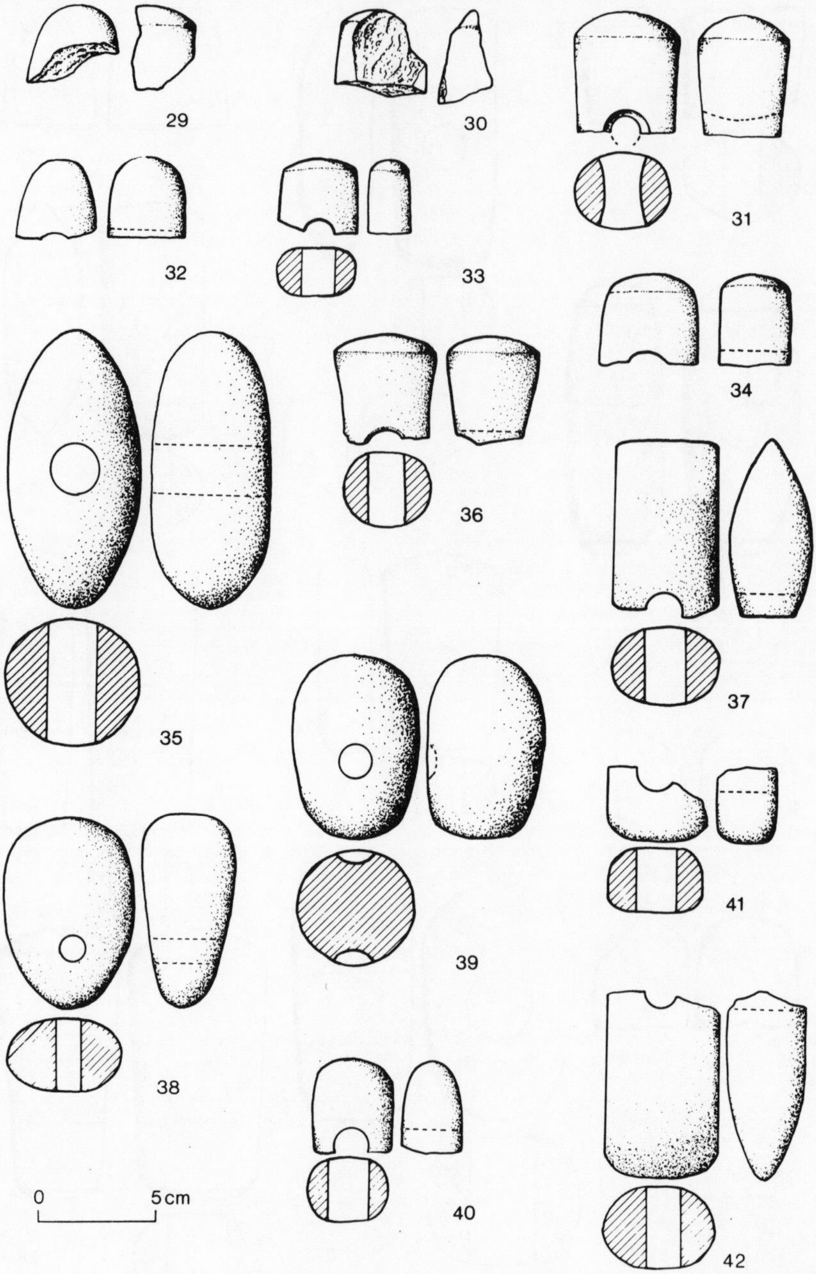

Figure 17.5: Orkney maceheads.

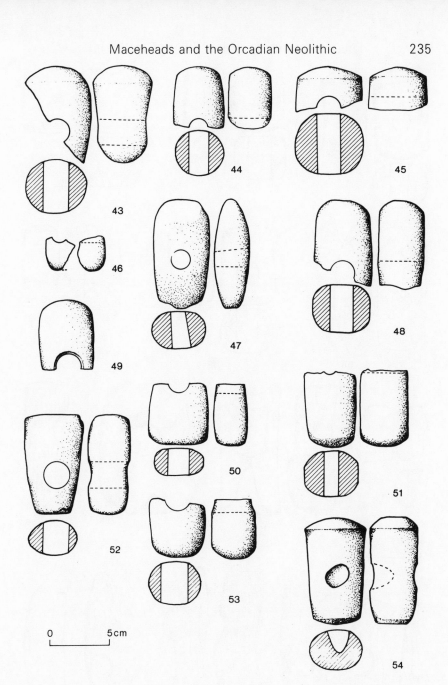

Figure 17.6: Orkney maceheads.

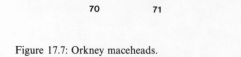

Figure 17.7: Orkney maceheads.

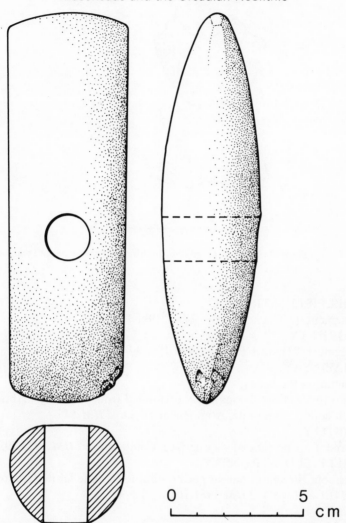

Figure 17.8: Cushion macehead (No. 75) from the Skaill collection.

transparency. A number of maceheads recorded in museum collections could not be located when the catalogue was being compiled; these are included in the catalogue but not illustrated. Each entry is ordered as follows: Provenance; Find Circumstances (where known); Type, Petrology and Collection; References. The following abbreviations have been used: *Hunt* – Hunterian Museum, Glasgow University; *Marischal* – Marischal Museum, Aberdeen University; *NMS* – National Museums of Scotland, Edinburgh; *Stromness* – Stromness Museum, Orkney; *THM* – Tankerness House Museum, Kirkwall, Orkney.

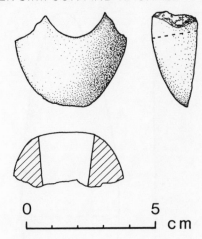

Figure 17.9: Fragment of Ovoid macehead (No. 76) from near the Stones of Stenness.

1. MILLFIELD, STRONSAY.
   Fragment. (?)Thames Pestle. *THM* 1981.164.
2. (?)ORKNEY.
   Fragment. ?Thames Pestle. *THM* 1985.134.
3. SHAPINSAY.
   'Found on the beach.'
   (?)Proto-Cushion. Incompletely perforated from both sides. Abraded at both ends. Camptonite, from igneous dyke. *THM* 546.
4. SANDAY.
   Ovoid. Part-perforated on one face. Camptonite. *THM* 1985.79.
5. MILLFIELD, STRONSAY.
   Cushion. Broken in half at perforation. Riebeckite felsite (according to *THM* Catalogue). *THM* 1981.163.
6. SANDAY.
   Ovoid. *THM* 52.
7. ISBISTER, SOUTH RONALDSAY.
   From cache against internal dry-stone wall of cairn.
   Orkney Pestle. Amphibolite. *Private coll.* Hedges 1983; J.L. Davidson and Henshall 1989.
8. TAVERSOE TUICK, ROUSAY.
   In chambered tomb.
   Orkney Pestle. Broken; three fragments survive. Amphibole-plagioclase gneiss. *NMS* EO 378. J.L. Davidson and Henshall 1989.
9. SKARA BRAE, SANDWICK.
   From House (found during excavations begun in 1861).
   Knobbed macehead. *NMS* HA 658. S. Piggott 1954, Figure 53.6.

10. TOFTS NESS, SANDAY.
  From settlement.
  Thames Pestle. Broken in half at perforation. Awaiting decision by Finds Disposal Panel. Hunter et al. forthcoming.
11. BARNHOUSE, STENNESS.
  From midden behind House 6.
  Cushion. Broken at perforation. Banded mudstone. Awaiting decision by Finds Disposal Panel.
12. BARNHOUSE, STENNESS.
  In ploughsoil.
  Unclassified. Unfinished. Hornfelde schist. Awaiting decision by Finds Disposal Panel.
13. BARNHOUSE, STENNESS (not illustrated).
  Fragment. Unclassified. (?)Gneiss. Awaiting decision by Finds Disposal Panel.
14. BARNHOUSE, STENNESS (not illustrated).
  In ploughsoil.
  Fragment. (?)Cushion. Volcanic rock. Awaiting decision by Finds Disposal Panel.
15. GRIND, TANKERNESS, ST. ANDREWS.
  Cushion. *THM* 1985.66.88. W.J. Gibson 1944, 25.
16. BAY OF STOVE, SANDAY.
  'Probably in an ancient structure.'
  Orkney Pestle. *Stromness*, unregistered. Roe 1979, 33, Figure 9k; Lamb 1980, No 70.
17. BOOKAN, SANDWICK.
  (?)Thames Pestle. Fragment. Acid gneiss. *NMS* AH 184. Callander 1931.
18. SMOOGRO, ORPHIR.
  'Found in a kitchen midden.'
  Cushion. Plagioclase amphibolite. *NMS* AH 152. W.J. Gibson 1944, 25.
19. LAMBANESS, SANDAY.
  Cushion. Broken at perforation. Quartz-amphibole-chlorite. *NMS* AH 33. Lamb 1980, No 236.
20. ROUSAY.
  Largs. Heavily pecked over central part of body. *NMS* AH 193.
21. BROUGH OF BIRSAY, BIRSAY.
  From House Site F.
  Proto-Cushion. Amphibolite. *NMS* HB 600. Curle 1982, Figure 600.
22. ORPHIR.
  Cushion. Basalt or basaltic andesite. *NMS* AH 42. W.J. Gibson 1944, 25.
23. BOOKAN, SANDWICK.
  (?)Ovoid. Fragment broken at perforation. Muscovite-granite. *NMS* AH 183. Callander 1931.

24. ORKNEY.
   Proto-Cushion. Microgranite. *NMS* AH 119.
25. BLOODY QUOY, DEERNESS.
   Proto-Cushion. Plagioclase amphibole. *NMS* AH 89. *Proc Soc Antiq Scotl* 23 (1889–90), 16, No 22.
26. WEST PULDRITE, EVIE.
   'In a field.'
   Thames Pestle. Fragment. Basic gneiss. Very heavily weathered: appears to have been water-rolled. *NMS* AH 254.
27. NEAR BIRSAY.
   Ovoid. Polished clayslate (old geological identification). *NMS* AH 131.
28. EGILSAY.
   Proto-Cushion. *NMS* AH 186. Lamb 1982, No 155.
29. RINYO, ROUSAY.
   From settlement.
   Unclassifiable. Fragment. Amphibole plagioclase. *NMS* HDA 126.
30. BOCKAN, SANDWICK.
   Unclassifiable. Fragment. Chalcedony. *NMS* AH 180. Callander 1931.
31. GRIND, TANKERNESS.
   'In a peat moss.'
   Orkney Pestle. Plagioclase microgranite. *NMS* AH 157.
32. BOOKAN, SANDWICK.
   (?)Ovoid.
33. BOCKAN, SANDWICK.
   (?)Proto-Cushion. Impure banded quartzite. *NMS* AH 177. Callander 1931.
34. BOCKAN, SANDWICK.
   (?)Proto-Cushion. Fine-grained gabbro(?). *NMS* AH 181. Callander 1931.
35. HEATHERBANK, WESTRAY.
   Bush Barrow. Abraded at both ends. Microgranite with quartz phenocrysts. *NMS* AH 129. Lamb 1983, No 175; *Proc Soc Antiq Scotl* 42 (1907–8), 9; Roe 1979, 34, Figure 10E.
36. ORKNEY.
   Orkney Pestle. Quartz dolerite. *Marischal* Acc. No 125. Kenworthy 1977.
37. KIRKWALL, ST OLA.
   Cushion. Fragment broken at perforation. Cross-bedded sandstone. *Hunt.* B.1914.638.
38. NOLTLAND CASTLE, WESTRAY.
   Ovoid. *Hunt.* B.1914.554.
39. BIRSAY.
   Ovoid. Part-perforated from both sides. *Hunt.* B.1914.554.

40. KINGSDALE, FIRTH.
Ovoid. Fragment broken at perforation. Diorite (hydrothermally altered and weathered). *Hunt*. B.1914.569.

41. BINSCARTH, FIRTH.
(?)Thames Pestle. Fine-grained basic gneiss. *Hunt*. B.1914.630.

42. YARPHA, ORPHIR.
Cushion. Fragment broken at perforation. *Hunt*. B.1914.604.

43. MUSSAQUOY, DEERNESS.
Ovoid. Broken at perforation. Granite gneiss. *Hunt*. B.1914.643.

44. YARPHA, ORPHIR.
Thames Pestle. Fragment broken at perforation. Megapegmatite. *Hunt*. B.1914.605.

45. HALLEY, DEERNESS.
(?)Thames Pestle. Fragment broken at perforation. Metabasalt. *Hunt*. B.1914.558.

46. HARRAY.
Unclassified. Fragment. Microgranite. *Hunt*. B.1914.588.

47. FIRTH.
Cushion. Metagabbro. *Hunt*. B.1914.580.

48. WHITLID, STRONSAY.
Thames Pestle. Metagabbro. *Hunt*. B.1914.834.

49. CUWEEN HILL, FIRTH.
Near Maes Howe-type passage tomb.
Thames Pestle. Granite. *Private coll.*

50. TANKERNESS, ST ANDREWS.
Thames Pestle. *THM* 113.

51. ST MAGNUS CATHEDRAL, ST OLA.
Found in use as a doorstop.
Thames Pestle. Camptonite, from a dyke(?). *THM* 1979.219.

52. CRANTIT, ST OLA.
Proto-Cushion. Gneiss. *THM* 214.

53. TANKERNESS, ST ANDREWS.
Thames Pestle. Camptonite. *THM* 66.

54. LIGHTHOUSE, NORTH RONALDSAY.
Orkney Pestle. Very irregular perforation begun on one side only. Metamorphic rock. *THM* 1976.231. Lamb 1980, No 253.

55. STENNESS.
'From a cist.'
Orkney Pestle. *Stromness* A187.

56. (?)ORKNEY.
Thames Pestle. Gneiss. *THM* 1983.212.

57. ORKNEY.
Thames Pestle. Granodiorite. *Stromness*, unregistered.

58. SKARA BRAE, SANDWICK.
From uppermost midden.
Cushion. Fragment. Gneiss. *NMS*, unregistered. Roe 1979, 33, Figure 9l;
I.F. Smith 1979, 15.

59. DOUNBY, BIRSAY OR SANDWICK.
(?)Thames Pestle. Fine-grained banded basic metamorphic rock,
probably an amphibole-plagioclase. *NMS*, unregistered.

60. RINYO, ROUSAY.
Thames Pestle. Broken at perforation. Garnet-amphibole-plagioclase.
NMS HDA 278.

61. SKARA BRAE, SANDWICK.
No specific provenance; among material donated to NMAS in 1914.
(?)Thames Pestle. Fragment. Hornblende schist. *NMS* HA 173.

62. ROUSAY (not illustrated).
Unclassified. Fragment. Fine-grained gabbro(?). *NMS*, unregistered.

63. SANDAY (not illustrated).
Thames Pestle. Diorite. *Hunt*. B.1914.813.

64. BROCH OF LINGRO, ST OLA (not illustrated).
Bush Barrow. Unfinished perforation. *Hunt*. B.1914.667. Missing.

65. 'MAINLAND' (not illustrated).
Unclassified. *Stromness* A.286. Missing. Note: this may be the specimen
listed as No 57 (Brundle personal communication).

66. HARRAY HILLS, HARRAY (not illustrated).
Unclassified. *Stromness* A.139. Missing. Note: this may be the specimen
listed as No 57 (Brundle personal communication).

67. KNAP OF HOWAR, PAPA WESTRAY.
From house.
Cetacean bone. *NMS* HD 2003. Traill and Kirkness 1937, 315, Figure 4.

68. KNAP OF HOWAR, PAPA WESTRAY.
From House 1. Primary midden in wall cove. Period I. Cetacean bone.
NMS, unregistered. A. Ritchie 1983, 79, Figure 14, 176.

69. KNAP OF HOWAR, PAPA WESTRAY.
From House 1. Primary midden in wall cove. Period I. Red deer antler.
NMS, unregistered. A. Ritchie 1983, 79, Figure 14, 189.

70. KNAP OF HOWAR, PAPA WESTRAY.
From house.
Red deer antler. *NMS* HD 2004. Traill and Kirkness 1937, 315, Figure
4.

71. SKARA BRAE, SANDWICK.
Hut 9.
Red deer antler. *NMS* HA 578. Childe 1931a, 60, Figure 17.

72. QUANTERNESS, KIRKWALL.
Maes Howe-type passage tomb.
Red deer antler. Fragmentary. *NMS*, unregistered. Renfrew 1979, 83,
Figure 35, 58.

73. CRANTIT, KIRKWALL.

Lower compartment of 'double-decker' stone cist with cremation and juvenile inhumation.

Red deer antler(?). Lost. Cursiter 1910.

74. ORKNEY.

Cetacean bone. *NMS* L.1933.2050. Note: currently also incorrectly labelled as HR 1314; from Skaill collection (Sheridan personal communication).

75. ORKNEY.

Cushion. *NMS* AH 255. Callander 1931, 95; W.J. Gibson 1944, 25.

76. STENNESS.

In ploughsoil. Ovoid. Fragment. Awaiting decision by Finds Disposal Panel.

18

Artefacts of Coarse Stone from Neolithic Orkney

Ann Clarke

INTRODUCTION

Artefacts of coarse stone are ubiquitous in prehistoric Orkney, and they form an important component of the surviving material culture from many sites. During the Neolithic in particular, stone was exploited to fulfil a wide variety of needs and its use pervaded many aspects of Neolithic life, from the quarrying of flagstone blocks as building stone to the manufacture of tools from beach cobbles for processing other raw materials. Stone was also used as a symbolic medium, as both structural slabs and hand-tools were decorated with linear patterns while other pieces were sculpted into complex three-dimensional objects.

Given the widespread use of coarse stone and its capability for post-depositional survival in comparison to organic materials, it is surprising that there has been little interest in artefacts made of this material. This is perhaps due to archaeologists' perception of such objects as being rather crude and uninteresting while, until recently, the tendency to concentrate excavation on sites of a non-domestic nature has also meant that few large assemblages of coarse stone artefacts have been recovered. Those settlement sites which were excavated – Skara Brae and Rinyo (Childe 1931a; Childe and Grant 1939; 1947) – are unfortunately difficult to study in great detail owing to the lack of contextual information associated with the finds. Excavations in Orkney over the last twenty years have increased the number of known Neolithic domestic sites from two to seven (see Table 18.1), and consequently large amounts of well-recorded data have now been recovered. Since most of these excavations have not been fully published, it is not possible to refer to detailed contextual information in this chapter, and there will also be little reference to internal site phasing and comparative site chronology. There are also interpretative problems, as the nature of the contexts and the size of the excavated area vary considerably between sites. Both of these factors can cause differences in the types of artefacts recovered and the numbers found. This paper will concentrate on the basic characteristics of coarse stone

Table 18.1: Coarse stone artefacts by site.

Type	1	2	3	4	5	6	7
Skaill knives	9	10	1059	278	***	399	106
Cobble tools	68	25	23	51	**	67	28
Stone discs	–	1	158	12	**	35	1
Flaked cobbles	3	–	6	9		5	3
Grinders	–	4	–	–		1	1
Borers	–	7	–	–		1	–
Ground end tools	8	–	–	–		1	–
Spatulate tools	3	–	–	–		1	–
Multi-hollowed stones	6	–	–	–		1	–
Sculpted stones	–	–	–	–		4	–
Ground slabs	20	–	–	–		–	–
Mortars	1	–	1	–	*	2	1

Key: 1. Barnhouse, Mainland; 2. The Knap of Howar, Papa Westray; 3. Skara Brae, Mainland (1972–3 excavations only); 4. The Links of Noltland, Westray (West Midden trench only); 5. Rinyo, Rousay (no numbers available, *** dominant, ** frequent, * present); 6. Pool Sanday; 7. Tofts Ness, Sanday.

assemblages from Neolithic settlement sites and chambered tombs with reference to resources, artefact-type and use, and social attitudes of exploitation.

The artefact-types discussed below form the majority of the coarse stone tools and objects which have been recovered from Neolithic sites in Orkney. However, objects such as ground stone axeheads, maceheads, querns and quern rubbers are not included in this chapter (see D.D.A. Simpson and Ransom this volume, Chapter 17, for a discussion of maceheads in Orkney).

RESOURCES

In Orkney, the solid geology is composed mainly of extensive flagstone and sandstone beds which form the gently shelving landscape typical of the islands. These are exposed around the coastline and are eroded, first into blocks, and then worked further by the sea to form the numerous cobble beaches. The sedimentary rocks vary in character across the islands from the soft, yellow Eday sandstones to the harder, black Rousay flags, and differences in bedding structure produce a range of finely-laminated to more homogenous materials. Other raw materials come from the erosion of volcanic dykes and lavas, while stone such as amphibolite, granite and quartzite is present in the deposits of glacial till. The raw materials are thus readily available in block, slab or cobble form, the selection of which is dependent on intended use. There is no evidence from any of the Neolithic assemblages to suggest that coarse stone was directly quarried for artefacts as opposed to structural stone, and there is also no evidence for the use of imported coarse stone; the stone which was available immediately around the site would have been exploited for most of the artefacts discussed below.

The artefact-types which are present in significant quantities can be divided into three main groups: flakes; cobble tools; and stone discs.

The flakes are of three main types: flakes manufactured for use; flakes produced as a by-product of tool manufacture; and flakes produced as a by-product of tool use. Those flakes which are manufactured directly for use are more commonly known as Skaill knives. These are primary or sometimes secondary flakes of sandstone which are detached from a parent cobble by throwing the cobble against an anvil stone. This method was first noted by Petrie (1868), and the flakes were named after the Bay of Skaill in Orkney, near which Skara Brae is situated. The resultant flake has a characteristic crushed scar on the thick proximal end and it is often squat in shape, enabling it to be held comfortably in the palm of the hand, leaving free a long, useful edge (Figure 18.1). It is unlikely that these flakes were ever hafted. The size range is large, although in large assemblages flakes with weights of 40 g to 80 g are most numerous. Very few of the flakes have been retouched, with the original edge sufficing for most needs, and where secondary working is present this is often undistinguished (Figure 18.1, 1). Some of the flakes, around twenty per cent of each assemblage, have traces of macroscopic edge damage in the form of light flaking, snapping and rounding, and it is probable that most of this damage was formed as a result of the use of these tools (Figures 18.1, 2, 18.1, 3, 18.1, 4). Experimental work has shown that such flakes are very efficient as butchery tools (A. Clarke 1990), and, although the potential functional repertoire of such tools has not been fully explored, it is likely that their use was confined to the processing of fairly pliant substances, particularly as the sandstone is a fairly soft rock. There is very little evidence for the curation of these flakes, and they can be viewed as highly disposable items which may have been used only once before being discarded.

Those flakes which are present as by-products of tool manufacture and use are less easily recognisable but, in general, they are much smaller than Skaill knives and have a smaller cortical component. At Skara Brae (1972–3, 1977 excavations) and the Links of Noltland, where detailed recovery techniques such as wet-sieving were used, there is evidence for such flake debris to occur in quantity in the middens. This suggests that tools were either made or used on or near the midden, or else that the working debris was discarded onto the middens.

The cobble tools are unmodified prior to use, and they are classed according to the type and location of wear traces. These tools are most often made from sandstone cobbles, but materials such as granites, amphibolites and quartz often form a significant component, and this is a feature particularly of the Neolithic period. The characteristic wear patterns include

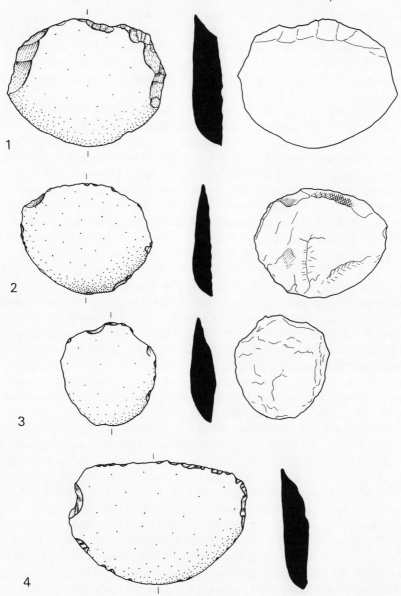

Figure 18.1: Skaill knives from the Links of Noltland, Westray. After pencil originals by M. O'Neil. Scale: 1:2

localised pecking on the faces and/or end faceting, as well as more random spreads of wear. Such tools can be used for a great variety of tasks from grinding and crushing to hammering, with each activity leaving characteristic wear traces. It is likely that many of the smaller cobbles which exhibit facial pecking and end facetting would have been used as hammerstones for flint knapping (A. Clarke forthcoming a).

A few cobbles have been modified prior to use by unifacial or bifacial flaking down one side to form a chopping edge (Figure 18.2, 1).

Large stone discs are another feature of Neolithic sites in the Northern Isles. They are made from shales or finely laminated sandstones, and have been chipped bifacially around the edge to shape. They are often large, but also have quite a wide size range. On many discs, it is possible to observe evidence of heat damage, often in the form of a reddish discoloration on the surface. From Pool, where a large number of stone discs were found, it was shown that this heat damage was most often located discretely around the edge on one or both faces of the disc, and that those which had been burnt were among the largest of the discs (A. Clarke forthcoming a). This suggests that the larger discs served as overhanging pot lids, used while the vessels were heated over the fire, whereas the smaller discs may have been associated with more permanent storage of materials in pots. Unfortunately, it was not possible to compare the diameters of the discs with those of the pots, as much of the pottery from this site was subject to post-depositional deformation (see MacSween this volume, Chapter 19).

Other artefact-types are present in much smaller numbers in comparison to the previous types. They tend to occur in small groups from an individual site, while at other sites they are represented by only a single piece.

From the Knap of Howar, there is a series of distinctive grinders and borers (A. Ritchie 1983), each of which has parallels from only two other sites. The borers are distinguished by the presence of an isolated, blunt, circular-sectioned knob on one end of the pebble, and it is likely that these were shaped before use (Figures 18.3, 2, 18.3, 3). Their function remains obscure, but the excavator noted that the direction of visible striations suggested their use as borers (A. Ritchie 1983, 56). The grinders are all very similar in form and size, having a smooth flat base and a domed upper face with discrete areas of pecking on both surfaces (Figure 18.3, 1). They are quite small tools, capable of being held in one hand, and it is likely that the flat base was formed prior to use; this distinguishes them from quern rubbers, which are not discussed here.

From Barnhouse, there are a number of artefacts which can be paralleled only at Pool. One type consists of a series of small, narrow, elongated pebbles, some of which have been ground down the sides but all of which have a ground end which may be blunted or faceted (Figures 18.4, 3, 18.4, 4). Another is the spatulate tool with a distinctive broad flat spatulate end formed on a small flat pebble (Figures 18.4, 1, 18.4, 2). Both types are small

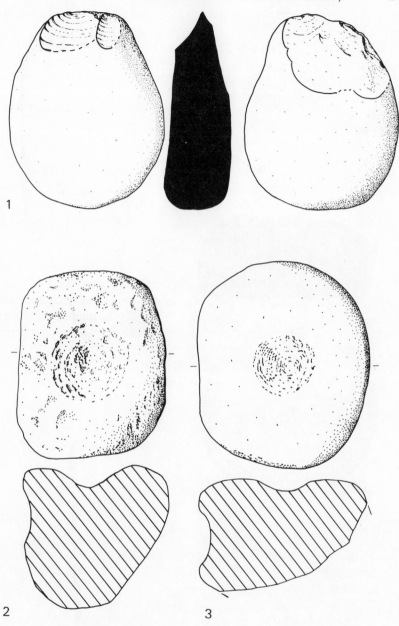

Figure 18.2: 1: Bifacially flaked cobble, Skara Brae; 2, 3: Multi-hollowed stones, Barnhouse.
Scale: 1:2.

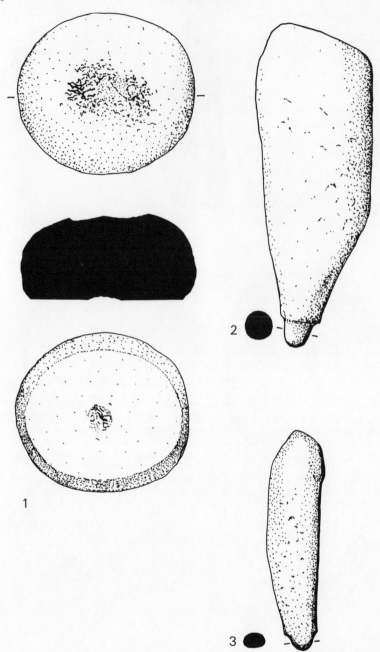

Figure 18.3: 1: Grinder; 2, 3: Borers. All from the Knap of Howar, Papa Westray. After
A. Ritchie 1983, Figures 15 and 16. Scale: 1:2.

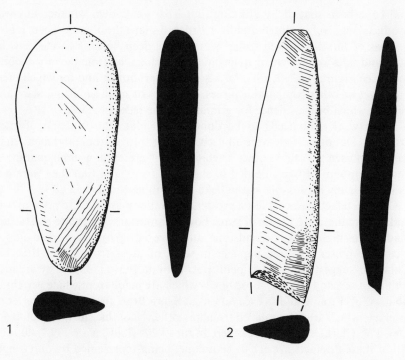

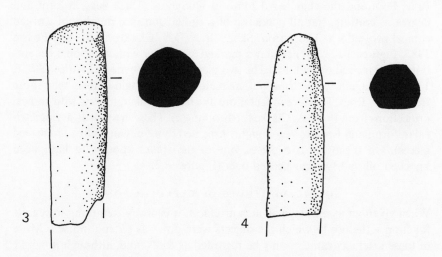

Figure 18.4: 1, 2: Spatulate tools; 3, 4; Ground end tools. All from Barnhouse. Scale: 1 : 1.

and have been shaped by grinding, but it is not known whether this was produced passively or intentionally in order to shape the objects. There is also a series of multi-hollowed stones which have deep hollows formed on the faces and sides and which are quite different in character from the other cobble tools (see Figures 18.2, 2, 18.2, 3). Also from Barnhouse, and for which there are as yet no other comparable pieces, is a series of small sandstone slabs and cobbles which bear evidence for grinding on the faces or sides.

Much work still needs to be done to elucidate the function of such artefacts. Doubtless they were all used as some form of tool, and many may have been used to fashion other artefacts. Their presence in small quantities, and the amount of work needed to shape them, suggest that they were not as immediately disposable as the flake and cobble tools.

Other artefact-types exhibit a greater amount of manufacture prior to use, and among these are the small stone bowls or mortars. These are most often made from small blocks of sandstone, and have a deep hollow worked on one face. The presence of red pigment in some of those from Skara Brae led Childe to suggest their use as paint pots (Childe 1931a, 134). They are also similar in size and form to those bowls which are made from whale vertebrae (ibid., 136). From Childe's excavations at Skara Brae, there is also a series of artefacts which are unparalleled from any other Neolithic site and even from David V. Clarke's excavations there in the 1970s (ibid., plates 39.2, 40, 41). All of these artefacts appear to be unique, being represented by only single objects, and some exhibit greater complexity in manufacture and form than is observed on the rest of the coarse stone assemblage. For the present, their functions must remain obscure.

Finally, there is a series of three-dimensional spiked objects from Skara Brae, Pool and the chambered tomb of Quoyness. These vary in form and degree of crafting, but all make use of a similar motif: a number of worked conical projections. Those from Skara Brae (D.V. Clarke, Cowie and Foxon 1985, Figures 3.22, 3.27) exhibit a marked symmetry with additional decoration either incised or sculpted. The two pieces from Quoyness (Figures 18.5, 1, 18.5, 2) are again symmetrical but are plainer and less rigid in form than those from Skara Brae. They are in fact more like the four plain objects with conical projections from Pool (A. Clarke forthcoming a). These are mostly asymmetrical in form, and two are very roughly executed (and may in fact be unfinished pieces). On the other two pieces, one of the spikes appears to have been knocked off and the scar pecked over (Figure 18.5, 3).

SOCIAL ATTITUDES OF EXPLOITATION

When given an assemblage of such artefacts, it is always tempting to regard function – the use to which the objects were put – as an end in itself. Most of these artefacts can certainly be regarded as tools, and, although it would be useful to have knowledge of their uses, it is unlikely that their full functional repertoire will ever be known. Even if a programme of experimen-

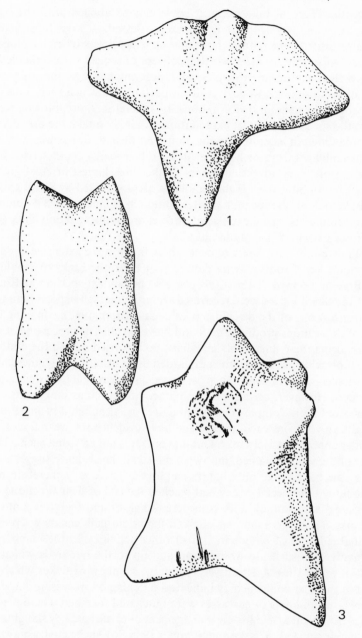

Figure 18.5: Sculpted objects. 1, 2: Quoyness, Sanday, after Henshall 1963; 3: Pool, Sanday.
Scale: roughly 1 : 2.

tal replication were to take place, it could not be applied until the basic patterns of assemblage formation had been assessed. A strict functionalist stance also attempts to reduce the rather ephemeral sets of archaeological data to a logical format. However, the concept of society is too complex to impose such reductionist principles, and over-emphasis on the utilitarian aspects of tool use tends to neglect the important role which such tools can play in observing social transformations. It is therefore more informative to examine the social attitudes of exploitation – that is, to take the broad view of how the different assemblages functioned in their widest sense.

The assemblages from each of the sites can be broadly characterised by a comparison of the relative frequencies of the three largest artefact groups (Table 18.1). All but two of the assemblages are dominated by Skaill knives, and cobble tools are frequent at all sites, although in much reduced numbers by comparison with the flake tools. Stone discs are frequent at only three sites and are not present at Barnhouse at all.

Skaill knives are most likely to occur in quantity in the extensive midden-deposits of a late Grooved Ware date, e.g. at Pool, the Links of Noltland, Skara Brae and Rinyo. These tools can also be context-specific: at Rinyo, most of the Skaill knives were recovered from the midden deposit filling the interior of just one of the dwellings (Childe and Grant 1947), while the first season of excavations produced no Skaill knives at all. The processing of raw materials using these flake tools may have been carried out on the middens and the tools which were used then discarded there. Alternatively, these tools and the associated debris may have been used elsewhere and then dumped on the midden. However, certain processing activities such as butchering may have involved more complex discard practices as, although a proportion of the Skaill knives from each assemblage have evidence for wear traces, the remainder appear relatively fresh and unworn. It is unlikely that such a large number of the tools remained unused, and instead the evidence suggests that many of the flakes were only lightly employed. These may therefore have been discarded not because they had reached the end of their functional life but perhaps because they were considered unclean and therefore unfit for further use. The large quantities of Skaill knives in middens may represent individual episodes of butchering, or of other activities, as the numbers of tools involved in such use would soon add up to the hundreds which are present at many sites. Alternatively, the large numbers of flakes which are present in the later contexts may indicate a batching of processing activities: perhaps large numbers of carcasses were butchered together. There is some evidence from Skara Brae for the management of cattle herds by slaughtering year-old animals (D.V. Clarke and Sharples 1985, 75); such activity may have been limited in time and space, thereby creating a concentration of tools and butchering waste.

The use of cobble tools remains fairly constant between the various assemblages, and this in part reflects the common practice of flint, chert or quartz knapping on all the sites.

The contrast in the occurrence of stone discs between sites is of interest. This may be a reflection of the different excavation of activity/depositional contexts, but, from Barnhouse, where extensive excavation was carried out, there are no stone discs at all. The presence of large numbers of stone discs compares with the dominance of Skaill knives at the sites of Skara Brae, Rinyo and Pool, and the majority of the discs are also associated with the latest middens from these sites. The discs are almost certainly associated with cooking or with storage in vessels and their varying representation in the assemblages has implications for the use of either different vessel coverage techniques or even of different cooking or storage strategies between the sites.

The assemblages can be differentiated further on the basis of the less common tool types, and in this respect the sites of Barnhouse, the Knap of Howar and Skara Brae stand out. Such differences could suggest that other types of processing activities were carried out at these sites, or that types of raw material other than coarse stone were used for these tools at other sites. It is unlikely that these patterns can be attributed directly to chronology: the houses at Barnhouse appear to be of the same period as the earlier houses at Skara Brae and Rinyo (Richards 1990), yet neither of the latter sites has the artefact-types which are specific to the assemblage at Barnhouse. Two of the artefact types, a spatulate piece and a ground end tool, do occur as single pieces in the latest Grooved Ware phase at Pool. The grinders and borers from the Knap of Howar which were thought, until recently, to be unique to an Unstan assemblage can now be paralleled by single pieces in later Grooved Ware contexts at Pool, Tofts Ness and the Links of Noltland. Thus, specific tools which are most frequent at the sites of the Knap of Howar or Barnhouse do appear at other sites in later contexts. As these artefacts are represented by only single objects, it could be argued that these were residual from earlier phases: Pool does have a phase of earlier Grooved Ware pottery similar to that found at Barnhouse (MacSween this volume, Chapter 19), and there is also an Unstan site under it from which the grinder and the borer may have derived. However, at Tofts Ness, there is no evidence for an Unstan pottery assemblage despite the presence of a grinder in the latest Neolithic phase. It is premature to characterise an Unstan coarse stone assemblage on the basis of only one excavated settlement site, particularly as there are great differences in artefact-types and quantity even amongst the six Grooved Ware assemblages.

The assemblage from Barnhouse is of interest, not only for its collection of tools which are uncommon to other sites but also for the lack of the most common Neolithic artefact-types. It could be argued that, being an inland site, the inhabitants of Barnhouse did not have immediate access to the abundant stone resources of the beaches and that other materials may have been substituted. However, the absence of extensive middens from this site and the scarcity of Skaill knives and stone discs could be closely associated, and point to great differences in activities between Barnhouse and the other Neolithic settlement sites. It is possible that certain types of raw material processing activities such as butchering, which were common to other Neolithic sites, were not carried out at Barnhouse at all.

Finds of coarse stone artefacts from chambered tombs are infrequent. At only nine tombs are such objects present (six Orkney-Cromarty, three Maes Howe type), and in most cases they are not directly associated with the use of the tomb but rather with infilling or external activity. Henshall has observed that artefacts of a specifically Grooved Ware type from Orkney-Cromarty tombs are only associated with filling and secondary activities (J.L. Davidson and Henshall 1989, 90). Finds of Skaill knives, cobble tools and stone discs are present in Orkney-Cromarty tombs, but these are not specific to either Grooved Ware or Unstan assemblages. The finds of ard points and flaked sandstone bars from these types of tomb are almost certainly derived from later activity (ibid., 80). It is interesting to note the presence of a lobate object from Taversoe Tuick which not only has parallels at Skara Brae (D.V. Clarke 1983) but is also similar to pieces from the Shetland sites of Jarlshof (Hamilton 1956), Sumburgh and Kebister (A. Clarke forthcoming c). These latter three sites are all Bronze Age, and the association of the lobate piece from Taversoe Tuick with a hollowed stone and a fragment of a slate cleaver raises the possibility that this deposit may also be assignable to post-Neolithic activity.

From the Maes Howe-type tombs, coarse stone artefacts appear to be more closely associated with the use of the tomb. From Quanterness, the cobble tools, worked flagstone, stone disc and quern rubber are like those artefacts found on most settlement sites, while from Cuween Hill there is a sandstone ball and from Quoyness there are two sculpted spiked objects and two stone discs, one of which is ground.

Coarse stone artefacts thus provide a surviving medium through which one can observe the cross-over of ritual and everyday practices. Objects which commonly occur on settlement sites are present in the tomb at Quanterness, while decorated objects, which are not tools as such, are also present in the tomb of Quoyness and at the settlement sites of Pool and Skara Brae. From Quoyness, there was also a small ground disc (Childe 1952), and a similar object was also recovered from Pool in the latest phase (A. Clarke forthcoming a). On two objects from Skara Brae, both functional and decorative worlds coincide: these are the Skaill knife and the ground edge flake, both of which have incised decoration on one face (A. Clarke, D.V. Clarke and Saville forthcoming). The former piece was recovered from a layer in the abandoned early phase house from which a set of other interesting artefacts were recovered (D.V. Clarke 1976a, 13). Until recently, it was supposed that Skara Brae was a special site inasmuch as some components of the material culture, particularly the decorative elements, were viewed as being of a non-domestic nature. With the presence of such similar objects from Pool, it is now less likely that the dichotomy of settlement and ritual sites can be maintained.

POST-NEOLITHIC ASSEMBLAGES FROM ORKNEY

The use of coarse stone for tools continued throughout the Bronze Age, and this period is characterised by the appearance of flaked sandstone bars (often referred to as chipped stone implements) and ard points. Such tools were in use during the Neolithic and Bronze Age in Shetland, where they are most certainly associated with arable activities; the ard points are stone shares for the simple ard plough (Rees 1986), while the flaked sandstone bars may have functioned as some form of mattock. Neither of these tools has been found in a Neolithic context from Orkney, despite clear evidence for ard marks at the Links of Noltland (D.V. Clarke and Sharples 1985, 73). It is possible that materials such as bone or wood were preferred for ard points during the Neolithic period in Orkney, although none survives. The selection of less durable raw materials than stone for arable tools may reflect the quality of the soil being cultivated, as at the Links of Noltland the ploughed soil was light and sandy (ibid., 72) while at Scord of Brouster on Shetland the soil was very stony (Romans 1986, 130) and would have been more easily cultivated by stone ard points. It is of interest that the first use of the stone ard points and flaked sandstone bars in Orkney was at the time when steatite vessels also appear in Orcadian funerary and settlement contexts. Outcrops of steatite are not present in Orkney, and its nearest source is Shetland (Sharman 1990). The presence on Orkney of both steatite and the new tool types in the Bronze Age may indicate a connection in this period between these islands and those of Shetland. The evidence from the metalwork of the Bronze Age, particularly in the later period, is also suggestive of contacts with Shetland (Øvrevik 1985, 143). Many of the cobble tools from Bronze Age sites are similar in form to those of the Neolithic period, while there is an increase in the use of bifacially-flaked cobbles and, at Tofts Ness, these form a distinct component of the whole assemblage (A. Clarke forthcoming a). Large stone discs and Skaill knives also continue in use on some sites.

The coarse stone assemblages from Iron Age sites are very similar to those of the same period from Shetland. Large and heavily worn cobbles are common to most assemblages, and are relatively easy to distinguish from the cobble tools of the preceding periods. Stone discs are much smaller in diameter than those of earlier periods, and probably encompassed a wider range of functions such as plugs and gaming counters as well as pot lids (Hamilton 1956). Hollowed stones, lamps, spindle whorls and perforated net-sinkers also appear, and the emphasis on stone tools for processing activities diminishes, although some Skaill knives are associated with Iron Age contexts, e.g. Tofts Ness (A. Clarke forthcoming a), Pierowall Quarry (Sharples 1984) and Calf of Eday (Calder 1939).

ANN CLARKE

CONCLUSIONS

Any study of material culture is hampered when only one aspect, in this case the coarse stone assemblage, is considered. Artefacts do not function on their own but are incorporated within the needs and requirements of society. To assess fully the role of coarse stone artefacts, it would be necessary, for example, to look at tools made from other raw materials, examine the evidence of butchery practices from the bone and compare the different types of soil which were cultivated. Unfortunately, it is not always possible to have access to such information, particularly as much of the organic evidence is subject to post-depositional alteration. It has been argued in this chapter that many aspects of Neolithic society can be explored through a consideration of the coarse stone artefact-types and their frequency and context of deposition. Since it is often only those assemblages of stone which survive with any integrity, then they must be viewed as a productive area of inquiry for any further work on the Neolithic of Orkney.

19

Orcadian Grooved Ware

Ann MacSween

INTRODUCTION

In his 1985 review article 'Circumstance not context: the Neolithic of Scotland as seen from the outside', Ian Kinnes summarised the fundamental problems which blight Scottish Neolithic pottery studies:

> Little work has been undertaken on fabric analyses so that no basis exists for speculation on wider exchange systems or further characterization of styles distinguished by form or decoration. [In] the absence of stratigraphic controls . . . relative chronology largely depends on the dangerous method of correlation with monuments and the available radiocarbon dates . . . The potential for regional analysis is here but . . . this is rendered even more difficult by the looseness of definitions involved (Sharples 1981, 39). These cannot be remedied until far more detailed study and classification is undertaken. (1985, 21–2)

One area which has suffered from the lack of a detailed study is Orkney, where two distinct pottery traditions, conventionally referred to as 'Unstan Ware' and 'Grooved Ware', have been recognised for the Neolithic. Although the two pottery styles are little understood, they are nevertheless included in any debate on either the development and chronology of Orcadian chambered tombs or the relationship between the cairns and other 'ritual' and domestic sites.

This chapter addresses some of the problems which Kinnes listed, with respect to Orcadian Grooved Ware, considering the stylistic details of the assemblages, Grooved Ware's relationship to Unstan Ware and the possibility of chronological differences among the Grooved Ware sub-styles.

The term 'Unstan Ware' has conventionally been used to refer to a series of plain and decorated round-based vessels, originally defined on the basis of the assemblages from Orcadian chambered tombs and named after the tomb at Unstan in Mainland Orkney (S. Piggott 1954, 248–9). Subsequent reassessments of the term (e.g. Henshall 1983b, Sharples 1981, MacSween forthcoming a) have resulted in disagreement over the homogeneity of 'Unstan Ware'. Since this chapter is not primarily concerned with the debate over the definition of 'Unstan Ware', the less contentious term 'round-based pottery tradition' will be used to distinguish this pottery from the flat-based 'Grooved Ware tradition'.

Grooved Ware has as its most common type a bucket-shaped vessel, decorated with either applied motifs or thick grooves incised into its walls. The decoration is usually restricted to the upper portion of a vessel. Stuart Piggott (1936, 191) was first to define Grooved Ware. He suggested that variants of one tradition could be recognised at sites as far apart as Clacton in Essex and Skara Brae in Orkney. Childe and Grant (1939, 24) accepted this north-south connection in discussing the pottery from their excavations at the settlement site of Rinyo on the Orcadian island of Rousay. Grooved Ware's wider distribution over southern Scotland was demonstrated by R.B.K. Stevenson (1946), W.L. Scott (1948) and Robertson-Mackay (1952).

Stuart Piggott (1954) proposed that the term 'Rinyo-Clacton Culture' should replace 'Grooved Ware Tradition', as he felt that elements apart from pottery, such as stone artefacts and house plans, were common to both the north and the south during the Later Neolithic. Isobel Smith (1956) and Wainwright and Longworth (1971) reverted to the use of the term 'Grooved Ware' arguing that although there are several sub-styles, 'the concept of a Rinyo-Clacton Culture was an overstatement of the evidence, and in retrospect rather misleading' (ibid., 236).

Others, for example David L. Clarke (1970, 268), have challenged the hypothesis that Grooved Ware represents a well-defined tradition of pottery manufacture. Clarke felt that the northern pottery developed from local Beacharra and Unstan traditions while the southern styles developed from the Fengate tradition.

Over the past twenty years, consideration of Unstan Ware and Grooved Ware from Orkney has focused more on their chronological relationship rather than on stylistic detail (e.g. Renfrew 1979, 205–8; J.L. Davidson and Henshall 1989, 64–78), probably due in part to the lack of large, well-stratified assemblages.

Recent excavations of domestic and funerary sites have, however, greatly increased the amount of Orcadian Neolithic pottery available for study. These sites comprise the settlements at the Knap of Howar, Papa Westray (A. Ritchie 1983), the Links of Noltland, Westray (D.V. Clarke, Hope and Wickham-Jones 1978; D.V. Clarke and Sharples 1985), Skara Brae (D.V. Clarke 1976a, 1976b) and Barnhouse (Richards 1989, 1990) in Mainland Orkney and Pool, Sanday (Hunter et al. forthcoming), and the chambered tombs at Isbister (Hedges 1983) and Quanterness (Renfrew 1979) in Mainland Orkney. The pottery sequence for Pool has been established (MacSween 1990), and is taken as the starting point for a review of Orcadian Grooved Ware.

THE POOL SEQUENCE

Between 1982 and 1988, excavations were carried out on the eroding settlement mound at Pool, Sanday, by Dr John Hunter of the University of Bradford on behalf of the then-named Scottish Development Department. Two main periods of occupation were identified, the earlier being Neolithic (4000–2000 BC) and the later being Iron Age (400–1200 AD).

In phasing the site, Hunter (Hunter et al. forthcoming) drew his divisions to reflect 'events' in the formation of the mound, which did not necessarily coincide with changes in settlement. The Neolithic deposits were divided into three phases: Phase 1, the earliest, a series of black tips; Phase 2, an overlying series of red tips; and Phase 3, a further series of black tips.

The Neolithic pottery assemblage comprised 10,000 sherds, representing a maximum 1,900 vessels. The pottery was studied independently of the phasing, and the phasing was not drawn up with respect to the pottery.

In the study, a morphological/technological approach was taken. This assumes that in recording change in a sequence, variations in manufacturing techniques and raw material choice are just as important as morphological changes.

At Pool, the Phase 1 occupation levels were only uncovered in the northern two square metres of the trench, and relatively little pottery (275 sherds) was recovered. Included in the assemblage are four sherds from decorated round-based bowls. Only two of the remaining Phase 1 sherds are decorated, one with cord impressions, the other with finger-impressions. The rim-types are either plain or flattened. No flat bases were recovered from either the Phase 1.1 or 1.2 contexts, the only identifiable basal sherd being from a round-based vessel. Over forty-five per cent of the sherds in Phase 1 are untempered, twenty per cent shell-tempered and the remainder are tempered with small amounts of gravel. Petrological analysis of local clays (MacSween 1990, 200–5) indicates that both primary clays, from the degrading cliff section adjacent to the site, and boulder clays were used.

The finer primary clays dominate the Phase 2 assemblage, and the majority of the pottery is shell-tempered. Although 'baggy' vessels (wide-mouthed vessels with slightly curving walls, around 12 cm in diameter at the rim, narrowing to around 5 cm at the base; see Figure 19.1) were recovered from contexts in Phases 2.2 and 2.3, flat-based vessels with straight-angled walls are most common. The latter have larger rim-diameters, averaging 20 cm and it appears that they were substantial, many having wall-thicknesses of over 1·5 cm. Plain, flattened and inverted rims, and rims with an internal bevel, are well represented. Incised decoration, confined largely to Phases 2.2 and 2.3, includes dots, chevrons and wavy lines.

The Phase 3 pottery differs from that of Phase 2 in fabric, form and decoration. Wares tempered with crushed sedimentary rock comprise seventy-five per cent of the assemblage. Clays with a substantial gravel

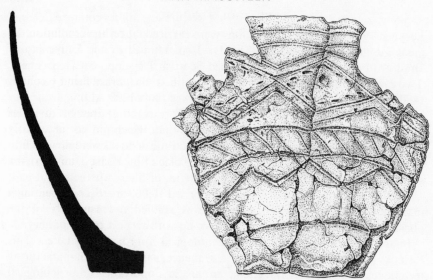

Figure 19.1: Vessel with incised decoration from Pool, Phase 2.

component, probably from glacial deposits (MacSween 1990, 200–5) were preferred. Only five per cent of the pottery is shell-tempered, and its contexts suggest that it is residual from Phase 2. The rock-tempered pottery is generally thinner-walled than the shell-tempered pottery of Phase 2, although the rim-diameters are similar. There are no baggy vessels, the common type being a bucket-shaped vessel. Decorative scalloped and notched rims appear (Figure 19.2), and applied decoration including ladder, lattice, trellis and fish-scale motifs is dominant. There is occasional incised decoration, but unlike the Phase 2 pottery, the incisions are deeper, true grooves, usually into a slip rather than into the vessel wall, and have been used as much to make the intervening areas stand out as to incise a pattern into the walls.

The Pool sequence, then, has three distinct assemblages, which can be distinguished on grounds of vessel morphology, decoration and fabric.

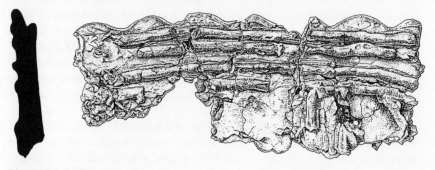

Figure 19.2: Scalloped rim with applied decoration from Pool, Phase 3.

Insofar as the small size of the Phase 1 assemblage allows comment, changes from Phase 1 to Phase 2 appear to represent gradual stylistic evolution. The Phase 3 assemblage, by contrast, differs in form, fabric, surface finish, technology and decoration.

That the ceramic changes from Phase 2 to Phase 3 are matched by a change in the nature of the tips suggests a hiatus in settlement, although the site's dating is not precise enough to indicate its length. A period of several decades, which would be long enough for the adoption of new potting techniques, would not be detected by radiocarbon or TL dating.

The Pool sequence is important for Orcadian Neolithic studies for two main reasons. First, it adds weight to the hypothesis that the round-based pottery tradition was in existence before Grooved Ware. Second, the simple round-based bowl/Grooved Ware dichotomy becomes complicated by the presence at Pool of a degree of technological and stylistic continuity between the round-based and flat-based pottery.

THE POOL SEQUENCE COMPARED WITH OTHER ORCADIAN NEOLITHIC ASSEMBLAGES

Pottery assemblages from other excavated Orcadian Neolithic sites were examined to determine whether the relationships noted in the Pool sequence could be recognised elsewhere. Although the assemblages from the funerary sites have been published and are synthesised in J.L. Davidson and Henshall (1989, 64–78), the only domestic assemblage to have been published fully is that from the Knap of Howar. Consequently, comments on the domestic assemblages from Rinyo, Skara Brae, the Links of Noltland and Barnhouse should be regarded as preliminary. Tables 19.1 and 19.2 summarise the main decorative and morphological attributes of the Grooved Ware assemblages cited in the text.

Comparisons with Pool Phase 1 pottery

Three Orcadian chambered tombs – Unstan (Clouston 1885), Taversoe Tuick ·(Henshall 1963, 234–6) and Isbister (Henshall 1983b) have produced large assemblages of round-based pottery. Shallow, collared, 'Unstan' bowls dominate each of these assemblages, but Henshall noted that other elements were more difficult to classify. She drew attention to a group of sherds from Isbister which, although apparently contemporary with the 'Unstan' bowls and other round-based pots, stood out because of their friability, the result of shell-tempering (ibid., 43). Among the shell-tempered pottery is a flat base which Henshall (J.L. Davidson and Henshall 1989, 77) suggested 'might be regarded as Grooved Ware, but the base is unusually narrow and thick'. The base closely resembles the 'baggy' vessels from Phase 2 at Pool. Again at Unstan and Taversoe Tuick, where both 'Unstan' bowls and a deeper, probably round-based form of bowl were found, a proportion of the assemblage was of a 'corky', presumably shell-tempered fabric (ibid., 166–7).

Table 19.1: Decorative motifs and their occurrence on Grooved Ware sites.

	1.	2.	3.	4.	5.	6.	7.	8.	9.	10.	11.	12.	13.	14.	15.
	≡	⋀⋀	∴	≈	◉	○	⫤	≋	⩘	═	═	⫸	‖‖	∞∞∞	∘∘
Pool 2	•	•	•	•		•									
Barnhouse	•	•	•	•			•	•	•						
Stenness	•	•		•											
Quanterness	•	•	•					•	•	•					•
Pool 3	•							•	•	•	•	•			
Links of Noltland	•							•	•	•	•	•	•		
Rinyo	•	•						•	•	•			•		•
Skara Brae	•				•	•		•	•	•				•	•
Raigmore, Inverness	•	•	•		•		•		•				•		
Knappers Farm, Dunbartonshire	•	•						•	•			•			
Balfarg, Fife	•	•					•		•	•	•				
Balfarg Riding School	•	•					•	•	•	•	•				
Tentsmuir/Brackmont, Fife	•	•							•	•	•				
Beech Hill House, Perthshire	•	•					•	•		•					
Luce Sands, Wigtown	•	•								•	•				
Yorkshire	•	•				•	•		•	•	•		•		
S. England	•	•							•	•	•		•		•

1. Incised parallel lines.
2. Incised chevrons.
3. Impressed dots.
4. Incised wavy lines.
5. Incised spirals.
6. Impressed finger-tip.
7. Linked cordons.
8. Wavy cordons.

9. Branching cordons.
10. Incised cordons.
11. Plain cordons.
12. Fish scale/trellis decoration.
13. Vertical panelling.
14. Chain-link cordons.
15. Bosses.

Henshall (1983a), in discussing the Knap of Howar assemblage, again distinguished between the more finely-made 'Unstan' bowls and a coarser range of pottery, much of the latter containing fragments of shell, both types occurring in each of the site's two phases. Round-based vessels dominate the assemblage, but two flat bases were also recorded. Henshall later noted that several body sherds did not fit into either the round-based bowl or the Grooved Ware traditions (J.L. Davidson and Henshall 1989, 77). Some of these were decorated with incised lines, for example random lines (A. Ritchie 1983, 69, Figure 11B), horizontal lines (ibid., 67, Figure 10.88) and vertical

Table 19.2: Decorative rim forms and their occurrence on Grooved Ware sites.

	1 ∿	2 ⌇	3 ⁄⁄⁄	4 ⌒⌒
Pool 2				
Barnhouse				
Stenness				
Quanterness				
Pool 3	•	•		
Links of Noltland	•	•		
Rinyo	•		•	•
Skara Brae	•		•	
Raigmore, Inverness	•			•
Knappers Farm, Dunbartonshire				
Balfarg, Fife				•
Balfarg Riding School				
Tentsmuir/Brackmont, Fife				
Beech Hill House, Perthshire				•
Luce Sands, Wigtown				
Yorkshire	•			•
S. England				

1. Scalloped.   3. Cable.
2. Notched.   4. Pinched.

lines (ibid., 67, Figure 10.84), again paralleled within the Pool Phase 2 incised pottery.

The assemblage from Rinyo on Rousay was thought by Childe (Childe and Grant 1947) to prove that 'Unstan Ware' preceded Grooved Ware. David V. Clarke (1983, 48) subsequently questioned these conclusions on the basis of the poor standards of excavation, the recording methods used and the fact that Childe's argument rested on the existence of two sherds from shallow, round-based vessels.

Childe (Childe and Grant 1947, 34–8) recognised eight layers in House G, five of which – 1 to 5 – he regarded as midden levels pre-dating the floor levels. The pottery from the later layers, 7 and 8, had applied decoration and was tempered with angular rock fragments. Rock-tempered pottery was also found in the earlier layers, but it was softer and tempered with rounded gravel. Where decoration could be determined, it was by incision (ibid., 37). In Phase 5a and below, Childe noted a corky or vesicular fabric, which became more common in the earlier levels and commented that it was similar to pottery from chambered tombs. The characteristic vessel-type was an undecorated, round-based bowl with a bevelled rim. Even if it cannot be proved unequivocally that 'Unstan bowls' were present at Rinyo, the sequence of 'corky wares' preceding rock-tempered Grooved Ware parallels the Pool sequence and suggests the presence of two chronologically and technologically distinct pottery traditions.

Thus where sequences have been established, it appears that round-based vessels and shell-tempering are characteristic of the early part of the Orcadian Neolithic sequence.

Comparisons with Pool Phase 2 incised wares

The Pool Phase 2 incised wares are more difficult to parallel in Orkney, and, until the excavations at Barnhouse, comparable material was restricted to pottery from Quanterness tomb (Henshall 1979) and Stenness henge (Henshall and Savory 1976), and occasional sherds from other sites (e.g. the Knap of Howar, above). At Quanterness, sherds from two vessels have incised decoration. One (Renfrew 1979, 76, Figure 33.2) has chevron decoration, while the other (ibid., 77, Figure 34.8b) exhibits part of a chevron and dot motif. At Stenness henge, three sherds (J.N.G. Ritchie 1976, Figures 6.5, 6.11, 6.16), also decorated with chevrons and parallel lines incised into a slip, were recovered.

Only the recently-excavated site of Barnhouse near the Stones of Stenness henge has produced a sizeable assemblage (c. 6,000 sherds) comparable to the Phase 2 assemblage (Richards 1989, 1990). The most common form of decoration comprises converging sets of curvilinear, parallel incised lines, a motif found on an estimated seventy per cent of the decorated sherds. The other common form of decoration is a pinched-up cordon, stabbed at alternate sides to produce a zigzagging effect. Occasionally, these two decorative forms are found together. Less common are incised chevrons, sometimes in combination with impressed dots. Applied decoration is rare, and confined to later phases of occupation.

A smaller but similar assemblage was recovered by Childe and Grant (1939) during their first season of excavations at Rinyo. Although pottery with applied ribs was found throughout the site, the earlier (Rinyo I) pottery, had incised ribs, similar to the Barnhouse pottery. Five such vessels were recovered, four having ribs incised with jabs (e.g. ibid., plate 21, b), the fifth (ibid., plate 22, b. 7) having a rib decorated with small slashes. All the incised pottery (eg. ibid., plate 22), a comparatively small number of relatively thin sherds, was found 'close to virgin soil under floors C and D' (ibid., 25).

At Skara Brae, Childe (1931b, 130–1) noted a chronological division in decorative styles. Applied decoration was found in Periods I, II and III, but incised relief and incision into a slip were only found early in the sequence, in Periods I and II. At Pool, several examples of incised relief similar to that found at Skara Brae were found in Phase 3.1.

Assemblages comparable to Pool Phase 3

The Pool Phase 3 assemblage is most similar to that from the Links of Noltland, East Midden Trench (also known as 'Grobust'; the remainder of the Links of Noltland pottery has not yet been examined in detail). The assemblages are remarkably close in terms of decorative elements and fabric.

Scalloped and notched rims are common, in combination with applied trellis and fish-scale decoration. The Links of Noltland applied Grooved Ware is, like the Pool applied ware, rock-tempered and usually slipped.

The pottery with applied decoration from Rinyo (the upper two levels of Area G) is more similar to that from Skara Brae than to the pottery from the Links of Noltland and Pool. Although certain elements, for example the use of branching decoration and scalloped rims, are found at all four sites, other elements such as the use of roundels, cable rims and vertical panelling are only found at Skara Brae and Rinyo.

SUMMARY OF THE ORCADIAN SEQUENCE

The following summary of Grooved Ware on Orkney must be regarded as a provisional model which will need refining as more assemblages are analysed in detail.

If the shell-tempered, flat-based pottery of Pool Phase 2 is taken as a starting point, then this appears to represent a point of technological continuity both with the Pool Phase 1 pottery and with the shell-tempered, round-based vessels from elsewhere in Orkney. The round-based pottery tradition on Orkney seems to pre-date and overlap with the flat-based tradition.

This early 'Grooved Ware' is characterised by 'baggy' vessels and larger vessels with slightly-angled sides. Decoration is by incision and based on chevrons and parallel lines. Some of the incised motifs from the Pool Phase 2 assemblage are parallelled at Quanterness, Stenness, the Knap of Howar and Barnhouse. At Barnhouse, it occurs on rock-tempered, slipped pottery and is accompanied by the use of relief decoration in the form of a pinched-up, wavy cordon.

This early relief decoration at Barnhouse finds parallels amongst the early-phase pottery with incised ribs from Rinyo and also, significantly, in pottery from mainland Scotland (see below). The Barnhouse material suggests that a gradual shift towards the use of relief decoration occurred, and this is confirmed by the Pool Phase 3 assemblage. (By this time, slipped, rock-tempered pottery was also in use at Pool.) Links between the Pool Phase 3 and Skara Brae assemblages are suggested by the shared use of relief decoration and, in particular, the use of incised relief decoration as found occasionally in the material from Pool Phase 3 and more often in Skara Brae Periods I and II. However, a divergence between Pool and Skara Brae can be distinguished in the more extensive and flamboyant use of applied decoration at Skara Brae, which is parallelled in the Rinyo late-phase material. The closest parallel to the Pool Phase 3 assemblage is to be found at the Links of Noltland.

DISCUSSION

Although recent excavations in Orkney have produced enough pottery to enable the construction of a general sequence for the Orcadian Neolithic,

many issues remain unresolved. The following section summarises the state
of knowledge and suggests areas for future research for four of these
issues.

Chronology

In drawing up a pottery sequence for the Orcadian Neolithic the radiocarbon
dates, summarised by Renfrew and Buteux (1985, 264–9), provide only a
broad timescale. Unfortunately, pottery from chambered tombs cannot be
easily related to the dates, due to the reorganisation of the chambers between
burials.

The dates from Pool and Barnhouse are useful in that, unlike dates from
chambered tombs, they relate to phases of activity which can be linked to a
specific pottery-type. The only radiocarbon dates for the Neolithic sequence
at Pool are for vegetable matter from Phase 2.3, the sub-phase containing the
majority of the incised wares (Gowlett et al. 1987; a sequence of TL dates,
covering the span of Neolithic activity at Pool, is awaited). At 2 sigma, the
calibrated dates fall within the period 3360–2705 CAL-BC. The radiocarbon
dates from Barnhouse range from 3495–2985 CAL-BC at 2 sigma, indicating
broad contemporaneity with Pool Phase 2.

Dates for the Period I village at Skara Brae range from 3380–2880 CAL-
BC (Birm-637) to 3180–2585 CAL-BC (Birm-791) at 2 sigma, overlapping
with the 'incised Grooved Ware' phases at Pool and Barnhouse, while
the dates for the Period II village range from 3295–2585 CAL-BC (Birm-788)
to 2580–1975 CAL-BC (Birm-433). Dates from material in the west Midden
at the Links of Noltland (2930–2595 CAL-BC (GU-1429) to 2495–2135
CAL-BC (GU-1430) at 2 sigma), indicate broad contemporaneity with the
Period II village at Skara Brae, and, from the close similarities between
the Pool Phase 3 pottery and that from the East Midden at the Links of
Noltland, dates in this range would be expected for the Phase 3 occupation
at Pool.

Although the available absolute dates support the pottery sequence, the
evidence does not provide a solution to the relationship between Grooved
Ware and the round-based pottery tradition. Dates from Isbister and the
Knap of Howar, for example, overlap with the dates for the incised Grooved
Ware at Barnhouse and Pool (Renfrew and Buteux 1985). Colin Richards
(personal communication) has suggested that this may be indicative of more
rapid change in Mainland Orkney, witnessed also in changes in domestic and
funerary structures, with the old traditions surviving for longer in the peripheral regions.

Many more well-contexted and well-dated sequences are needed to resolve
the issues raised by the dating evidence. In particular, the excavation of
further early domestic sites may help to clarify the relationship between
round-based vessels and incised Grooved Ware.

The relationship between Orcadian Grooved Ware and that of the rest of Britain

That the later applied Grooved Ware motifs such as trellis and fish-scale decoration as well as notched and scalloped rims are a development local to Orkney has so far been confirmed by petrological analyses. Williams (1979, 1982) analysed thin sections of pottery from Skara Brae, Rinyo, Quanterness and the Stones of Stenness and concluded that it could have been made on or near the sites, as it almost certainly was at Pool (Browell 1986; MacSween, Hunter and Warren 1989). Williams also noted that variation in non-dyke materials of sections from different sites indicated that a single production centre within Orkney was unlikely (Williams 1982, 11).

The issue of the origins of the incised Grooved Ware and the early applied cordons must remain unresolved. Although the Pool pottery suggests some continuity with the round-based tradition of pottery production in terms of fabric and decoration, the reason for the switch from round- to flat-based pottery is not clear.

Radiocarbon dates are unhelpful in resolving the question of Grooved Ware origins, apart from consistently indicating that the Scottish dates are earlier than those from the south of England. The Barnhouse dates, for example, are almost a millennium earlier than those from Durrington Walls, which centre on 2000 BC. Again, dates from Balfarg in Fife, Quanterness and Stenness, centring on 2900 BC, support an early date for the Scottish material.

As has been noted above, several of the motifs found on Orcadian Grooved Ware, notably branching decorated cordons and parallel wavy lines, are recurring elements in southern Scottish assemblages such as Beech Hill House (MacSween forthcoming b), Tentsmuir (Longworth 1967), Balfarg (Henshall and Mercer 1981), Balfarg Riding School (Henshall forthcoming), Raigmore (D.V. Clarke personal communication), Knappers Farm (Mackay 1950) and Luce Sands (McInnes 1964). At present, Grooved Ware sequences for the northern mainland are lacking, and it is not out of the question that this area may prove to be the point of inspiration for the applied decoration found on pottery from Orkney and southern Scotland.

Grooved Ware and chambered tombs

Henshall (1985) noted that in no area of Britain outwith Orkney is Grooved Ware associated with the primary levels of chambered tombs, although the presence of possible Grooved Ware has occasionally been recorded in such tombs, for example at Unival, North Uist (W.L. Scott 1948, plate 7). Even for Orkney, the argument rests on the assemblage from Quanterness. In fact, applied Grooved Ware forms only a very small part of the Quanterness assemblage, comprising three out of a possible twenty-six vessels. One vessel (Renfrew 1979, 76, Figure 33.4) was decorated with branching cordons and

applied bosses, another (ibid., Figure 33.1) with a plain cordon and an incised
zigzagging cordon, and a third with a single cordon parallel to the rim. No
examples of scalloped or notched rims or trellis or fish-scale decoration have
been found in a chambered tomb and where artefacts associated elsewhere
with applied Grooved Ware pottery have been found in tombs, for example
at Quoyness, they have not been associated with primary activity on the site.
Thus, available evidence suggests that by the later phases of occupation of
Skara Brae, the Links of Noltland, Pool and Rinyo, the tombs were either not
being used, or pottery was not being placed in them. Excavation of
chambered tombs on the northern mainland of Scotland is needed to
determine whether this situation is peculiar to Orkney or is a more widespread phenomenon.

Function and decoration

Where large, well-stratified sequences of Grooved Ware have been recovered,
there is considerable variation in form, size and decoration among the
assemblages. The complexities behind the choice and arrangement of motifs
on a vessel have been the subject of various studies (e.g. Richards and
Thomas 1984), but no such study has been carried out on the Orcadian
material. The question of whether there was a set repertoire of motifs, used
in similar combinations from site to site, is important in assessing both inter-
and intra-site relationships between pottery and communities which made
and used it.

An understanding of vessel function is important in interpreting the assemblages further. Scalloped and notched rims, for example, are extremely
impractical, and their use may have been largely restricted to the storage or
cooking of 'special' foods. Colin Richards (personal communication) has
suggested that the restriction of decoration to a band around the upper part
of a vessel may indicate that it was set into the ground and used for storage:
an *in situ* example was uncovered during the excavations at Barnhouse. An
initial estimate of vessel function can be made by analysis of vessel morphology and the presence or absence of sooting (Rice 1987, 208–41), but pro-
grammes of residue analysis would complement such studies.

CONCLUSIONS

Although a chronological difference between the round-based pottery
tradition and Grooved Ware has been suspected in the past, the Pool assemblage suggests that round-based pottery was indeed earlier. Dates from the
Knap of Howar and Isbister, however, indicate a degree of overlap between
the round-based pottery tradition and the flat-based incised wares. At Pool,
pottery which has traditionally been classified as 'Grooved Ware' divides into
an incised and an applied decorated assemblage, separated temporally. The
assemblage from Barnhouse indicates that applied decoration, in the form of
raised decorated cordons, was being added to the repertoire of motifs by

around 3000 BC. Assemblages with similar decorative characteristics to the Barnhouse material are well-paralleled in slightly later sites in southern Scotland. The later, 'high relief' style of decoration found at Pool Phase 3, the Links of Noltland, Skara Brae and Rinyo appears to have been a development restricted to Orkney.

Inevitably, the scheme outlined above will need to be refined with new assemblages and more dates. It should be considered as a working model, but may serve to add some detail to the Orcadian Neolithic pottery sequence, providing hypotheses against which future work can be considered.

ACKNOWLEDGEMENTS

I wish to thank the following people for allowing me to use unpublished data from their excavations and artefact research: John Hunter (Pool), Anna Chudecka (Pool pottery illustrations), Colin Richards (Barnhouse – excavations and pottery), David V. Clarke (the Links of Noltland excavations), Alison Sheridan (the Links of Noltland pottery), Sylvia Stevenson (Beech Hill House excavations) and Gordon Barclay (Balfarg Riding School). I am afraid that, for obvious reasons, I have had to take the liberty of quoting Audrey Henshall's forthcoming paper on the pottery from the excavations at Balfarg Riding School without her permission, and hope that she does not mind!

Thanks also to John Barber, John Hunter, V.J. McLellan, Colin Richards and Christina Unwin who read and discussed drafts of my paper, and Alison Sheridan and Niall Sharples for their help and encouragement through all the stages of its rather prolonged production.

20

Neolithic Pottery From Barbush Quarry, Dunblane, Perthshire, With Notes On The Earlier Neolithic Pottery of Eastern and Central Scotland

Trevor G. Cowie

INTRODUCTION

Discoveries of Earlier Neolithic pottery are still rare enough in lowland Scotland to merit attention, and the primary aim of this chapter is to publish a small group comprising sherds recovered on at least three different occasions from the locality of Barbush Quarry near the north edge of Dunblane, in the former county of Perthshire (now in Stirling District, Central Region). In preparing this paper, the author took the opportunity to catalogue all finds of Earlier Neolithic pottery from eastern and central Scotland, many of them previously unpublished in detail, but owing to the constraints of space, this wider survey will appear elsewhere (see Table 20.1, Figure 20.1; Cowie forthcoming).

FINDS FROM BARBUSH QUARRY, DUNBLANE (FIGURE 20.2)

In November 1981, a corn-drying kiln was discovered during the removal of sand from the quarry at NN 7835502305, and subsequently excavated (Barclay, Brooks and Rideout 1982); in the course of the excavation, the owners of the quarry, Messrs I. and K. Fleming, reported that they had in their possession a small collection of artefacts from the general area of the quarry, and through the good offices of Mr Gordon Barclay these were subsequently presented to the then-named National Museum of Antiquities of Scotland. In addition to the pottery catalogued here (Cat. Nos 1–11, 24–5), the collection included a spindle whorl, several flint flakes and a fragment of a jet or cannel-coal bracelet (*Proc Soc Antiq Scotl* 114 (1984), 597). Subsequent research revealed that among the Museum's existing collections there was already a small group of objects from Barbush donated in 1947 and 1952 by Mr and Mrs A. Fleming respectively: these included a large sherd of what is now considered to be Neolithic pottery (Cat. No. 23: *Proc Soc Antiq Scotl* 81 (1946–7), 194); several sherds of later prehistoric pottery and a segment of a cannel-coal armlet said to have been found 'with burnt material on the saddle between the two summits of the Knock of Barbush'

Table 20.1: List of Neolithic pottery findspots from eastern and central Scotland (Tayside, Fife and Central Regions). The site numbers correspond with those mapped in Figure 20.1.

Site	References
1. Boysack Mills, Inverkeilor, Angus	Reynolds, Ralston and Haggarty 1977; RCAHMS 1978b, 9, no. 26; Close-Brooks 1984, 91–2, Fig. 4; Kinnes 1985, 46.
2. Douglasmuir, Inverkeilor, Angus	RCAHMS 1978b, 15, no 91; Kendrick and Gregson 1980; Kendrick 1980, 12, 14; Kendrick 1982, 136; Kinnes 1985, 48.
3. Balbirnie, Markinch, Fife	J.N.G. Ritchie 1974, 15, 18–20, cat. no. 29; Mercer 1981, 132–3.
4. Balfarg henge, Markinch, Fife	Mercer 1981; Kinnes 1985, 49; Mercer, Barclay, Jordan and Russell-White 1988.
5. Balfarg Riding School, Markinch, Fife	Barclay 1983b; Barclay 1983c; Barclay 1984; Barclay 1985; Kinnes 1985, 46, 49; Barclay and Russell-White forthcoming.
6. Barns Farm, Dalgety, Fife	Watkins 1982; Kinnes 1985, 46.
7. Brackmont Mill, Leuchars, Fife	Longworth 1967; Kinnes 1985, 49.
8. Calais Muir, Dunfermline, Fife	H. Beveridge 1886, 244–52; Watkins 1982, 113; Kinnes 1985, 46.
9. Clatchard Craig, Abdie, Fife	McInnes 1969, 26; Close-Brooks 1986, 125, 150–3; Kinnes 1985, 46.
10. Easter Kinnear, Kilmany, Fife	Driscoll 1989.
11. Kinloch Farm, Collessie, Fife	Barber 1982; Kinnes 1985, 49.
12. Scotstarvit, Ceres, Fife	Bersu 1948; Kinnes 1985, 49.
13. Tentsmuir, Leuchars, Fife	Longworth 1967; Mercer 1981, 132; Kinnes 1985, 49.
14. Barbush Quarry, Dunblane, Perthshire	Barclay, Brooks and Rideout 1982; Barclay 1983a, 253; Kinnes 1985, 45.
15. Beech Hill House, Coupar Angus, Perthshire	S.J. Stevenson 1990; S.J. Stevenson forthcoming.
16. Croft Moraig, Dull, Perthshire	S. Piggott and D.D.A. Simpson 1971; Kinnes 1985, 45.
17. Cultoquhey, Fowlis Wester, Perthshire	Henshall 1972, 475 (PER 4) with further site references; Kinnes 1985, 46.
18. Grandtully, Logierait, Perthshire	McInnes 1969, 22, 28; Kinnes 1985, 49; D.D.A. Simpson and J.M. Coles 1990.
19. Inchtuthil, Caputh, Perthshire	Abercromby, Ross and Anderson 1901, 182–242; Pitts and St Joseph 1985.

Table 20.1: Continued

	Site	References
20.	Moncreiffe, Dunbarney, Perthshire	Stewart 1985.
21.	Monzie, Crieff, Perthshire	Young and Crichton Mitchell 1939; Donations *Proc Soc Antiq Scotl* 100 (1967–68), 201.
22.	North Mains, Strathallan, Perthshire	Barclay 1983a; Kinnes 1985, 45.
23.	Pitnacree, Logierait, Perthshire	J.M. Coles and D.D.A. Simpson 1965; Henshall 1972, 167–72; Kinnes 1979, 11; Kinnes 1985, 46.
24.	Strageath, Crieff, Perthshire	Frere and Wilkes 1989, 269, Fig. 135.
25.	Bannockburn, Stirling, Stirlingshire	Tavener 1987.
26.	Bantaskine, Falkirk, Stirlingshire	Donations *Proc Soc Antiq Scotl* 50 (1915–16), 255; Callander 1929, 35, 56–7, 81, Fig. 38.
27.	Mumrills, Falkirk, Stirlingshire	MacDonald and Curle 1929, 544, Fig. 107.
28.	Nether Kinneil, Bo'ness, West Lothian	Sloan 1982.

(NN 786027); and a fragment of a large, calcined flint knife apparently found with a cremation burial on the south-west slope of the hill (NN 785026) (*Proc Soc Antiq Scotl* 86 (1951–2), 210, with additional unpublished details from National Museums of Scotland (NMS) catalogue). Nor were these the first archaeological finds made in the area by the Fleming family, for in 1937, near the highest part of the largest sand knoll at Barbush (at NN 78530264), Mr Andrew Fleming had found a hoard of ninety-three silver pennies, mainly of Edward I–II, and now thought to have been concealed between 1333 and 1336 AD (Kerr 1939; Mayhew 1975, 35).

In 1986, following mechanical stripping of topsoil preparatory to further quarry operations, an area of greyish/black sandy soil was observed at NN 784020 and reported to Mrs Lorna Main, Regional Archaeologist for Central Region. Some 45 to 60 cm of topsoil and subsoil had already been removed prior to archaeological inspection of the site, and the area had been heavily disturbed by machinery. However, salvage excavation revealed eight patches of charcoal-flecked, dark grey soil lying within a broader area of grey soil with a total surviving extent of some 10 × 9 m. The patches varied in depth from 6–16 cm but lacked clearly-defined edges or bases, the largest measuring some 115 cm × 158 cm. From these frustratingly amorphous features were

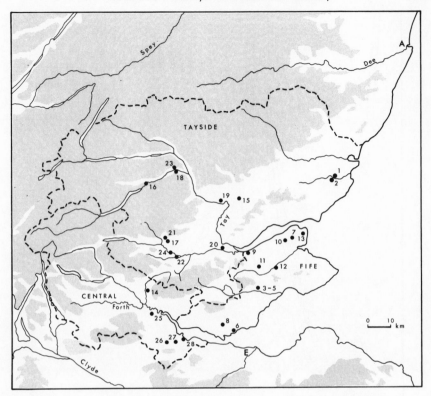

Figure 20.1: Map showing area covered by survey: the numbers correspond to those in
Table 20.1.

retrieved a number of sherds of Neolithic pottery described below (see Cat.
Nos 12–22).

Finally, brief mention may be made of the discovery of a slab-lined pit
investigated by Mrs Main at NM 783021, possibly comparable with Iron Age
graves excavated at Broxmouth, East Lothian (Main 1984; cf. Hill 1982,
179–80), and also a number of items of worked stone from the general quarry
area, including a broken mortar and a possible stone loom-weight from NN
785025, the latter now in the Smith Museum, Stirling (Main 1986).

THE NEOLITHIC POTTERY FROM BARBUSH QUARRY (FIGURE 20.3)

The group of Neolithic pottery from Barbush comprises a sizeable portion of
a bowl, twenty-three sherds and nine fragments with a total weight of 915 g.
Much of the assemblage consists of featureless body pieces, but in all but a
few instances, their fabric is sufficiently diagnostic to leave their Earlier
Neolithic attribution in no doubt despite the unsatisfactory circumstances of
their recovery. While the exact nature of the context of the pottery and the

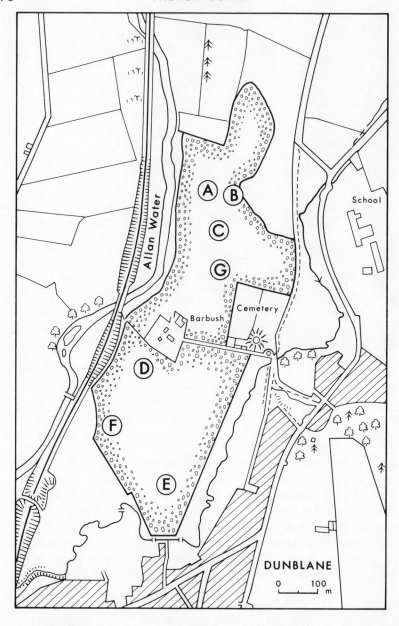

Figure 20.2: Barbush Quarry, Dunblane: location map. The following archaeological discoveries
have been plotted: A: coin hoard 1937; B: Iron Age pottery; C: Bronze Age
cremation; D: corn-drying kiln; E: Neolithic pottery; F: ?Iron Age grave; G: stone
loom-weight.

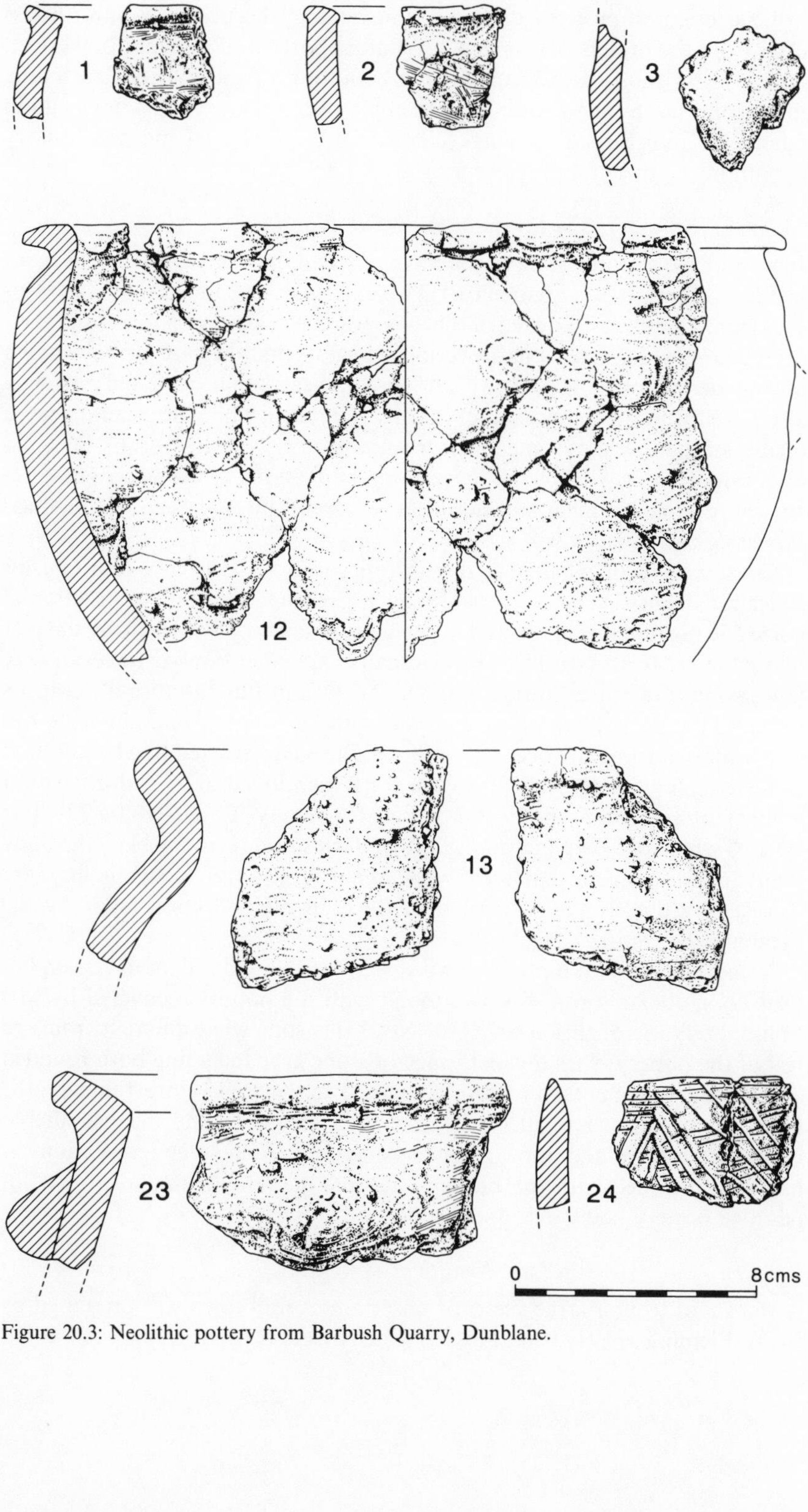

Figure 20.3: Neolithic pottery from Barbush Quarry, Dunblane.

original circumstances of its deposition remain obscure, it is nevertheless clear from the presence of such a substantial portion of a lugged bowl (Cat. No. 12) and the relatively unabraded condition of most pieces, including those collected by the Flemings, that much of the pottery must have lain in relatively undisturbed original contexts until revealed by the quarry operations (rather than representing a residual scatter).

Earlier Neolithic (Cat. Nos 1–22)

In view of the featureless nature of most of the pieces, only a few sherds merit invidual attention (see Figure 20.3). Two externally-expanded rims (Cat. Nos 1–2) from an unlocalised area of the quarry are very similar in form, and their orientation, which is reasonably certain, suggests that they are probably from unshouldered bowls. However, Cat. No. 3 indicates that carinated pots may also have formed a component of the original range, while the generally good quality of the fabric of some of the featureless sherds (Cat. Nos 4–11) would also be in keeping with such a suggestion, even if none of the pieces possesses the exceptional thinness and hardness or careful burnish seen on the finest Neolithic carinated bowls.

Conservation of what at first sight appeared to be a very unpromising collection of sherds and shattered fragments resulted in the reconstruction of a sizeable portion of the rim and upper body of a heavy bowl bearing the scar of a large lug (Cat. No. 12). The externally-expanded rim has traces of very faint, wide transverse fluting, but it is felt that in this instance at least, its formation is most likely to be a result of the process of moulding the rim rather than a deliberate decorative effect. The reconstructed bowl was found in the course of Mrs Main's salvage work mentioned above, along with a number of featureless body sherds and fragments (Cat. Nos 14–22). For reasons which defy explanation simply in terms of a recovery bias, the body sherds retrieved from that area, while again of generally good quality, are consistently thicker (10–12 mm) than those in the collection made by the Flemings (8–9 mm).

A single large sherd representing a vessel with everted rim, of uncertain but possibly globular form, was also found with the pottery recovered by Mrs Main: the fabric of this vessel (Cat. No. 13) is somewhat different from the rest of the pottery, with a wider range of stone grits including both rounded and angular fragments in a hard, laminated clay matrix. Unfortunately, the sherd has been severely affected by fire after breakage, and this has altered its surface texture and appearance considerably. With some reservations, it has been included with the Earlier Neolithic material, some possible comparative pottery being discussed below.

?Late Neolithic (Cat. No. 23)

A rim sherd from a large vessel of uncertain overall form was presented by Mr A. Fleming in 1947 (Cat. No. 23): when first accessioned, this pot was felt not to be prehistoric, but there would now seem to be no telling reasons why, despite its somewhat unusual form and atypically hard fabric, it should not be catalogued as Neolithic. Typologically, the heavy thickened rim with its broad internal bevel suggests a relatively late Neolithic date, since one strand in the sequence of ceramic development was undoubtedly the elaboration of the rims of vessels – ultimately resulting in the use of the bevel as a major 'platform' for ornament, as seen especially in the Late Neolithic 'Impressed Ware' assemblages in southern Scotland (cf. McInnes 1969, 22).

Grooved Ware (Cat. Nos 24–5)

Among the collection of random finds made by the Flemings was a single rim sherd of Grooved Ware (Cat. No. 24) from a sizeable vessel with an upright pointed rim, decorated on the exterior with fine horizontal lines just below the lip, overlapping with what appears to have been a chevron pattern made up of oblique incised lines. A plain body sherd has also tentatively been included in this category.

DISCUSSION

Barbush Quarry: circumstance not context

The Barbush Quarry pottery group highlights several of the problems which frustrate the study of Earlier Neolithic pottery over so much of lowland Scotland: these include the small size of the assemblage and its component pieces, the dearth of diagnostic features and the virtual absence of reliable contextual information (cf. Kinnes 1985, 21). It is a prime example of how our material is all too often the product of circumstance. Perhaps with the benefit of hindsight, one could claim that Barbush represents a missed opportunity for fuller investigation of a potentially rewarding area, but it would be more profitable to apply some of the lessons of this site elsewhere. For example, comparable suites of fluvio-glacial knolls in the region might bear careful scrutiny by means of fieldwalking, particularly if undertaken in conjunction with an assessment of museum records and collections (particularly lithic collections) and the results of aerial survey.

Earlier Neolithic pottery

The featureless nature of the bulk of the Earlier Neolithic pottery from Barbush Quarry severely limits any attempt to place the material in any wider ceramic context. Superficially, fairly close comparisons can, however, be made between some of the Barbush Quarry fabrics and groups of sherds from several sites in the region, such as Croft Moraig (16: see Table 20.1 for references to this and other sites numbered in parentheses) and North Mains (22), Perthshire; Bantaskine (26) in Stirlingshire, and further afield too, for example at Linlithgow, West Lothian (Stones 1989, fiche 11: G9–10), the Catstane, Midlothian (Cowie 1978, 197) and Balfarg Riding School (5), Fife.

Reporting on the pottery from the sites at North Mains, the writer noted that sherds of several of the fabric groups represented at that suite of sites could be compared macroscopically with examples of all three fabrics recognised at Pitnacree (23), Perthshire (in Barclay 1983a, 252–3); among the Barbush sherds too, there are a number (especially Cat. Nos 14–20) which bear close comparison with the quartz-gritted fabric found at Pitnacree (J.M. Coles and D.D.A. Simpson 1965, 42, Group C).

At the moment, while holding out the promise of rewarding results, such comparisons on the basis of fabric alone are unsupported by detailed petrological work: there is clearly a growing need for broad-based research on this and other aspects of Neolithic pottery manufacture, production and distribution in Scotland. In the absence of statistically-valid domestic assemblages, however, the time is not yet right for such work on the Neolithic pottery of lowland Scotland, although some of the avenues of enquiry are clear enough and a variety of pilot projects could usefully be undertaken. What, for example, were the processes of clay preparation and pottery manufacture that led to the production of the very distinctive Earlier Neolithic fabrics characterised by mica-speckled surfaces? This is such a recurrent feature that one wonders if it could possibly reflect a very widespread adherence to a particular early technical tradition – indeed, almost a potting recipe – that eventually broke down as regional ceramic styles became established. The possible chronological implications of this suggestion might bear further investigation in the light of Herne's recent reappraisal of the 'Grimston bowl', which suggested that the actual currency of classic carinated bowls may have been more restricted than formerly thought, with a date range of c. 4000–3500 BC (Herne 1988, 23–4).

The bevelled rims of Cat. Nos 1–2 from Barbush lack precise parallels among the pottery from the region under review, nor does the form appear to be easy to match elsewhere. However, the presumed overall form of the vessels concerned, plain, somewhat globular small bowls with little elaboration of the rim, occurs more widely (e.g. vessels from Bicker's Houses, Bute: Henshall 1972, 416, no. 2, or Luce Sands, Wigtownshire: McInnes 1964, Cat. No. 32. The large, lugged bowl, Cat. No. 12, and the everted rim sherd, Cat. No. 13, will be discussed below.

Despite the absence of telling evidence of the presence of carinated vessels, the generally good quality of much of the Barbush pottery (in particular that represented by Cat. Nos 1–11 and 14–22) is thus comparable with the range of fabrics found in larger groups falling within the so-called 'Grimston/Lyles Hill series', among which carinated vessels predominate (cf. I.F. Smith 1974, 106–8). However, the present writer shares the reservations expressed by Kinnes (1985, 22) and more recently Herne (1988) regarding the suitability of 'Grimston/Lyles Hill' as a portmanteau term, at least when the evidence is of this quality; and, for the present, much of our Earlier Neolithic pottery is perhaps best described simply as being in the 'bowl style' (cf. Kinnes 1985,

21), to use a suitably neutral, all-embracing term for material that would formerly have been described as being in the 'Western Neolithic' tradition.

Returning to Barbush Quarry, the originally lugged bowl, Cat. No. 12, and the everted rim sherd, Cat. No. 13, contrast with the remainder of the Earlier Neolithic material from that site on account of their generally heavy proportions and coarse fabrics. A significant group of comparable and similarly distinctive pottery was recovered from a series of pits and scoops located in the course of sampling excavations to the west of the Balfarg Henge (5), Fife. This group predominantly comprises what, despite the near-absence of reconstructable profiles, appears to be a range of deep and heavy bowl forms in well-made but coarse fabrics, often bearing obvious signs of tooling of the surfaces and a low standard of finish.

The two Barbush vessels and the larger group of heavy bowls from Balfarg augment what has hitherto been a relatively restricted range of related pottery mainly from southern Scotland: this includes the much smaller bowl from Oatslie Sandpit, near Roslin, Midlothian (R.B.K. Stevenson 1948, 294–5), portions of vessels from Knappers, Dunbartonshire (MacKay 1948, 236–7, cat. no. 5; Ritchie and Adamson 1981, 184–7, cat. nos 1–2, with details of comparative material in the Clyde area), and rim sherds from two large vessels found in the course of excavations on the Roman civilian settlement at Inveresk (Henshall in Thomas 1988, fiche 1: G10–11). Although less pronounced, the everted rims of sherds from Knappers (Ritchie and Adamson 1981, 184, cat. no. 2) and Balfarg Riding School (5) (unpublished) provide the best parallels for Barbush Cat. No. 13. This accumulating range of unshouldered, relatively coarse, heavily-proportioned pottery may be seen as analogous, rather than directly related, to the so-called Towthorpe style of Yorkshire, which appears to have been current as a ceramic tradition complementary to the Grimston style in that region during much of the fourth millennium BC (Manby 1988).

Relatively coarse, thick-walled vessels do form a component of assemblages of Earlier Neolithic pottery (e.g. East Finnercy, Aberdeenshire: Henshall 1983c, 30, 42). It is thus perhaps arguable that the group of heavy bowls from Balfarg simply represents one extreme of a range of Bowl pottery manufacture: however, not only are the rim- and wall-thicknesses considerably greater than those found on the heavy component of early assemblages, but also the fabric is quite different in composition and texture, inviting comparison instead with the generally coarser wares of the Later Neolithic. While the ancestry of the vessel shapes is hardly in doubt, the heaviness of the rim-forms and the relative coarseness and thickness of the fabrics appear to reflect changing methods and techniques of manufacture. Typologically, such vessels may lie behind the development of the thick-rimmed heavy bowls which form a major element of the Scottish Late Neolithic Impressed Ware assemblages – a development that principally involved further elaboration of the rim to provide a major 'platform' for decoration (cf. Barbush Cat. No.

23). However, further work is required in Northern Britain to permit a more objective assessment of these differences.

Dating

Radiocarbon determinations for so-called Grimston/Lyles Hill pottery in Britain and Ireland appear to range from the late fifth to the mid-third millennium BC. However, recent reappraisal of the dating evidence for carinated bowl assemblages suggests that the actual currency of carinated bowls, if strictly defined, may have been more restricted, and possibly limited to the first half of the fourth millennium BC (Herne 1988, 23–4), and much of the evidence for the supposed prolonged currency of such bowls has been called into question (ibid., 14–15). Until a range of dates became available from the North-East, the date of 3705–3510 CAL-BC (GaK-601) from the pre-mound surface at Pitnacree virtually underpinned Neolithic chronology in lowland Scotland, but to this may now be added several relevant dates from other sites in the region under review, including Douglas-muir (2), Angus; Balfarg Riding School (5) and Barns Farm (6), Fife, and North Mains, Perthshire (22). The early dating of the carinated bowl assemblages has been reinforced by several new radiocarbon dates from the West of Scotland (Newton, Islay: McCullagh 1991; Machrie Moor, Arran: Haggarty forthcoming), and the date of 3020–2775 CAL-BC (I-4705) from Auchategan, Cowal, Argyll (Marshall 1978, 43) now looks increasingly isolated (cf. Kinnes 1985, 23, illustration 4).

In the area under review, the reassessment of the dates for carinated bowls has implications for the supposed association of Earlier Neolithic sherds and coarse ware in the so-called 'Flat Rim Ware' tradition at Croft Moraig (16), Perthshire, in particular, and the grounds for associating the two groups of pottery at that site now look weak. Only three 'Western Neolithic' sherds were found as opposed to twenty-six sherds of coarse pottery, and the former are now more economically interpreted as residual. While Stuart Piggott and Derek Simpson were right to draw attention to the coarse component of Earlier Neolithic assemblages, at least some of the coarse pottery at Croft Moraig invites more ready comparison with undecorated Grooved Ware (Henshall in Mercer 1981, 132).

The group of heavy plain bowls found at Balfarg, which it has been suggested may be analogous to the Towthorpe style, can be dated firmly to the mid- to later fourth millennium BC as a result of two radiocarbon determinations from pits containing sherds of this type at Balfarg Riding School (5) – one of the dates being obtained from a carbonised cereal grain actually embedded in the wall of a rim sherd!

Pit (2050) Charcoal   3605–3385 CAL-BC (GU-2606)

Pit (2212) Cereal grain 3675–3545 CAL-BC (UtC-1302)

The lower end of the date-range of these vessels is uncertain, although there is some decidedly weak evidence to suggest that such pottery may still have been current in both Northern England and Scotland as late as the first half of the third millennium BC (cf. Henshall in Thomas 1988, fiche 1: G11).

Grooved Ware

Finally, mention may be made of the rim sherd of Grooved Ware from Barbush Quarry (Cat. No. 24). Audrey Henshall's discussion of the sizeable assemblage from Balfarg Henge (4), coupled with her forthcoming report on the Grooved Ware from Balfarg Riding School (5), render much further comment on this class of pottery unnecessary. The recent recovery of a small group of Grooved Ware sherds from the pre-cairn ground surface at Beech Hill House, Coupar Angus (15), Perthshire, extends the regional distribution north of the Tay, and suggests that it is now only a matter of time before some of the broad gaps in the Scottish mainland distribution pattern begin to close. In any case, that distribution has to take into account a variety of plain vessels that were formerly classed under the portmanteau heading of 'Flat Rimmed Ware' – for example at Croft Moraig (16), Moncrieffe (20) and Monzie (21), all in Perthshire – because, in the light of the sizeable assemblages now available from the region, such pots can now plausibly be seen to be related to the undecorated component of Grooved Ware assemblages (Henshall in Mercer 1981, 132; but see also Audrey Henshall's prescient observations in 1972, 182).

ACKNOWLEDGEMENTS

I am most grateful to Mrs Lorna Main for allowing me to publish details of the pottery recovered in the course of her investigation of sites at Barbush Quarry, and to Rosemary Cowie for reconstructing the surviving portions of the lugged bowl from Barbush from what seemed a most unpromising collection of sherds and fragments crushed by quarry machinery. I am also indebted to Marion O'Neil and Sylvia Stevenson, respectively, for preparing the maps and pottery illustrations which accompany this chapter.

CATALOGUE OF NEOLITHIC POTTERY FROM BARBUSH QUARRY, DUNBLANE, PERTHSHIRE

Notes to catalogue entries:

1. Items marked with an asterisk are illustrated in Figure 20.3
2. Descriptions. Sherds are defined as having both their external and internal surfaces surviving; fragments have only one of these surfaces surviving, and crumbs are arbitrarily $10\,mm^2$ or less and retain no formal features. The position and orientation of most pieces is uncertain. Where rim diameters are given, these must usually be assumed to be approximate.

3. See introduction for details of the circumstances of discovery: only the findspot of Cat. Nos 12–22 can be located with any certainty.

4. Current locations of pottery (March 1990): 1–11, 23–5: Department of Archaeology, National Museums of Scotland, Edinburgh (NMS), currently based at the Royal Museum of Scotland, Queen Street, Edinburgh. 12–22: With excavator, pending disposal to Smith Museum, Stirling.

Earlier Neolithic

*1. Rim sherd; externally-expanded rim from vessel of uncertain overall form, probably an unshouldered bowl; most of the top of the rim has flaked away to a consistent depth, indicating that the rim was partly formed by the addition of extra clay; light reddish-brown (5YR 6/4) and grey external surface; dark grey core; reddish-brown (5YR 5/3) internal surface; fine hard clay matrix with moderate amount of gritting with speckled rock, including mica, breaking surface in places; 37 mm × 33 mm; 9 mm thick; rim-diameter uncertain, but between 200 and 240 mm. National Museums of Scotland (NMS) catalogue no. EO 1123.

*2. Rim sherd; externally-expanded rim from vessel of uncertain overall form, probably an unshouldered bowl similar to Cat. No. 1; dark grey (10YR 4/1) or dark greyish-brown (10YR 4/2) throughout; fabric very similar to Cat. No. 1; 40 × 36 mm; 9 mm thick; rim diameter uncertain, but between 200 and 240 mm. NMS EO 1124.

*3. Body sherd with gentle carination; reddish-brown/brown external surface, dark grey core and internal surface; fabric similar to Cat. No. 1; 48 × 42 mm; 8–10 mm thick. NMS EO 1126.

4–9. Nine body sherds, only two of which appear to be from the same vessel; reddish-brown external surfaces, grey/dark grey cores; grey or dark brown internal surfaces; fabric generally similar to Cat. No. 1; largest sherd 35 × 32 mm; 8 mm average thickness. NMS EO 1128–33.

10–11. Two body sherds; grey throughout; compact, slightly gritty fabric; larger sherd 23 × 23 mm, 9 mm thick. NMS EO 1134–5.

12–22, from NN 784020

*12. Portion of the rim and upper body of a heavy lugged bowl, reconstructed from approximately twenty sherds and fragments; the rim is externally-expanded with very faint wide transverse fluting, probably the result of moulding of the rim; on the exterior, the former presence of a lug is betrayed by a slight swelling in the clay and a prominent elongated scar approximately 18 mm high by 55 mm in width set 50 mm below the rim at the maximum girth of the vessel; above the site of the lug there is a broad shallow groove in the external surface of the vessel – possibly the result of pressure on the clay when applying the lug; dark grey (10YR 4/1), brown (7.5YR 5/2) and reddish-brown (5YR 5/4) external surface, dark grey (10YR 4/1) core and internal surface; very compact, hard clay matrix with dark grey stone grits breaking the surface expecially on the lower surfaces; both internal and external surfaces bear traces of horizontal tool or wipe marks. Maximum surviving height 135 mm; thickness of wall 12–15 mm; estimated original height c. 170 mm; estimated rim-diameter 240 mm.

*13.   Rim sherd from vessel of uncertain overall form, probably globular, with everted rounded rim; reddish-yellow (5YR 6/6) and pale brown (10YR 6/3) external surface with some dark grey patches; pale brown internal surface; hard coarse fabric with profuse grits up to 10 mm; horizontal tooling marks on interior; grits stand proud on interior of rim where surfaces abraded; apparently re-fired; 80 × 70 mm; 14–15 mm thick; estimated rim-diameter 350 mm.

14–20. Four body sherds and eight fragments, from several vessels; reddish or reddish-brown external surfaces, grey cores, brown or grey-brown internal surfaces; hard fine clay matrix with quartz grits, prominent in breaks, but surfaces well-smoothed; largest 35 × 30 mm, 10–12 mm thick.

21.   Large body sherd, with tooling or wipe marks over both surfaces; reddish-brown external and internal surfaces; core reddish and dark grey; surfaces well-smoothed, but profuse rounded and angular grits visible in section, possibly same vessel as Cat. No. 13; 62 × 64 mm; 10·5–12 mm thick.

22.   Fragment; position and orientation uncertain, but possibly from flattened or sagging base near basal angle; reddish external surface, grey/brown internal surface; 29 × 19 mm; 19 mm thick.

?Late Neolithic

*23.   Rim sherd, from vessel of uncertain overall form with externally expanded rim with broad internal bevel; below the rim is a prominent applied oval lug; tool or fingernail marks under the rim and below the lug probably incorporated during manufacture; very hard coarse fabric with profuse dark grey stone grits breaking surface especially around bevel; 63 × 105 mm; 12 mm thick at break; estimated rim-diameter 280 mm. NMS MEA 5.

Grooved Ware

*24.   Rim sherd, composed of two joining pieces; pointed rim from vessel probably of upright bucket-shaped form; dark grey external surface, reddish internal surface; decorated: irregular series of fine horizontal incisions immediately below exterior of rim; these are partly overlain, partly cut by oblique incised lines probably part of a chevron arrangement around upper part of vessel; 41 × 60 mm; 9·5–11 mm thick; estimated rim-diameter 300 mm. NMS EO 1125.

25.   Body sherd composed of two joining pieces, possibly Grooved Ware; building joint; grey and light brown surfaces, grey core; undecorated; 45 × 45 mm; 10 mm thick. NMS EO 1127.

21

Significant Form: Ceramic Styles in the Earlier Neolithic of Southern England

Rosamund M.J. Cleal

Look at the dust on the mantlepiece, for example, the dust which, so they say, buried Troy three times over, only fragments of pots utterly refusing annihilation. (Virginia Woolf, 'The Mark on the Wall', in *Monday or Tuesday*)

THE BACKGROUND

There is some confusion about the classification of the pottery of the fourth and third millennia BC in southern Britain. This is partly because the development of the classification has led to a confusing use of type-names. A summary of the situation as it stands is therefore called for.

Essentially, the classification has developed since the mid-1920s, with fairly few major steps along the way, and is largely the result of work by two leading figures: Stuart Piggott and Isobel Smith. The seminal work on the subject is Piggott's paper of 1931. In this, he defined two major groups of Neolithic pottery, 'Windmill Hill Ware' and 'Peterborough Ware', the former being recognised as earlier than the latter. He also suggested that they should be known as 'Neolithic A' and 'Neolithic B' wares, to avoid the use of type-site names which could give a misleading impression of uniformity to a tradition which displayed considerable local variation (S. Piggott 1931, 71).

Twenty-three years later, in *Neolithic Cultures of the British Isles*, Piggott presented a more detailed discussion of British Neolithic pottery styles, which differed in some respects from the earlier version (1954, 66–75). The term 'Neolithic A' was abandoned in favour of 'Western Neolithic' to indicate the common Continental background of the large, and quite varied, group of related styles now recognised. 'Windmill Hill', as well as being used by Piggott as a name for a culture which covered the whole of southern Britain south of a line from the Wash to the Severn (ibid., 17, Figure 1), denoted a ceramic tradition which was a subdivision of the 'Western Neolithic' group of wares, and itself developed regional variants, 'Whitehawk', 'Abingdon' and 'East Anglian' (ibid., table II). The division of a Windmill Hill tradition into three sub-styles was taken further by Isobel Smith in her Ph.D. thesis

(1956), and, although unfortunately unpublished, this has remained the classic work on the subject for over thirty years, establishing criteria for the three sub-styles of 'Windmill Hill' ware – 'Abingdon', 'Whitehawk' and the East Anglian style renamed as the 'Mildenhall'. However, Piggott's suggestion that the Windmill Hill tradition showed development through time from a stage with predominantly plain vessels, including deep, bag-shaped forms, as represented in the early fills of the ditches at Windmill Hill itself, to the three heavy-rimmed decorated sub-styles (S. Piggott 1954, 70–2, table II), did not survive the detailed analysis of Windmill Hill carried out by Dr Smith. Although supporting Piggott's observations, Smith rejected his interpretation that real chronological change was represented. Her reasons are convincing, and include the fact that a sherd of Abingdon Ware (i.e. in Piggott's terms a variant of developed Windmill Hill Ware) occurs low in the primary fill (I.F. Smith 1965, 14).

The fact that the classification has developed in stages, with one stage superseding the previous one, has not always been appreciated, leading to some confusion in the use of terms. Thus 'Windmill Hill' could be used as a generic term for Earlier Neolithic pottery in southern Britain, as a regional style of decorated pottery divided into sub-styles, as an early stage in that tradition without sub-styles, and, finally, as a minor variant identified at the type-site although not now confined to it. The degree of confusion to which this has led is perhaps indicated by the fact that a version of Piggott's plain Windmill Hill Ware has re-emerged recently in a basic guide to earlier prehistoric pottery (A.M. Gibson 1986, 14–15).

Two landmarks which ought also to be described are Isobel Smith's article of 1974 and Alasdair Whittle's contribution in 1977. In the former, Dr Smith argued that the generic terms formerly employed for Earlier Neolithic pottery were no longer appropriate, so that 'Western Neolithic' and 'Windmill Hill' should be abandoned in that sense, while the type-site names for regional styles should be retained as still fulfilling a useful purpose (I.F. Smith 1974, 106). Smith used, therefore, the names 'Hembury', 'Abingdon' and 'Grimston/Lyles Hill', and illustrated the distributions of at least the first and last, which clearly overlap (ibid., Figure 14). More importantly, Smith also made the point that the existence of stylistic variations and overlapping distributions might be explained by the type of activities that caused the movement of gabbroic ware from its source, a movement then only recently recognised, and that the way to elucidate this was through detailed typological and petrological studies.

Dr Whittle, in his volume on the continental relations of the Neolithic in southern Britain, took a broad view and described large-scale regional styles: 'South-Western' (the former Hembury Ware), 'Decorated' (formerly Windmill Hill) and 'Eastern' (more or less equivalent to Grimston/Lyles Hill), essentially, as he acknowledged, the same as those defined by his predecessors (Whittle 1977, 84). The renaming of the styles is telling, being related to a move from the particular and local to the regional and general. In part, of course, this is justified, as the work is mainly concerned with Britain in relation to the continent and therefore needs to deal in the large scale. In part, however, it is unfortunate in its suggestion of internally coherent styles over large areas, as this has aided in deferring the search for any internal inconsistency. The line suggested by Smith, of detailed typological and petrological studies, has not been followed.

WHY CLASSIFY?

At least three assumptions would seem to underlie the exercise of classification and must be shared by most of those who use classifications of any pottery. First, it is assumed that there was some sort of classification of ceramic containers in use by the makers and users of the pottery studied, that is, that they were not made and used entirely at random. In studying a contemporary society, this would be termed the 'folk classification' (Rice 1987, 277–82). Second, it is assumed that the prehistoric 'folk classification' is approachable through the vessels, that is, that their place within it is reflected in at least some attributes which were tangible at the time, and survive deposition. Third, it is assumed that our perceptions about the pots we study are relevant to the understanding of the 'folk classification'.

There are of course flaws inherent in each of these points, but it seems reasonable to assume that anyone who classifies prehistoric pottery must partly subscribe to all three. As the classificatory approach is almost universal in Neolithic pottery studies, and is not one which it is proposed to abandon here, these flaws, and certain qualifying remarks, must be made clear.

The first point – that classifications of objects, and the world in general, are virtually universal – appears fairly uncontroversial. However, classifications used by contemporary societies are difficult enough to identify, and indeed vary in use even within quite small social groups. Kempton, for instance, discovered differences between the folk classifications of ceramics employed by potters, female non-potters and male non-potters in communities in present-day Mexico, although these were differences of detail rather than completely different classifications (Kempton 1981). However, certain features of contemporary folk classifications do suggest positive ways of approaching the problem of prehistoric folk classifications. In particular, there appears to be a universal tendency for pots to be classified according to their actual or projected use, even to the extent of the names of individual vessels being changed if their use is changed, such as upon damage occurring to the pot (Rice 1987, 278). This appears at first a depressing possibility, but this is not the case if one acknowledges that the practical goal of the archaeologist is not an exact replication of a folk classification but an approximation of it: not the exact role or roles filled by particular forms but the general shape of the classification, for example its range of forms and sizes or the differentiation in decorative treatment of some forms over others. In this area, the third point mentioned above, that of our perceptions of the pottery we study, is relevant. Even if in folk classifications, perhaps including those used during the Neolithic, pots are moved from class to class on the basis of changing use, there are still factors which will undoubtedly influence use and are perhaps accessible to us. This is not to suggest that our aim should (or even could) be to elucidate the exact function of any particular vessel or form, but rather to establish the most likely ranges of use, and to incorporate these into our attempt to reconstruct the general shape of the folk classification, even if that turns out to be relatively unspecialised, with therefore little physical differentiation between classes.

If one legitimate aim of classification is to discern at least the broad outlines of the folk classification of the pottery makers, another is to isolate the existence of different pottery types which may relate to the existence of different social groups or units, from large-scale regional groups down to micro-traditions within communities. The former has perhaps been the uppermost of the two aims in the development of Earlier Neolithic pottery classification in the British Isles, and is inherent in the identification of regional styles, although often the exercise of identification is carried out without making its aim explicit. Micro-traditions, on the other hand, recognisable in contemporary pottery assemblages (e.g. Longacre 1981, 62–3), have not been successfully identified, probably because little emphasis has been placed on looking for them.

AN APPROACH TO CLASSIFICATION

The existing classifications of Earlier Neolithic pottery in southern Britain are heavily dependent on the following features: the presence of decoration (regardless of type), the heaviness and elaboration of the rim, and the presence of a carination. In very simple terms, the Windmill Hill regional style (i.e. Whittle's Decorated Style, Whittle 1977, 85–94), is characterised by heavy rims and a high proportion of decoration, generally on carinated vessels; the Grimston/Lyles Hill, more or less equivalent to Whittle's Eastern Style (ibid., 82–5, Figure 13) by carinated bowls and S-profiled bowls, often of open forms; and the Hembury (Whittle's South-Western, ibid., 77–82, Figure 12) by a range of bowls, including carinated and uncarinated forms, most of which, like those of the Grimston/Lyles Hill style, are undecorated. Even this simplification of the present classification does illustrate the emphasis on some features of form over others (particularly the primacy of carination), and the overriding importance of decoration. Features which are of only minor importance in the classification are size, proportion and form other than presence of a carination.

Anyone who has had to deal with large assemblages of Earlier Neolithic pottery, or even with small groups or stray finds, is likely to be aware of the difficulties of dealing with the material and the self-fulfilling nature of the regional styles as presently defined. The tendency will always be to look for local parallels, and they will often be found, while similar forms or even close parallels in other regions may easily be overlooked.

The response to this which will be outlined below is the logical product of two processes: on the one hand, that of dealing with Neolithic pottery within the traditional framework, and, on the other, that of attempting to replicate and use Earlier Neolithic pottery vessels. The response is thus firmly grounded in, and engendered by, close contact with the artefact-type involved.

The way in which Neolithic pottery is treated, in virtually all publications, is firmly two-dimensional, above and beyond the limitations of the printed page alone. It is certainly not intended here to suggest that the conventions of traditional pottery illustration should be abandoned, as a strictly applied convention is obviously vital to the comparison of assemblages; but one could give a fuller impression of the pottery by other methods, in addition to the normal conventions. It is, for instance, not common to illustrate pots as whole, lifelike vessels except, rarely, on book-covers (e.g. I.F. Smith 1981, Healy 1988), although this type of treatment does occur in reports on pottery of later periods (e.g. Platt and Coleman-Smith 1975, Figures 121–34). Neither is it common practice to give calculations of volume for reconstructable vessels, although predicted volume is more likely to be accurate for incomplete round-based forms than for incomplete flat-based pots in which the point at which the form is truncated often cannot be predicted with confidence. Even so, calculation of volume is much more common in reports on flat-based pots of later periods. In the conventional treatment, stress is laid on features which show well in cross-section, such as very minor variations in profile, but which would be much less obvious to the viewer of the pot itself. Conversely, little attention is paid to those features which most strike the viewer of a vessel, principally the overall shape and proportions of the pot and the location of the decoration.

The solution to this problem of two-dimensionality is in part simply a change in methodology. At the most basic level, it can be suggested that a method of classification is needed in which the pot can be treated as an object, rather than primarily as a 'Windmill Hill'-style bowl, or even as one of Herne's 'Carinated Bowls' (1988). Complex methods have been developed for recording vessel shape (e.g. as summarised in Rice 1987, 219–222), but Anna Shepard's method, described in the 1950s, still appears one of the easiest to apply, and is one which relates to vessel use, in that its primary divisions are related to restriction (Shepard 1954, 224–32). This method, with some modification, is here tentatively applied to five published assemblages of Earlier Neolithic pottery, using a three-part classification. The main modification is the introduction of 'Open', 'Neutral' and 'Closed' as a layer in the descriptive hierarchy, and the omission of geometric shape descriptors. The former was added because this three-fold division is already in common

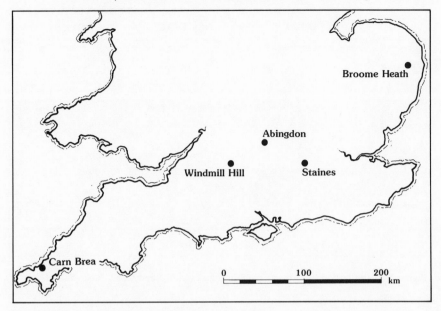

Figure 21.1: Location of sites mentioned in text.

use (since Whittle 1977) and does relate to body proportions; in fact, the absence of this relationship from the Shepard classification might be regarded as a failing of that system. The latter was omitted partly because it was found to be difficult to apply with any degree of confidence, and partly because the investment in time needed to apply it seemed unlikely to be rewarded by a high degree of information about the assemblages, as the shapes represented in British Earlier Neolithic pottery are limited.

The material used in the study (Figure 21.1) comprises five assemblages: three from central southern Britain which are traditionally assigned to the Decorated Style (Abingdon, Oxfordshire: Avery 1982; Staines, Surrey: Robertson-Mackay 1987 and Windmill Hill, Wiltshire: I.F. Smith 1965), a single assemblage of the South-Western Style (Carn Brea, Cornwall: I.F. Smith 1981), and the assemblage from Broome Heath, Norfolk (Wainwright 1972), the identification of which as an Eastern Style assemblage by Whittle has been queried by Herne (1988, 15). Figure 21.2 illustrates the various vessel form categories as used in the study. Figures 21.3 to 21.6 and Tables 21.1 to 21.4 summarise the analytical results, in the form of presence/absence charts and percentage data respectively: the variables covered are not only vessel form but also mouth : depth ratios (see Figures 21.3 and 21.4), attachments (i.e. lugs, handles and cordons: see Figure 21.5) and location of decoration (see Figure 21.6).

This treatment, although crude, did bring out both similarities which

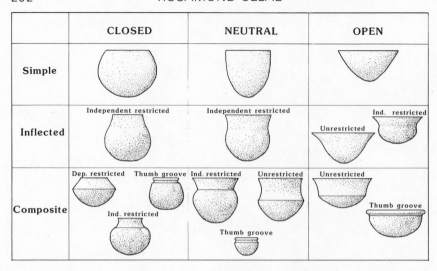

Figure 21.2: Illustration of forms as given in Figures 21.3, 5 and 6 and Tables 21.1–4.

would be expected, and those which would not, between the assemblages. In addition, Table 21.5 gives the Jaccard Coefficients (a measure of similarity) for every possible combination of two sites regarding the incidence of specific form-types. This suggests not only that the pairs Abingdon and Windmill Hill, and Staines and Windmill Hill, have a moderately higher degree of similarity than most of the others, but also that there is a greater than expected similarity between both Staines and Windmill Hill on the one hand and Broome Heath on the other, mainly in Neutral and Closed forms. This would seem to support Herne's assertion that 'a concern with decorative style hides a fundamental unity [between Broome Heath and the Decorated Style assemblage from Hurst Fen]' (ibid., 15). An underlying aspect brought out by the analysis is that on the whole there is greater inter-assemblage similarity displayed in Neutral and Closed forms than in Open forms.

Figures 21.3, 21.5 and 21.6 while only illustrating the occurrence of mouth : depth ratios, attachments and the location of decoration within each class of vessel form, nevertheless do give some indication of patterns which would be difficult to discern without a systematic approach such as this. For instance, restricted vessels with mouth diameters less than depth, which could be termed jars, are rare (Figure 21.3; see under Closed, Inflected, Independent Restricted). They are recorded both at Abingdon and Windmill Hill. Conversely, Figure 21.3 also shows the occurrence of closed forms with mouth diameters much wider than vessel depth at Broome Heath. This preference is shown by no other assemblage: no forms with mouth : depth ratios greater than 2 : 1 could be identified at Abingdon, Windmill Hill or Staines, despite the fact that profiles of shallow vessels are more likely to be reconstructable,

OPEN

	Simple					Inflected				Composite				Complex
	Unrestricted					Un restricted		Ind		Unrestricted				
	S	R	H	IE	T	S	R	S	R	S	R	H	TG	R
Abingdon														
Windmill Hill	▲◊ ▼♦	▲▼			▼						▼	▲▼	▲	
Staines		▲▼				▼								
Broome Heath	▲◊					♦	▼♦▼	▼	▼♦		▼♦			▼
Carn Brea	◊ ▼♦									□				

NEUTRAL

	Simple				Inflected			Composite						Complex		
	Unrestricted				Independent restricted			Unrestricted				Ind restricted		Un restricted		Ind
	S	R	H	T	S	R	T	S	R	H	TG	R	T	R	H	R
Abingdon	▲▼	▲		■					▼	▲						
Windmill Hill	▲■ ▼♦	▲▼	▲		▼					▼						
Staines	▲▼	▼			▲					▲▼				▼		
Broome Heath		▼♦			▼			▲▼	▼♦			▼				
Carn Brea	▲▼				▲▼											

CLOSED

	Simple				Inflected			Composite								Complex		
	Unrestricted				Independent restricted			Ind restricted		Dependent restricted						Ind restricted		Dep restricted
	S	R	H	IE	S	R	H	R	TG	T	S	R	H	IE	R	IE	R
Abingdon		▲	▲		■		■					▲					
Windmill Hill	▲■ ▼	▲■ ▼♦	▲	▲		■			▼		▲	▲,					
Staines	▲	▲			▲	▲					▲						
Broome Heath	▼♦	▼			▲▼	▼		▲■ ▼			▲	▲ ▼♦			♦		▲
Carn Brea																	

KEY

S	Simple		■	1:2-1:1		♦	2:1-2.5:1
R	Rolled-over						
H	Heavy		▲	1:1-1.5:1		◊	2.5:1-3:1
T	"T" shaped						
IE	Internally extended		▼	1.5:1-2:1		□	3.5:1-4:1
TG	Thumb groove						

Figure 21.3: Incidence of mouth: depth ratios by form and site.

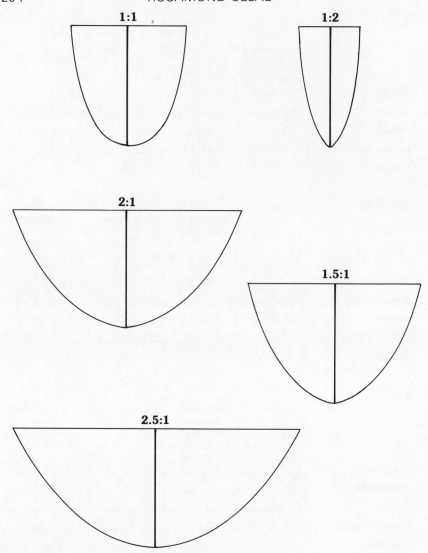

Figure 21.4: Illustration of mouth: depth ratios.

and therefore recorded, than those of deep forms (see Figure 21.4 for illustrations of mouth: depth ratios). High mouth: depth ratios are also a feature of
the open vessels at Broome Heath, as would be expected, and are identifiable
in five of the eight forms, whereas they are identifiable in only one at
Windmill Hill and none at Staines and Abingdon. The contrast between these
differences of detail and the similarity in forms between these assemblages
(Table 21.5) may be a reflection of the distance, both geographical and in

OPEN

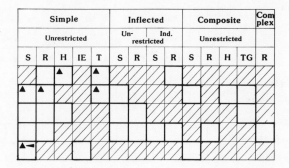

| | Simple | | | | | Inflected | | | | Composite | | | | Complex |
| | Unrestricted | | | | | Un-restricted | | Ind. restricted | | Unrestricted | | | | |
	S	R	H	IE	T	S	R	S	R	S	R	H	TG	R
Abingdon			▲		▲									
Windmill Hill	▲	▲			▲									
Staines														
Broome Heath														
Carn Brea	▲◄													

NEUTRAL

| | Simple | | | | Inflected | | | Composite | | | | | | Complex | | |
| | Unrestricted | | | | Independent restricted | | | Un-restricted | | | | Ind. | | Un-restricted | | Ind. |
	S	R	H	T	S	R	T	S	R	H	T	R	T	R	H	R
Abingdon				▲						▲■						
Windmill Hill	▲	▲	▲●			▲				■			●			
Staines	●						▲									
Broome Heath																
Carn Brea	▲●				■											▲

CLOSED

| | Simple | | | | Inflected | | | Composite | | | | | | | | Complex | | |
| | Unrestricted | | | | Independent restricted | | | Ind. restricted | | | Dep. restricted | | | | | Ind. restricted | | Dep. restricted |
	S	R	H	IE	S	R	H	R	TG	T	S	R	H	IE	R	IE	R
Abingdon		▲	▲■		▲		■						▲				
Windmill Hill	▲	▲●	▲●		▲						▲	▲		▲			
Staines	●																
Broome Heath	●																
Carn Brea	▲																

KEY

S	Simple	◄	Trumpet lug
R	Rolled-over		
H	Heavy	▲	Other lug
T	"T" shaped		
IE	Internally extended	■	Handle
TG	Thumb groove	●	Cordon

Figure 21.5: Incidence of attachments by form and site.

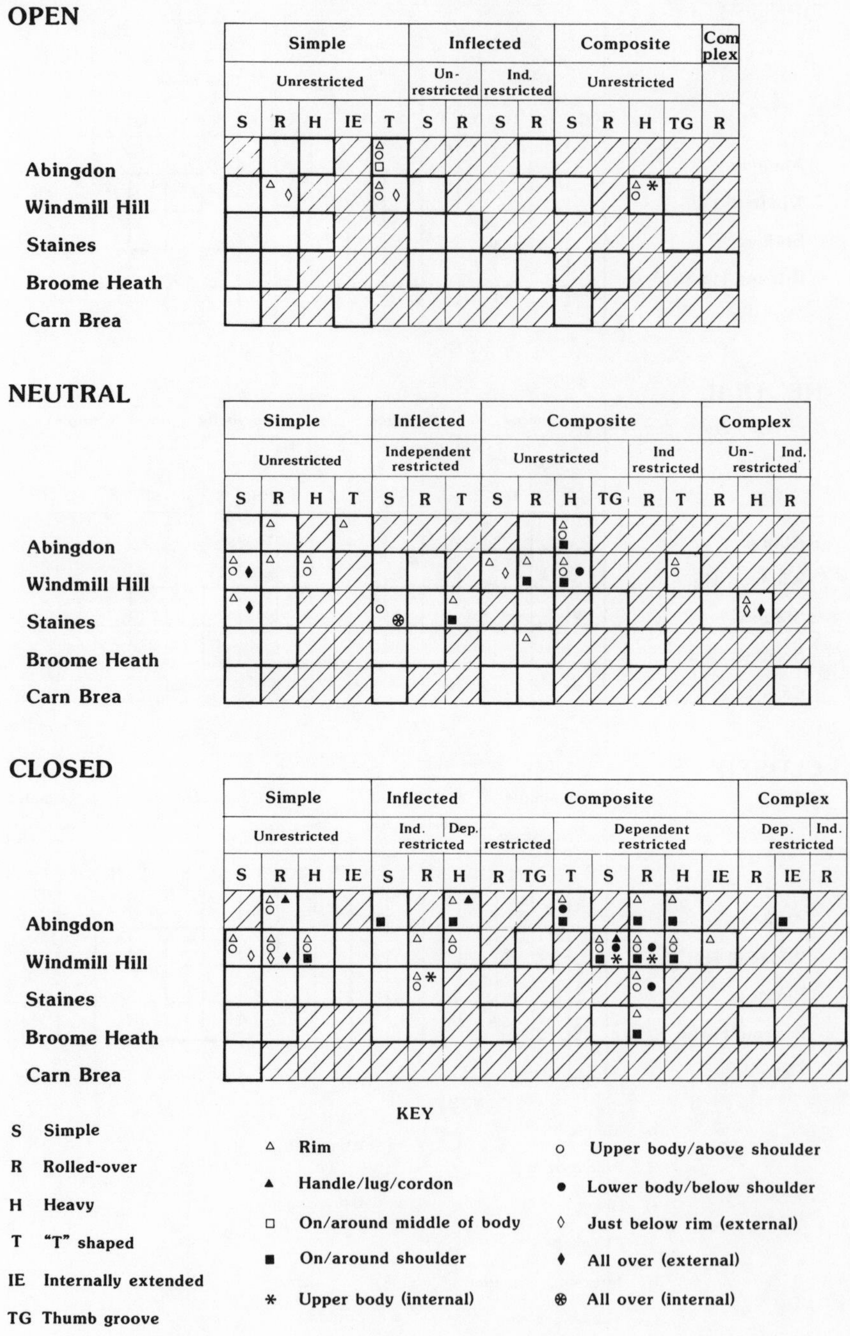

OPEN

	Simple					Inflected				Composite				Com plex
	Unrestricted					Un-restricted		Ind. restricted	Unrestricted					
	S	R	H	IE	T	S	R	S	R	S	R	H	TG	R

Abingdon
Windmill Hill
Staines
Broome Heath
Carn Brea

NEUTRAL

	Simple				Inflected			Composite						Complex		
	Unrestricted				Independent restricted			Unrestricted				Ind restricted		Un-restricted		Ind. restricted
	S	R	H	T	S	R	T	S	R	H	TG	R	T	R	H	R

Abingdon
Windmill Hill
Staines
Broome Heath
Carn Brea

CLOSED

	Simple				Inflected				Composite							Complex	
	Unrestricted				Ind. restricted		Dep. restricted		restricted		Dependent restricted					Dep. restricted	Ind. restricted
	S	R	H	IE	S	R	H	R	TG	T	S	R	H	IE	R	IE	R

Abingdon
Windmill Hill
Staines
Broome Heath
Carn Brea

KEY

△	Rim		o	Upper body/above shoulder
▲	Handle/lug/cordon		●	Lower body/below shoulder
□	On/around middle of body		◊	Just below rim (external)
■	On/around shoulder		♦	All over (external)
✱	Upper body (internal)		⊛	All over (internal)

S   Simple
R   Rolled-over
H   Heavy
T   "T" shaped
IE Internally extended
TG Thumb groove

Figure 21.6: Incidence of location of decoration by form and site.

Table 21.1: Form, by percentage, at **Broome Heath**

	CLOSED	NEUTRAL	OPEN
SIMPLE	9·5% (9)	4·2% (4)	4·2% (4)
INFLECTED	Independent restricted 15·8% (15)	Independent restricted 3·2% (3)	Unrestricted 10·5% (10); Independent restricted 6·3% (6)
COMPOSITE	Dependent restricted 15·8% (15); Independent restricted 8·4% (8)	Unrestricted 11·6% (11); Independent restricted 1·1% (1)	Unrestricted 6·3% (6)
COMPLEX	2·1% (2)		1·1% (1)

Table 21.2: Form, by percentage, at Carn Brea

	CLOSED	NEUTRAL	OPEN
SIMPLE	6·25% (5)	43·75% (35)	12·5% (10)
INFLECTED	Independent restricted	Independent restricted 1·25% (1)	Independent restricted
COMPOSITE	Independent restricted	Independent restricted; Unrestricted 2·5% (2)	Unrestricted 31·2% (25); 1·25% (1)
COMPLEX	Dependent restricted	1·25% (1)	Unrestricted

Table 21.3: Form, by percentage, at Staines

	CLOSED	NEUTRAL	OPEN
SIMPLE	28% (25)	17% (15)	Independent restricted — 19% (17)
INFLECTED	Independent restricted — 12% (11)	Independent restricted — 8% (7); Unrestricted — 1% (1); Thumb groove — 5% (4)	Unrestricted — 3% (3); Thumb groove — 2% (2)
COMPOSITE	Independent restricted — 1% (1); Dependent restricted — 1% (1)		
COMPLEX		Independent restricted — 2% (2)	

Table 21.4: Form, by percentage, at Windmill Hill

	CLOSED	*NEUTRAL*	*OPEN*
SIMPLE	37·0% (47)	28·3% (36)	11·0% (14)
INFLECTED	Independent restricted 2·4% (3)	Independent restricted 1·6% (2)	Independent restricted
COMPOSITE	Independent restricted 0·8% (1); Thumb groove 1·6% (2)	Independent restricted 0·8% (1); Unrestricted 5·5% (7) 2·4% (3)	Unrestricted 0·8% (1)
COMPLEX	Dependent restricted 5·5% (7)	Unrestricted 1·6% (2)	Thumb groove 0·8% (1)

Table 21.5: Jaccard coefficients for incidence of Open, Neutral and Closed forms

Incidence of forms as per Figures 21.3, 5 and 6; Jaccard Coefficient calculated for each pair of sites, using the formula $S_J = a/(a + b + c)$, where a, b and c represent the number of occurrences, thus:

$$\begin{array}{ccc} & \text{Site} & 2 \\ & + & - \\ \text{Site } 1 + & a & b \\ - & c & \end{array}$$

The higher the Jaccard coefficient value, the more similar the pair of assemblages.

Site pair	Open forms	Neutral forms	Closed forms
Abingdon/Staines	0·25	0·27	0·33
Abingdon/Windmill Hill	0·22	0·40	0·43
Abingdon/Broome Heath	0·20	0·33	0·21
Abingdon/Carn Brea	0·00	0·25	0·00
Staines/Windmill Hill	0·44	0·39	0·54
Staines/Broome Heath	0·33	0·45	0·55
Staines/Carn Brea	0·13	0·27	0·13
Windmill Hill/Broome Heath	0·25	0·6	0·4
Windmill Hill/Carn Brea	0·25	0·4	0·08
Broome Heath/Carn Brea	0·10	0·5	0·11

stylistic terms, between Broome Heath and the Decorated assemblages. It certainly suggests a much more complex situation than is indicated by the traditional framework, in which Broome Heath would have to be considered primarily as an Eastern Style site, or as a Decorated one, in the case of the latter the very name necessarily excluding it despite numerous formal similarities.

Although occurrences of size classes (by mouth-diameter) were recorded for each form, no clear patterns emerged, and the results are not presented here; it is perhaps more likely that if there are positive relationships between some vessel forms and some sizes, this would show in terms of volume rather than mouth diameter. However, it was noted that 'cups' (external diameter less than 120 mm) occurred in a wide range of forms, including Open, Neutral and Closed Composite forms, in all but the Carn Brea assemblage.

Simple logic might suggest that a positive relationship should exist between simple rims and the presence of handling aids, since simple rims offer no assistance in manipulating the vessel, in contrast to extended or heavy rims. This is clearly true in the case of the Carn Brea assemblage, which is dominated by simple rims and has handling aids on most forms. However, the converse cannot be shown to be true: although non-simple rims can certainly act as handling aids, nevertheless lugs, handles and cordons are represented on most Neutral and Closed forms, irrespective of rim form, from Windmill Hill and Abingdon, although few are identifiable at Staines

(Figure 21.5). Among Open forms, handling aids are represented only on Simple forms, and only at Windmill Hill, Staines and Carn Brea, although they do occur on forms with simple and non-simple rims. Cordons, a rare feature in all assemblages, are represented only on Neutral and Closed Simple forms, at Windmill Hill, Staines, Broome Heath and Carn Brea. Handles too are represented only on Neutral and Closed forms, at Abingdon, Windmill Hill and Carn Brea.

An alternative method of presenting the data on shape was also attempted for four of the sites (Tables 21.1 to 21.4 and Figure 21.2). Although this is a crude representation of assemblages formed over perhaps several generations, it does indicate differences between them which may represent long-term preferences for certain vessel forms. For instance, Broome Heath shows a clear emphasis on Inflected and Composite forms, as opposed to Simple ones, in sharp contrast to Carn Brea, which is dominated by Simple forms. These are perhaps very obvious differences, but the method also highlights, for instance, the importance of Inflected forms, especially Closed, at Staines, in contrast to a rarity of all Inflected forms at Windmill Hill. Because of the difficulty of restoring profiles and the occurrence of quite a high proportion of carinated vessels in which it cannot be determined whether the form is Open or Neutral, a hybrid entry has been allowed in these Tables. This demonstrates not only the very great contrast between Carn Brea and the other assemblages, which is obvious from a cursory glance at the pottery, but also the different preferences in Composite vessels between Broome Heath and Windmill Hill. The former assemblage, as well as having a high proportion of Composite vessels, also shows a preference for Closed Composite forms, a preference not apparent at Windmill Hill. Both Broome Heath and Staines share a preference for Inflected Independent Restricted forms – again, as suggested above, an indication of nuances of relationship not allowed for in the conventional framework.

This analysis is presented not as a definitive treatment of the material, but simply as an illustration of what might be achieved by a systematic approach, as opposed to the traditional approach of parallel-seeking and assigning assemblages to established regional styles.

SUMMARY AND CONCLUSIONS

The classification of Earlier Neolithic pottery in southern Britain, it is argued, is in need of a review in which it may be necessary to discard the regional styles as presently formulated. It is possible that they may survive the exercise, but it would seem to be important to adopt an approach, perhaps along the lines suggested above, in which the existence of regional styles is not assumed *a priori*.

In addition, one can argue that we are not presently viewing pots enough as objects, but are influenced too much by the two-dimensional view of them presented by the traditional schemes. We should be aware of the various ways in which pots may be viewed and used, and of the limitations and freedoms presented by the medium. Very simple modifications to the way we treat pots, such as the introduction of volume as a standard attribute in pottery reports, would greatly assist in engendering a view of pots as functioning objects. Other means might include the calculation, as standard treatments, of ratios for mouth : depth, maximum diameter : depth, or upper-body : lower-body measurements where possible. Perhaps we could also include, as a standard item rather than an optional extra, three-dimensional reconstructions of the main elements in, for instance, whole sites, or elements of sites, as is sometimes done for pottery of later periods, illustrated from non-standard viewpoints (e.g. isometrically rather than full-face).

The suggestion of a standardised approach to description is fundamental to the argument presented here. It would seem necessary, both to the question of spatial difference, and also to chronological change, to be able to chart differences and similarities in concrete terms. This is not to argue that the particular system outlined here is necessarily the most appropriate, but rather that this type of methodology is a means to improve our understanding of the pottery. Of course, it may be argued that one could go on adding attributes to be studied without adding greatly to the value of the classification, and that is partly true. However, it is quite clear that, in the traditional classification, some features are undervalued or ignored altogether despite the fact that, on the evidence both of analogy with contemporary pottery-using communities and a consideration of pots as objects, such features are clearly important. If we are to progress at all, these must be integrated into new classifications.

Inherent in this is the suggestion that the use of type-site identifications should be abandoned, or at least not accorded the primary position which they now occupy. Type-site identifications of styles suggest entities which are internally consistent, even if, as in Cunliffe's Iron Age style zones, two names are employed to show the range within the style (Cunliffe 1978, Chapter 3). This would seem not to be appropriate to Earlier Neolithic pottery, which might be envisaged as part of a much more fluid network of movement and exchange, in which pots (and perhaps their makers) may travel long distances. Rather than Kinnes' model of overlapping Neolithic 'style zones' (1978, Figure 38), I would postulate a network with altogether looser connections, in which none of the major sites is wholly single-style and in which pots, and possibly pot-makers, moved from region to region. To come full circle, this is clear perhaps at Windmill Hill, a site which, although published before the current emphasis on fabric, suggests the contribution of pottery-making groups from nearby, a moderate distance, and long distance. The variety in both fabric and style at Windmill Hill offers great scope for the application of techniques such as neutron activation analysis of fabric or multivariate analysis of form and decoration. One may have to break the habits of thought which are encouraged by the traditional regional style framework in order to appreciate the full complexity of the relations represented. The pottery of the Earlier Neolithic has much still to offer, and we owe it to its makers to utilise to the full all its richness and variety.

ACKNOWLEDGEMENTS

I am grateful to Christopher Gingell for his valuable comments on this chapter, and to Elizabeth James for the illustrations. Responsibility for the opinions expressed must, of course, lie with the author alone.

Definition of terms used in Figures 21.2, 21.3, 21.5 and 21.6 and Tables 21.1 to 21.4

Overall form

Open: mouth diameter exceeds maximum body diameter
Neutral: mouth diameter and maximum body diameter approximately equal
Closed: maximum body diameter exceeds mouth diameter

Type of profile

Simple: lacks inflection and corner points
Inflected: possesses one inflection point
Composite: possesses one corner point
Complex: possesses more than two inflection points, or corner points, or has a combination of both

Degree of restriction

Unrestricted: No corner point or inflection point above equator
Dependent
Restricted: The diameter at the corner point or inflection point is the same as that of the equator (i.e. usually is the same point – only in complex contours may not be)
Independent
Restricted: An inflection point or corner point is present above the equator and is less than it (i.e. in contrast to dependent restricted forms, the diameter of the inflection/corner point is separate from – or independent of – that of the equator)

Part 4
Regional Studies

22

The Hebridean Neolithic

Ian Armit

INTRODUCTION

As in later periods of prehistory, the Hebrides in the Neolithic have suffered from a persistent lack of archaeological interest. Work on the nature and development of Scottish Neolithic societies has tended to concentrate on better-known Orcadian and Shetland evidence. This same concentration on one focal area has occurred in recent decades for the Atlantic Scottish Iron Age. Recent work on the Western Isles and Argyll, however, has begun to stress the value which lies in the study of relationships between distinct regional trajectories of development (e.g. Armit 1990a, Nieke 1990). Perhaps the same widening of regional awareness might have beneficial effects for our understanding of the Scottish Neolithic.

This chapter attempts to present the Western Isles and the wider Hebridean zone as an additional and complementary focus for research to the Northern Isles and to assess the potential gains to be made from the comparisons and contradictions of disparate regional models. The data used will be those from the Western Isles, defined in their modern political sense. The limitations of space prevent any wide-ranging discussion of all the elements of the Hebridean Neolithic and require a concentration on one aspect of the data: in this case the settlement evidence. The major part of the following discussion will be concerned with this. The final part of the chapter will assess the potential of regional studies within the wider Scottish Neolithic.

THE SETTLEMENTS

Five Neolithic settlement sites are now known in the Western Isles (Figure 22.1), two having been identified and excavated within the past five years. Distinct patterns in the settlement evidence are now building up which enable some discussion of the nature of domestic settlement in the Hebridean Neolithic.

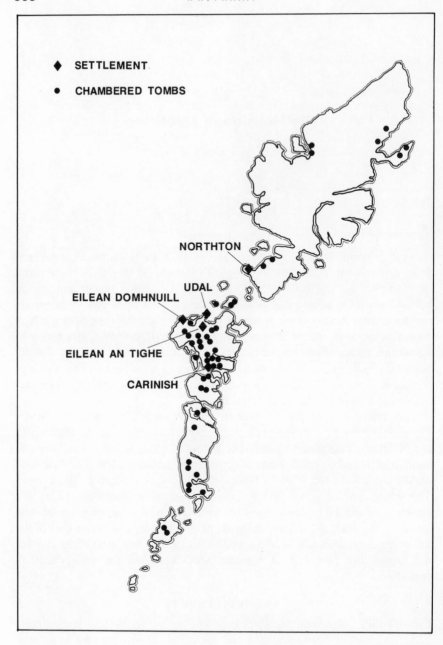

Figure 22.1: The Hebridean Neolithic – chambered tombs and settlements.

Eilean Domhnuill, Loch Olabhat

The most significant Neolithic settlement site presently known in the Western Isles is the site of Eilean Domhnuill, an islet in Loch Olabhat in the north-west of North Uist (Figure 22.2). This site has been the focus of four seasons of excavation since 1986 as part of the Loch Olabhat Research Project, a landscape project focusing on the excavation and survey of sites in the area centred on Loch Olabhat (Armit 1986, 1987, 1988, 1990c).

The circumstances of the discovery of this site are detailed in the first interim report (Armit 1986). The site had initially been regarded as a standard example of an Iron Age island dun or broch, appearing as a low, flat, stony islet in a shallow loch. An earlier *sondage* by the local antiquary Erskine Beveridge (1911) had revealed nothing to distinguish the site structurally from the many Iron Age sites he had examined in the area, and Beveridge failed to realise the Neolithic date of the pottery which he had found (cf. Henshall 1972). The initial season of the present work was focused on the adjacent promontory, Eilean Olabhat, with only a small trial trench excavated on Eilean Domhnuill, to access the nature of any structures present. The quantities of Neolithic pottery recovered from Eilean Domhnuill demonstrated, from the initial excavation, that the site was exclusively of Neolithic date.

Eilean Domhnuill is a multi-phase, partially waterlogged settlement site. There is no evidence of any outcrop rock in the excavated areas, and all of the deposits which form the parts of the islet so far excavated are anthropogenic. Most comprise midden material and structural and occupation debris. The site had been occupied over a prolonged period during the Neolithic, and the excavations carried out between 1986 and 1990 have revealed twelve phases of this occupation. There is every indication that quantities of material remain unexcavated in the lower, waterlogged layers. The excavated phases reveal the artificial definition of the islet by palisades and revetments and control of access through an elaborate entrance. Whether the islet was wholly man-made or originally simply a consolidated outcrop, it was a wholly artificial and structured environment for much of its use, created and maintained by a Neolithic community.

One of the principal results of the excavation has been the recovery of a number of house plans and evidence for house construction. Three major episodes can be defined from the structural sequence, and these are divided into twelve Phases (numbered latest to earliest as excavated – Figure 22.3). The earliest excavated series comprises Phases 12–5, a long period of occupation during which many successive houses occupied the site and substantial midden-deposits accumulated. Preservation of these structures is poor, with the building of each house destroying its predecessor. This period of occupation was associated with a timber causeway and an elaborate entrance façade which was altered on a number of occasions. Figure 22.4 shows a reconstruc-

Figure 22.2: Eilean Domhnuill, Loch Olabhat, North Uist.

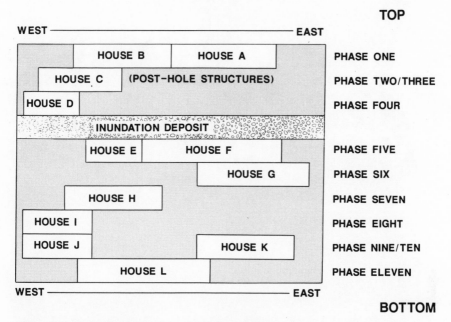

Figure 22.3: Eilean Domhnuill, Loch Olabhat: schematic section

tion drawing by Alan Braby which draws on the evidence of a number of elements from the early phases. During this period, the loch level rose consistently, necessitating the remodelling of the entrance works and eventually drowning the site (covering it in a sealing layer of loch silt) and forcing temporary abandonment.

These early excavated phases at Eilean Domhnuill display a range of structural elements. The principal structural features comprise stone alignments which define the extent of floor-deposits. These are very fragmentary and are commonly displaced: the structures which they represent appear to have been relatively slight and there is little evidence to suggest that coursed walls were ever present. These alignments partially delineate domestic structures: their 'interiors' contain hearths and occupation debris and are generally distinct from surrounding deposits. There is a lack of substantial post-holes in this phase, and, although some do occur, principally in Phase 5, most of the negative features are slight stake-holes, with charred stakes themselves often present in the lower levels. Wattlework hurdle fragments, found both on land and in the underwater trench excavated in 1989, suggest that this was a common structural element.

The structures are rectilinear or elongated oval in shape, and their size can seldom be determined with any precision; most extend into the north section which delimits the extent of the excavated area. The Phase 7 house measures

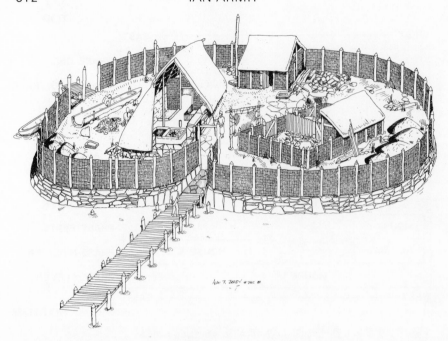

Figure 22.4: Eilean Domhnuill, Loch Olabhat: artist's reconstruction (by Alan Braby).

approximately 9 × 5·5 m externally, and the surviving parts of the other houses suggest that this may have been representative.

After an abandonment of unknown duration, the site was reoccupied by a succession of slight structures associated with a stone causeway. These form the second major episode of occupation and are still unambiguously Neolithic. The later of these Phases, Phase 2/3, contained a large number of substantial post-holes of a greater scale than any in the earlier deposits. These formed no recognisable structure and were broadly contemporary with a boulder-defined structure containing a hearth.

The final structures to occupy the site were two substantial and conjoined rectilinear buildings with stone and earth walls. The larger of these houses measures approximately 9 × 5·5 m externally (about 6·5 × 4 m internally), the same dimensions as the earlier Phase 7 house, while the smaller measures about 7 × 5 m (about 4 m × 3 m internally). These were again associated with the stone causeway, but the ceramics appear slightly different, hinting perhaps at a slightly later, although still Neolithic, date. The closest parallels for the Phase 1 structures are the Neolithic houses from the Knap of Howar (A. Ritchie 1983). In both cases, two conjoined rectilinear structures dominate a settlement with earlier occupation. The location of the two sites is very different however, and the Knap of Howar structures are somewhat larger: similarities of form may well be superficial.

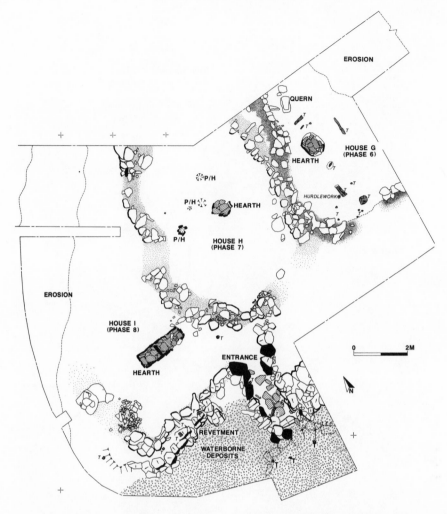

Figure 22.5: Eilean Domhnuill, Loch Olabhat: simplified plan of the houses of Phases 6, 7 and 8.

The ceramic assemblage from the excavated parts of Eilean Domhnuill totals some 20,000 sherds, the majority decorated (Figure 22.7), providing a vast resource for the study of ceramic development and variation in a well-contextualised assemblage. By contrast, the lithic assemblage is impoverished and there are indications that locally-available quartz was used as a substitute for better-quality material. Other common finds include saddle querns, pieces of pumice and wooden structural elements (including a piece of non-indigenous wood, possibly North American larch or spruce, collected as flotsam). Rarer finds include a single stone bead, a piece of rope, two

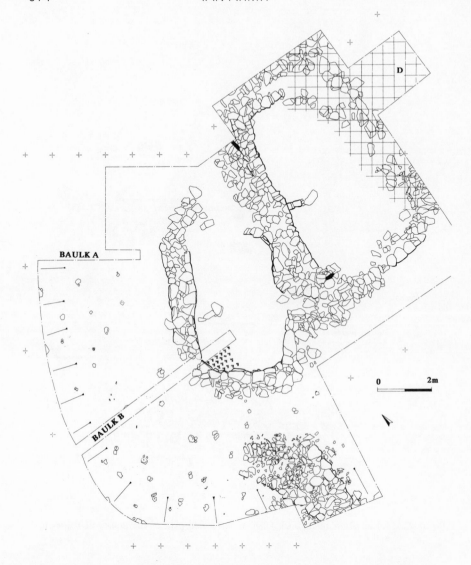

Figure 22.6: Eilean Domhnuill, Loch Olabhat: simplified plan of the houses of Phase 1.

decorated ceramic phallic-shaped objects, worked bone and a decorated stone ball.

Eilean Domhnuill appears to have been a settlement site, but its precise role and status in the economy and settlement system of its builders remains hazy. There is evidence suggesting agricultural processing on the islet: a number of saddle querns were recovered which indicate the processing of grain (although the context of many of these in house walls suggests that

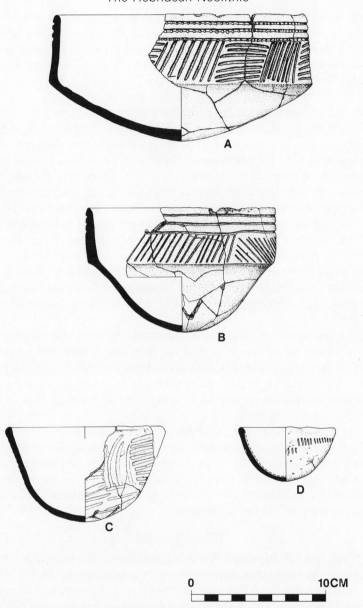

Figure 22.7: Eilean Domhnuill, Loch Olabhat: examples of Unstan bowls from the site.

some at least may have arrived on the site as building stone). There is little evidence that animals were kept on the islet: the preservation of untrampled, thin, ash lenses across the site suggests little post-depositional disturbance by stock. Despite the fact that vast quantities of pottery are found on the site, there is no evidence at present for its manufacture (although simple firing hearths or pits can be hard to distinguish from domestic cooking facilities). Similarly, despite well-preserved wood from the waterlogged contexts, there are, at present, no wood chips identified which would be expected from wood-working *in situ* (Skinner personal communication). The lithic assemblage has yet to be examined in detail, but there are indications (e.g. beach cobble hammerstones) that knapping took place on the site.

As yet, it appears that Eilean Domhnuill may have been only one, although possibly the main, component of a range of sites with different specific functions utilised by its builders and inhabitants. Limited excavations on the loch shore have produce no evidence for activity there. It might well be the case that a related complex of sites occupied specific, diverse, resource-based areas encompassing machair, lowland and hills, and that functionally-specialised sites remain to be found. With our current limited knowledge of Neolithic economic practices and of the nature of the change from Mesolithic to Neolithic, it would be unwise to assume that a sudden sedentism developed or that single domestic centres need have appeared. If this hypothesis is valid, it may help to account for the repeated rebuilding of the domestic structures; perhaps we are witnessing the annual or seasonal re-establishment of the settlement.

The persistent rise of the loch level during the Phases so far excavated has been remarked on above. It is possible that this drastic, and apparently relatively rapid, loch-level rise may have been initiated by anthropogenic factors. Deforestation of the site catchment, for example, or progressive over-exploitation of soils, may have contributed to a greater flow of water and sediment into the loch.

It was the final inundation of the islet which appears to have preserved the Neolithic deposits from disturbance by later occupation. The walls around Eilean Olabhat, an Iron Age site in the same loch, show that later prehistoric loch levels were such as to have virtually drowned the Neolithic site. This fortuitous circumstance of preservation has enabled a widening of our perception of early settlement in the west.

Bharpa Carinish

The other recently identified Neolithic settlement site in North Uist lies adjacent to the chambered tomb at Bharpa Carinish (Crone 1989). This site is soon to be published (Crone forthcoming), so no attempt will be made to provide detailed interpretation here. Some specific comparisons of this settlement with various features at Eilean Domhnuill, however, might be useful.

The settlement evidence at Carinish comprised a series of occupation deposits, principally ash and charcoal, a spread of ceramic material and occasional structural fragments including stake-holes, hearths and a stone alignment. No coherent structure plans could be discerned, and the structural elements were reminiscent of the early phases at Eilean Domhnuill. The difference between the two sites was that at Carinish a relatively short-lived occupation seems to be represented, in contrast to the great depth of material at Eilean Domhnuill. Ceramic forms appear identical, although the Carinish assemblage was relatively small, comprising some 500 sherds (Armit and MacSween forthcoming). It has been suggested that the lack of substantial structures may relate to a ritual function associated with the use of the chambered tomb (Crone 1989), but, given the similarity of structural elements to those at Eilean Domhnuill, a more mundane domestic function seems likely.

Eilean an tighe

Eilean an Tighe is a small natural islet in a large loch in North Uist. In the 1940s, Sir Lindsay Scott excavated a series of small Neolithic structures on part of the islet and concluded that they represented the remains of a potter's workshop (W.L. Scott 1951a). Derek Simpson has already drawn attention to the lack of ceramic wasters on the site as evidence against Scott's interpretation (1976, 222), and the accumulating evidence from Eilean Domhnuill and Carinish suggests that the slight stone structures at Eilean an Tighe may well have been the remains of domestic structures: the presence of large quantities of ash at the latter site again corresponds to the floor-deposits at the other two settlements.

Viewed in this light, Eilean an Tighe is a close parallel for Eilean Domhnuill: both produced vast quantities of ceramics of identical forms; both have evidence for slight, boulder structures with extensive ash deposits; both lie on islets in inland lochs; both are of broadly similar dimensions. The lack of a causeway at Eilean an Tighe is not evidence of any functional difference, since the timber causeway belonging to the earlier excavated phases at Eilean Domhnuill would not have been visible had it not been rebuilt in stone at a late stage in the occupation.

Northton

The fourth major Neolithic settlement in the Western Isles lies on the south Harris machair at Northton, stratified below deposits yielding Beaker ceramics and structures (D.D.A. Simpson 1976). The site preserved few structural elements, although 'one short length of dry stone walling' was found and other boulders had clearly been brought to the site (ibid., 221). The ceramic range closely parallels that from Eilean Domhnuill and the other settlement sites. The available evidence suggests that this site is a further example of a Hebridean Neolithic settlement pattern of slight, transient structures with occupation most visibly demonstrated by the deposition of large quantities of ceramics.

Other settlement sites

There are other sporadic instances of sites which may be Neolithic settlements in the Western Isles. The most important of these is the site at the Udal, which has been recorded as yielding Hebridean-style pottery (Kinnes 1985, 49). The pottery, however, has not been published, and details of typology cannot presently be verified. Similarly, the claims made for the existence on the site of structures 'of fairly elaborate building style' (Crawford n.d., 7) cannot be assessed without publication of the evidence. If it is indeed a Neolithic site, it would represent a machair context with more definite structural evidence than is recorded elsewhere.

There is a record in the *Proc Soc Antiq Scotl* for 1904–5 of the discovery of a sherd of Hebridean Ware on Pigmies Isle, a small tidal islet off the north-west of the Butt of Lewis (MacKenzie 1905). No associated deposits are recorded, although there is later activity on the site. This rather scant record does suggest the possibility of a further Neolithic islet settlement.

Finally, the ongoing Sheffield University programme of survey and excavation in the Hebrides has produced a few sherds resembling Hebridean Neolithic pottery on Barra (SEARCH 1989).

SUMMARY AND DISCUSSION

The discovery of the Neolithic date of Eilean Domhnuill has opened up new possibilities for the definition of early settlement patterns in the Western Isles, particularly for North Uist where the main concentration of Hebridean funerary architecture also occurs (Armit 1990b, Chrisp 1990). The excavations at Eilean Domhnuill grew out of a wider reassessment of Hebridean prehistoric settlement, and their results fed back into that re-evaluation. There is now evidence to suggest that many of the islet settlements in the inland parts of the Western Isles, and most visibly in North Uist, may date to the earlier rather than later prehistoric period (Armit 1990d, Chapter 12). In addition, many Neolithic islet settlements may now be entirely submerged, as Eilean Domhnuill was for so long. More may lie unrecognised as simple featureless islets if, unlike Eilean Domhnuill, a stone causeway was never built.

Machair settlement is likely to have been an important element of Neolithic settlement in the Western Isles. The sites at Northton and the Udal have demonstrated the potential of this environment, especially significant since it lends itself to the preservation of different materials to the acidic inland soils. Much of the Neolithic machair has now been lost to coastal erosion, however, and it is important to maximise the archaeological resources directed towards any such sites located in the future.

A further and almost wholly unexplored environment is Neolithic cave occupation. The ceramic assemblage from Ulva Cave in the Inner Hebrides, recovered as a by-product of the excavation of pre-Neolithic deposits, has affinities with the Unstan and Hebridean styles from the Western Isles (Armit forthcoming).

It is possible that substantial inland landscapes of Neolithic and Bronze

Age date lie buried under the peat of the Western Isles, with numerous islet settlements as their surviving visible elements. The excavations at Bharpa Carinish (Crone 1989), where preliminary survey located field walls associated with a chambered cairn, indicate the possibilities of simple sub-surface probing to locate settlement sites and field systems. That survey was located in an area adjacent to a chambered cairn, but similar surveys based around inland islet settlements may have equally important results. The unusual inland site at Steinacleit in Lewis may well represent Neolithic settlement, in this case exposed by peat-cutting (RCAHMS 1928, no. 18, 8), and it should be remembered that the Callanish stones were, until relatively recently, partially buried in the peat (Ashmore 1983).

Overall, the pattern which is emerging for Neolithic settlement in the Western Isles is one of slight, small-scale structures with large quantities of ceramics as the only indicator of extensive occupation. There seems to have been a general unspoken feeling that finally a western Skara Brae would emerge, fitting the pattern seen in the north. In fact, the Hebridean settlement picture has been with us for some time but has gone unrecognised. There is no indication of monumental Neolithic architecture such as we see in the Orkneys and elsewhere, nor of the solid settlement structures of the Scord of Brouster area in Shetland (Whittle 1986). No indication of clustered settlement is apparent in the west, again in contrast to parts of the Orcadian Neolithic settlement picture. The closest settlement parallels between the two island groups are the Phase 1 (last phase) structures on Eilean Domhnuill (Armit 1988) with the Knap of Howar structures in the Orkneys (A. Ritchie 1983). In the Western Isles, the apparent transience of the known settlements further emphasises the contrast between the houses of the living and the cairns for the dead with their monumentality and permanence. The hints from Eilean Domhnuill that the known settlements may be elements within more dispersed settlement systems emphasise the lack of a clearly-defined home base for the Neolithic communities of the area. The realisation of this possibility may open up new avenues in the interpretation of the role of funerary architecture in Hebridean Neolithic societies.

The dating of these Neolithic settlements is not yet clear, although processing of additional samples in the near future may help to resolve the situation. A bone sample from the later of two Neolithic phases at Northton gave a date of 3105–2905 CAL-BC (BM-705). Dates from the Udal structures are reputed to be 'ca. 21–2300 B.C.' (sic, Crawford n.d., but presumably referring to an uncalibrated radiocarbon timescale). The four Neolithic dates from Bharpa Carinish range from c. 3350 to c. 2650 CAL-BC (Crone personal communication).

An initial series of radiocarbon dates from Eilean Domhnuill is shortly to be processed, but, at present, the parallels of the ceramic assemblage at Carinish and Northton are the only means of dating. Similarly, dates from

Neolithic contexts at Ulva Cave are shortly to be obtained (Bonsall personal communication).

In the domestic structures and in the apparent dispersal of activity areas, the settlement patterns of the Hebridean Neolithic appear little different from their Mesolithic predecessors in the Inner Hebrides. The nature of the transition from Mesolithic to Neolithic in western Scotland has recently been explored elsewhere, revealing possible factors of continuity which have not previously been apparent (Armit and Finlayson forthcoming). The Mesolithic settlement excavated on Rhum (Wickham-Jones 1990), for example, is not dissimilar in its structural elements to Hebridean Neolithic settlements, including later, Neolithic evidence from the same site. Later Neolithic settlement too, in the conventionally-defined Beaker period, displays structures of a similar nature to those of the preceding Mesolithic and Neolithic (e.g. D.D.A. Simpson 1976, Shepherd 1976).

A striking feature of Hebridean Neolithic settlement is the use of islets in shallow lochs. Eilean an Tighe was set on a natural islet formed of outcrop, but Eilean Domhnuill was substantially, perhaps wholly, artificial and delimited at various times by stone revetments and timber palisades. This locational preference seems to have set a pattern in Hebridean settlement which survived throughout prehistory (Armit 1990d).

There is little evidence for more than sporadic contacts between the Northern and Western Isles during the Neolithic. Despite the shared occurrence of 'Unstan bowls' and some other associated pottery, the development of pottery styles does not appear to follow the same pattern in the two areas. The putative 'Unstan'/Grooved Ware progression or dichotomy is not a feature of the western ceramic record. Grooved Ware is not present in the Western Isles in any quantity, the exceptions being one vessel at the chambered tomb of Unival and sherds from the excavations at Callanish (listed in Kinnes 1985, 49–50). The striking dominance of Beaker pottery in the later Hebridean Neolithic finds no reflection in the north. Hebridean styles similarly are not a feature of the northern ceramic assemblages. The Maes Howe-type passage tombs of the north again have no western equivalents: whatever social transformations were associated with the development of these monuments, we cannot see a parallel process in the chambered tombs of the west.

The realisation that there need be no single Scottish Neolithic is not a new one; indeed, it was stressed by Kinnes in his recent overview of the subject (ibid., 16). This chapter has suggested that significant differences may exist in the pattern of Neolithic societies between the Northern and Western Isles. A further regional variant may be represented by the settlement at Balbridie, which currently appears alien to recognised regional traditions (Ralston 1982). It may well be that the construction of regional sequences of development and the relationships and articulation of these sequences may be the best means available of advancing our overall understanding of the complexities of the period.

ACKNOWLEDGEMENTS

I would like to thank Mr Alan Braby for permission to use his drawings for the illustrations which accompany this chapter. Preliminary drafts were read by Dr Bill Finlayson, Professor D.W. Harding and Diane Nelson, and their comments are gratefully acknowledged. I would also like to thank Dr Anne Crone for allowing me to make reference to her work at Bharpa Carinish in advance for its full publication.

Much of this chapter has been based on the work at Eilean Domhnuill, Loch Olabhat, funded by the National Museums of Scotland, the Russell Trust, the Society of Antiquaries of Scotland and the Munro Trust.

23

Aspects of Regionalisation in the Scottish Neolithic

Niall M. Sharples

INTRODUCTION

This chapter originated as a discussion at the end of an analysis of the Neolithic tombs and ceramics of Scotland. It was intended to show that the Scottish Neolithic could be divided into discrete regional units, and the purpose of the discussion was to define these units and discuss their significance. However, on examining the evidence (most of which, needless to say, derives from Audrey Henshall's work), it became increasingly clear that this was not going to be possible. The most striking features of the Scottish Neolithic appeared to be the lack of similarity between the regions, and the fact that most of the diagnostic regional traits were normally restricted to a very specific locale within each region. This might simply be the result of differential survival of the evidence and archaeological research, but this seems more and more unlikely. Why, for instance, are most of the classic examples of Clyde, Hebridean, Clava, Camster and Stalled tombs concentrated in quite specific areas within a larger region and why do the stone circles of the western seaboard concentrate in clusters when those on the east are dispersed throughout the landscape?

To explore these questions, it was necessary to look in detail at the Orcadian evidence. It is arguable that one of the major problems of Scottish archaeology is the disproportionately large amount of resources spent on excavating, researching and arguing about Orkney. Nevertheless, the results of this effort and the quality of the surviving archaeology enable an exploration of problems which are seldom even visible in other areas.

I shall begin by re-examining some aspects of the Orcadian settlement evidence and by speculating on the Neolithic colonisation of the islands. I shall then use these speculations to order and assess the evidence for Neolithic settlement in the three regions of the western seaboard of Scotland: the Western Isles, the Clyde and the South-West. By doing this, I hope to make clear how the problems identified above – of regional variation and local concentrations – have historical reality and are not merely a product of archaeological practice.

One of the principal problems in understanding the nature of the Orcadian Neolithic has been the isolation of two contemporary but very different sets of material culture. The contrasts between these two units can be summarised as a series of oppositions, thus:

- Bookan tombs
- Maes Howe tombs
- Grooved Ware
- Village settlements
- Rich agricultural land
- Central locations

- Tripartite tombs
- Stalled tombs
- Unstan bowls
- Isolated houses
- Poor agricultural land
- Peripheral locations

This dichotomy can be shown to operate from at least the middle of the fourth millennium BC to the beginning of the third millennium BC and cannot be resolved by isolating geographically discrete territories (see Hedges 1984).

I have recently argued (Sharples 1985) that the Maes Howe tombs were an architectural innovation designed to facilitate the integration of the hitherto dispersed and independent communities of the Early Neolithic. They attracted a large number of people to a variety of ceremonies which were initially focused on burial. Rituals included the symbolic reclassification of individuals and their integration into a much larger community. Central to this interpretation was the link between large passage tombs and the prime agricultural land of the islands.

Upon reflection, a more convincing explanation would appear to emerge from considering the relationship between the Grooved Ware/Maes Howe complex and the farmland with which the monuments and settlements are associated (Fraser 1983, 263–9). While superficially these glacial till and extensive shell-sand machair deposits appear to be rich and/or easy to cultivate, in fact they would have been very problematic landscapes for early agricultural communities.

The glacial till of central Mainland Orkney would be physically difficult to cultivate and would require constant attention to drainage. The two excavated Grooved Ware settlements on clay soils, Barnhouse (Richards 1990) and Rinyo (Childe and Grant 1939, 1947) have clearly been built with this problem in mind, both being equipped with complicated drainage systems. All the drains are clay-lined flagstone constructions, but at Rinyo a bark lining was also recorded (Childe and Grant 1939, 18). Similar elaborate drains were also found at Skara Brae, but here, in a well-drained sand dune, they could have a more symbolic function (see D.V. Clarke and Sharples 1985, 65). Admittedly, the settlements' drainage is not crucial to the agricultural exploitation of the landscape, but it does indicate a sophisticated understanding of hydraulic engineering.

The occupation of the machair systems would create different problems. Soils developed on shell sand are deficient in essential nutrients and have a tendency to suffer cataclysmic deflation when the surface is broken. These problems can best be solved by the creation of thick middens which fertilise the soil and, by creating a topsoil, stabilise it. At the Links of Noltland, one of the areas excavated was part of a field which had been repeatedly ard-cultivated and heavily fertilised with midden (ibid., plate 4.10). The large midden surrounding the settlement at Skara Brae (D.V. Clarke 1976a; 1976b) was effectively a bank of fertiliser, of some symbolic importance to the community, as without it the settlement would probably have ceased to exist. Such a response to the problems of farming machair is found throughout prehistory. There are similar semi-subterranean Bronze Age settlements encased in midden at Jarlshof, and Late Iron Age examples all along the west coast of the Uists.

The factor linking the clay-based and machair-based settlements is not the technical innovations needed to facilitate arable agriculture, but the social resources necessary to achieve the solution. Both landscapes require intensive agricultural production, and it is likely that these societies would be closely-integrated, endogamous communities.

It is therefore possible that the development of Maes Howe passage tombs and the Grooved Ware tradition was closely related to a number of economic and social innovations which enabled the creation of villages. These social transformations were necessary for the intensive exploitation of difficult but potentially very productive ecosystems. As argued elsewhere (Sharples 1985), Maes Howe tombs performed this integrative function by acting as the theatre where the symbolic breaking-up and intermixing of individuals took place.

In contrast one can suggest, on the basis of the marginal position of the Stalled tombs and their rigid internal subdivision (Richards this volume, Chapter 5), that these functioned in a very different manner. They could well be territorial markers dividing the landscape into units, and would suggest a social system of rigidly-segmented, exogamous communities. This is supported by the isolated nature of the one 'Unstan' settlement so far identified, the Knap of Howar (A. Ritchie 1983), and the nature of the decoration on Unstan bowls. This is broken into panels of decoration which perhaps symbolically complement the divisions of the tombs (Hodder 1984).

The close relationship of material culture to specific agricultural practices suggests that the cultural affiliations of different groups or individuals could be transformed very quickly. This type of fluid but complex cultural cat-egorisation has been clearly demonstrated by Leach in the highlands of Burma (1954) and by Bloch in Madagascar (1982). In both areas, marriage patterns, tribal identity, settlement structure and material culture are closely related with the nature of the agricultural economy. Furthermore, in both areas, the dichotomy lies in the varying labour-intensity of agricultural practices in differing environments (i.e. wet rice vs. dry rice and garden cultivation).

These studies demonstrate that very different economic and cultural systems can exist in close proximity. They also show that certain individuals, families and larger communities can maintain their cultural identity when dealing with the other side, and can move from one system to the other. Such a complicated relationship between culture and economy may best explain the overlapping and interconnected nature of the Orcadian pattern as suggested above.

If one accepts that the Late Neolithic dichotomy emphasised by the Maes Howe and Stalled tombs has evolved from an existing Early Neolithic dichotomy, represented by Tripartite and Bookan tombs, then one can legitimately suggest that this dichotomy may derive from the nature of the Neolithic colonisation of Orkney. Two points need to be stressed:

1. The initial impetus for the agricultural settlement of Orkney came from the adjacent areas of mainland Scotland. The earliest Bookan and Tripartite tombs clearly have a familial relationship with the Camster tombs of Caithness (see for example, Richards this volume, Chapter 5), and certain examples are more or less identical on either side of the Pentland Firth.

2. These settlers were probably not entering a totally empty landscape. Most of the Hebrides had been colonised several millennia before the Neolithic occupation of Scotland, and it is difficult to believe that the absence of Mesolithic settlement in Orkney is a result of anything other than the lack of coordinated fieldwork.

Understanding the nature of the Neolithic settlement, therefore, depends on understanding the relationship of the hunter-gatherer and farmer. In general, one could envisage colonists, deriving from adjacent and only recently-colonised areas, where there may have been a marked increase in population, moving into less heavily-populated areas of the Orkneys where there were light soils conducive to arable agriculture. In Orkney, the distribution of these simple tombs suggests that these areas were the smaller islands north and south of the Mainland. Possible reasons for this preference are an open scrub woodland cover (caused by the effects of wind-blown salt water), and the absence of intractable till deposits. This would leave a community of hunter-gatherers in the Mainland, and perhaps smaller groups on the other islands, to be assimilated slowly into the agricultural way of life. Such communies could well acquire aspects of Neolithic culture before abandoning completely their hunter-gatherer subsistence strategies.

Over time, those communities developed in the Orkney Mainland, and 'used' their more flexible social structure to create village communities which maximised the economic potential of the landscape. The more established agricultural communities on other islands, in contrast, became restricted by a social structure which emphasised territorality. In these areas, individual farmsteads were the primary units of agricultural production. Where the area of cultivable land was naturally restricted, as on Rousay, this resulted in a particularly elaborate form of unrestrained megalithic construction which can perhaps be explained as competitive emulation between communities under severe economic stress.

BROADER APPLICATIONS

By linking the Orcadian patterns of the Late Neolithic to a structural dichotomy created by the initial Neolithic colonisation, one can interpret the distribution of tombs, stone circles and Mesolithic settlement in general terms thus:

1. Primary agricultural settlement could be expected to occur in the areas outside the main areas of Mesolithic settlement.

2. Concentrations of elaborate traditional tombs emerge in landscapes where the light soils capable of supporting agricultural practices were restricted.

3. The development of complicated Late Neolithic communities occurred in landscapes which may have been unsuitable for early agriculturalists. These were areas where marginalised hunter-gatherer communities survived alongside the earliest agricultural communities.

The remainder of this chapter concentrates on examining the archaeological record for the Neolithic occupation of the west coast of Scotland, where all of these patterns occur.

THE WESTERN ISLES

Taking into account the growing evidence for settlement as described by Armit (this volume, Chapter 22), the principal evidence for early prehistoric occupation in the Western Isles remains the distribution of chambered tombs. These are scattered fairly evenly along the edge of the coastal plain on Barra, South Uist and Benbecula, with sporadic occurrences on Lewis and Harris, notably on the sandstone outcrops around Stornoway. The principal feature of the distribution is, however, a major concentration of monuments on the island of North Uist (Henshall 1972, maps 4 and 5).

That the underlying distribution of tombs is related to the agricultural potential of the soils is demonstrated in Lewis by their clustering around Stornoway. However, the concentration of tombs on North Uist, like that on Rousay, cannot be explained in this manner. Comparison of this distribution with that of later prehistoric settlements (Armit 1990b) has clearly shown that tombs are considerably over-represented on North Uist.

Explanation of the settlement of the Western Isles is hindered by the presence of large areas of machair along the western fringes of the long island. It is still unclear whether this wind-blown sand deposit existed in the Neolithic period. One could suggest that the conditions were intially favourable to agricultural settlements along the west coast of the long island, as this was a relatively treeless landscape with light, easily-cultivated soils. However, there was little scope for expansion into the inhospitable hinterland, and it is likely that the productivity of these soils deteriorated very quickly. Consequently, throughout the islands, and on North Uist in particular, there would have been increasing pressure on resources which could temporarily be kept in check by the construction of ever larger chambered tombs. The occupation of possibly defended island settlements at Eilean Domhnuill and Eilean an Tighe, and the development of richly-decorated Hebridean Wares, could likewise symbolise the increasing pressure between communities.

It is significant that the development of the one major complex of ritual monuments on the Western Isles occurs not on North Uist but on the west coast of Lewis. A group of about twelve stone circles and standing stones occurs around the major complex at Callanish. This complex is established in an area of very poor land, and it is difficult to believe that Early arable agriculture was ever capable of sustaining a community large enough to construct or justify the building of these monuments. It might have been possible, temporarily, to sustain a substantial community by exploiting marine resources. The stone circles are distributed around a complex of sea lochs with sheltered anchorages, and this area is also noted for its important salmon rivers. It may be no mere coincidence, then, that Early Mesolithic settlement of the area was dense enough to show up in the local pollen diagrams (Bohncke 1988).

THE CLYDE REGION

As pointed out by Hughes (1988), a similar variability of tomb density and agricultural potential is evident here. Most of the megaliths are found scattered across the less agriculturally-favourable landscapes of the Highland zone, such as Argyll, Bute and Islay, and there is a noticeable concentration on the island of Arran. This distribution is particularly remarkable when compared with that of Mesolithic settlement and polished stone axeheads (ibid., Figures 2 and 4), which concentrate on the adjacent Ayrshire mainland, with only sporadic occurrences in the areas favoured by chambered tombs. The latter correspond to the distribution of heavy clay soils, a significant feature of the Ayrshire coastal plain.

Particularly important is the situation in north Argyll around Oban (Pollard 1990). The continued occupation of the Oban caves into the Neolithic and the use of chambered tombs in adjacent but separate areas around Loch Nell and the Moss of Achnacree (ibid., Figure 2) suggest that hunter-gatherer subsistence strategies continued into the Neolithic period in close proximity to communities using chambered tombs.

Hughes used the distribution of tombs and Mesolithic lithic scatters to argue that Arran had a special position for the Neolithic inhabitants of the region, thanks to its perhipheral but important role as a summer hunting

ground for the Mesolithic communities on the Ayrshire coast, and its traditional importance to Mesolithic groups as a source of pitchstone, an
important lithic resource. This position was transformed by the arrival of
Neolithic settlers into a role as an island of the ancestors, to mediate 'between
life and death by bringing the linear progression of human life within the
cyclical patterns of the natural world' (Hughes 1988, 52).

I would argue, however, that the pattern represents a similar situation to
that in Orkney. The initial agricultural settlement can be seen as the result of
expansion from an adjacent area (in this case, the South-West: see below).
Settlement largely occurred in areas peripheral to the major Mesolithic
settlement on the Ayrshire coastal plain, partly (one assumes) because of
potential conflicts, but also because the landscapes exploited by both groups
were significantly different. Once settlement occurred, developments took a
number of different paths. In Arran, as in Rousay, the concentration of
tombs is dominated by typologically late examples, which in this case are
elongated, multi-compartment tombs of Clyde type. A process similar to that
suggested for Rousay and North Uist can be postulated. In Ayrshire, our
knowledge of Neolithic activity is unfortunately almost non-existent,
although it seems likely that the distribution of stone axeheads represents the
development of indigenous arable agriculture. Monuments are conspicuous
by their absence, but it may be that they are present but incorrectly classified
and dated. The recent debate on the chronology of the earthen mounds
of north Ayrshire (Linge 1987; J.G. Scott 1989) shows the potential for
reinterpretation of many monuments in the area.

Stone circles and henges are at present restricted to the western part of the
region. There are two significant concentrations of these monuments: one in
Arran at Machrie Moor, and one at Kilmartin in Mid Argyll. Topologically,
both areas stand out as unusual landscapes. Machrie Moor is one of the few
extensive areas of lowland moorland on Arran, and Kilmartin is a large
expanse of fluvio-glacial terrace on the edge of a large area of bog, which may
have been a coastal marsh when the monuments were erected. Both of these
areas would have been superficially attractive zones for continued hunter-
gatherer use, and at Machrie Moor there is good evidence, from pollen
analysis (Robinson 1983), for Mesolithic settlement. The discovery of
Grooved Ware and ard-marks preceding the construction of a stone circle in
recent excavations at Machrie (Haggarty forthcoming) is also analogous to
the situation on Orkney. It suggests that these communal monuments were
created by communities with a social structure more open to the development
of innovative economic and cultural ideas.

THE SOUTH-WEST

The South-West of Scotland is a very important area, as it highlights key
issues influencing views of the colonisation and subsequent development of
the Neolithic in the rest of Scotland. The burial monuments are particularly

interesting, as three distinct forms are present, namely Bargrennan tombs (discussed by Murray this volume, Chapter 3, and concentrating in the Galloway uplands), Clyde cairns (present on the coastal plain and river valleys of Wigtownshire and West Kirkcudbright) and non-megalithic long barrows (occurring in similar coastal and riverine locations in Dumfriesshire and West Kirkcudbright, Henshall 1972; Kinnes this volume, Chapter 7). Our understanding of these distributions is enhanced by the considerable number of lithic scatters documented in this area. These concentrate on the coastal plain, but recent research has also shown that Mesolithic scatters extend up the valleys into the high ground between Kirkcudbright and Ayrshire (Edwards et al. 1983). Unfortunately, there is no eqivalent distribution of Neolithic settlements to which this can be compared.

The principal feature distinguishing this region from the others examined in this chapter, and the adjacent Clyde region in particular, is the coincident distribution of Mesolithic settlement and burial monuments (Clyde and non-megalithic types). It is common to find tombs and lithic scatters in close juxtaposition. Furthermore, the typology of the tombs is very important. The tombs (excluding the Bargrennan group for the moment) are, with one exception, simple boxes or cists which have been made only slightly more complex by the later addition of porches or elaborate façades. These have been understandably compared to wooden prototypes, and the close similarities between Cairnholy I (S. Piggott and Powell 1949) and the wooden structure below the cairn at Lochhill (Masters 1981b) is convincing. It might be argued, therefore, that this area is one of the few in Scotland where the indigenous Mesolithic inhabitants adopted and transformed aspects of Neolithic culture and then expanded to influence adjacent areas (another possible area is the region around Inverness).

The transformation of timber mortuary structures into rectangular cists could well have been influenced by an existing, but as yet undocumented, tradition of Mesolithic burial in cists, but a great deal more exploration of both Mesolithic and Neolithic sites in the area will be necessary before this can be established. The shift from rectangular cairns (associated with non-megalithic chamber structures) to oval or circular cairns (associated with Clyde tombs) is more clearly explicable if one accepts that the cairns are homologies of the domestic structures of the different communities (see Hodder 1990 and Sherratt 1990 for an extended discussion of this point). Certainly, Early Neolithic structures of rectangular form are known in Britain, and, in Scotland, the Balbridie building (Ralston 1982) is roughly contemporary with the Lochhill mortuary structure. Similarly, Mesolithic tent structures comparable in size and shape to the primary mounds at Mid Gleniron were found at Morton (J.M. Coles 1971). The only Early Neolithic structures known in western Scotland are the post-settings at Auchategan (Marshall 1978) which were interpreted by the author as round houses (but see Herne 1988, 21 for an alternative interpretation). The association of rectangular cairns and chambered tombs seems to occur quite late in the Neolithic development of the South-West. They appear to be structural additions to early tombs or integral to the construction of the larger, later tombs which occur in the Clyde region.

In the South-West, the one distinctive group of tombs of apparently late date is the Bargrennan tombs. These simple passage tombs can be interpreted as idiosyncratic developments from the simple Clyde chambers of the coastal zone. The surrounding cairns are, however, much larger, suggesting communal cooperation in their construction, and the presence of a long passage indicates a significantly different purpose. These tombs could conceivably be explained as the monuments of displaced and/or isolated hunter-gatherer communities which gradually developed a more integrated social system, allowing them to farm the inhospitable upland landscape in which they are situated. While this provides some parallels with Orkney, the agricultural capacity of the landscape restricted the development of any important Later Neolithic monuments.

The distribution and form of the Late Neolithic monuments of the South-West show a similarly marked contrast to the regions previously discussed. Stone circles are common, small, and dispersed throughout the fertile, low-lying river valleys and coastal plain. This pattern, and the absence of any sizeable foci, is strongly reminiscent of the pattern visible throughout eastern Scotland, and confirms the ceramic associations between the two areas. These monuments could well have developed fairly early during the Neolithic, and represent a fusion of Neolithic and Mesolithic systems which does not seem to have occurred in the other regions of the west coast.

CONCLUSION

This chapter has covered a large area of land and a wide variety of monuments, in what some might feel is a rather cavalier fashion. In justification, I would say that sweeping overviews are possible, so long as their limited objectives are firmly kept in view. It is only by acting thus that one can begin to explain why monuments in geographically separate and culturally-distinct regions share certain structural similarities. It is also the only way in which one can highlight the features which give a region such as Orkney a unique position in the archaeological record. This chapter has tried to show that similarities in monumental design between different regions do not necessarily result from contact between the populations of each region. The Neolithic colonisation of Britain would have to occur with a certain predictable regularity in each region. Once this happened, the environmental, social and cultural constraints on development were such as to limit the responses that were available to different communities. Each community had a cultural history which dictated certain standard reactions to the pressures that would be created by population growth and soil deterioration. The creation of multi-compartment 'gallery-graves', passage tombs and stone circles were all fairly predictable mechanisms for solving these problems, as they utilise a symbolic medium which is embedded in the population's cultural history.

In closing, I should emphasise, however, that the similarities which exist should not disguise the many differences which also exist. Each response, though governed by history, was a unique and individual response to a set of particular circumstances.

Bibliography

Abercromby, J., Ross, T. and Anderson, J. 1902. Account of the excavation of the Roman station at Inchtuthil, Perthshire, undertaken by the Society of Antiquaries of Scotland in 1901, *Proc Soc Antiq Scotl* 36 (1901–2), 182–242.

Adler, M.A. and Wilshusen, R.H. 1990. Large-scale integrative facilities in tribal societies: cross-cultural and south-western US examples, *World Archaeol* 22, 133–46.

Allen, J.R. 1882. Notes on some undescribed Stones with Cup-markings in Scotland, *Proc Soc Antiq Scotl* 16 (1881–2), 79–143.

Anderson, J. 1868. On horned cairns of Caithness: their structural arrangement, contents of chambers, etc., *Proc Soc Antiq Scotl* 7 (1866–8), 480–512.

Anderson, J. 1883. *Scotland in Pagan Times: the Iron Age*, Edinburgh.

Armit, I. 1986. *Excavations at Loch Olabhat, North Uist, 1986. First Interim Report*, Edinburgh, Edinburgh Univ. Archaeol. Dept Project Paper 5.

Armit, I. 1987. *Excavation of a Neolithic Settlement Site at Loch Olabhat, North Uist, 1987. Second Interim Report*, Edinburgh, Edinburgh Univ. Archaeol. Dept Project Paper 8.

Armit, I. 1988. *Excavations at Loch Olabhat, North Uist, 1988. Third Interim Report*, Edinburgh, Edinburgh Univ. Archaeol. Dept Project Paper 10.

Armit, I. 1990a. Brochs and beyond in the Western Isles, *in* I. Armit (ed.) *Beyond the Brochs*, Edinburgh, 41–70.

Armit, I. 1990b. Monumentality and elaboration: a case study in the western Isles, *Scott Archaeol Rev* 7, 84–95.

Armit, I. 1990c. *The Loch Olabhat Project 1989. Fourth Interim Report*, Edinburgh, Edinburgh Univ. Archaeol. Dept Project Paper 12.

Armit, I. 1990d. *Later Prehistoric Settlement Patterns in the Western Isles of Scotland*, unpublished Ph.D. thesis, Edinburgh Univ.

Armit, I. forthcoming. The Neolithic pottery, *in* J.C. Bonsall, Excavations at Ulva Cave.

Armit, I. and Finlayson, W. forthcoming. Hunter-gatherers transformed: the transition to farming in Northern and Western Europe.

Armit, I. and MacSween, A. forthcoming. The pottery *in* A. Crone.

Ashbee, P. 1966. The Fussell's Lodge long barrow, *Archaeologia* 100, 1–80.

Ashbee, P. 1970. *The Earthen Long Barrow in Britain*, London.

Ashmore, P.J. 1983. Callanish: making a stone stand again, *in* M. Magnusson (ed.) *Echoes in Stone*, Edinburgh, 41–4.

Ashmore, P.J. 1986. Neolithic carvings in Maes Howe, *Proc Soc Antiq Scotl* 116, 57–62.

Atkinson, R.J.C. 1962. Fishermen and farmers, in S. Piggott (ed.) *The Prehistoric Peoples of Scotland*, London, 1–38.

Atkinson, R.J.C. 1965. Wayland's Smithy, *Antiquity* 30, 126–33.

Atkinson, R.J.C. 1972. Burial and population in the British Bronze Age, *in* F.M. Lynch and C. Burgess (eds), 107–16.

Atkinson, R.J.C., Piggott, C.M. and Sandars, N.K. 1951. *Excavations at Dorchester, Oxon.*, Oxford.

Avery, M. 1982. The Neolithic causewayed enclosure, Abingdon, *in* H.J. Case and A.W.R. Whittle (eds) *Settlement Patterns in the Oxford Region: Excavations at the Abingdon Causewayed Enclosure and Other Sites*, Oxford, Council Brit. Archaeol. Res. Rep. 44.

Barber, J.W.A. 1982. The investigation of some plough truncated features at Kinloch Farm, Collessie in Fife, *Proc Soc Antiq Scotl* 112, 524–33.

Barber, J.W.A. 1988. Isbister, Quanterness and the Point of Cott: the formulation and testing of some middle range theory, *in* J.C. Barrett and I.A. Kinnes (eds), 57–62.

Barber, J.W.A. forthcoming. Excavations at the chambered tomb at the Point of Cott, Westray, Orkney.

Barber, J.W.A. and Angell, I.O. forthcoming. Corbelling and the Irish stone roof series.

Barclay, G.J. 1983a. Sites of the third millennium bc to the first millennium ad at North Mains, Strathallan, Perthshire, *Proc Soc Antiq Scotl* 113, 122–281.

Barclay, G.J. 1983b. *Balfarg Riding School [First] Interim Report*, unpublished MS, Scott. Devel. Dept/Anc. Mons, Edinburgh.

Barclay, G.J. 1983c. *Balfarg Riding School Second Interim Report*, unpublished MS, Scott. Devel. Dept/Anc. Mons, Edinburgh.

Barclay, G.J. 1984. *Balfarg Riding School Third Interim Report*, unpublished MS, Scott. Devel. Dept/Anc. Mons, Edinburgh.

Barclay, G.J. 1985. *Balfarg Riding School Fourth Interim Report*, unpublished MS, Scott. Devel. Dept/Hist. Buildings Mons Dir., Edinburgh.

Barclay, G.J. 1989a. Henge Monuments: reappraisal or reductionism? *Proc Prehist Soc* 55, 260–2.

Barclay, G.J. 1989b. Ballagan, burial mound, *Discov Excav Scotl* 1989, 28.

Barclay, G.J. 1990. The clearing and partial excavation of the cairns at Balnuaran of Clava, Inverness-shire, by Miss Kathleen Kennedy, 1930–1, *Proc Soc Antiq Scotl* 120, 17–32.

Barclay, G.J., Brooks, M. and Rideout, J.S. 1982. A corn-drying kiln at Barbush Quarry, Dunblane, Perthshire, *Proc Soc Antiq Scotl* 112, 583–6.

Barclay, G.J. and Maxwell, G.S. 1991. The excavation of a Neolithic long mortuary enclosure within the Roman legionary fortress at Inchtuthil, Perthshire, *Proc Soc Antiq Scotl* 121.

Barclay, G.J. and Russell-White, C.J. (eds) forthcoming. Excavations in the ceremonial complex of the fourth to second millennium BC at Balfarg/Balbirnie, Glenrothes, Fife, *Proc Soc Antiq Scotl*.

Barclay, G.J. and Tolan, M. 1990. Trial excavation of a terrace-edge enclosure at North Mains, Strathallan, Perthshire, *Proc Soc Antiq Scotl* 120, 45–54.

Barnatt, J. 1989. *Stone Circles of Britain: Taxonomic and Distributional Analyses and a Catalogue of Sites in England, Scotland and Wales*, Oxford, Brit. Archaeol. Rep. 215.

Barnwell, E.L. 1867. Marked stones in Wales, *Archaeol Cambrensis* 13, 150–6.

Barrett, J.C. 1988a. The living, the dead, and the ancestors: Neolithic and Early Bronze Age mortuary practices, *in* J.C. Barrett and I.A. Kinnes (eds), 30–41.

Barrett, J.C. 1988b. Fields of discourse: reconstituting a social archaeology, *Critique of Anthropology* 9, 313–39.

Barrett, J.C. 1989. Food, gender and metal: questions of social reproduction, in M.L. Sørensen and R. Thomas (eds) *The Bronze Age – Iron Age Transition in Europe, Volume 2*, Oxford, Brit. Archaeol. Rep. Int. Ser. 483, 304–20.

Barrett, J.C. forthcoming. *Towards an Archaeology of Ritual*.

Barrett, J.C. and Kinnes, I.A. (eds) 1988. *The Archaeology of Context in the Neolithic and Bronze Age: Recent Trends*, Sheffield.

Barth, F. 1975. *Ritual and Knowledge among the Baktaman of New Guinea*, New Haven.

Bateman, T. 1861. *Ten Years' Diggings in Celtic and Saxon Grave-Hills*, London.

Beckensall, S. 1983. *Northumberland's Prehistoric Rock Carvings*, Rothbury.

Bersu, G. 1948. 'Fort' at Scotstarvit Covert, Fife, *Proc Soc Antiq Scotl* 82 (1947–8), 241–63.

Beveridge, E. 1911. *North Uist*, Edinburgh.

Beveridge, H. 1886. Notice of two cemeteries, containing cists and urns, on the Estate of Pitreavie, near Dunfermline, *Proc Soc Antiq Scotl* 20 (1885–6), 240–52.

Binford, R.L., Binford, S.R., Whallon, R. and Hardin, M. 1970. *Archaeology at Hatchery West*, Washington, D.C., Memoirs Soc. American Archaeol. 24.

Birks, H.H. 1975. Studies in the vegetational history of Scotland IV: pine stumps in Scottish blanket peats, *Phil Trans Roy Soc Lond* 270B, 181–223.

Bishop, A.C., Woolley, A.R., Kinnes, I.A. and Harrison, R.J. 1977. Jadeite axes in Europe and the British Isles: an interim study, *Archaeol Atlantica* 2, 1–8.

Blier, S. 1987. *The Anatomy of Architecture*, Cambridge.

Bloch, M. 1982. Death, women and power, in M. Bloch and J. Parry (eds) *Death and the Regeneration of Life*, Cambridge, 211–20.

Boast, R. 1987. Rites of passage: topological and formal representation, *Planning and Design* 14, 451–66.

Bohncke, S.J.P. 1988. Vegetation and habitation history of the Callanish area, Isle of Lewis, Scotland, in H.H. Birks, H.J.B. Birks, P.E. Kaland and D. Moe (eds) *The Cultural Landscape – Past, Present and Future*, Cambridge, 445–61.

Bourdieu, P. 1977. *Outline of a Theory of Practice* (trans. R. Nice), Cambridge.

Bourdieu, P. 1979. Symbolic power, *Critique of Anthropology* 4, 77–85.

Bowen, E.G. and Gresham, C.A. 1967. *History of Merioneth, Volume 1*, Dolgellau.

Bradley, R.J. 1982. Position and possession: assemblage variation in the British Neolithic, *Oxford J Archaeol* 1, 27–38.

Bradley, R.J. 1984. *The Social Foundations of Prehistoric Britain: Themes and Variations in the Archaeology of Power*, London.

Bradley, R.J. 1985. *Consumption, Change and the Archaeological Record*, Edinburgh, Edinburgh Univ. Archaeol. Dept. Occ. Paper 13.

Bradley, R.J. 1989a. Darkness and light in the design of megalithic tombs, *Oxford J Archaeol* 8, 251–9.

Bradley, R.J. 1989b. Deaths and entrances: a contextual analysis of megalithic art, *Curr Anthropology* 301, 68–75.

Bradley, R.J. 1990. Perforated stone axe-heads in the British Neolithic: their distribution and significance, *Oxford J Archaeol* 9, 299–304.

Bradley, R.J. 1991. Rock art and the perception of landscape: avenues to analysis, *Cambridge Archaeol J* 1, 77–101.

Bradley, R.J. and Chapman, R. 1984. Passage graves in the European Neolithic – a theory of converging evolution, *in* G. Burenhult, 348–59.

Bradley, R.J. and Chapman, R. 1986. The nature and development of long-distance relations in later Neolithic Britain and Ireland, in A.C. Renfrew and J.F. Cherry (eds), *Peer Polity Interaction and Socio-Political Change*, Cambridge, 127–36.

Bradley, R.J. and Edmonds, M. 1988. Fieldwork at Great Langdale, Cumbria, 1985–7: preliminary report, *Antiq J* 68, 181–209.

Bradley, R.J. and Edmonds, M. in press. *Production, Circulation and Consumption: a Study of Stone Axe Making in Neolithic Britain*, Cambridge.

Bradley, R.J. and Gardiner, J. (eds) 1984. *Neolithic Studies: a Review of Some Current Research*, Oxford, Brit. Archaeol. Rep. 133.

Bradley, R.J. and Hodder, I. 1979. British Prehistory: an integrated view, *Man* 14, 93–104.

Braithwaite, M. 1982. Decoration as ritual symbol, in I. Hodder (ed.), *Symbolic and Structural Archaeology*, Cambridge, 80–8.

Brewster, T.C.M. 1980. *The Excavation of Garton and Wetwang Slacks*, unpublished microfiche, Nat. Mons. Record, London.

Brewster, T.C.M. 1984. Hutton Buscel, *Curr Archaeol* 94, 331–2.

Brindley, A., Lanting, J.N. and Moore, W.G. 1983. Radiocarbon dates from the Neolithic burials at Ballintruer More, Co. Wicklow and Ardcony, Co. Tipperary, *J Ir Archaeol* 1, 1–9.

Briscoe, G. 1957. Swale's Tumulus, a combined Neolithic A and Bronze Age barrow at Worlington, Suffolk, *Proc Cambridgeshire Antiq Soc* 50, 101–12.

Britnell, W.J. and Savory, H.N. 1984. *Gwernvale and Penywyrlod: Two Neolithic Long Cairns in the Black Mountains of Brecknock*, Cardiff, Cambrian Archaeol Monog 2.

Browell, K.M. 1986. *Stratigraphic Feasibility Study of Thin Section Petrology for the Examination of Orcadian Neolithic Ceramics from Pool, Sanday*, unpublished BSc dissert, Bradford Univ.

Brydon, J. 1870. Notice of the opening of a burial cairn at Shaws, Selkirkshire, *Proc Soc Antiq Scotl* 8 (1868–70), 352–5.

Bunzel, R. 1929. *The Pueblo Potter: a Study of Creative Imagination in Primitive Art*, New York.

Burenhult, G. 1980. *The Archaeological Excavation at Carrowmore Co. Sligo, Ireland: Excavation Seasons 1977–9*, Stockholm, Theses and Papers in North-European Archaeol 9.

Burenhult, G. 1984. *The Archaeology of Carrowmore: Environment, Arch-*

aeology and the Megalithic Tradition at Carrowmore, Co. Sligo, Ireland, Stockholm, Theses and Papers in North-European Archaeol 14.

Burgess, C. 1990. The chronology of cup-marks and cup-and-ring marks in Atlantic Europe, *Revue Archéologique de l'Ouest*, Supplément 2, 157–71.

Burgess, C. and Miket, R. (eds) 1976. *Settlement and Economy in the Third and Second Millennia BC*, Oxford, Brit. Archaeol. Rep. 33.

Burl, H.A.W. 1976. *The Stone Circles of the British Isles*, New Haven.

Burl, H.A.W. Report on the excavation of a Neolithic mound at Boghead, Speymouth Forest, Fochabers, Moray, 1972 and 1974, *Proc Soc Antiq Scotl* 114, 35–73, fiche 1: A2–C10.

Calder, C.S.T. 1939. Excavations of Iron Age dwellings on the Calf of Eday in Orkney, *Proc Soc Antiq Scotl* 73 (1938–9), 167–85.

Calder, C.S.T. 1956. Report on the discovery of numerous Stone Age house-sites in Shetland, *Proc Soc Antiq Scotl* 89 (1955–6), 340–97.

Calder, C.S.T. 1963. Cairns, Neolithic houses and burnt mounds in Shetland, *Proc Soc Antiq Scotl* 96 (1962–3), 37–86.

Callander, J.G. 1929. Scottish Neolithic pottery, *Proc Soc Antiq Scotl* 63 (1928–9), 29–98.

Callander, J.G. 1931. Notes of (1) certain prehistoric relics from Orkney and (2) Skara Brae: its culture and its period, *Proc Soc Antiq Scotl* 65 (1930–1), 78–114.

Callander, J.G. and Grant, W.G. 1935. A long stalled cairn, the Knowe of Yarso, in Rousay, Orkney, *Proc Soc Antiq Scotl* 69 (1934–5), 325–51.

Carter, S.P. 1989. Soil Science, *Scott Devel Dept/Hist Buildings Mons Dir, Archaeol Operations and Conservation Ann Rep* 1989, 46.

Carter, S.P., Haigh, D., Neil, N.R.J. and Smith, B. 1984. Interim report on the structures at Howe, Stromness, Orkney, *Glasgow Archaeol J* 11, 61–73.

Case, H.J. 1969. Settlement patterns in the North Irish Neolithic, *Ulster J Archaeol* 32, 3–26.

Case, H.J. 1973. A ritual site in North-East Ireland, *in* G.E. Daniel and P. Kjaerum (eds), 173–96.

Cavanagh, W.G. and Laxton, R.R. 1990. Vaulted construction in French megalithic tombs, *Oxford J Archaeol* 9, 141–67.

Chapman, R. 1981. The emergence of formal disposal areas and the 'problem' of megalithic tombs in prehistoric Europe, *in* R. Chapman, I.A. Kinnes and K. Randsborg (eds), 71–81.

Chapman, R., Kinnes, I.A. and Randsborg, K. (eds) 1981. *The Archaeology of Death*, Cambridge.

Chappell, S.J. 1987. *Stone Axe Morphology and Distribution in Neolithic Britain*, Oxford, Brit. Archaeol. Rep. 177.

Cherry, J. 1978. Generalisation and the archaeology of the state, in D. Green, C. Haselgrove and M. Spriggs (eds), *Social Organisation and Settlement*, Oxford, Brit. Archaeol. Rep. Int. Ser. 47, 411–37.

Cherry, J. 1981. Pattern and process in the earliest colonisation of the Mediterranean islands, *Proc Prehist Soc* 47, 41–68.

Childe, V.G. 1931a. *Skara Brae, a Pictish Village in Orkney*, London.

Childe, V.G. 1931b. Final report on the excavations at Skara Brae, *Proc Soc Antiq Scotl* 65 (1930–1), 27–77.

Childe, V.G. 1933. Scottish megalithic tombs and their affinities, *Trans Glasgow Archaeol Soc* 8, 120–37.

Childe, V.G. 1934. Neolithic settlement in the west of Scotland, *Scot Geographical Mag* 50, 18–24.

Childe, V.G. 1935a. *The Prehistory of Scotland*, London.

Childe, V.G. 1935b. Some sherds from Slieve na Caillighe, *J Roy Soc Antiq Ire* 65, 320–4.

Childe, V.G. 1946. *Scotland Before the Scots*, London.

Childe, V.G. 1952. Re-excavation of the chambered cairn of Quoyness, Sanday, on behalf of the Ministry of Works in 1951–2, *Proc Soc Antiq Scotl* 86 (1951–2), 121–39.

Childe, V.G. 1962. The earliest inhabitants, in F.T. Wainwright (ed.) *The Northern Isles*, Edinburgh, 9–25.

Childe, V.G. and Graham, A. 1943. Some notable prehistoric and Medieval monuments recently examined by the Royal Commission on Ancient and Historical Monuments of Scotland, *Proc Soc Antiq Scotl* 77 (1942–3), 31–49.

Childe, V.G. and Grant, W.G. 1939. A Stone Age settlement at the Braes of Rinyo, Rousay, Orkney (first report), *Proc Soc Antiq Scotl* 73 (1938–9), 6–31.

Childe, V.G. and Grant, W.G. 1947. A Stone Age settlement at the Braes of Rinyo, Rousay, Orkney (second report), *Proc Soc Antiq Scotl* 81 (1945–7), 16–32.

Chrisp, H. 1990. *The Chambered Cairns of North Uist*, unpublished MA dissert, Edinburgh Univ.

Clare, T. 1987. Towards a reappraisal of henge monuments: origins, evolution and hierarchies, *Proc Prehist Soc* 53, 457–78.

Clarke, A. 1990. The Skaill knife as a butchering tool, *Lithics* 10, 16–27.

Clarke, A. forthcoming. a. The coarse stone assemblages from Pool and Tofts Ness, in J.R. Hunter, S. Dockrill, J.M. Bond and A.N. Smith (eds).

Clarke, A. forthcoming. b. The coarse stone assemblage from Barnhouse, in C.C. Richards (ed.) *The Late Neolithic Settlement Complex of Barnhouse*.

Clarke, A. forthcoming. c. The coarse stone assemblage, in O.A. Owen and C.E. Lowe (eds) *Kebister, Shetland: the Archaeology of a Prehistoric and Medieval Farmstead*.

Clarke, A., Clarke, D.V. and Saville, A. forthcoming. A decorated Skaill knife from Skara Brae.

Clarke, A. and Griffiths, D. 1990. The use of bloodstone as a raw material for flaked stone tools in the west of Scotland, *in* C. Wickham-Jones, 149–56.

Clarke, D.L. 1970. *Beaker Pottery of Great Britain and Ireland*, Cambridge.

Clarke, D.V. 1976a. *The Neolithic Village at Skara Brae, Orkney, Excavations 1972–3: an Interim Report*, Edinburgh.

Clarke, D.V. 1976b. Excavations at Skara Brae: a summary account, *in* C. Burgess and R. Miket (eds), 233–50.

Clarke, D.V. 1983. Rinyo and the Orcadian Neolithic, *in* A. O'Connor and D.V. Clarke (eds), 45–56.

Clarke, D.V., Cowie, T.G. and Foxon, A. 1985. *Symbols of Power at the Time of Stonehenge*, Edinburgh.

Clarke, D.V., Hope, R. and Wickham-Jones, C. 1978. The Links of Noltland, *Curr Archaeol* 6, 44–6.

Clarke, D.V. and Sharples, N.M. 1985. Settlements and subsistence in the third millennium bc *in* A.C. Renfrew (ed.), 54–82.

Clifford, E.M. 1936. Notgrove long barrow, Gloucestershire, *Archaeologia* 86, 119–62.

Close-Brooks, J. 1984. Pictish and other burials, *in* J.G.P. Friell and W.G. Watson (eds) *Pictish Studies: Settlement, Burial, and Art in Dark Age Northern Britain*, Oxford, Brit. Archaeol. Rep. Brit. Ser. 125, 87–114.

Close-Brooks, J. 1986. Excavations at Clatchard Craig, Fife, *Proc Soc Antiq Scotl* 116, 117–84, fiche 1: B1–C14.

Clough, T.H. McK. and Cummins, W.A. (eds) 1979. *Stone Axe Studies*, London, Council Brit. Archaeol. Res. Rep. 23.

Clough, T.H. McK. and Cummins, W.A. (eds) 1988. *Stone Axe Studies, Volume 2*, London, Council Brit. Archaeol. Res. Rep. 67.

Clouston, R.S. 1885. Notice of the excavation of a chambered cairn of the Stone Age, at Unstan, in the Loch of Stennis, Orkney, *Proc Soc Antiq Scotl* 19 (1884–5), 341–51.

Coles, F.R. 1894. The cairns of Kirkudbrightshire, *Trans. Dumfriesshire Galloway Natur Hist Antiq Soc* 10 (1893–4), 59–66.

Coles, F.R. 1897. A record of the kistvaens found in Stewartry of Kirkcudbright, *The Reliquary and Illustrated Archaeologist* 3, 1–19.

Coles, F.R. 1908. *A Classification of the Carved Stone Balls Peculiar to Scotland*, unpublished MS, National Museums of Scotland, Edinburgh.

Coles, J.M. 1971. The early settlement of Scotland: excavations at Morton, Fife, *Proc Prehist Soc* 37, 284–366.

Coles, J.M. and Coles, B.J. 1990. Part II: the Sweet Track date, in J. Hillam, C.M. Groves, D.M. Brown, M.G.L. Baillie, J.M. Coles and B.J. Coles, Dendrochronology of the English Neolithic, *Antiquity* 64, 210–20.

Coles, J.M. and Simpson, D.D.A. 1965. The excavation of a Neolithic round barrow at Pitnacreee, Perthshire, Scotland, *Proc Prehist Soc* 31, 34–57.

Coles, J.M. and Simpson, D.D.A. (eds) 1968 *Studies in Ancient Europe*, Leicester.

Collingwood, W.G. 1901. Tumulus at Grayson-lands, Glassonby, Cumberland, *Trans Cumberland Westmorland Antiq Archaeol Soc* 1, 295–9.

Collins, A.E.P. 1954. The excavation of a double horned cairn at Audleystown, Co. Down, *Ulster J Archaeol* 17, 7–56.

Collins, A.E.P. 1959. Further work at Audleystown long cairn, Co. Down, *Ulster J Archaeol* 22, 21–7.

Collins, A.E.P. 1960. Knockmany Chambered Cairn, Co. Tyrone, *Ulster J Archaeol* 23, 2–6.

Collins, A.E.P. 1976. Dooey's Cairn, Ballymacaldrack, County Antrim, *Ulster J Archaeol* 39, 1–12.

Collins, A.E.P. and Waterman, D.M. 1955. *Millin Bay: a Late Neolithic Cairn in Co. Down*, Belfast.

Conwell, E.A. 1866. Examination of ancient sepulchral cairns on the Loughcrew hills, County of Meath, *Proc Roy Ir Acad* 9, 355–78.

Coombs, D.G. 1976. Callis Wold round barrow, Humberside, *Antiquity* 50, 130–1.

Cooney, G. 1990. The place of megalithic tomb cemeteries in the Irish Neolithic, *Antiquity* 64, 741–53.

Corcoran, J.X.W.P. 1966. Excavation of three chambered cairns at Loch Calder, Caithness, *Proc Soc Antiq Scotl* 98 (1964–6), 1–75.

Corcoran, J.X.W.P. 1969a. The Cotswold-Severn Group: 2. Discussion, *in* T.G.E. Powell et al. (eds), 73–104.

Corcoran, J.X.W.P. 1969b. Excavation of two chambered cairns at Mid Gleniron Farm, Glenluce, Wigtownshire, *Trans Dumfriesshire Galloway Natur Hist Antiq Soc* 46, 29–90.

Corcoran, J.X.W.P. 1972. Multi-period construction and the origins of the chambered long cairn in western Britain and Ireland, *in* F.M. Lynch and C. Burgess (eds), 31–63.

Cowie, T.G. 1978. Excavations at the Catstane, Midlothian 1977, *Proc Soc Antiq Scotl* 109 (1977–8), 166–201.

Cowie, T.G. forthcoming. A survey of Neolithic pottery from eastern and central Scotland, *Proc Soc Antiq Scotl.*

Crawford, I. n.d. *The West Highlands and Islands, A View of 50 Centuries, the Udal (North Uist) Evidence*, unpublished MS, Cambridge Univ.

Crone, A. 1989. Excavation and survey at Bharpa Carinish, North Uist, 1989, *Scott Devel Dept/Hist Buildings Mons Dir, Archaeol Operations and Conservation Ann Rep* 1989, 7–10.

Crone, A. forthcoming. The excavation of Neolithic features and a Bronze Age enclosure at Bharpa Carinish, North Uist.

Cummins, W.A. and Moore, C.N. 1973. Petrological identification of stone implements from Lincolnshire, Nottinghamshire and Rutland, *Proc Prehist Soc* 39, 219–55.

Cunliffe, B.W. 1978. *Iron Age Communities in Britain*, London.

Curle, A.O. 1930. Examination of a chambered cairn by the Water of Deugh, Stewartry of Kirkcudbright, *Proc Soc Antiq Scotl* 64 (1929–30), 272–5.

Curle, A.O. 1982. *Pictish and Norse Finds from the Brough of Birsay*, Edinburgh, Soc. Antiq. Scotl. Monog. 1.

Cursiter, J.W. 1910. Notice of a stone cist of unusual type found at Crantit, near Kirkwall, *Proc Soc Antiq Scotl* 44 (1909–10), 215–7.

Daniel, G.E. 1950. *The Prehistoric Chamber Tombs of England and Wales*, Cambridge.

Daniel, G.E. 1958. *The Megalith Builders of Western Europe*, London.

Daniel, G.E. 1962. The megalith builders, in S. Piggott (ed.) *The Prehistoric Peoples of Scotland*, London, 39–72.

Daniel, G.E. and Kjaerum, P. (eds) 1973. *Megalithic Graves and Ritual*, Copenhagen, Jutland Archaeol. Soc. Publ. 11.

Darvill, T. 1987a. *Prehistoric Gloucestershire*, Gloucester.

Darvill, T. 1987b. *Prehistoric Britain*, London.

Davidson, D.A. and Jones, R.L. 1985. The environment of Orkney, *in* A.C. Renfrew (ed.), 10–35.

Davidson, J.L. and Henshall, A.S. 1989. *The Chambered Cairns of Orkney*, Edinburgh.

Davidson, J.L. and Henshall, A.S. 1991. *The Chambered Cairns of Caithness*, Edinburgh.

Davies, O. 1936. Excavations at Dun Ruadh, *Proc Belfast Natur Hist Phil Soc* 1, 50–75.

de Valéra, R. 1960. Mound of the Hostages, Tara, Co. Meath, *Proc Prehist Soc* 26, 241–2.

Driscoll, S. 1989. Easter Kinnear, *Discovery Excav Scotl 1989*, 17.

Earnshaw, J. 1973. The site of a medieval post-mill and prehistoric site at Bridlington, *Yorks Archaeol J* 45, 19–40.

Edmonds, M. 1989. *The Gift of Stones: the Production and Consumption of Neolithic Stone Axes in Britain*, unpublished Ph.D. thesis, Reading Univ.

Edmonds, M. and Thomas, J.S. 1987. The Archers: an everyday story of country folk, in A.G. Brown and M. Edmonds (eds) *Lithic Analysis and Later British Prehistory*, Oxford, Brit. Archaeol. Rep. 167, 187–99.

Edmonds, M., Sheridan, J.A. and Tipping, R. forthcoming. Survey and excavation at Creag na Caillich, Killin, Perthshire, *Proc Soc Antiq Scotl*.

Edwards, K.J., Ansell, M. and Carter, B.A. 1983. Mesolithic sites in south-west Scotland and their importance as indicators of inland penetration, *Trans Dumfriesshire Galloway Natur Hist Antiq Soc* 58, 9–15.

Eliade, M. 1959. *The Sacred and the Profane: the Nature of Religion*, New York.

Eogan, G. 1963. A Neolithic habitation-site and megalithic tomb in Townleyhall townland, Co. Louth, *J Roy Soc Antiq Ire* 93, 37–81.

Eogan, G. 1984. *Excavations at Knowth, Volume 1*, Dublin, Roy. Ir. Acad. Monog. Archaeol. 1.

Eogan, G. 1986. *Knowth and the Passage-tombs of Ireland*, London.

Eogan, G. 1990. Diffuse picking in megalithic art, *Revue Archéologique de l'Ouest*, Supplément 2, 120–40.

Eogan, G. and Richardson, H. 1982. Two maceheads from Knowth, Co. Meath, *J Roy Soc Antiq Ire* 112, 123–38.

Essene, E.J. and Fyfe, W.S. 1967. Omphacite in Californian metamorphic rocks, *Contributions to Mineralogy and Petrology* 15, 1–23.

Evans, C. 1988. Monuments and analogy: the interpretation of causewayed enclosures, in C. Burgess, P. Topping, C. Mordant and M. Maddison (eds) *Enclosures and Defences in the Neolithic of Western Europe*, Oxford, Brit. Archaeol. Rep. Int. Ser. 403, 47–74.

Evans, E.E. 1938. Doey's Cairn, Dunloy, Co. Antrim, *Ulster J Archaeol* 1, 59–78.

Evans, E.E. 1939. Excavations at Carnanbane, County Londonderry: a double horned cairn, *Proc Roy Ir Acad* 45C, 1–12.

Evans, E.E. 1940. Sherds from a gravel pit, Killaghy, Co. Armagh, *Ulster J Archaeol* 3, 139–41.

Evans, E.E. 1953. *Lyles Hill: a Late Neolithic Site in County Antrim*, Belfast.

Evans, J. 1872. *The Ancient Stone Implements, Ornaments and Weapons of Great Britain*, London.

Evans, J. 1897. *The Ancient Stone Implements, Ornaments and Weapons of Great Britian*, 2nd ed., London.

Fenton, M.B. 1984. The nature of the source and manufacture of Scottish battle-axes and axe-hammers, *Proc Prehist Soc* 50, 217–44.

Fenton, M.B. 1988. The petrological identification of stone battle-axes and axe-hammers from Scotland, *in* T.H. McK. Clough and W.A. Cummins (eds), 92–136.

Feustel, R. and Ulrich, H. 1965. Totenhütten der Neolithischen Walternienburger Gruppe, *Alt Thüringen* 7, 105–202.

Fleming, A. 1972. Vision and design: approaches to ceremonial monument typology, *Man* 7, 57–73.

Fleming, A. 1973. Tombs for the living, *Man* 8, 177–93.

Fraser, D. 1983. *Land and Society in Neolithic Orkney*, Oxford, Brit. Archaeol. Rep. 117.

Frere, S.S. and Wilkes, J.J. 1989. *Strageath, Excavations within the Roman Fort 1973–86*, London, Britannia Monog. Ser. 9.

Gates, T. 1982. A long cairn on Dod Hill, Ilderton, Northumberland, *Archaeol Aeliana* 10, 210–11.

Gibson, A.M. 1984. Problems of Beaker assemblages: The north British Material, *in* R. Miket and C. Burgess (eds), 74–96.

Gibson, A.M. 1986. *Neolithic and Early Bronze Age Pottery*, Princes Risborough.

Gibson, W.J. 1944. Maceheads of 'Cushion' type in Britain, *Proc Soc Antiq Scotl* 78 (1943–4), 16–25.

Giot, P-R. 1983. The megaliths of France, *in* A.C. Renfrew (ed.) *The Megalithic Monuments of Western Europe*, London, 18–29.

Giot, P-R., L'Helgouac'h, J. and Monnier, J-L., 1979. *Préhistorie de la Bretagne*, Rennes.

Goldstein, L. 1981. One-dimensional archaeology and multi-dimensional people: spatial organisation and mortuary analysis, *in* R. Chapman, I.A. Kinnes and K. Randsborg (eds), 53–69.

Goldsworthy, A. 1990. *Hand to Earth*, Leeds.

Gowlett, J.A., Hedges, R.E.M., Law, I.A. and Perry, C. 1987. Radiocarbon dates from the Oxford AMS system: Archaeometry datelist 5, *Archaeometry* 29, 143.

Graves, C.P. 1989. Social space in the English Medieval parish church, *Economy and Society* 18, 297–322.

Gray, A.F. 1956 *Notes on Some of the Antiquities and Other Landmarks in the Parish of Ballantrae, Ayrshire*, unpublished MS, Nat Mons Record, Edinburgh.

Green, S.W. and Zvelebil, M. 1990. The Mesolithic colonisation and agricultural transition of south-east Ireland, *Proc Prehist Soc* 56, 57–88.

Greenwell, W. 1890. Recent researches in barrows in Yorkshire, Wiltshire, Berkshire, etc., *Archaeologia* 52, 1–72.

Greenwell, W. and Rolleston, G. 1877. *British Barrows*, Oxford.

Grinsell, L.V. 1982. *Dorset Barrows Supplement*, Dorchester.

Grogan, E. 1989. *The Early Prehistory of the Lough Gur Region: Neolithic and Bronze Age Settlement Patterns in North Munster South of the River Shannon*, unpublished Ph.D. thesis, Nat. Univ. Ire.

Grøn, O. 1989. General spatial behaviour in small dwellings: a preliminary study in ethnoarchaeology and social psychology, in C. Bonsall (ed.) *The Mesolithic in Europe*, Edinburgh, 99–105.

Haggarty, A. forthcoming. Excavations on Machrie Moor, Arran.

Hamilton, J.R.C. 1956. *Excavations at Jarlshof, Shetland*, Edinburgh.

Harden, J. 1989. Corrimony burial mound, *Discovery Excav Scotl* 1989, 27.

Harding, A.F. 1981. Excavations in the prehistoric ritual complex near Milfield, Northumberland, *Proc Prehist Soc* 47, 87–135.

Harding, A.F. and Lee, G.E. 1987. *Henge Monuments and Related Sites of Great Britain: Air Photographic Evidence and Catalogue*, Oxford, Brit. Archaeol. Rep. 175.

Harding, D.W. (ed.) 1982. *Later Prehistoric Settlement in South-East Scotland*, Edinburgh, Univ. Edin. Dept Archaeol. Occas. Pap. 8.

Harry, W.T. 1952. An unusual appinitic sill near Killin, Perthshire, *Geol Mag* 89, 41–8.

Hartnett, P.J. 1957. Excavation of a passage grave at Fourknocks, Co. Meath, *Proc Roy Ir Acad* 58C, 197–277.

Hartnett, P.J. 1971. The excavation of two tumuli at Fourknocks (sites II and III), Co. Meath, *Proc Roy Ir Acad* 71C, 35–89.

Hawkes, C.F.C. 1954. Archaeological theory and method: some suggestions, *J Anthropological Archaeol* 1, 132–59.

Hay, G. 1957. *The Architecture of Scottish Post-Reformation Churches 1560–1843*, Oxford.

Healy, F. 1988. *Spong Hill, Part 6, 7th to 2nd Millennia bc*, Dereham, East Anglian Archaeol Rep 39.

Hedges, J.W. 1983. *Isbister, a Chambered Tomb in Orkney*, Oxford, Brit Archaeol Rep 115.

Hedges, J.W. 1984. *Tomb of the Eagles: a Window on Stone Age Tribal Britain*, London.

Hedges, J.W. and Parry, G.W. 1980. A Neolithic multiple burial at Sumburgh Airport, Shetland, *Glasgow Archaeol J* 7, 15–26.

Henshall, A.S. 1963. *The Chambered Tombs of Scotland, Volume 1*, Edinburgh.

Henshall, A.S. 1966. The second report of cist burials at Parkburn sand-pit, Lasswade, Midlothian, *Proc Soc Antiq Scotl* 98 (1964–6), 204–14.

Henshall, A.S. 1968. Scottish dagger graves, *in* J.M. Coles and D.D.A. Simpson (eds), 173–95.

Henshall, A.S. 1972. *The Chambered Tombs of Scotland, Volume 2*, Edinburgh.

Henshall, A.S. 1974. Scottish chambered tombs and long mounds, in A.C. Renfrew (ed.) *British Prehistory: a New Outline*, London, 137–64.

Henshall, A.S. 1978. Manx megaliths again: an attempt at structural analysis, in P. Davey (ed.) *Man and Environment in the Isle of Man, Volume 1*, Oxford, Brit Archaeol Rep 54, 171–6.

Henshall, A.S. 1979. Artefacts from the Quanterness cairn, *in* A.C. Renfrew (ed.), 75–93.

Henshall, A.S. 1983a. Pottery: catalogue and discussion, *in* A. Ritchie, 59–73.

Henshall, A.S. 1983b. The pottery, *in* J.W. Hedges, 33–46.

Henshall, A.S. 1983c. The Neolithic pottery from Easterton of Roseisle, Moray, *in* A. O'Connor and D.V. Clarke (eds), 19–44.

Henshall, A.S. 1985. The chambered cairns, *in* A.C. Renfrew (ed.), 83—117.

Henshall, A.S. forthcoming. The Grooved Ware pottery, *in* G. Barclay and C. Russell-White.

Henshall, A.S. and Mercer, R. 1981. Report on the pottery from Balfarg, Fife, *in* R. Mercer, 128–33.

Henshall, A.S. and Savory, L. 1976. Small finds from the 1973–4 excavations: pottery, *in* J.N.G. Ritchie, 22–5.

Herity, M. 1973. Irish Sea and Scandinavian passage graves, *in* G.E. Daniel and P. Kjaerum (eds), 129–35.

Herity, M. 1974. *Irish Passage Graves*, Dublin.

Herity, M. 1982. Irish decorated Neolithic pottery, *Proc Roy Ir Acad* 82C, 247–404.

Herity, M. 1987. The finds from Irish court tombs, *Proc Roy Ir Acad* 87C, 103–281.

Herne, A. 1988. A time and a place for the Grimston Bowl, *in* J.C. Barrett and I.A. Kinnes (eds), 9–29.

Hill, P.H. 1982. Broxmouth hillfort excavations, 1977–8: an interim report, *in* D.W. Harding (ed.), 141–88.

Hillam, J., Groves, C.M., Brown, D.M., Baillie, M.G.L., Coles, J.M. and Coles, B.J. 1990. Dendrochronology of the English Neolithic, *Antiquity* 64, 210–20.

Hillier, B. and Hanson, J. 1984. *The Social Logic of Space*, Cambridge.

Hirst, P.Q. 1985. Constructed space and the subject, in R. Fardon (ed.) *Power and Knowledge*, Edinburgh, 171–80.

Hodder, I. 1978. The maintenance of group identities in the Baringo district, western Kenya, in D. Green, C. Haselgrove and M. Spriggs (eds) *Social Organisation and Settlement, Volume 1*, Oxford, Brit. Archaeol. Rep. Int. Ser. 47, 47–73.

Hodder, I. 1979. Social and economic stress and material culture patterning, *American Antiquity* 44, 446–54.

Hodder, I. 1982. *Symbols in Action*, London.

Hodder, I. 1984. Burials, houses, women and men in the European Neolithic, *in* D. Miller and C. Tilley (eds) *Ideology, Power and Prehistory*, Cambridge, 51–68.

Hodder, I. 1989. This is not an article about material culture as text, *J Anthropological Archaeol* 8, 250–69.

Hodder, I. 1990. *The Domestication of Europe: Structure and Contingency in Neolithic Societies*, Oxford.

Hope-Taylor, B. 1977. *Yeavering: an Anglo-British Centre of Early Northumbria*, London.

Hornsby, W. and Stanton, R. 1917. British barrows near Brotton, *Yorkshire Archaeol J* 24, 263–8.

Howell, J.M. 1981. The typology of Scottish stone axes, *Scott Archaeol Forum* 11, 15–24.

Hughes, I. 1988. Megaliths: space, time and the landscape – a view from the Clyde, *Scott Archaeol Rev* 5, 41–56.

Hunter, J.R., Dockrill, S., Bond, J.M. and Smith, A.N. (eds) forthcoming. *Archaeological Investigations on Sanday, Orkney*, Edinburgh, Soc. Antiq. Scotl. Monog.

Hunter, J.R. and MacSween, A. 1991. A sequence for the Orcadian Neolithic, *Antiquity* 65.

Ingold, T. 1986. *The Appropriation of Nature*, Manchester.

Innes, C. 1860. Notice of a tomb on the Hill of Roseisle, Morayshire, recently opened; also of the chambered cairns and stone circles at Clava, on Nairnside, *Proc Soc Antiq Scotl* 3 (1857–60), 46–50.

Jackson, D.A. 1976. The excavation of Neolithic and Bronze Age sites at Aldwincle, Northants, 1967–71, *Northamptonshire Archaeol* 11, 12–70.

Jobey, G. 1968. Excavations of cairns at Chatton Sandyford, Northumberland, *Archaeol Aeliana* 46, 5–50.

Jobey, G. 1977. A Food Vessel burial on Dour Hill, Byrness, Northumberland, *Archaeol Aeliana* 5, 204–7.

Johnston, D.A. 1990. Biggar Common, *Discovery Excav Scotl* 1990, 37.

Johnston, S. 1989. *Prehistoric Irish Petroglyphs: Their Analysis and Interpretation in Anthropological Context*, Ann Arbor.

Jones, V., Bishop, A.C. and Woolley, A.R. 1977. Third supplement of the Catalogue of jade axes from sites in the British Isles, *Proc Prehist Soc* 43, 287–93.

Jones, V.J., Stevenson, A.C. and Batterbee, R.W. 1989. Acidification of lakes in Galloway, south-west Scotland: a diatom and pollen study of the postglacial history of the Round Loch of Glenhead, *J Ecology* 77, 1–23.

Joussaume, R. (ed.) 1990. *Mégalithisme et Société*, La-Roche-sur-Yon.

Keatinge, T.H. and Dickson, J.H. 1979. Mid-Flandrian changes in vegetation on Mainland Orkney, *New Phytologist* 82, 585–612.

Kempton, W. 1981. *The Folk Classification of Ceramics*, London.

Kendrick, J. 1980. *Douglasmuir, The Excavations of an Early Iron Age Settlement and a Neolithic Enclosure 1979–80. Preliminary Report*, unpublished report, Scott Devel Dept/Anc Mons, Edinburgh.

Kendrick, J. 1982. Excavations at Douglasmuir, 1979–80, *in* D.W. Harding (ed.), 136–40.

Kendrick, J. and Gregson, M. 1980. Douglasmuir, *Discovery Excav Scotl 1980*, 38.

Kenworthy, J.A. 1977a. A reconsideration of the 'Ardiffery' finds, Cruden, Aberdeenshire, *Proc Soc Antiq Scotl* 108 (1976–7), 80–93.

Kenworthy, J.A. 1977b. A mace-head from Orkney, *Proc Soc Antiq Scotl* 108 (1976–7), 366–7.

Kenworthy, J.A. 1981. The flint adze-blade and its cultural context, *in* J.N.G. Ritchie and H.C. Adamson, 189–93.

Kerr, R. 1939. Two hoards of silver coins found at Bridge of Don, Aberdeen, and at Dunblane, Perthshire, *Proc Soc Antiq Scotl* 73 (1938–9), 51–4.

Kilbride-Jones, H.E. 1973. On some aspects of Neolithic building techniques in Orkney, *Acta Praehistorica et Archaeologica* 4, 75–96.

Kinnes, I.A. 1975. Monumental function in British Neolithic burial practices, *World Archaeol* 7, 16–29.

Kinnes, I.A. 1978. The earlier prehistoric pottery, in J. Hedges and D. Buckley, Excavations at a Neolithic causewayed enclosure, Orsett, Essex, 1975, *Proc Prehist Soc* 44, 219–308.

Kinnes, I.A. 1979. *Round Barrows and Ring-ditches in the British Neolithic*, London.

Kinnes, I.A. 1981. Dialogues with death, *in* R.W. Chapman, I.A. Kinnes and K. Randsborg (eds), 83–91.

Kinnes, I.A. 1985. Circumstances not context: The Neolithic of Scotland as seen from outside, *Proc Soc Antiq Scotl* 115, 15–57.

Kinnes, I.A. 1988. Megaliths in action: some aspects of the Neolithic Period in the Channel Islands, *Archaeol J* 145, 13–59.

Kinnes, I.A. 1991. *Non-Megalithic Long Barrows and Related Monuments in Britain*, London.

Kinnes, I.A. forthcoming. *Round Barrows, Enclosures and Graves in the British Neolithic*.

Kinnes, I.A., Schadla-Hall, T., Chadwick, P. and Dean, P. 1983. Duggleby Howe reconsidered, *Archaeol J* 140, 83–108.

Lamb, R.G. 1980. *The Archaeological Sites and Monuments of Sanday and North Ronaldsay*, Edinburgh.

Lamb, R.G. 1982. *The Archaeological Sites and Monuments of Rousay, Egilsay and Wyre*, Edinburgh.

Lamb, R.G. 1983. *The Archaeological Sites and Monuments of Papa Westray and Westray*, Edinburgh.

Larick, R. 1985. Spears, style and time among the Maa-speaking pastoralists, *J Anthropological Archaeol* 4, 206–20.

Lawson, T.J. 1981. The 1926–7 excavations of the Creag nan Uamh bone caves, near Inchnadamph, Sutherland, *Proc Soc Antiq Scotl* 111, 7–20.

Leach, E.R. 1954. *Political Systems of Highland Burma: A Study of Kachin Social Structure*, London.

Leask, H.G. 1977. *Irish Churches and Monastic Buildings, Volume 1*, Dundalk.

Lewis, G. 1980. *Day of Shining Red: an Essay on Understanding Ritual*, Cambridge.

L'Helgouac'h, J. 1965. *Les Sépultures mégalithiques en Armorique*, Rennes.

Linge, J. 1987. Re-discovering a landscape: the barrow and motte in north Ayrshire, *Proc Soc Antiq Scotl* 117, 23–32.

Longacre, W. 1981. Kalinga Pottery: an ethnoarchaeological study, in I. Hodder, G. Isaac, and N. Hammond (eds) *Pattern of the Past*, Cambridge, 49–66.

Longworth, I.H. 1967. Further discoveries at Brackmont Mill, Brackmont Farm and Tentsmuir, Fife, *Proc Soc Antiq Scotl* 99 (1966–7), 60–92.

Lucas, A.T. 1986. The social role of relics and reliquaries in ancient Ireland, *J Roy Soc Antiq Ire* 116, 5–37.

Lynch, A. 1988. Poulnabrone – a stone in time, *Archaeol Ire* 2, 105–7.

Lynch, F.M. 1967. Barclodiad y Gawres, comparative notes on the decorated stones, *Archaeol Cambrensis* 116, 1–22.

Lynch, F.M. 1969. The megalithic tombs of North Wales, *in* T.G.E. Powell et al. (eds), 107–48.

Lynch, F.M. 1970. *Prehistoric Anglesey*, Llangefni.

Lynch, F.M. 1973. The use of the passage in certain passage graves as a means of communication rather than access, *in* G.E. Daniel and P. Kjaerum (eds), 147–61.

Lynch, F.M. 1974. Cup and ring marked stone at Llwydiarth Esgob, *Trans Anglesey Antiq Soc* 1974, 118–21.

Lynch, F.M. 1975. Excavations at Carreg Samson megalithic tomb, Mathry, Pembrokeshire, *Archaeol Cambrensis* 124, 15–35.

Lynch, F.M. and Burgess, C. (eds) 1972. *Prehistoric Man in Wales and the West*, Bath.

M'Bain, J. 1929. *The Merrick and the Neighbouring Hills*, Ayr.

MacBryde, I. 1978. *Wil-im-ee Moor-ing*: or, where do axes come from? *Mankind* 11, 354–82.

McCormick, F. 1986. Animal bones from prehistoric Irish burials, *J Ir Archaeol* 3 (1985–6), 37–48.

McCullagh, R. 1991. Excavation at Newton, Islay. *Glasgow Archaeol J* 15 (1988–9), 23–52.

MacDonald, G. and Curle, A.O. 1929. The Roman fort at Mumrills near Falkirk, *Proc Soc Antiq Scotl* 63 (1928–9), 396–575.

Macdonald, J. 1882. Illustrated notices of the ancient stone implements of Ayrshire (first series), *Archaeol and Historical Collections of Ayr and Wigtown*, III, 66–81.

Macdonnall, D. 1986. *Theories of Discourse*, Oxford.

McDowall, J.K. 1947. *Carrick Gallovidian*, Ayr.

McInnes, I.J. 1964. The Neolithic and Early Bronze Age pottery from Luce Sands, Wigtownshire, *Proc Soc Antiq Scotl* 97 (1963–4), 40–81.

McInnes, I.J. 1968. Jet sliders in Neolithic Britain, *in* J.M. Coles and D.D.A. Simpson (eds), 137–44.

McInnes, I.J. 1969. A Scottish Neolithic pottery sequence, *Scott Archaeol Forum* 1, 19–30.

McInnes, I.J. 1971. Settlements in later Neolithic Britain, *in* D.D.A. Simpson (ed.), 113–30.

Mackay, R.R. 1948. Neolithic pottery from Knappers Farm, near Glasgow, *Proc Soc Antiq Scotl* 82 (1947–8), 234–7.

Mackay, R.R. 1950. Grooved Ware from Knappers Farm, near Glasgow, and from Townhead, Rothesay, *Proc Soc Antiq Scotl* 84 (1945–50), 180–3.

MacKenzie, W.C. 1905. Notes on the Pigmies Isles, at the Butt of Lewis, with the results of the recent exploration of the Pigmies Chapel there, *Proc Soc Antiq Scotl* 39 (1904–5), 248–58.

MacKie, E. 1972. Radiocarbon dates for two Mesolithic shell heaps and a Neolithic axe factory in Scotland, *Proc Prehist Soc* 38, 412–6.

MacKie, E. 1976. The Glasgow conference on ceremonial and science in prehistoric Britain, *Antiquity* 50, 136–8.

MacKie, E. 1977. *The Megalith Builders*, Oxford.

M'Leod, A.G. 1940. Recent excavations carried out at Borland Castle Hill, Cumnock, South Ayrshire, *Proc Soc Antiq Scotl* 74, (1939–40), 136–7.

MacSween, A. 1990. *The Neolithic and Late Iron Age Pottery from Pool, Sanday, Orkney*, unpublished Ph.D. thesis, Bradford Univ.

MacSween, A. forthcoming. a. The pottery from the Point of Cott, in J.W.A. Barber.

MacSween, A. forthcoming. b. The pottery from Beech Hill House, *in* S. Stevenson, A kerbed cairn at Beech Hill House, Coupar Angus, Perth and Kinross.

MacSween, A., Hunter, J.R. and Warren, S.E. 1988. Analysis of coarse wares from the Orkney Islands, in E.A. Slater and J.O. Tate (eds) *Science and Archaeology, Glasgow, 1987: Proceedings of a Conference on the Application of Scientific Techniques to Archaeology*, Oxford, Brit. Archaeol. Rep. 196, 95–106.

McVicar, J.B. 1982. The spatial analysis of axe size and the Scottish axe distribution, *Archaeol Revs from Cambridge* 1(2), 30–45.

MacWhite, E. 1946. A new view on Irish Bronze Age rock scribings, *J Roy Soc Antiq Ire* 76, 59–80.

Main, L. 1984. Barbush, *Discovery Excav Scotl 1984*, 46.

Main, L. 1986. Barbush, *Discovery Excav Scotl 1986*, 6.

Manby, T.G. 1963. The excavation of the Willerby Wold long barrow, East Riding of Yorkshire, England, *Proc Prehist Soc* 29, 173–205.

Manby, T.G. 1974. *Grooved Ware Sites in Yorkshire and the North of England*, Oxford, Brit. Archaeol. Rep. 9.

Manby, T.G. 1975. Neolithic occupation sites on the Yorkshire Wolds, *Yorkshire Archaeol J* 47, 23–59.

Manby, T.G. 1976. The excavation of the Kilham long barrow, East Riding of Yorkshire, *Proc Prehist Soc* 42, 111–59.

Manby, T.G. 1979. Typology, materials, and distribution of flint and stone axes in Yorkshire, in T.H. McK. Clough and W.A. Cummins (eds), 65–81.

Manby, T.G. 1988. The Neolithic in Eastern Yorkshire, in T.G. Manby (ed.) *Archaeology in Eastern Yorkshire. Essays in honour of T.C.M. Brewster F.S.A.*, Sheffield, 35–87.

Mann, L. MacL. 1914. The carved stone balls of Scotland: a new theory as to their use, *Proc Soc Antiq Scotl* 12 (1913–4), 407–20.

Manning, C. 1985. A Neolithic burial mound at Ashleypark, Co. Tipperary, *Proc Roy Ir Acad* 85C, 61–100.

Marshall, D.N. 1976. The excavation of Hilton cairn, *Trans Buteshire Natur Hist Soc* 20, 9–27.

Marshall, D.N. 1977. Carved stone balls, *Proc Soc Antiq Scotl* 108 (1976–7), 40–72.

Marshall, D.N. 1978. Excavations at Auchategan, Glendaruel, Argyll, *Proc Soc Antiq Scotl* 109 (1977–8), 36–74.

Marshall, D.N. 1983. Further notes on carved stone balls, *Proc Soc Antiq Scotl* 113, 628–30.

Marshall, D.N. and Taylor, I.D. 1977. The excavation of the chambered cairn at Glenvoidean, Isle of Bute, *Proc Soc Antiq Scotl* 108 (1976–7), 1–39.

Masters, L.J. 1973. The Lochhill long carn, *Antiquity* 47, 96–100.

Masters, L.J. 1981a. The Druid's Grave, Kyle and Carrick District, Strathclyde Region: the rediscovery of a chambered tomb, *Trans Dumfriesshire Galloway Natur Hist Antiq Soc* 56, 10–17.

Masters, L.J. 1981b. Chambered tombs and non-megalithic barrows in Britain, in J.D. Evans, B.W. Cunliffe and A.C. Renfrew (eds) *Antiquity and Man: Essays in Honour of Glyn Daniel*, London, 161–76.

Masters, L.J. 1984. The Neolithic long cairns of Cumbria and Northumberland, *in* R. Miket and C. Burgess (eds), 52–74.

Masters, L.J. 1989. The early settlers, *in* D. Omand (ed.) *The New Caithness Book*, Wick.

Maté, I.D. 1988. Soil science, *Scott Devel Dept/Hist Buildings Mons Dir, Archaeol Operations and Conservation Ann Rep* 1988, 40–1.

Mayhew, N.J. 1975. The Aberdeen Upperkirkgate hoard of 1886, *Brit Numis J*, 45, 33–50.

Meillassoux, C. 1972. From reproduction to production, *Economy and Society* 1, 93–105.

Meillassoux, L. 1973. On the mode of production of the hunting band, in P. Alexandre (ed.) *French Perspectives in African Studies*, Oxford, 187–203.

Mercer, R.J. 1980a. *Hambledon Hill – a Neolithic Landscape*, Edinburgh.

Mercer, R.J. 1980b. *Archaeological Field Study in Northern Scotland, Volume 1, 1976–79, with Contribution by J.M. Howell*, Edinburgh, Edinburgh Univ. Archaeol. Dept Occ. Paper 4.

Mercer, R.J. 1981. The excavation of a late Neolithic henge-type enclosure at Balfarg, Markinch, Fife, Scotland, *Proc Soc Antiq Scotl* 111, 63–171.

Mercer, R.J. 1985. *Archaeological Field Survey in Northern Scotland, Volume 3, 1982–3, with Contribution by P.N. Hill*, Edinburgh, Edinburgh Univ. Archaeol. Dept Occ. Paper 11.

Mercer, R.J. forthcoming, *Archaeological Field Survey in Northern Scoltand, Volume 4*, Edinburgh, Edinburgh Univ. Archaeol. Dept Occ. Paper.

Mercer, R.J. and Tipping, R. 1989. Sketewan, *Edinburgh Univ Archaeol Dept Ann Rep 1989*, 24.

Miket, R. 1985. Ritual enclosures at Whitton Hill, Northumberland, *Proc Prehist Soc* 51, 137–48.

Miket, R. and Burgess, C. (eds) 1984. *Between and Beyond the Walls*, Edinburgh.

Miller, D. 1985. *Artefacts as Categories*, Cambridge.

Milne, J. 1892. Traces of early man in Buchan, *Trans Buchan Field Club* 2 (1891–2), 101–8.

Mills, C. 1988. Environmental archaeology, *Scott Devel Dept/Hist Buildings Mons Dir, Archaeol Operations and Conservation Ann Rep* 1988, 40.

Mills, C. 1989. Environmental archaeology, *Scott Devel Dept/Hist Buildings Mons Dir, Archaeol Operations and Conservation Ann Rep* 1989, 44–5.

Moore, C.N. 1979. Stone axes from the East Midlands, *in* T.H. McK. Clough and W.A. Cummins (eds), 82–6.

Moore, H.L. 1986. *Space, Text and Gender*, Cambridge.

Moore, J.W. 1964. Excavations at Beacon Hill, Flamborough Head, East Yorkshire, *Yorkshire Archaeol J*, 41, 191–202.

Moore, P.D. 1973. The influence of prehistoric cultures upon the initiation and spread of blanket bog in upland Wales, *Nature* 241, 350–3.

Morris, I. 1987. *Burial and Ancient Society: the Rise of the Greek City State*, Cambridge.

Morris, R.H. 1912. Notes on the spiral ornament in Wales, *Archaeol Cambrensis* 12, 249–62.

Morris, R.W.B. 1977. *The Prehistoric Rock Art of Argyll*, Poole.

Morris, R.W.B. 1989. The prehistoric rock art of Great Britain: a survey of all sites bearing motifs more complex than simple cup-marks, *Proc Prehist Soc* 55, 45–88.

Morrison, A. 1980. *Early Man in Britain and Ireland*, London.

Mortimer, J.R. 1905. *Forty Years' Researches in the British and Saxon Burial Mounds of East Yorkshire*, London.

Morton, W.R.M. and Scott, J.H. 1954. Report on the human skeletal remains found at Audleystown, 1952, *Ulster J Archaeol* 17, 37–53.

Müller, J. 1988. *The Chambered Cairns of the Northern and Western Isles*, Edinburgh, Edinburgh Univ. Archaeol. Dept Occ. Paper 16.

Murray, J. forthcoming. Megaliths again: a view from the Solway, *Scott Archaeol Rev* 8.

Nash Williams, V.E. 1950. *The Early Christian Monuments of Wales*, Cardiff.

Newbigin, N. 1936. Excavations of a long and a round cairn on Bellshiel Law, Redesdale, *Archaeol Aeliana* 13, 293–309.

Newell, P.J. 1988. A buried wall in peatland by Sheshader, Isle of Lewis, *Proc Soc Antiq Scotl* 118, 79–93.

Nieke, M. 1990. Fortifications in Argyll: retrospect and future prospect, in I. Armit (ed.) *Beyond the Brochs*, Edinburgh, 131–42.

Nielsen, P.O. 1977. Die Flintbeile der Frühen Trichterbecherkultur in Dänemark, *Acta Archaeologica* 48, 61–138.

O'Connor, A. and Clarke, D.V. (eds) 1983. *From the Stone Age to the 'Forty-five. Studies Presented to R.B.K. Stevenson*, Edinburgh.

O'Kelly, C. 1973. Passage grave art in the Boyne Valley, Ireland, *Proc Prehist Soc* 39, 354–82.

O'Kelly, M.J. 1952. Excavation of a cairn at Moneen, Co. Cork, *Proc Roy Ir Acad* 54C, 121–59.

O'Kelly, M.J. 1982. *Newgrange: Archaeology, Art and Legend*, London.

O'Kelly, M.J. 1989. *Early Ireland*, Cambridge.

O'Kelly, M.J., Lynch, F.M. and O'Kelly, C. 1978. Three passage graves at Newgrange, Co. Meath, *Proc Roy Ir Acad* 78C, 249–352.

Ó Ríordáin, S.P. 1947. Excavation of a barrow at Rathjordan, Co. Limerick, *J Cork Hist Archaeol Soc* 52, 1–4.

Ó Ríordáin, S.P. 1948. Further barrows at Rathjordan, Co. Limerick, *J Cork Hist Archaeol Soc* 53, 19–31.

Ó Ríordáin, S.P. 1954. Lough Gur excavations: Neolithic and Bronze Age houses on Knockadoon, *Proc Roy Ir Acad* 56C, 297–459.

O'Sullivan, M. 1986. Approaches to passage tomb art, *J Roy Soc Antiq Ire* 116, 68–83.

Øvrevik, S. 1985. The second millennium and after, *in* A.C. Renfrew (ed.), 131–49.

Pacitto, A.L. 1972. Rudston Barrow LXII: the 1968 Excavation, *Yorkshire Archaeol J* 44, 1–22.

Parkyn, E.A. 1915. *An Introduction to the Study of Prehistoric Art*, London.

Patrick, R.W.C. 1874. Note on some explorations in a tumulus called the Courthill, in the parish of Dalry and County of Ayr, *Proc Soc Antiq Scotl* 10 (1872–4), 281–5.

Peltenburg, E. 1982. Excavations at Balloch Hill, Argyll, *Proc Soc Antiq Scotl* 112, 142–214.

Petersen, F. 1972. Traditions of multiple burial in later Neolithic and Early Bronze Age England, *Archaeol J* 129, 22–55.

Petrie, G. 1868. Notice of ruins of ancient dwellings at Skara, Bay of Skaill, in the parish of Sandwick, Orkney, recently excavated, *Proc Soc Antiq Scotl* 7 (1866–8), 201–19.

Pierpoint, S. 1980. *Social Patterns in Yorkshire Prehistory 3500–750 bc*, Oxford, Brit Archaeol Rep 74.

Piggott, S. 1931. The Neolithic pottery of the British Isles, *Archaeol J* 88, 67–158.

Piggott, S. 1936. Grooved Ware, in S.H. Warren, S. Piggott, J.G.D. Clark, M.C. Burkitt, H. Godwin and M.E. Godwin, Archaeology of the submerged land surface of the Essex coast, *Proc Prehist Soc* 2, 191–201.

Piggott, S. 1948. The excavation at Cairnpapple Hill, West Lothian, 1947–8, *Proc Soc Antiq Scotl* 82 (1947–8), 68–123.

Piggott, S. 1954. *The Neolithic Cultures of the British Isles*, Cambridge.

Piggott, S. 1956. Excavations in passage-graves and ring cairns of the Clava group, 1952–3, *Proc Soc Antiq Scotl* 88 (1954–6), 173–207.

Piggott, S. 1962. *The West Kennet Long Barrow Excavations 1955–6*, London.

Piggott, S. 1972. Excavation of the Dalladies long barrow, Fettercairn, Kincardineshire, *Proc Soc Antiq Scotl* 104 (1971–2), 23–47.

Piggott, S. and Daniel, G.E. 1951. *Ancient British Art*, Cambridge.

Piggott, S. and Powell, T.G.E. 1949. The excavation of three Neolithic chambered tombs in Galloway, 1949, *Proc Soc Antiq Scotl* 83 (1948–9), 103–61.

Piggott, S. and Simpson, D.D.A. 1971. Excavation of a stone circle at Croft Moraig, Perthshire, Scotland, *Proc Prehist Soc*, 37, 1–15.

Pitts, L.F. and St Joseph, J.K. 1985. *Inchtuthil. The Roman Legionary Fortress Excavations 1952–65*, London, Britannia Monog. Ser. 6.

Platt, C. and Coleman-Smith, R. 1975. *Excavations in Medieval Southampton 1953–69*, Leicester.

Plunkett, T. and Coffey, G. 1898. Report on the excavation of Topped Mountain cairn, *Proc Roy Ir Acad* 4 (1896–8), 651–8.

Pollard, A. 1990. Down through the ages: a review of the Oban cave deposits, *Scott Archaeol Rev* 7, 58–74.

Powell, T.G.E. 1966. *Prehistoric Art*, London.

Powell, T.G.E., Corcoran, J.X.W.P., Lynch, F.M. and Scott, J.G. (eds) 1969. *Megalithic Enquiries in the West of Britain*, Liverpool.

Powell, T.G.E. and Daniel, G.E. 1956. *Barclodiad y Gawres: the Excavation of a Megalithic Chambered Tomb in Anglesey*, Liverpool.

Price, R.J. 1983. *Scotland's Environment During the Last 30,000 Years*, Edinburgh.

Proudfoot, E. 1965. Bishop's Cannings, Roughridge Hill, *Wiltshire Archaeol Mag* 60, 133.

Pryor, F. 1984. *Excavation at Fengate, Peterborough, England: the Fourth Report*, Northampton.

Ralston, I.B.M. 1982. A timber hall at Balbridie Farm, *Aberdeen Univ Rev* 168, 238–49.

Ramsden, P. 1991. Alice in the Afterlife: a glimpse in the mirror, in D.R. and D.A. Counts (eds) *Coping with the Final Tragedy: Cultural Variation in Dying and Grieving*. Amityville, New York, 27–41.

RCAHMS 1911. The Royal Commission on the Ancient and Historical Monuments and Constructions of Scotland, *Inventory of the Ancient Monuments and Constructions for the County of Caithness*, Edinburgh.

RCAHMS 1912. The Royal Commission on the Ancient and Historical Monuments and Constructions of Scotland, *Fourth Report and Inventory of Monuments and Constructions in Galloway, Volume 1, County of Wigtown*, Edinburgh.

RCAHMS 1914. The Royal Commission on the Ancient and Historical Monuments and Constructions of Scotland, *Fourth Report and Inventory of Monuments and Constructions in Galloway, Volume 2, Stewartry of Kirkcudbright*, Edinburgh.

RCAHMS 1928. The Royal Commission on the Ancient and Historical Monuments and Constructions of Scotland, *The Outer Hebrides, Skye and the Small Isles*, Edinburgh.

RCAHMS 1963. The Royal Commission on the Ancient and Historical Monuments of Scotland, *Stirlingshire. An Inventory of the Ancient Monuments*, Edinburgh.

RCAHMS 1978a. The Royal Commission on the Ancient and Historical Monuments of Scotland, *Lanarkshire: Prehistoric and Roman Monuments*, Edinburgh.

RCAHMS 1978b. The Royal Commission on the Ancient and Historical Monuments of Scotland, *The Archaeological Sites and Monuments of Scotland, 4: The Lunan Valley and the Montrose Basin, Angus District, Tayside Region*. Edinburgh.

RCAHMS 1979. The Royal Commission on the Ancient and Historical Monuments of Scotland, *The Archaeological Sites and Monuments of Scotland, 6: Easter Ross*, Edinburgh.

RCAHMS 1981. The Royal Commission on the Ancient and Historical Monuments of Scotland, *The Archaeological Sites and Monuments of Scotland, 14: South Carrick*, Edinburgh.

RCAHMS 1983. The Royal Commission on the Ancient and Historical Monuments of Scotland, *The Archaeological Sites and Monuments of Scotland, 17: North Carrick*, Edinburgh.

RCAHMS 1987. The Royal Commission on the Ancient and Historical Monuments of Scotland, *The Archaeological Sites and Monuments of Scotland, 16: East Rhins*, Edinburgh.

RCAHMS 1988. The Royal Commission on the Ancient and Historical

Monuments of Scotland, *Inventory of Ancient Monuments in Argyll, Volume 6: Mid Argyll and Cowal*, Edinburgh.

RCAHMS 1990. The Royal Commission on the Ancient and Historical Monuments of Scotland, *North-East Perthshire: an Archaeological Landscape*, Edinburgh.

RCAHMS in press. The Royal Commission on the Ancient and Historical Monuments of Scotland, *South-East Perthshire*, Edinburgh.

RCAM 1921. The Royal Commission on Ancient Monuments (Wales and Monmouthshire), *Inventory of Ancient Monuments: County of Merioneth*, Cardiff.

RCAM 1937. The Royal Commission on Ancient Monuments (Wales and Monmouthshire), *Inventory of Ancient Monuments: Anglesey*, Cardiff.

RCAMS 1946. The Royal Commission on the Ancient Monuments of Scotland, *Inventory of the Ancient Monuments of Orkney and Shetland, Volumes 1 and 2*, Edinburgh.

Rees, S. 1986. Stone implements and artefacts, *in* A.W.R. Whittle (ed.), 75–91.

Reid, R.W. and Fraser, J.R. 1924. Short stone cist found in the parish of Kinneff and Catterline, Kincardineshire, *Proc Soc Antiq Scotl* 58 (1923–4), 27–40.

Renfrew, A.C. 1976. Megaliths, territories and populations, in S.J. de Laet (ed.) *Acculturation and Continuity in Atlantic Europe*, Brugge, Dissertationes Archaeologicae Gandenses 16, 298–320.

Renfrew, A.C. (ed.) 1979. *Investigations in Orkney*, London.

Renfrew, A.C. (ed.) 1985. *The Prehistory of Orkney*, Edinburgh.

Renfrew, A.C. and Buteux, S. 1985. Radiocarbon dates from Orkney, *in* A.C. Renfrew (ed.), 263–74.

Reynolds, D. Ralston, I. and Haggarty, G. 1977. Boysack Mills, *Discovery Excav Scotl 1977*, 5.

Rice, P.R. 1987. *Pottery Analysis. A sourcebook*, Chicago.

Richards, C.C. 1985. *The Orkney Survey Project: an Interim*, unpublished MS, Glasgow Univ. Archaeol. Dept.

Richards, C.C. 1988. Altered images: a re-examination of Neolithic mortuary practices in Orkney, *in* J.C. Barrett and I.A. Kinnes (eds), 42–56.

Richards, C.C. 1989. Barnhouse, Stenness, *Discovery Excav Scotl* 1989, 66–7.

Richards, C.C. 1990. Postscript: the Late Neolithic settlement complex at Barnhouse Farm, Stenness, in A.C. Renfrew (ed.), *The Prehistory of Orkney*, 2nd edn, Edinburgh, 305–16.

Richards, C.C. forthcoming. The Neolithic house in Orkney, in R. Samson (ed.) *The Social Archaeology of Houses*, Edinburgh.

Richards, C.C. and Thomas, J.S. 1984. Ritual activity and structured deposition in later Neolithic Wessex, *in* R.J. Bradley and J. Gardiner (eds), 189–218.

Richardson, J.T. and Richardson, J.S. 1902. Prehistoric remains at Gullane, *Proc Soc Antiq Scotl* 36 (1901–2), 654–8.

Ricoeur, P. 1971. The model of the text: meaningful action considered as a text, *Social Research* 38, 529–62.

Ritchie, A. 1983. Excavation of a Neolithic farmstead at Knap of Howar, Papa Westray, Orkney, *Proc Soc Antiq Scotl* 113, 40–121.

Ritchie, A. forthcoming. Excavation at Holm of Papa Westray North, Orkney, *Proc Soc Antiq Scotl*.

Ritchie, J.N.G. 1970a. Excavation of the chambered cairn at Achnacreebeag, *Proc Soc Antiq Scotl* 102 (1969–70), 31–55.

Ritchie, J.N.G. 1970b. Beaker pottery in south-west Scotland, *Trans Dumfriesshire Galloway Natur Hist Antiq Soc* 47, 123–46.

Ritchie, J.N.G. 1974. Excavation of the stone circle and cairn at Balbirnie, Fife, *Archaeol J* 131, 1–32.

Ritchie, J.N.G. 1976. The Stones of Stenness, Orkney, *Proc Soc Antiq Scotl* 107 (1975–6), 1–60.

Ritchie, J.N.G. and Adamson, H.C. 1981. Knappers, Dunbartonshire: a reassessment, *Proc Soc Antiq Scotl* 111, 172–204.

Ritchie, J.N.G. and MacLaren, A. 1972. Ring-cairns and related monuments in Scotland, *Scott Archaeol Forum* 4, 1–17.

Ritchie, J.N.G. and Ritchie, A. 1981. *Scotland: Archaeology and Early History*, London. Revised 1991, Edinburgh.

Ritchie, P.R. 1959. A chambered tomb at Isbister, South Ronaldsay, Orkney, *Proc Soc Antiq Scotl* 92 (1958–9), 25–32.

Ritchie, P.R. 1968. The stone implement trade in third-millennium Scotland, *in* J.M. Coles and D.D.A. Simpson (eds), 117–36.

Ritchie, P.R. 1987. Current research on Scottish stone axes, *Scott Archaeol Gazette* 14, 8–14.

Ritchie, P.R. and Scott, J.G. 1988. The petrological identification of stone axes from Scotland, *in* T.H. McK. Clough and W.A. Cummins (eds), 85–91.

Robertson-Mackay, R. 1952. Grooved Ware from Knappers Farm, near Glasgow, and from Townhead, Rothesay, *Proc Soc Antiq Scotl* 84 (1949–50), 180–4.

Robertson-Mackay, R. 1987. The Neolithic causewayed enclosure at Staines, Surrey: excavations 1961–3, *Proc Prehist Soc* 53, 23–128.

Robinson, D.E. 1983. Possible Mesolithic activity in the west of Arran: evidence from peat deposits, *Glasgow Archaeol J* 10, 1–6.

Roe, F.E.S. 1968. Stone maceheads and the latest Neolithic cultures of the British Isles, *in* J.M. Coles and D.D.A. Simpson (eds), 145–72.

Roe, F.E.S. 1979. Typology of stone implements with shaft-holes, *in* T.H. McK. Clough and W.A. Cummins (eds), 23–48.

Romans, J.C.C. 1986. Soils, *in* A.W.R. Whittle (ed.), 125–31.

Ruggles, C. 1984. *Megalithic Astronomy: A New Archaeological and Statistical Study of 300 West Scottish Sites*, Oxford, Brit. Archaeol. Rep. 123.

Ryan, M. 1980. Prehistoric burials at Clane, Co. Kildare, *J Co Kildare Archaeol Soc* 16, 108–14.

Ryan, M. 1981. Poulawack, Co. Clare; the affinities of the central burial structure, in D. Ó Corráin (ed.), *Irish Antiquity: Essays and Studies Presented to Professor M.J. O'Kelly*, Cork, 134–46.

Saville, A. 1990. *Hazelton North, Gloucestershire: Excavations 1979–82*, London, English Heritage Archaeol. Rep. 13.

Saville, A. and Sheridan, J.A. forthcoming. A hoard of flint axeheads and other flint artefacts from Auchenhoan, near Campbeltown, Strathclyde Region, *Proc Soc Antiq Scotl*.

Scott, J.G. 1956. The chambered cairn at Brackley, Kintyre, *Proc Soc Antiq Scotl* 89 (1955–6), 22–54.

Scott, J.G. 1969. The Clyde Cairns of Scotland, *in* T.G.E. Powell et al. (eds), 175–222.

Scott, J.G. 1976. Raised mortuary structures, unpublished paper given at conference on *Neolithic Burial Practices in Northern Britain*, Edinburgh Univ.

Scott, J.G. 1989. The hall and motte at Courthill, Dalry, Ayrshire, *Proc Soc Antiq Scotl* 119, 217–8.

Scott, W.L. 1948. The chamber tomb of Unival, North Uist, *Proc Soc Antiq Scotl* 82 (1947–8), 1–49.

Scott, W.L. 1951a. Eilean an Tighe: A pottery workshop of the second millennium BC, *Proc Soc Antiq Scotl* 85 (1950–1), 1–37.

Scott, W.L. 1951b. The colonisation of Scotland in the second millennium BC, *Proc Prehist Soc* 17, 16–82.

SEARCH 1989. Sheffield Environment and Archaeology Research Campaign in the Hebrides, *The Western Isles Project, Second Interim Report* Sheffield Univ. Archaeol. and Prehist. Dept.

Shand, P. and Hodder, I. 1990. Haddenham, *Curr Archaeol* 118, 339–42.

Shanks, I.M. and Tilley, C. 1982. Ideology, symbolic power and ritual communication: a reinterpretation of Neolithic mortuary practices, in I. Hodder (ed.), *Symbolic and Structural Archaeology*, Cambridge, 129–54.

Sharman, P. 1990. *Tuquoy Steatite Report*, unpublished MS, Scott. Devel. Dept/Hist. Buildings Mons Dir. (Archaeol. Operations and Conservation), Edinburgh.

Sharples, N.M. 1980. *The Excavation by J.X.W.P. Corcoran of the Ord North, Lairg, Sutherland, in 1967*, unpublished MA dissert, Glasgow University.

Sharples, N.M. 1981. The excavation of a chambered cairn, the Ord North, at Lairg, Sutherland, by J.X.W.P. Corcoran, *Proc Soc Antiq Scotl* 111, 21–62.

Sharples, N.M. 1984. Excavations at Pierowall Quarry, Westray, Orkney, *Proc Soc Antiq Scotl* 114, 75–125.

Sharples, N.M. 1985. Individual and community: the changing role of megaliths in the Orcadian Neolithic, *Proc Prehist Soc* 51, 59–76.

Sharples, N.M. 1986. Radiocarbon dates from three chambered tombs at Loch Calder, Caithness, *Scott Arch Rev* 4, 2–10.

Sharples, N.M. 1990. *Miltown of Clava: Interim Report*, unpublished MS, Scott. Devel. Dept/Hist. Buildings Mons Dir. (Archaeol. Operations and Conservation), Edinburgh.

Shennan, S.J. 1983. Monuments: an example of archaeologists' approach to the massively material, *Roy Anthropological Inst Newsletter* 59, 9–11.

Shepard, A.O. 1954. *Ceramics for the Archaeologist*, Washington D.C., Carnegie Institution Publication 609.

Shepherd, I.A.G. 1976. Preliminary results from the Beaker settlement at Rosinish, Benbecula, *in* C. Burgess and R. Miket (eds), 209–20.

Sheridan, J.A. 1985. *The Role of Exchange Studies in 'Social Archaeology', with Special Reference to the Prehistory of Ireland from the Fourth to the Early Second Millennium bc*, unpublished Ph.D. thesis, Cambridge University.

Sheridan, J.A. 1986a. Megaliths and megalomania: an account, and interpretation, of the development of passage tombs in Ireland, *J Ir Archaeol* 3 (1985–6), 17–30.

Sheridan, J.A. 1986b. Porcellanite artifacts: a new survey, *Ulster J Archaeol* 49, 19–32.

Sheridan, J.A. 1989. Biggar Common, *Discovery Excav Scotl* 1989, 60.

Sheridan, J.A., Cooney, G. and Grogan, E. in press. Stone axe studies in Ireland, *Proc Prehist Soc* 58.

Sherratt, A. 1990. The genesis of megaliths: monumentality, ethnicity an social complexity in the Neolithic of North-West Europe, *World Archaeol* 22, 147–67.

Shotton, F.W. 1972. The large stone axes ascribed to north-west Pembrokeshire, *in* F.M. Lynch and C. Burgess (eds), 85–91.

Simpson, D.D.A. (ed.) 1971. *Economy and Settlement in Neolithic and Early Bronze Age Europe*, Leicester.

Simpson, D.D.A. 1976. The later Neolithic and Beaker settlement at Northton, Isle of Harris, *in* C. Burgess and R. Miket (eds), 221–32.

Simpson, D.D.A. 1988. The stone maceheads of Ireland, *J Roy Soc Antiq Ire* 118, 27–52.

Simpson, D.D.A. 1991. The stone maceheads of Ireland: Part 2, *J Roy Soc Antiq Ire* 119, 113–26.

Simpson, D.D.A. and Coles, J.M. 1990. Excavations at Gradtully, Perthshire, *Proc Soc Antiq Scotl* 120.

Simpson, D.D.A. and Thawley, J.E. 1972. Single grave art in Britain, *Scott Archaeol Forum* 4, 81–104.

Simpson, J.Y. 1865. On ancient sculpturings of Cups and Concentric Rings etc., *Proc Soc Antiq Scotl* 6 (1864–5), monog. as appx, 1–140.

Sloan, D. 1982. Nether Kinneil, *Curr Archaeol* 84, 13–15.

Smith, A.G. 1981. The Neolithic, *in* I.G. Simmons and M.J. Tooley (eds) *The Environment in British Prehistory*, London, 125–209.

Smith, I.F. 1956. *The Decorative Art of Neolithic Ceramics in South-Eastern England*, unpublished Ph.D. thesis, Univ. London.

Smith, I.F. 1965. *Windmill Hill and Avebury. Excavations by Alexander Keiller 1925–39*, Oxford.

Smith, I.F. 1971. Causewayed enclosures, *in* D.D.A. Simpson (ed.), 89–112.

Smith, I.F. 1974. The Neolithic, in A.C. Renfrew (ed.) *British Prehistory*, London, 100–36.

Smith, I.F. 1979. The chronology of British stone implements, *in* T.H. McK. Clough and W.A. Cummins (eds), 13–22.

Smith, I.F. 1981. The Neolithic pottery, in R.J. Mercer, Excavations at Carn Brea, Illogan, Cornwall, 1970–3, *Cornish Archaeol* 20, 1–204.

Smith, J. 1895. *Prehistoric Man in Ayrshire*, London.

Smith, J.A. 1876. Notes of small ornamented balls found in different parts of Scotland, *Proc Soc Antiq Scotl* 11 (1875–6), 29–62.

Smith, W.C. 1963. Jade axes from sites in the British Isles, *Proc Prehist Soc* 29, 133–72.

Sockett, E. 1971. A Bronze Age barrow at Mount Pleasant, near Normanby, North Riding, *Yorkshire Archaeol J* 43, 33–9.

Stevenson, R.B.K. 1946. Jottings on Early Pottery, *Proc Soc Antiq Scotl* 80 (1945–6), 141–3.

Stevenson, R.B.K. 1948. Notes on some prehistoric objects, *Proc Soc Antiq Scotl* 82 (1947–8), 292–5.

Stevenson, S.J. 1990. A kerbed cairn at Beech Hill House, Coupar Angus, Perth and Kinross, *Scott Devel Dept/Hist Buildings Mons Dir, Archaeol Operations and Conservation Ann Rep* 190, 10–14.

Stewart, M.E.C. 1959. Strath Tay in the Second Millennium B.C. – a field survey, *Proc Soc Antiq Scotl* 92, 71–84.

Stewart, M.E.C. 1985. The excavation of a henge, stone circles and metal working area at Moncrieffe, Perthshire, *Proc Soc Antiq Scotl* 115, 125–50.

Stones, J.A. (ed.), 1989. *Three Scottish Carmelite Friaries. Excavations at Aberdeen, Linlithgow and Perth 1980–6.* Edinburgh, Soc. Antiq. Scotl. Monog. Ser. 6.

Sweetman, D. 1976. An earthen enclosure at Monknewton, Slane, Co. Meath, *Proc Roy Ir Acad* 76C, 25–72.

Tavener, N. 1987. Bannockburn: the pit and post alignments excavated in 1984 and 1985, *Scott Devel Dept/Hist Buildings Mons Dir, Central Excavation Unit and Ancient Monuments Laboratory Annual Report*, 1987, 71–6.

Taylor, J.J. 1983. An unlocated Scottish gold ore source or an experiment in alloying? *in* A. O'Connor and D.V. Clarke (eds), 57–64.

Thomas, J.S. 1984. A tale of two polities: kinship, authority and exchange in the Neolithic of south Dorset and north Wiltshire, *in* R.J. Bradley and J. Gardiner (eds), 161–76.

Thomas, J.S. 1988. The social significance of Cotswold-Severn burial practices, *Man* 23, 540–59.

Thomas, J.S. 1990. Monuments from the inside: the case of Irish megalithic tombs, *World Archaeol* 22, 168–78.

Thomas, J.S. 1991. *Rethinking the Neolithic*, Cambridge.

Thomas, J.S. forthcoming. The hermeneutics of megalithic space, in I.M. Shanks and C. Tilley (eds) *Interpretive Archaeology*, London.

Thomas, J.S. and Whittle, A.W.R. 1986. Anatomy of a tomb – West Kennett revisited, *Oxford J Archaeol* 5, 129–56.

Thornby, Canon 1902. Ring-marked stones at Glassonby and Maughanby, *Trans Cumberland Westmorland Antiq Archaeol Soc* 2, 380–3.

Thorpe, I.J. and Richards, C.C. 1984. The decline of ritual authority and the introduction of Beakers into Britain, *in* R.J. Bradley and J. Gardiner (eds), 67–86.

Thorpe, O.W. and Thorpe R.S. 1984. The distribution and sources of archaeological pitchstone in Britain, *J Archaeol Sci* 11, 1–34.

Tilley, C. 1990. *Reading Material Culture*, Oxford.

Traill, W. and Kirkness, W. 1937. Hower, A prehistoric structure on Papa Westray, Orkney, *Proc Soc Antiq Scotl* 71 (1936–7), 309–21.

Trigger, B. 1990a. Monumental architecture: a thermo-dynamic explanation of symbolic behaviour, *World Archaeol* 22, 119–32.

Trigger, B. 1990b *A History of Archaeological Thought*, Cambridge.

Tuan, Y-F. 1977. *Space and Place: the Perspective of Experience*, London.

Turner, V. 1967. *The Forest of Symbols*, Ithaca.

Turner, V. 1969. *The Ritual Process*, Harmondsworth.

Turner, V. 1974. *Dramas, Fields and Metaphors*, Ithaca.

Twohig, E. Shee 1981. *The Megalithic Art of Western Europe*, Oxford.

Twohig, E. Shee 1990. *Irish Megalithic Tombs*, Princes Risborough.

Van Gennep, A. 1960. *The Rites of Passage*, London.

Vyner, B.E. 1984. The excavation of a Neolithic cairn at Street House, Loftus, Cleveland, *Proc Prehist Soc* 50, 151–95.

Vyner, B.E. 1986. Evidence for mortuary practices in the Neolithic burial mounds and cairns of northern Britain, *Scott Archaeol Rev* 4, 11–16.

Waddell, J. 1974. On some aspects of the Late Neolithic and Early Bronze Age in Ireland, *Ir Archaeol Res Forum* 1, 32–8.

Wainwright, G.J. 1971. The excavation of a Late Neolithic enclosure at Marden, Wiltshire, *Antiq J* 51, 177–239.

Wainwright, G.J. 1972. The excavation of a Neolithic settlement on Broome Heath, Ditchingham, Norfolk, *Proc Prehist Soc* 38, 1–97.

Wainwright, B.J. and Longworth, I.H. 1971. *Durrington Walls: Excavations 1966–68*, London.

Walker, I.C. 1968. Easterton of Roseisle: a forgotten site in Moray, *in* J.M. Coles and D.D.A. Simpson (eds), 95–115.

Watkins, T.W. 1982. The excavation of an Early Bronze Age cemetery at Barns Farm, Dalgety, Fife, *Proc Soc Antiq Scotl* 112, 48–141.

Weiss, K.M. 1973. *Demographic Models for Anthropology*, Washington, D.C., Memoirs Soc. American Archaeol. 27.

Whimster, R. 1981. *Burial Practices in Iron Age Britain*, Oxford.

Whittle, A.W.R. 1977. *The Earlier Neolithic of Southern England and its Continental Background* Oxford, Brit. Archaeol. Rep. Int. Ser. 35.

Whittle A.W.R. (ed.) 1986. *Scord of Brouster: an Early Agricultural Settlement on Shetland. Excavations 1977–9*, Oxford, Oxford Univ. Cttee Archaeol. Monog. 9.

Whittle, A.W.R. 1988. *Problems in Neolithic Archaeology*, Cambridge.

Whittle, A.W.R. forthcoming. Excavations at Silbury Hill, north Wiltshire, *Proc Prehist Soc*.

Wickham-Jones, C. 1981. Flaked stone technology in northern Britain, *Scott Archaeol Forum* 11, 36–42.

Wickham-Jones, C. 1986. The procurement and use of stone for flaked tools in prehistoric Scotland, *Proc Soc Antiq Scotl* 116, 1–10.

Wickham-Jones, C. 1990. *Rhum: Mesolithic and Later Sites at Kinloch, Excavations 1984–6*, Edinburgh, Soc. Antiq. Scotl. Monog. 7.

Wickham-Jones, C. and Collins, G.H. 1978. The sources of flint and chert in northern Britain, *Proc Soc Antiq Scotl* 109 (1977–8), 7–21.

Williams, D.F. 1979. Petrological analysis of pottery, *in* A.C. Renfrew (ed.), 94–6.

Williams, D.F. 1982. Aspects of prehistoric pottery-making in Orkney, in I. Freestone, C. Johns and T. Potter (eds), *Current Research in Ceramics: Thin Section Studies*, London, Brit. Mus. Occ. Paper 32, 9–13.

Wilson, G. 1878. Notes on the ancient stone implements of Wigtownshire, *Archaeol and Historical Collections of Ayr and Wigtown*, I, 1–30.

Woodham, A.A. and Woodham, M.F. 1957. The excavation of a chambered cairn at Kilcoy, Ross-shire, *Proc Soc Antiq Scotl* 90 (1956–7), 102–17.

Woodman, P.C. 1989. A review of the Scottish Mesolithic: a plea for normality! *Proc Soc Antiq Scotl* 119, 1–32.

Woodman, P.C. in press. Excavations at Mad Man's Window, Co. Antrim, and a reassessment of some flintworking sites in North-East Ireland, *Proc Prehist Soc* 58.

Woolley, A.R., Bishop, A.C., Harrison, R.J. and Kinnes, I.A. 1979. European Neolithic jade implements: a preliminary mineralogical and typological study, *in* T.H. McK. Clough and W.A. Cummins (eds), 90–6.

Yates, M. 1984a. Groups of small cairns in northern Britain – a view from south-west Scotland, *Proc Soc Antiq Scotl* 114 (1984), 217–34.

Yates, M. 1984b. *Bronze Age Round Cairns in Dumfries and Galloway*, Oxford, Brit. Archaeol. Rep. 132.

Young, A. and Crichton Mitchell, M. 1939. Report on excavation at Monzie, *Proc Soc Antiq Scotl* 73 (1938–9), 62–70.

Index